The Collected Papers of James Meade

Volume I: Employment and Inflation

Also from Unwin Hyman

The Collected Papers of James Meade

Volume II: Value, Distribution and Growth
edited by Susan Howson   004 445073 7

Volume III: International Economics
edited by Susan Howson   004 445074 5

Volume IV: The Cabinet Office Diary of James Meade 1944–46
edited by Susan Howson and Donald Moggridge   004 445075 3

The Collected Papers of James Meade

Volume I: Employment and Inflation

Edited by

SUSAN HOWSON

University of Toronto

London
UNWIN HYMAN
Boston   Sydney   Wellington

Published by the academic division of
Unwin Hyman Ltd
15/17 Broadwick Street, London W1V 1FP, UK

Allen & Unwin Inc.,
8 Winchester Place, Winchester, Mass. 01890, USA

Allen & Unwin (Australia) Ltd,
8 Napier Street, North Sydney, NSW 2060, Australia

Allen & Unwin (New Zealand) Ltd
in association with the Port Nicholson Press Ltd,
60 Cambridge Terrace, Wellington, New Zealand

First published in 1988

British Library Cataloguing in Publication Data

Meade, J. E.
    The collected papers of James Meade.
    Vol. I: Employment and inflation
1. Great Britain – Economic policy
I. Title   II. Howson, Susan
330.941'082   HC256
ISBN 0–04–331115–6

Library of Congress Cataloging-in-Publication Data

Meade, J. E. (James Edward), 1907–
    The collected papers of James Meade.
Includes index.
Contents: v. 1. Employment and inflation.
1. Unemployment – Collected works.
2. Unemployment – Great Britain – Collected works.
3. Keynesian economics – Collected works.
I. Howson, Susan, 1945–
II. Title.
HD5710.M43 1988   330.1   87–15288
ISBN 0–04–331115–6 (v. 1. : alk. paper)

Typeset in 10 on 11 point Times by Nene Phototypesetters Ltd
and printed in Great Britain by Biddles of Guildford

Contents

Editorial Preface

When Meade gave his inaugural lecture as Professor of Commerce at the London School of Economics in February 1948, he reminded his listeners:

> My main concern in economics has always been, not with descriptive or institutional studies, but with theoretical analysis and, in particular, with the contribution which economic analysis has to make to the solution of problems of practical economic policy. ['Financial policy and the balance of payments', *Economica*, vol. 15, 1948, p. 101]

James Meade has also written on a very wide range of problems in most fields of economics: Keynesian unemployment theory, national income accounting, exchange-rate theory, open economy macro-economics, international trade, price theory and welfare economics, growth theory, economic development, problems of income distribution, some aspects of industrial organisation, and, throughout his career, the control of inflation. The main problem in putting together this edition of Meade's Collected Papers has, therefore, been to organise the material. This includes not only academic articles, essays, lectures and pamphlets, but also unpublished papers on policy problems written either for the Labour Party in the 1930s, while Meade was teaching in Oxford, or during his period of government service, 1940–7, in the Economic Section of the Cabinet Offices, of which he was Director 1946–7.

In this edition a selection of Meade's published and unpublished papers has been organised in five categories corresponding to the five parts of his introductory textbook, *An Introduction to Economic Analysis and Policy* (Oxford: Clarendon Press, 1936; second edition, London: Oxford University Press, 1937). I have called these Employment and Inflation; Price Theory and Policy; Distribution; Growth and Development; and International Economics. Volume I contains the first category. In this way theory and policy papers can be juxtaposed: for example, a memorandum on the control of inflation written for the Budget Committee of the Treasury in 1946 appears in this volume beside Meade's inaugural lecture as Professor of Political Economy in the University of Cambridge on the same subject twelve years later. Several of Meade's writings cover two or more of the five categories; in this volume two such papers ('Public Works in their International Aspect' and 'Outline of Economic Policy for a Labour Government') have been included on the grounds that their overriding concern is with the problem of unemployment.

I have followed two simple criteria for the selection of published papers: major articles in major academic journals on the one hand, and essays, lectures, and pamphlets that present Meade's policy proposals and his analyses of their effects, on the other. The unpublished papers have been selected mainly from the Meade Papers in the British Library of Political and Economic Science, which include at least the first drafts of his Labour Party papers and copies of forty-five papers which he chose to take with him when he left government service in 1947. These memoranda often exist in more than one version, but research in Labour Party sources and the Public Record Office reveals that the version in Meade's papers is in almost all cases the final version from his own hand. I have indicated the reasons for the selection of individual documents in introductory notes to the papers reproduced below. The notes also include information on the sources of the documents. Apart from the correction of minor inconsistencies of spelling and obvious typographical errors and the completion or correction of bibliographical references, the papers appear as they were originally typed or printed.

In this volume, Meade's most important papers on theoretical and applied aspects of employment and inflation, written over five decades (1932–1985), are preceded by his own account of his life, originally written to accompany his Nobel Memorial Lecture in 1977. I should like to thank Professor Meade and the Nobel Foundation for permission to include this as well as Meade's Nobel Lecture, 'The Meaning of "Internal Balance"'. The memoranda written by Meade in the Economic Section are Crown Copyright and are reproduced by permission of the Controller of Her Majesty's Stationery Office. I am also grateful to the Fabian Society, Oxford University Press, Cambridge University Press, the Wincott Foundation, the Institute of Economic Affairs, and the editors of *The Economic Journal*, the *Review of Economic Studies*, *Oxford Economic Papers*, *Nationaløkonomisk Tidsskrift* and *Lloyds Bank Review* for permission to republish articles and pamphlets. Finally, I very much wish to acknowledge the generous assistance with the research for this edition I have received from Dr Angela Raspin of the British Library of Political and Economic Science, Dr Stephen Bird of the Labour Party, the Warden and Fellows of Nuffield College, Oxford, the Humanities and Social Sciences Committee of the University of Toronto, and, most of all, Professor Meade.

Susan Howson
December 1986

1

James Meade

Professor Meade wrote this account of his life on the occasion of his Nobel Memorial lecture, 'The Meaning of "Internal Balance"', delivered in Stockholm on 8 December 1977 (see Chapter 21 below). He has added a postscript (in 1986) to bring the story up to date.

Born on 23 June 1907, I was brought up in the City of Bath in England. At school – Lambrook School (1917–1921) and Malvern College (1917–1926) – my education was concentrated on the Latin and Greek languages. At the University – Oriel College, Oxford (1926–1930) – I continued my classical education until 1928. I then moved over for two years to the newly started School of Philosophy, Politics and Economics.

My interest in economics had the following roots. Like many of my generation I considered the heavy unemployment in the United Kingdom in the inter-war period as both stupid and wicked. Moreover, I knew the cure for this evil, because I had become a disciple of the monetary crank, Major C. H. Douglas, to whose works I had been introduced by a much loved but somewhat eccentric maiden aunt. But my shift to the serious study of economics gradually weakened my belief in Major Douglas's A + B theorem, which was replaced in my thought by the expression MV = PT.

In 1930 I was elected to a Fellowship at Hertford College, Oxford, with freedom in the first year to continue my study of economics as a post-graduate student. As a result of having lived as a child next door to his great aunt, I aready knew Dennis Robertson who invited me to go to Trinity College, Cambridge, as his student for the academic year 1930/31. This resulted in the intellectually most exciting year of my life.

At Cambridge I made a close friendship with Richard Kahn and became a member of the 'Circus' with him, Piero Sraffa and Joan and Austin Robinson, which discussed Keynes' *Treatise on Money* and stimulated the start of its translation into the *General Theory*. Keynes appeared at the week-ends when Richard Kahn reported to him our discussions of the week and when we met on Monday evenings at the Political Economy Club in Keynes' rooms in King's College. Thus I abandoned the formula MV = PT for I = S.

To spend this particular year reading essays to Dennis Robertson as one's supervisor and simultaneously enjoying membership of the group round Keynes was indeed an intellectual treat.

From 1931 to 1937 I was a Fellow and Lecturer in Economics at Hertford College, Oxford. The teaching of economics as a regular subject for examination was relatively new in Oxford and we were a young group of enthusiasts, including, in addition to Eric Hargreaves, my old tutor at Oriel College, Roy Harrod, Henry Phelps Brown, Charlie Hitch, Robert Hall, Lindley Fraser and Maurice Allen. My job was to teach the whole corpus of economic theory, but there were two subjects in which I was especially interested, namely the economics of mass unemployment and international economics. In the 1930s one was aware of two great evils – mass unemployment and the threat of war. I thought – and I still think – that the government of the United Kingdom could in those days have altered the course of world history by listening to Keynes on employment policy and by backing to the hilt the League of Nations for the preservation of peace. In Oxford there was a strong branch of the League of Nations Union with Gilbert Murray as its chairman and Margaret Wilson as its secretary. In 1933 Margaret and I were married. Was there some positive feedback between my interest in Margaret and my interest in international affairs?

Margaret had close links with Geneva where she had spent some years as a student while her parents had been wardens of the Quaker Hostel there and where she had gone back as secretary to Gilbert Murray. At the end of 1937 I joined the Economic Section of the League of Nations in Geneva as editor of the World Economic Survey and produced the two issues for 1937/38 and 1938/39. These were the seventh and eighth issues of the Survey, which had been preceded in 1931 by a prototype volume entitled *The Course and Phases of the World Depression*, prepared by Bertil Ohlin. The preparation of the World Economic Survey was backed by the more specialised volumes written by the established members of the section, including Rasminsky, Tirana, Nurkse and Hilgerdt. Haberler with Marcus Fleming as his assistant had just produced *Prosperity and Depression*; and Tinbergen with Polak as his assistant, followed by Koopmans, were busy applying statistical tests to the theories outlined by Haberler. Loveday, the Director of the Economic Section, seemed to have the knack of picking his team.

After the outbreak of war, in April 1940, we left Geneva with our three children aged 4 years, 2 years and 2 weeks only to become part of the disordered refugee crowds fleeing across France from the German army. After some adventures we reached England, where I became a member of the Economic Section of the War Cabinet Secretariat. I remained a member of the section till 1947, becoming Director in 1946. Under the inspiring war-time leadership of Lionel Robbins and in close co-operation with Keynes in the Treasury the Section became an influential body, having the day-to-day task of giving advice at a moment's notice on any economic problem ranging from points-rationing for foodstuffs to the price policies of nationalised industries. For myself three major tasks stand out. First and foremost in 1940 and 1941 Richard Stone and I prepared the first official estimates of the UK national income and expenditure, and we did so in a form which constituted what was, I believe, the first true double-entry social accounts prepared for any country. Second, there were the discussions and drafts leading up to the White Paper on Employment Policy of 1944, in which the UK government accepted the maintenance of employment as an obligation of governmental policy. Third, there were the discussions, state papers and conferences leading up to the post-war international financial and economic settlement, namely the International Monetary Fund, the International Bank for Reconstruction and Development and the General Agreement on Tariffs and Trade. I was especially concerned with the last of these.

In 1947 I became Professor of Commerce at the London School of Economics, where Lionel Robbins was our leader in the economics department with its large and rich team of economic colleagues. Of these I will mention only Professor A. W. H. Phillips to whom I owe an immense intellectual debt of gratitude for education in the treatment of dynamic systems. There I embarked on an over-ambitious project. My interest in economics has always been in the whole corpus of economic theory, the interrelationships between the various fields of theory and their relevance for the formulation of economic policy. In Oxford before the war I had, with this interest in mind, written a short text-book entitled *An Introduction to Economic Analysis and Policy*. It was now my intention to rewrite this work. I realised that it might be necessary to do so in more than one volume. So, as I was appointed at the LSE to teach international economics, I started on *The Theory of International Economic Policy*. It grew into my two books *The Balance of Payments* and *Trade and Welfare* with their two mathematical appendices. The former examined the international relations between a number of national economies constructed on the Keynesian model; the latter applied the theory of economic welfare to international transactions.

These books took up practically the whole of my ten years at the LSE; but even so they did not cover the whole of the international problem, there being little or no reference in them to the international aspects of economic growth or of dynamic disequilibrium. My original project was over-ambitious; but the part which I did manage to cover was sufficient eventually to gain for me the Nobel award.

In 1957 I moved from London to the chair of Political Economy in Cambridge, which I held till 1967, when I resigned to become a Senior Research Fellow of Christ's College, Cambridge. I relinquished that Fellowship on retirement age in 1974. During these years I set out to continue my over-ambitious project, planning to write one or two volumes on the domestic aspects of economic theory and policy. So far I have written four volumes in this series: *The Stationary Economy, The Growing Economy, The Controlled Economy,* and *The Just Economy*. But even so I have managed only to make a beginning. The frontiers of knowledge in the various fields of our subject are expanding at such a rate that, work as hard as one can, one finds oneself further and further away from an understanding of the whole. I believe this experience to illustrate the basic problem of our subject. Sane economic policy must take into account simultaneously all aspects of the economy; but a soundly based understanding of the whole and of the relationship between its parts becomes more and more difficult, if not impossible, to attain.

How then should a seventy-year old best use his remaining years? Since 1974 I have taken time off to act as full-time chairman of a committee set up by the Institute for Fiscal Studies to examine the structure of direct taxation in the United Kingdom, the committee consisting of a number of first-rate economic theorists and of leading practitioners in tax law, accountancy and administration. I have learned as much in the last three years as in any other comparable period of my life, but with an added realisation of how little over half a century of study one has in fact managed to learn of the whole range of economic policy issues.

Such in brief outline has been my intellectual development. But whatever I may have achieved would have been impossible without the advantages of my family background: a loving mother, a father concerned only to give me the best start in life, a wife who gives unfailing support, and four happily married children providing seven lively grandchildren.

Postscript, October 1986

What has happened in the nine years which have elapsed since the above words were written?

A notable change is that our children have now provided an eighth lively grandchild.

Intellectually my work has been concentrated on the development of the ideas presented in my Stockholm lecture on 'The Meaning of "Internal Balance"'. In that lecture I discussed the possibility of a new Keynesian approach to our macro-economic problems by concentrating Keynesian financial policies on the control of the *money* value of total national income in combination with a radical reform of wage-fixing institutions to promote the *real* target of 'full employment'.

I have worked on these ideas with a number of able and enthusiastic colleagues in Cambridge including economists and control engineers (David Vines, Martin Weale, Jan Maciejowski, Peter Westaway, Nicos Christodoulakis, and Andy Blake). Reports on the first stage of this work have appeared in book form – *Stagflation, Volume 1: Wage-Fixing* (1982) and *Volume 2: Demand Management* (1983).

By that time we had already increased the financial targets from two (control of inflation and of the balance of payments) to three by the addition of control of the distribution of the national resources between consumption and investment for future growth. Since that time the team has done much work in four main fields:

(1)   the design of different combinations and forms of monetary, fiscal, and foreign exchange-rate policies in order to achieve different combinations and forms of control over money incomes, the balance of payments, and the distribution of resources between consumption and capital investment;

(2)   ways to allow for the formation of expectations and for their effects on the consequential developments in the economy;

(3) modifications of an existing fully complete macro-economic model of the United Kingdom economy (the National Institute for Economic and Social Research model) in certain ways which are needed if it is to be used for the simulation of the effects of our various combinations of policies rather than for forecasting purposes; and

(4) the actual application of various policy designs and treatments of expectations to the modified model.

It is hoped that this second stage of the team's work will be completed in 1987, which for me personally would be a most welcome celebration of four score years of existence and of a decade of concentrated work since my Stockholm lecture.

2

Public Works in their International Aspect

Written in 1932 and published by the New Fabian Research Bureau in January 1933, this pamphlet is reprinted here without the introduction by H. B. Butler, the Director of the International Labour Office, the first chapter, which was added by A. A. Evans of the ILO, and the final chapter on 'Schemes of public works', which was also included at the instigation of Evans and others at the ILO (Meade Papers 2/3).

II General Issues and Problems of Administration

It has frequently been argued that unemployment and the other evils, which are caused by cyclical fluctuations in trade, may to a large extent be avoided by a policy on the part of public authorities of concentrating their expenditure on capital developments and renewals in periods of unemployment and bad trade, and cutting down such expenditure in times of good trade. The international aspect of a public works policy is, however, too often neglected. What agreements are necessary between nations to make any such policy really effective? What are the possibilities of international co-operation in undertaking works on roads, railways, electricity schemes, etc., which cut across national frontiers and are common to many nations?

The possibility of there being a policy of public works, as distinct from works undertaken merely for relief of unemployment, depends upon the international body, the governments, municipalities or public utility companies planning in advance. For the policy means that, when trade is beginning to be depressed and unemployment to increase, because the orders of private businesses are slackening, public authorities should press forward with their plans of development. These plans must have been prepared and postponed in good times; for there are very few undertakings of any importance which can be undertaken at a few months' notice. This policy involves important problems of administration, which are certainly not insoluble, but which differ from country to country and which cannot be discussed in very great detail here. Apart from questions of the administration of international works proper, which will be discussed later, there are certain general administrative difficulties.

(1) A central government, which has decided upon a policy of public works, must ensure that municipalities and public utility companies, who may be responsible for a very large proportion of the public works to be undertaken, do form plans in advance.

(2) In the second place, even if the central government can assure that plans are ready, it must have some means of deciding when such works should be pressed on and when postponed. Movements in the general price index or in the number of workers unemployed are possible criteria. But, as we shall see, so many considerations of the international economic position of the country concerned should affect its public works policy, that it would probably be best for the authorities of a single country to take no automatic criterion as a guide to the proper time to spend money on public works, but rather to judge every moment on its merits, on the general assumption that expenditure on public works should be increased, when prices and employment fall.

(3) In the third place the central government must find means actually to postpone or speed up expenditure on public works at the desired moment. In as far as the central government is responsible for the works, there is no difficulty here. In as far as municipalities or other authorities are responsible, if the moral persuasion of the central government is not sufficient, it must, by providing grants-in-aid or loans at low rates of interest to the authorities concerned, provide some incentive for increased expenditure in bad times, and by withdrawing such incentives and even by the imposition of special taxation delay such expenditure in good times.

(4) There is a fourth difficulty, which is more apparent than real, but which will occur to any body which is expected to undertake a policy of public works, namely, that in the nature of things works undertaken by public authorities are for the most part incapable of being postponed or brought forward in time; for instance, as the population in any district grows, new houses must be provided and, when new houses are built, the municipality concerned must extend its electricity, gas and water supplies appropriately. It cannot choose the time at which this shall be done. To some extent this is true; but there is a very large amount of public development which, *so long as authorities plan in advance*, would be capable of postponement or of speeding up. In nearly every country there is a large amount of slum clearance work to be undertaken, which history has proved to be capable of postponement and which a little town planning would prove to be capable of being tackled on a large scale. Again, the development of motor roads, the supply of electricity to new districts, the renewal of roads, bridges and railway equipment – all these things and many others are capable to some degree of being postponed or brought forward in time. But there may well be a real cost in postponing public works and concentrating them in certain times of bad trade. For instance, a railway station may become very congested in a time of good trade, if some necessary extension is being postponed. Since a policy of public works is being undertaken to avoid worse evils and may depend upon such postponement, such advance planning and postponement of works is worthwhile.

III Public Works as an Instrument of Stabilisation

Our next task is to see how a trade boom or depression can be caused, and to discuss their fundamental characteristics, in order to see whether a policy of public works can do anything to mitigate such fluctuations. In this chapter the discussion will relate to a single country, disregarding its connection with the rest of the world. Such a discussion is merely a necessary preliminary to the international aspect of the problem.

There are many causes which may start a trade boom or a trade depression, but all trade booms and all trade depressions have many features in common. There may be an important invention, which means that at the current rate of interest industrialists wish to invest a great deal of money in machinery and equipment of a new kind. This may well lead to a general trade boom. For in this case more money may be spent upon this new capital equipment without there being an equivalent reduction in the amount spent on other capital goods or on consumption goods. In the first place, when the invention takes place, persons, whether they are industrialists directly interested or simply members of the public, may invest in the new opening for capital money, which they had idle at deposit in the banks; this would cause an increased flow of money spent on such goods without a diminution of expenditure elsewhere. Secondly, those directly interested in the new form of capital development may borrow more insistently from the banks, who may thus be induced to lend money more freely and to increase the amount of credit they give, thus again causing an additional expenditure of new money. But in the third place, when once this additional expenditure on capital goods is started, it will begin to finance itself. For those who produce capital goods will have larger incomes and will therefore be enabled to save more money; companies producing capital goods will add money to their reserves when their receipts increase; more taxes will be paid to the state and, since more hands will be taken on in industries producing capital goods, state expenditure on unemployment relief will fall, so that there will be an increased budget surplus. At the same time those producing capital goods will increase their expenditure on consumption goods, so that these persons too will be able to save more money; companies producing goods for consumption will put more money to reserve; the tax receipts of the state will rise still more, while expenditure on unemployment relief will fall further, as more are employed in producing goods for consumption. Now all these sources – namely, increased savings by individuals, purchase of securities by companies to add to their reserves, and the increased budget surplus due to the rise in tax receipts and the fall in expenditure – will represent an increased demand for securities and will provide funds, by which the increased expenditure on capital goods can be financed.

But at this point it must be realised that the price of all goods and of ordinary shares will be rising. The price of capital goods will be rising because there is an increase in the total amount spent on them; the price of consumption goods will be rising because those producing capital goods have more to spend on them; and since industry will have become more profitable, the price of ordinary shares will be moving up. This upward movement of prices provides a further very strong incentive for increases in expenditure. Thus every business concern will have a strong inducement to speed up expenditure on capital goods, because industry has become more profitable and because the price of capital goods is rising, so that it expects to buy them cheaper now than in the future. When prices are rising no one will desire to hold money, but rather to hold goods or securities, since, if bought and held for a time, they can be sold for a money profit. Merchants will therefore increase their stocks, business concerns of every kind will increase their holdings of raw materials, and private individuals will desire to hold ordinary shares, rather than money. Such action will still further increase the rise in prices and in the total amount spent on goods.

Thus a typical boom will have started. What means could have been taken to stop it? The banks could have raised interest rates by raising their discount rates and by selling securities in the market, which would have depressed their price. Such a rise in interest rates would make it less profitable to borrow money for capital developments, and, if carried out on a large enough scale and soon enough, would have prevented the boom. But, as we have seen, once the boom has started, the fact that prices are rising will provide so large an incentive for increased expenditure on capital goods, that movements in the rate of interest will not control such expenditure. Here is the great opportunity of control through public works; if, as soon as the boom starts, public authorities postpone their expenditure at the same time that the banks raise interest rates, the rise in prices might be stopped. Such expenditure should simply be postponed to an extent and for a time sufficient to stop the rise in prices and to allow the banks by raising interest rates to regain control. Thus there must be close co-ordination between a public works policy and monetary policy.

What happens during the depression? A time comes when the expenditure on new capital goods for the purposes of the invention, which we are supposing to have started the boom, ceases, because all the new capital necessary for the invention is installed. This decrease in expenditure on capital goods will mean that the price of capital goods begins to fall. The fall in the incomes of those producing these capital goods will mean that they decrease their expenditure on consumption goods, so that the price of consumption goods also falls. For the same reason industry as a whole will become less profitable, so that the price of ordinary shares will fall. But, as we have already seen, a great deal of expenditure on new capital goods was taking place, simply because prices were rising so quickly, and this expenditure will cease, causing prices to fall still more rapidly. As soon as prices begin to fall, there will be every incentive to reduce expenditure on goods and to hold money instead. Thus merchants will sell stocks of goods without replacing them, since they are falling in money value. Companies will postpone investment in machinery, because industry is less profitable and because the price of machines is falling and will be lower in the future; and private individuals, since the price of shares is falling, will sell shares and hold money instead. All these things will add still further to the fall in prices.

Now in this case the depression might have been prevented at the very outset, if the banks had lowered interest rates by lowering their discount rates and by purchasing securities in the open market and so raising their price. For such a lowering of the rate of interest at which persons can borrow would, if sufficiently large, have induced persons to start borrowing money for further capital developments. But in this case as well, as soon as prices begin to move, the rate of interest itself will lose its power of control over the amount spent on new capital goods. For when prices of capital goods are falling, persons will not spend more on capital goods simply because of a fall in the rate of interest at which they can borrow money. Further, when the price of finished commodities is falling, and no one knows how far the fall is going, persons will not be willing to extend their capital equipment. When their price is falling, merchants will not be willing to hold larger stocks because the rate of interest at which they can borrow money is lowered, since the expected fall in price of the commodities may outweigh any fall in interest rates.[1] But if at this point public authorities determine to borrow for public works and to spend more on capital goods, at the same time that the banks are lowering interest rates, they will thereby be able to stop the fall in the price of capital goods and also, by maintaining the expenditure on consumption goods of those producing capital goods, to stop the fall in price of consumption goods, and so also the fall in profits and in share prices. Such extra expenditure on public works should be undertaken on a sufficient scale to prevent prices falling. It need only last sufficiently long to enable the banks by lowering interest rates to stimulate expenditure by ordinary private business again, and then the expenditure on public works can be diminished, as that of private business increases.

IV Certain Objections

We are now in a position to meet certain objections which are frequently made to a policy of this nature.

In the first place it is frequently argued that the extra borrowing by the state for public works will take funds of an exactly equivalent amount from private industry, so that there will be no net increase in business activity. Whether this is so or not depends upon the action of the banks. If public works are undertaken at a time when private industry cannot be stimulated by low interest rates and an easy money policy, then public borrowing for public works will provide just the opening for new funds which is required. But if, at a time when the state is undertaking a policy

---

[1] The attempts of the Federal Reserve System in the USA throughout 1932 to improve the situation by purchasing securities and lowering interest rates have not been as yet successful; for the fact that prices are still falling so rapidly in the USA has meant that low interest rates have little power to stimulate expenditure on capital goods. If this policy, however, had been coupled for a time with one of planned capital development by the Federal and State governments and municipalities, the result would have been very different.

of public works, the banks are not adopting an easy money policy but are keeping interest rates high, then it is quite possible that the increased expenditure on public works will be accompanied by an exactly equivalent decrease in expenditure on capital developments on the part of private industry.

It is for this reason that a close co-ordination of monetary policy and the public works policy is so necessary. But it by no means follows that the whole expenditure on the public works should be financed by new money provided by the banks; for once the monetary policy of the banks has brought it about that the expenditure on public works does represent additional expenditure on capital equipment, funds to finance these works will automatically be released. A numerical example will perhaps best illustrate this. Suppose that £100 millions a year is being spent on public works and that this does represent additional expenditure on capital equipment. Then, since more persons are being employed directly on the works or in producing the necessary raw materials, there will be a decrease of (e.g.) £25 m. in the state's expenditure on unemployment benefit; the contractors will be making larger profits and will therefore save (e.g.) £10 m. more a year and pay £5 m. more a year in taxes. Thus those engaged directly on the public works or in producing the raw materials for them will be receiving £100 m. more a year in income, but will be spending £60 m. more a year on consumption goods, since of this £100 m. £15 m. a year are being saved or paid in taxes and £25 m. a year are merely taking the place of unemployment relief, which was already being spent on consumption goods. But this additional £60 m. expenditure per year on consumption goods will cause greater employment and profits in these industries; this will mean (e.g.) a further diminution of £20 m. a year in unemployment benefit, a further increase in savings or in sums put to reserve by companies producing consumption goods of (e.g.) £10 m. a year, and a further increase in tax payments of (e.g.) £10 m. a year. Thus there will be a further increase of £20 m. expenditure per year on consumption goods due to this increase of £60 m. in the amount spent per year on consumption goods by those engaged on the public works, since of this £60 m. £40 m. a year only is saved, paid in taxes, or put to reserve by companies, or takes the place of previous expenditure of unemployment benefit. Of the additional £20 m. expenditure a year on consumption goods again a certain amount will be passed on as further expenditure on goods for consumption, and the rest will again be saved, or paid in taxes, or take the place of unemployment benefit. This process of ever-diminishing waves of expenditure must continue, until the whole of the £100 m. additional expenditure per year on public works is 'held up' in the form of increased individual savings, or additional sums put to reserve by companies, or additional tax payments, or diminution of other state expenditure. Thus the increase in the budget surplus, plus the increased savings of individuals, plus the increased sums put to reserve by companies, because of the extra activity caused by the expenditure of £100 m. a year on public works, must be equal to £100 m. a year, so that these sources of additional funds will be just sufficient to finance the public works.

Secondly, it is argued that expenditure on public works will as a matter of fact provide very little employment owing to the necessity of providing raw materials and of allowing for the profits of the contractors and others who will be concerned in the works. This argument entirely neglects the fact that the number of workers actually employed on the public works is one of the least important effects on employment, since consideration must be taken of those who are employed in providing the raw materials and also in meeting the extra money demand for consumption goods brought about by this policy. It must be realised that a policy of public works with a co-ordinated monetary policy may be the means of preventing a general depression.

Thirdly, it is often objected that public works are very costly. In so far as this policy is simply one of postponing works from good to bad times, this argument has little validity; for in bad times, especially if the banks are co-operating in lowering rates of interest, the public authorities will be able to borrow at a much cheaper rate than in good times, and further in such times the price of materials and of labour is likely to be low. Thus the works will probably be undertaken at a cheaper price. Possibly by concentrating the works at given times less efficient labour will have to be taken on; there will be some cost to be borne, because the works are not spread evenly over time, and there will be the real inconvenience – as we have seen above – of postponing works. But the policy is certainly worth this price. If however public works of general utility, which would not otherwise have been undertaken, are undertaken in bad times simply for the relief of unemployment, they will be as effective as any other works in preventing a general depression, if accompanied by an expansionist monetary policy.

In this case it is argued that the state is undertaking works at a great cost, which are 'unproductive'. The cost of such works, however, cannot simply be determined by the direct charge they put on the budget. For since, if they are successful, they will cause a decrease in unemployment and an increase in tax receipts, they will actually be the direct cause of some relief to the budget, and at the same time they will probably bring in some net revenue to the state, even if their actual 'productivity' is small. Thus they may cause no net charge on the budget. Suppose that a policy of public works together with an easy money policy had been undertaken by all countries in 1930 on a scale sufficiently large to arrest the development of the depression; could anyone in 1932 seriously maintain that they had been 'costly' or added any strain to the nations' budgets even if all the work undertaken had been entirely unproductive? But even if such works did impose some net charge on the budget in future years in payment of interest on the debt so incurred, the necessary increase in taxation, while it has certain disadvantages, is by no means a 'burden' on the society to be measured directly by the amount of interest to be paid, since the payment simply represents a transfer of income by taxation within the country from one person to another.

We may conclude then that, if a policy of public works simply means the postponement of works from good to bad times, these works are likely to be undertaken actually at a lower cost; that if the public works undertaken in bad times are special works of general utility undertaken to create employment, even then they are not likely to add any appreciable burden to the budget, if they are co-ordinated with an easy money policy and are carried out on a sufficient scale to stop the depression; and thirdly that a budgetary 'burden' is not a direct burden to be measured by the increase in taxation necessary to meet it. But, while a state should not shrink from borrowing in times of depression in order to undertake schemes of capital development, it should certainly not hesitate in good times from taxing heavily to repay these loans.

V   The Necessity for International Co-operation

In the previous three chapters the main arguments in favour of public works have been considered without reference to the fact that no single country is an isolated unit. From this point we must turn to the international aspect of public works. In this chapter we shall discuss why international co-operation is as desirable in a policy of public works as in a monetary policy.

We have seen that a policy of public works undertaken together with an easy money policy will raise prices and will also raise the money incomes of all those engaged in production. If such a policy is adopted in one country alone, it is therefore likely to lead to certain difficulties. There will probably be an increased purchase of imported raw materials in connection with the public works; both workers and others in the country in which the policy is being pursued will spend more on foreign commodities, because they will have larger money incomes, and also because the price of home-produced goods will have risen. At the same time the purchase on the part of foreigners of goods produced in the country in question will fall off, since prices in that country have risen. For these reasons the amount spent on imports into the country adopting a policy of public works will rise, while the amount received for its exports will fall.

This will lead to certain difficulties. If the country in question is on the gold standard, which prevents its exchange rate with other countries from fluctuating, it will immediately begin to lose gold to other countries to pay for the increase in its imports and the decrease in its exports. This cannot continue for long, and it will be obliged to raise its interest rates, in order to attract loans from abroad or to induce its own citizens to lend less to others, in order by this means to finance the decrease in its exports and increase in its imports. But this rise in interest rates will discourage private business from borrowing for capital developments at home, and will therefore largely counteract the effect of the expenditure of money by public authorities on public works. This does not necessarily mean that it will be impossible for a country in these circumstances to act alone. It could by raising a tariff, at the same time that it adopted a policy of low interest rates and public works at home, prevent any net increase in the amount spent by it on imports. It could take a strict control, other than by raising interest rates, of the amount which it lent abroad; by putting a special tax on incomes derived from abroad, it might be able so to lessen the incentive to lend abroad, that it could by this means pay for the increase in its imports. Finally something might be done by one country alone, if it indulged in a policy of public works, while at the same time it allowed the rate of interest in the country to rise. For the rise in the rate of interest would provide an incentive for its citizens to lend less abroad or for foreigners to lend more to it, so that thereby it could finance its increased imports. The rise in the rate of interest would, however, discourage some expenditure on capital development by private industry; and for there to be any net increase in the amount spent on capital goods, the amount spent on public works by public authorities at the higher rate of interest would have to be sufficient not only to make up for the decrease in the amount invested by private business in capital developments, but also to provide some net increase. Thus in this case the expense of public works would be great since the rate of interest would be high, and to some extent such expenditure would take the place of capital development by private business. Moreover, the policy might become semi-permanent, since in these circumstances the banks could not stimulate private business again by low interest rates.[2]

The position would however be quite different, if all countries had decided to adopt a policy of low interest rates and of public works at the same time. Since in this case prices would have been raised in every country, there would not be any incentive for one country, simply because its price level had risen, to buy more from another than before. Since money incomes would have risen in all countries, there would be an equal incentive in every country to spend more on the goods of other countries, so that no country would lose gold, so long as appropriate rates of expenditure on public works had been adopted in each country. It is generally recognised that, if an attempt is made by monetary policy to avoid unemployment or to stabilise prices, all countries must co-operate and raise and lower interest rates together at appropriate rates, to avoid exchange difficulties. *It should be equally clearly realised that such international co-operation is desirable, and for the same reasons, in the case of a policy of public works.*

We must next turn our attention to the case of a country which alone undertakes a policy of public works together with an easy money policy, but which is not on any fixed international monetary standard, so that its exchange rates can fluctuate. In this case the rise in its money incomes and prices will again lead to an increase in the amount spent on its imports and to a fall in the amount of its exports. However, in this case this will cause a depreciation of its exchange rate, so that a unit of its currency will purchase less of foreign currencies. Foreign goods will become more expensive to its citizens, while its own goods, since foreigners can purchase its currency with less of their own, will be cheaper to foreigners. Thus its imports wil be restricted again and its exports stimulated.

For this reason such a country will be in a much easier position to act alone in a national policy of public works. But there are still important

---

[2] Quite possibly Great Britain was in this position between 1925 and 1931.

difficulties, which would be avoided by an international policy of public works. In the first place, the fact that it was the known policy of the country to maintain prices, employment and money incomes by this policy, while prices and money incomes are falling elsewhere, would mean that it was well known that the currency of this country would over a period of time depreciate in terms of other currencies. It would therefore pay speculators to sell the currency of the country in question and buy that of other countries. This speculation would make the currency of the country depreciate still further, and such a speculative movement might cause it to depreciate out of all relation to any depreciation naturally to be expected from the movement in relative prices and incomes. Such speculative depreciation, by raising the price of the goods it imports, might even seriously endanger the standard of living of its members, if it relied for a large proportion of its consumption upon imported goods. At the least such a policy in a single country is likely to give rise to serious inconveniences due to fluctuations in its rate of exchange.

But, in the second place, the existence of international debts may raise serious difficulties in the case of a single debtor country alone adopting a policy of public works not financed by an external loan, even if it is not on an international monetary standard. For if a country has to pay fixed sums of money every year in interest on government or private debts, these sums are likely to be expressed in terms of the currencies of the creditor countries. In this case, as its currency depreciates in terms of other currencies, this will again stimulate its exports and cut off its imports, but at the same time it will mean that it has to pay more in its own currency to meet the interest payment expressed in other currencies; for this reason the depreciation of its currency might have to go a very long way before it could manage to adopt this policy of public works without failing to pay the interest on its external debt. It is possible, if the debt payment is large relative to the volume of its foreign trade, and if a depreciation in its rate of exchange does not greatly stimulate its exports or restrict its imports, that it will be impossible for it to adopt this policy of public works simply and solely by allowing the rate of exchange to go against it and yet at the same time meet the interest payment on its debt.

In the third place, while it is certain that the depreciation of a single country's currency in terms of other currencies will cause an increase in the value of its exports in terms of its own currency, and while it is certain that the depreciation of its currency will by raising their price restrict the volume of its imports, yet, if the rise in the price of these goods only slightly reduces the amount purchased, a greater total amount of money may be spent on them. The depreciation of the country's currency, while it will increase the value of its exports, may not decrease, but may increase the value of its imports. If it imports goods which it cannot well do without, the depreciation of its currency will seriously increase the amount it has to pay for its imports, and this will intensify its difficulties.

It is therefore most desirable, if not essential, that even when there is not an international monetary standard such as the gold standard, there should nevertheless be international co-operation in any policy of public works, as in any monetary policy. For in this case, if all countries adopt the policy at the same time, there would be no need for any fluctuations in exchange rates, since prices and money incomes would rise in every country at the same time.

VI Debtor and Creditor Countries

There remains one more question of the utmost importance in any international policy of public works. When a world depression starts some countries will be much more severely hit than others. In the first place debtor countries with debts fixed in terms of money will be faced by great difficulties. For suppose that a country, owing £10 m. per annum in interest on debt, has been importing goods worth £90 m. and exporting goods worth £100 m., the excess of its exports over its imports being used to pay the interest on its debt. Suppose, then, in a world depression that the total value of world trade is halved. Then if the value of its imports and of its exports were halved in each case, so that it was importing £45 m. and exporting £50 m. it would now only have a surplus of £5 m. from which to pay the interest of £10 m. This country will therefore lose gold; or else it must borrow more from other countries; or it must reduce its prices and costs so as to import less and export more; or it must let its exchange depreciate in an attempt to stimulate its exports and cut off its imports at the cost of adding to the burden of its debt in terms of its own currency; or else it must raise tariffs to reduce its imports, and by exchange restrictions attempt to secure as much foreign exchange as it can to pay its debt; or else it must default. But a country cannot go on for long meeting such a situation by an export of gold, and the worse its situation becomes, the less willing are creditors to lend to it, since it is already experiencing great difficulty in paying the interest on existing loans. At first tariffs will be raised, as in all debtor countries in this depression; Australia tried the method of exchange depreciation, Germany that of lowering prices and costs by decree and that of exchange restriction; while some debtors have defaulted.

Also those countries which produce commodities which are already 'overproduced' relative to other commodities and whose supply is not so quickly restricted as that of other commodities, will also be in particular difficulties in the depression. The prices of raw materials and of many agricultural products, such as wheat, wool, rubber, etc., have fallen much more severely than the prices of manufactured commodities, because these things are relatively overproduced and because their supply is not readily cut down with a fall in their prices. For this reason the countries producing these commodities will suffer a very severe reduction in the value of their exports, while the value of their imports will not fall so quickly. They will therefore find themselves in the same kind of exchange difficulties as the debtor countries. When they are also debtor countries, as in most cases they are (cf. Australia, Argentina, Brazil and many of the East European countries), their plight will be very serious.

Now these countries, namely the debtors and those the prices of whose export products have fallen most severely, will probably be suffering most severely from the depression; for their central banks will have had to raise interest rates very severely to attract foreign funds, which will very largely have restricted their internal activity. It is therefore often proposed that the creditor countries should relieve the exchange situation by lending more freely to the debtor countries by means of state guaranteed loans, and that the debtor countries should use these funds for schemes of public works in their countries to absorb their unemployed. Several schemes of this nature have been proposed. It is essential therefore to examine this principle.

Now there is no doubt at all that such schemes would give temporary relief in a period of depression. For the lending of money to the debtor countries would ease the exchange position of those countries; they could therefore indulge in expenditure on public works, which would absorb the unemployed and raise prices and money incomes in these countries. The increase in their importation of raw materials and of consumption goods and any fall in their exports, due to the rise in their prices and incomes, would be financed by the increased lending to them on the part of the creditors. But such action might only intensify future difficulties. For, as the debtor countries borrowed more, the amount which they would have to pay in interest would accumulate, and their exchange position would become worse. In any future periods of difficulty their situation might be very much worse because of this action.

This situation can perhaps be best illustrated by the history of Germany between 1925 and 1930. During these years Germany was enabled to meet her reparations liability by borrowing from creditor countries, mainly from America. In fact, she borrowed more than her total reparation liability payable during these years. These funds were used to a large extent by States and municipalities for expenditure on developments, which could be undertaken largely without regard to the rate of interest demanded on the loan; some of the funds were used for rationalisation of Germany's main industries, which certainly might have had the result of helping her to produce and sell in the international markets those goods which the creditors would have wanted. Germany might thereby have been able to meet the interest on her loans as well as the reparation payments, *had the creditor countries, when Germany's exports began to expand, shown themselves ready to see their imports increase and exports decrease*. But this they were unwilling to do. Both England and the United States of America have, since the slump of 1930, attempted to obtain a more favourable balance of trade by significantly raising tariffs; as soon as Germany developed an export suplus other countries attempted to 'protect their balance of trade'.

This history should serve as a warning. Loans made to debtor countries by creditor countries for the pupposes of public works should not be allowed, unless these works will be such as to improve the position of these countries in the export market, so as to enable them to pay the interest on the loan. Even in this case, this policy should not be adopted, unless the creditor countries consciously agree to allow an increase in their importation from the debtor countries in the future and to allow an unfavourable balance of trade to develop, so that the debtors can pay the interest on their loans. And this is largely a question of tariffs; creditor countries must show their willingness to lower their tariffs to enable the debtor countries to meet their debts, as soon as the debtors get into exchange difficulties. Naturally in cases in which these conditions can be fulfilled, such a policy is most desirable. *But it would be disastrous if this policy of further lending were undertaken simply for the temporary relief it provides, since the future intensified difficulties of the debtor countries, which could be directly traced to this policy, would undoubtedly very seriously discredit the whole cause of a sane public works policy.*

What help then can the creditor countries provide in this situation? There is one method by which they can not only help the debtor countries but at the same time relieve their own position in the depression. The creditor countries should themselves indulge in a vigorous policy of public works together with an expansionist monetary policy. For such a policy will, as we have seen, cause them to spend more on imported goods of every kind. This would immediately relieve the strain on the exchanges of debtor countries, and would enable them to pay their debts. It would lead to the removal of exchange restrictions and remove the main incentive to raise tariffs. Or, if that is not enough, the creditor countries mut be willing at the same time to lower their tariffs and so allow the debtor countries to develop a favourable balance of trade.

Such a policy on the part of creditor countries, in so far as they are not on an international monetary standard, should be accompanied by an attempt to maintain the value of their currency rather than to let it depreciate. For the less the currency of creditor countries depreciates as they raise prices and money incomes by a policy of public works, the greater the incentive for those countries to buy more goods from the debtor countries and the less the incentive of the debtor countries to purchase from the creditors.

As a contrast to this helpful policy on the part of creditor countries during a depression, we may compare the policy of Great Britain during the first half of 1932. In this country following the imposition of tariffs an attempt was made, by the purchase of gold by the Bank of England and by the purchase of foreign currencies first by the Bank and then indirectly through the Exchange Equalisation Account, to keep the value of the pound low in the foreign exchange market, and thereby to cheapen our exports in the world's markets, and to restrict our importation of commodities. At the same time prices in this country continued to fall, without any attempt through a vigorous public works policy together with the cheap money policy to stop this. The Government has on the contrary attempted to practice 'economy'. Now it may have been the intention of the authorities by this means so to increase exports and decrease imports that we could lend more abroad to help the weak countries. But the very fact that Great Britain tried thus to buy less from them and to sell more cheaply to them caused a further fall of world prices, more unemployment and business losses abroad. Our increased foreign lending was probably to a considerable extent used simply to finance budget deficits and business losses abroad caused by this policy of attempting to throw more goods on the world markets and to take less off them. What a difference our policy might have had on world prices and world trade, if we had maintained the value of the pound as much as we could, at the same time that we raised prices and incomes at home by a policy of public works!

In a depression, therefore, creditor countries should go ahead with a public works policy and raise prices and incomes in their own countries, thereby relieving the strain on the debtors' exchange position; further, they should be willing at this period to see an increase in their imports in order to aid the weaker countries. This does not mean that debtor countries may never go forward with a policy of public works. For as soon as the exchange difficulties have been removed by the action of the creditor countries, it will be possible for the debtor countries, having experienced an increased demand for their exports, to go forward themselves with a public works policy together with a monetary policy of low interest rates.

Now such a policy, in which the creditor countries go ahead sooner and on a larger scale than the debtors in their public works policy, may seem to lead to a further discrepancy between the standard of living of the creditor countries, which is likely to be already high, and that of the debtor countries, which is likely to be low; while the obvious policy of undertaking public works in debtor countries financed by loans from creditor countries would seem to lessen this discrepancy. But the contrast is very unreal. For a short time it may be true. But as soon as the debtor countries have to pay the interest on the loans, if those loans have not been used to develop their capacity to produce goods for export which creditors would be willing to buy, they would be in a very much worse relative position than they would have been in, had the loans not been made. For in any attempt to develop the value of their exports and cut down their imports to pay the debt, they would be compelled to reduce wages, raise interest rates and therefore face severe unemployment, and to raise the price of their imports by the imposition of tariffs. Whereas if in the first place the creditor countries had relieved their position by buying from them instead of lending to them, none of these results would have followed.

This policy of international agreement as to the timing of public works, whereby the creditor countries agree to go ahead sooner than and on a larger scale than debtor countries, would need international co-operation. It does not by any means exclude the policy of developing international public works or schemes common to many nations, which works are the ideal means of seeing that all nations move together in a policy of public works; nor is it inconsistent with the policy of creditor countries agreeing together to guarantee loans to debtor countries for the purpose of expenditure on public works, so long as those works are such as to increase the ability of the debtor countries to sell cheaply in the export market goods that are not over-produced, *and so long as creditors declare themselves ready in the future to face an increase in the value of their imports without a corresponding increase in the value of their exports of commodities.*

We have seen then the reasons why international agreement in a public works policy is so desirable. It is not, however, to be assumed that no country can therefore do anything significant alone by a national public works policy. An important creditor country with a strong exchange position might alone be able not only to help itself but to help other countries considerably by such a policy. Any country which has no debts fixed in terms of other countries' currencies might help itself considerably by such a policy, if it allowed its exchanges to depreciate; and it might do so even without any exchange depreciation, if it is a large country spending a small proportion of its income on imports from the rest of the world, so that a considerable rise in its incomes and prices would cause a very small increase in the amount it spent on imports.

VII   The Organisation of International Co-operation

The next problem is to decide what type of organisation is best fitted to serve the purposes required for an international policy of public works. We need a body which fulfils the following conditions:

(1) It must be representative of as many nations as possible, both debtor and creditor.

(2) It must represent the governments of the nations concerned, in order to ensure that actual steps are taken to advance and postpone expenditure on capital developments. It must have the services of representatives of the central banks of the nations concerned, to ensure co-ordination with the nations' monetary policies, on the principles outlined above. It must include representatives of the workers of these countries, to ensure that conditions of work on such capital developments are consistent with the standards set in those countries. Finally it must be able to obtain the services of experts to examine and report on the technical and economic possibilities of the different schemes of international works and of national works in countries which desire to float loans on the international market, with or without the guarantee of creditor countries, for their undertaking. We have already discussed the main economic conditions which schemes of this type should fulfil.

(3) The functions of any such international body would be to provide an organisation, in which the countries concerned would deposit all the possible information concerning schemes of capital development, which they were undertaking at the time, which they had already planned but were postponing, and which they were planning or simply considering as possible fields of action in the future. It should also provide an organisation for the planning and consideration of international works, or should examine schemes of international developments prepared by such bodies as, in the case of road development, the Permanent International Association of Road Congresses or the International Office of Motor Roads. It should examine or submit to examination by experts those plans of a national character in countries which desired international loans for their financing, and should report whether these schemes satisfied the required economic and technical conditions. Finally, it should recommend to governments to what degree, having regard to the

strength of their exchange positions, they should postpone or advance expenditure, should recommend to governments of creditor countries those loans to the countries in a weak exchange position, which they considered to be fit objects of some international guarantee, and finally should report on the monetary policies desirable in different countries for the success of their other proposals.

Before outlining a possible form of organisation to meet these requirements, it is necessary to recount briefly what has recently been done in the international sphere in this field,[3] in order to understand the present administrative position. In January 1931 the Governing Body of the International Labour Organisation passed a resolution, in which was expressed 'the possibility of Governments coming to an agreement through the appropriate organs of the League of Nations with a view to joint execution of extensive public works of an international character'. In April 1931 a memorandum was submitted by the International Labour Office to the Governing Body drawing attention to the possibility of extensive public works of an international character, and the Director of the International Labour Office was authorised to submit this in his own name to the Commission of Enquiry for European Union. This body considered the problem to be mainly a financial one and drew the attention of its Committee on Credit Problems to the work done by the International Labour Office in this sphere. The proposals, which had been made by the International Labour Office, were discussed by the Committee on Credit Problems; this committee suggested that the Committee of Enquiry on General Questions relating to Public Works and National Technical Equipment, set up by the Communications and Transit Organisation of the League of Nations, should, with the addition of representatives of the International Labour Office, be the proper body to examine proposals submitted to the League by governments, and that the Financial Committee of the League would then have to consider from the financial point of view those proposals which were already so approved from the technical and economic point of view. This proposal met with the approval of the Assembly and the Council of the League.

In October 1931 the Committee of Enquiry on General Questions relating to Public Works and National Technical Equipment met and circularised all States Members of the League and Soviet Russia and Turkey, asking them to give information of schemes of work, which they contemplated undertaking. In April 1932 the committee met again to examine schemes submitted by governments, and in May its report on these schemes was submitted to the Council of the League. The Council reserved its opinion until it should receive a further report from the Committee, in order that it might be able to give its opinion upon a larger number of schemes at the same time. In September 1932 the Committee presented a second report to the Council, which, in accepting the report, passed a resolution to the effect that the Commission of Experts, who were responsible for the preparation of the agenda of the World

---

[3] See the report of the Director of the International Labour Office to the Sixteenth Session of the International Labour Conference, 1932, pp. 37–39.

Economic Conference, should be asked to examine the reports of the Committee of Enquiry on General Questions relating to Public Works and National Technical Equipment, with a view to the inclusion of this problem in the agenda of the Conference.

This then is the administrative position at the moment: schemes are submitted by governments to the Committee on General Questions relating to Public Works and National Technical Equipment, which examines their technical merits and their economic 'productivity'. This committee reports to the Council of the League that it approves of certain of the schemes. The Financial Committee of the League will then presumably – unless a new administrative mechanism is suggested at the World Economic Conference [in 1933] – be asked to state what measures should be adopted for financing these schemes, when international loans are desired.

This organisation has many disadvantages, due mainly to the fact that it has been employed as a temporary method of dealing with the problem; for it was necessary to move quickly in order to see what could be done in the immediate future, and therefore to make use of any existing organisations which could be employed for that purpose. The main objections to this general form of organisation are:

(1) It makes difficult the proper co-ordination of public works policies, monetary policies and policies of lending to foreign governments. Although the Bank for International Settlements provides some means for co-operation among the central banks in their monetary policies, this is not at all co-ordinated with public works policies. Again, although in the Financial Committee of the League there is an organisation which deals with policies of international lending and which by the nature of its personnel is in close contact with the Bank for International Settlements, yet it is desirable that there should be much closer co-ordination of policies of international lending on long and short terms and of those of international public works. At the moment the Council of the League will presumably receive separate reports from the Financial Committee and the Committee on General Questions relating to Public Works and National Technical Equipment; plans for international co-operation in this field should be examined together in their financial, technical and general economic setting by some joint body, before they come before such a body as the Council of the League.

(2) This form of organisation is almost bound to interest itself solely in actual international public works, or public works in particular countries, for which international loans are required. For unless the schemes are discussed by a body on which the governments of the creditor countries are represented, and which can discuss the policy in all its broadest economic aspects, very little emphasis will be laid on the desirability of extensive schemes in creditor countries; the organisation is likely to become simply an organisation through which weak countries ask for loans. Throughout the history of attempts to obtain international co-operation in a public works policy too little emphasis has been laid on the desirability of obtaining agreement among creditor countries to undertake expenditure in their own countries at the right moment, and

too much on the possibilities of floating loans to aid weaker countries to absorb their unemployed on public works. Any organisation should be one which is likely to be able to stress the first type of policy more strongly.

(3) It will be difficult to use with any effect a permanent institution of this kind, as an instrument in avoiding fluctuations in trade and employment, unless the representatives of the governments agreeing in such a policy are actually present and able to commit their respective governments to certain forms of action.

If then it is really desired to obtain a degree of stability of trade and employment by means of co-ordinated monetary policies and policies of advancing or postponing all types of controllable expenditure on capital developments, then some permanent international body, competent to deal with these problems together and with the greatest possible powers of taking effective action, should be set up. It would be most desirable that such a body should be definitely a League of Nations organisation to ensure co-ordination with the other organs of the League and to provide means of co-operation between its secretariat and the Secretariat of the League and of the International Labour Office; and it should be possible to provide a constitution, by which such countries as the USA could co-operate in the work of such a technical body, and by which other countries, which were members of the League, need not necessarily be represented on it. For membership of such an organisation, while it should be as universal as possible, should also be confined to those nations which state their belief in some degree of stabilisation of employment through monetary control and a control of expenditure on planned capital development. Only if these constitutional difficulties proved too great should the body be officially dissociated from the League.

In the following paragraphs an attempt is made to sketch a suitable organisation for such a body. It should consist of a permanent Conference consisting of representatives of all the governments of the States Members of the organisation. Each government should also appoint a representative of the central bank of its country and a representative of labour. These representatives should have the right to speak, but not to vote; for, to make the body as effective as possible, only the government delegates should be allowed to vote. The Conference would meet once a year; but the main work of the organisation would be directed or undertaken by an executive committee, modelled on the lines of the Council of the League or the Governing Body of the International Labour Organisation; it would consist of the delegates; i.e. the government delegates and the representatives of the central banks and of labour, of the most important industrial and financial countries as permanent members, together with a number of delegates of the other countries, elected for a period of years by the members of the Conference other than the permanent members of the executive committee. This executive committee would meet frequently, and by means of delegating work to special expert committees would fulfil the functions which we have discussed above. The Executive Committee and the Conference would submit its resolutions and recommendations direct to States Members through their government representatives. Such a body would need some secretariat of its own; but this should not need to be very large, if the League of Nations, the International Labour Office and the Bank for International Settlements were all to provide it with information and to undertake research for it.

It is clear that this organisation is bound to overlap to some extent on its financial side with the Financial Committee of the League and with the Bank for International Settlements, since an international policy of public works cannot possibly be conducted successfully if it is not closely co-ordinated with monetary policy in general and with international long-term financing in particular. Some co-ordination between these bodies would clearly be essential. Probably the representation of each central bank on the new organisation would in fact provide sufficient contact with the Financial Committee of the League and the Bank for International Settlements, since the personnel of both the latter bodies would in fact be to some extent the same as the representatives of the banks on the new body. However, some form of closer official co-ordination could be devised, if it were necessary.

It would be difficult precisely to limit the functions of this body. For instance, since practically all the loans floated by governments or municipalities in the international market would be described as for purposes of capital development or public works, and since further, as we have seen, a sane public works policy depends upon the whole problem of international lending, it would be difficult to prevent the new body from taking over all the functions in this field of the Financial Committee of the League. Presumably the new organisation would set up a Financial Committee of its own, which would in fact be composed to some considerable extent of the same persons as the Financial Committee of the League, but it is, I think, essential that the new body should not simply make use of reports of the Financial Committee of the League, but should have financial experts representing central banks on its Executive Committee and on its Conference. A possible solution would be that the Financial Committee of the League should work for and report to the Council of the League, as well as to the new body. But the question immediately arises whether, if, in the interests of obtaining stability of world trade by some measures of planned control, a body has been instituted competent to deal with problems of control of expenditure on capital developments, of monetary policy and of international lending, it is logically possible to prevent that body from discussing tariff questions, budgetary problems, problems of immigration, problems of international combines, valorisation schemes for single commodities, etc. For how can budgetary problems be separated from monetary problems or problems of state expenditure on capital developments? How can tariff questions be separated from the exchange questions involved in foreign loans and the payment of interest on such loans? Such considerations would lead one to imagine a permanent body organised on the above lines, competent to discuss and pass resolutions and form agreements on all major economic problems, a body which would in the economic field fulfil those functions, which the League is already designed to fulfil in the political field.

Such is probably the ideal development of any such body; but such ideas must not blind one to the fact that this is only the logical development in the direction of greater co-ordination of many existing institutions, which are already doing good work. Nor must one for a moment imagine that such an elaborate organisation would be necessary before any solid advance can be made in the direction of an effective international policy of public works, co-ordinated with an international money policy. Any international committee, even the existing organisation, might do a great deal in this field; it is however essential that any such action should be co-ordinated with the monetary policy adopted at the same time, and also that the policy should be adopted in accordance with the general economic considerations, discussed above.

Finally the nature of any international organisation instituted for this purpose might require modification in view of any decisions made at the World Economic Conference, at which, as we have already seen, the problems of international public works will most probably be discussed. But whatever decisions that Conference makes in the sphere of monetary policy, whether it determines that an international gold standard is desirable, whether it determines that each country should adopt its own standard, whether or not it decides that some price index should be stabilised, co-operation will still be desirable through some international body on the lines laid down above in a policy of public works to achieve whatever stability is desired; this much I hope is sufficiently clear from the earlier discussion of the problem.

3

The Amount of Money and the Banking System

From The Economic Journal, *vol. 44 (1934), pp. 77–83*

The object of this note is to illustrate the factors which determine how much the amount of money will be affected in different types of banking system by given changes in that system. I have confined the inquiry to three types of banking system, but the method could easily be extended to cover other types. Finally, I have attempted, by means of statistical material taken from the Macmillan Report [Committee on Finance and Industry, *Report,* Cmd 3897 (London: HMSO, 1931)], to illustrate the results for the English banking system for the years 1925 to 1930.

I

1. The first banking system which I have considered is of the following type: No gold coin is in circulation, and the Central Bank alone issues notes. The Central Bank keeps a certain proportion of its note issue and a certain proportion of its deposit liabilities to member banks covered by gold. Member banks keep a certain proportion of their deposit liabilities covered by reserves, i.e. by notes or by deposits with the Central Bank; and they also keep a certain proportion of their reserves in the form of deposits with the Central Bank. The amount of money is defined as the total deposit liabilities of the member banks + the amount of notes held by the public. The public keep a certain proportion of their money in the form of notes.

Let G = the amount of gold,

       N = the total note issue, of which N_1 is held by member banks and N_2 by the public,

       B = the deposit liability of the Central Bank to the member banks,

       D = the deposit liabilities of the member banks,

       M = the amount of money,

       l = the proportion of its note issue which the Central Bank covers with gold,

m = the proportion of its deposit liability to member banks which the Central Bank covers with gold,

n = the proportion of their deposit liabilities which member banks cover with reserves,

p = the proportion of their reserves which member banks hold in the form of deposits with the Central Bank,

and q = the proportion of their money which the public holds in the form of notes.

Then:

$$G = lN + mB,$$
$$N = N_1 + N_2,$$
$$nD = N_1 + B,$$
$$B = p(N_1 + B),$$
$$M = N_2 + D,$$

and $N_2 = qM.$

It follows that

$$M = \frac{G}{n(1 - q)(l - p[l - m]) + lq} \,. \tag{i}$$

Let

$$\frac{1}{n(1 - q)(l - p[l - m]) + lq} = t_1.$$

2. If the Central Bank keeps the same proportion of its liabilities, whether they be notes issued or deposit liabilities, covered by gold, l will be equal to m. Let $l = m = l'$.

Then

$$M = \frac{G}{l'(n + q - qn)} \,. \tag{ii}$$

Let

$$\frac{1}{l'(n + q - qn)} = t_2.$$

It is interesting to note that p, the proportion of their reserves which member banks hold in the form of deposits with the Central Bank, disappears from this equation. This is, of course, exactly what one would expect. If the member banks substitute deposits with the Central Bank for part of their holding of notes, this will have no further effect if the Central Bank keeps the same proportion of gold against notes and against deposit liabilities. It will only have further repercussions if these two proportions are different.

3. Let us suppose that the Central Bank prints an amount of notes equal to its holding of gold + a given fiduciary issue, and maintains a given proportion between the notes so issued but not in circulation and its deposit liabilities to member banks. Let K = the fiduciary issue and k =

the proportion between 'notes in the banking department' and Central Bank deposit liabilities to member banks.

Then

$$M = \frac{G + K}{n(1 - q)(1 - p[1 - k]) + q} .$$ (iii)

Let

$$\frac{1}{n(1 - q)(1 - p[1 - k]) + q} = t_3.$$

In this case it is to be noticed that an alteration in p will affect M. This is naturally so, because now, if the member banks substitute notes for deposits with the Central Bank, this will affect the proportion k between the Central Bank's notes in the banking department and its deposit liabilities.

Up to this point it has been assumed that the member banks keep the same proportion of their deposit liabilities covered by reserves, whether these are 'time' or 'sight' liabilities. This may not be the case. Let D_1 be the amount of current accounts and D_2 the amount of deposit accounts; let n_1 be the proportion of current accounts covered by reserves and n_2 the proportion of deposit accounts covered by reserves. Let r be the proportion of their deposits which the public keep on current account.

Then

$$D_1 = r(D_1 + D_2)$$

and

$$n = \frac{n_1 D_1 + n_2 D_2}{D_1 + D_2}$$

so that

$$n = n_2 + r(n_1 - n_2).$$

II

In order to determine how sensitive the amount of money is to given changes, it is necessary to differentiate equations (i), (ii) and (iii) in respect to all the possible variables. The results of this process are shown in Table I.

Table I

	1	2	3
dM/dG	t_1	t_2	t_3
dM/dn	$-(1 - q)(l - p[l - m])t_1 M$	$-(1 - q)l't_2 M$	$-(1 - q)(1 - p[1 - k])t_3 M$
dM/dq	$-\{l - n(l - p[l - m])\}t_1 M$	$-(1 - n)l't_2 M$	$-\{1 - n(1 - p[1 - k])\}t_3 M$
dM/dl	$-(n[1 - q][1 - p] + q)t_1 M$	—	—
dM/dm	$-np(1 - q)t_1 M$	—	—
dM/dl'	—	$-\frac{1}{l'} M$	—
dM/dk	—	—	$-np(1 - q)t_3 M$
dM/dp	$+n(1 - q)(l - m)t_1 M$	0	$+n(1 - q)(1 - k)t_3 M$

All the proportions are $+^{ve}$ and lie between 1 and 0, and l will always in fact be $> m$. It follows that the derivatives are all of the sign shown in the table. In the case of each of the three types of banking system

$$\frac{dM}{dn_1} = r\,\frac{dM}{dn}, \quad \frac{dM}{dn_2} = (1-r)\,\frac{dM}{dn} \quad \text{and} \quad \frac{dM}{dr} = (n_1 - n_2)\,\frac{dM}{dn}.$$

III

The third thing which I wish to do is to make some attempt to measure these quantities for England from the years 1925 to 1930.

Table II

	G	N	R	B	D	N_1	$N_2 = N - N_1$	$p = \dfrac{B}{N_1 + B}$	$n = \dfrac{N_1 + B}{D}$	$q = \dfrac{N_2}{N_2 + D}$	$l' = \dfrac{G}{N + B}$	$k = \dfrac{R}{B}$	r
1925	145	382	26·7	71·3	1603	104	278	0·405	0·109	0·148	0·32	0·374	0·576
1926	149	375	27·6	68·4	1609	103	272	0·4	0·107	0·145	0·336	0·404	0·573
1927	150	373	32·0	66·5	1657	105	268	0·388	0·103	0·139	0·341	0·481	0·562
1928	163	372	46·9	65·7	1709	105	267	0·385	0·1	0·135	0·372	0·714	0·558
1929	147	362	44·5	62·8	1738	104	258	0·377	0·096	0·129	0·346	0·709	0·541
1930	155	358	56·7	64·9	1741	104	254	0·384	0·097	0·127	0·366	0·875	0·529
Av.	151·5	370	—	66·6	1693	—	266·1	0·389	0·102	0·137	0·347	0·592	0·556

Table II gives the necessary information for these calculations. R measures 'notes in the banking department' of the Bank of England. G, N, R, B, D, N_1 and N_2 are all measured in £ million. G, N, R and B are annual averages of the monthly averages of the columns headed respectively 'Gold Coin and Bullion', 'Notes in Circulation', 'Notes in Banking Department' and 'Other Deposits: Bankers' in the Macmillan Report, pp. 302–3. D and N_1 are taken from the columns headed 'Total Deposits' and 'Cash in Hand' in Table 3 on p. 296 of the Macmillan Report. r is taken from the column headed 'Proportion of Current Accounts to Total' on p. 37 of the Macmillan Report.

It is to be observed that the proportions p, n, q, l' and r are all fairly stable, while the proportion k shows a very large change over these years. This is largely, no doubt, to be explained by the changes made by the Currency and Bank Notes Act of 1928. But even between the years 1929 and 1930 there is a large fluctuation in k. On the other hand, l' is fairly stable. This suggests that while formally the English banking system is of our third type, in fact it is more similar to the second type examined above.

In order to see how much more or less sensitive our banking system would become to given changes in its structure, it is useful to assume certain values for n_1, n_2, l and m. Let us suppose, as has often been suggested, that the joint-stock banks hold a smaller proportion of reserves against deposit accounts and a larger proportion against current accounts. Let us suppose further that the proportion to be kept against deposit accounts is 3 per cent and that the proportion to be kept against current accounts is chosen in such a way that for the average of the years

1925 to 1930 the same proportion between reserves and total deposits would have been maintained. Then, since $n = n_2 + r(n_1 - n_2)$, we have

$$\cdot102 = \cdot03 + \cdot556(n_1 - \cdot03),$$

or
$$n_1 = \cdot16.$$

Similarly, let us suppose that the Bank of England had maintained a proportion of 37·5 per cent of its notes backed by gold, and that it had chosen to back such a proportion of its deposit liabilities by gold as would have enabled it to maintain the same note circulation and deposit liabilities to bankers as it did maintain from 1925 to 1930. Then we have

$$lN + mB = l'(N + B)$$

$$\cdot375 \times 370 + m66\cdot6 = \cdot347(370 + 66\cdot6),$$

or
$$m = \cdot195.$$

In Table III these proportions are used to calculate values for Table I.

Table III

$\dfrac{dM^1}{dG}$	$\dfrac{dM}{dn}$	$\dfrac{dM}{dq}$	$\dfrac{dM}{dl}$	$\dfrac{dM}{dm}$	$\dfrac{dM}{dl'}$	$\dfrac{dM}{dk}$	$\dfrac{dM}{dp}$	$\dfrac{dM}{dn_1}$	$\dfrac{dM}{dn_2}$	$\dfrac{dM}{dr}$
1 12·8	$-3\cdot37\,M$	$-4\cdot4\,M$	$-2\cdot44\,M$	$-\cdot438\,M$	—	—	$\cdot203\,M$	$-1\cdot88\,M$	$-1\cdot5\,M$	$-\cdot438\,M$
2 12·8	$-3\cdot84\,M$	$-3\cdot99\,M$	—	—	$-2\cdot88\,M$	—	0	$-2\cdot13\,M$	$-1\cdot71\,M$	$-\cdot5\,M$
3 4·74	$-3\cdot44\,M$	$-4\cdot33\,M$	—	—	—	$-\cdot163\,M$	$\cdot171\,M$	$-1\cdot91\,M$	$-1\cdot53\,M$	$-\cdot447\,M$

[1] The three figures in this column represent t_1, t_2 and t_3, and are calculated by means of the proportions given in Table II from equations (i), (ii) and (iii). t_1 and $t_2 = \dfrac{M}{G}$. They should, therefore, be equal to $\dfrac{N_2 + D}{G}$, which is equal to 12·9, calculated from Table I $t_2 = \dfrac{M}{(G + K)} = \dfrac{N_2 + D}{(G + 260)}$, since K is the fiduciary issue. $\dfrac{M}{(G + K)}$ calculated directly from Table I $= 4\cdot72$. These calculations provide a check on some of the work. I suspect, however, that the correspondence between the two methods of calculating t_2 is largely accidental, since the fiduciary issue (*i.e.* the notes in circulation + notes in the Banking Department – the amount of gold held by the Bank of England) was not fixed at £260 m. until 1928. I have used the figures for t_1, t_2 and t_3 given in Table III for the purpose of calculating the other figures in Table III.

There are certain comments to be made on this table. All the figures in line 1 and all those in the columns headed $\dfrac{dM}{dn_1}, \dfrac{dM}{dn_2}$ and $\dfrac{dM}{dr}$ are in a sense arbitrary and fictitious: they represent the sensitiveness of the amount of money to given changes, in the first place on the assumption that during the years 1925–30 the Bank of England had maintained certain arbitrarily chosen proportions between gold and notes issued and between gold and deposit liabilities, and in the second case on the assumption that the joint-stock banks maintained certain arbitrarily chosen proportions between current accounts and reserves and between deposit accounts and reserves. Thus in fact, since there is no difference between these proportions and $n_1 = n_2$, $\dfrac{dM}{dr} = 0$.

These figures should be taken, therefore, to represent what would have happened if the English banking system had been different in certain ways from what it was in the years 1925–30.

Secondly, all of the figures in Table III are, of course, calculated on the assumption that one factor is altered and that all the other factors are independent and constant. In many cases it is permissible to assume that the proportions are independent of one another; if the joint-stock banks decide to maintain a larger proportion of reserves to deposits, this is not likely to affect the proportion of notes held by the public to their total holding of money. But there are two important cases in which independence cannot be assumed. In the first place, a change in the amount of money may cause a change in prices or money incomes.[1] If a country is part of an international system, this in turn will probably affect its gold reserves. Thus a change in any of the proportions would probably affect G if the exchanges were fixed. For this reason the figures in Table III must not be interpreted as measuring the change in the amount of money, which would, in fact, have followed a given change in one of the proportions during the years 1925–30; but rather they are simply measures of the sensitiveness of the English banking system during those years (i.e. measures of what would have occurred if everything else had remained the same). In the second place, if the Central Bank is taking a conscious control of the monetary position – as it quite properly should do – it may not maintain l, m, l' or k constant, but may consciously vary them to offset changes in the other factors. It is necessary, however, to assume that certain proportions – l and m, or l' or k, for instance – are kept constant by the Central Bank in order to be able to calculate the figures of Table III at all. Thus all the figures in all the columns – except in those headed $\dfrac{dM}{dl}$, $\dfrac{dM}{dm}$, $\dfrac{dM}{dl'}$ and $\dfrac{dM}{dk}$ – are calculated on the assumption that the Bank of England was maintaining certain proportions constant. As I have said above, l' was much more constant than k during the years 1925–30, while l and m are purely fictitious quantities. Thus line 2 is probably the best measure for the actual position in England during those years.

Thirdly, it is interesting to make certain comments on the figures. First, it is clear that, whichever type of banking system England had adopted, the sensitiveness of the system to given changes would not have been very different in most cases. In the case, however, of a change in the amount of gold, with the first or second type of system the change in the amount of money would have been about thirteen times,

---

[1] It is not my purpose in this note to discuss at all whether this must be so, or in what way the change is caused.

while with the third type of system it would have been only about five times the change in the amount of gold. Secondly, the introduction of different percentages of reserves against deposit or current accounts would not, *with the arbitrary chosen figures of* 3 *per cent against deposit and* 16 *per cent against current accounts*, have made the banking system very sensitive to changes in the proportion of deposits held on current or deposit accounts. Thus, if during those years persons had elected to hold 56·6 per cent instead of 55·6 per cent of their deposits on current account, the amount of money would have been decreased by about one half of one per cent. Thirdly, it is interesting to observe how sensitive the amount of money is to changes in q, the proportion of their money which the public hold in the form of notes. Mr Hawtrey has argued that a boom is stopped and a depression starts largely because q increases as wages rise and a large proportion of the national dividend goes to those classes who hold a large proportion of their money in the form of currency. Table III shows that if q had increased from 13·7 per cent to 14·7 per cent, the total amount of money would have decreased by about 4 per cent. However, in order to test the importance of Mr Hawtrey's theory it is necessary to show not only how sensitive the amount of money is to changes in q, but also that q increases in the later phases of a boom. Table II shows that q was falling steadily in England from 1925 to 1930. But this period was a peculiar one in England, and to test the theory it would be interesting to calculate $\dfrac{dM}{dq}$ and movements in q for other countries and for other times, in which the phases of the trade cycle were more typical.

4

Outline of Economic Policy for a
Labour Government

By 1935, when this paper was written, Meade had prepared several memoranda for the Policy Subcommittee of the National Executive Committee of the Labour Party, having first been approached by Hugh Dalton, chairman of the subcommittee, in the autumn of 1932. He hoped that this paper would appear as a New Fabian Research Bureau pamphlet, but G. D. H. Cole and E. F. M. Durbin recommended against publication (Meade Papers 2/7 and 2/9, Dalton Papers 2/1, British Library of Political and Economic Science, and Elizabeth Durbin, New Jerusalems: The Labour Party and the Economics of Democratic Socialism, *1985, p. 197).*

Objects of Policy

§ 1.   The first objective of economic policy should be to cure unemployment and then to preserve a high level of employment. This objective is not only the most important, but it should take precedence in time over other objectives. The internal monetary, budgetary and industrial policy of the government should be devised in the first place to attain this objective.

§ 2.   The second objective of the government will be to devise a foreign exchange policy and tariff policy, which will enable the government to carry out the objective mentioned in §1 without getting into serious difficulties in the foreign exchange market, while obtaining the maximum advantages from foreign trade.

§ 3.   The third objective of economic policy should be to socialise certain industries which are in need of reorganisation in order that they may be more efficiently managed. Such industries are those which are naturally monopolistic and which require centralised control to be run efficiently in the interests of consumers.

§ 4.   The fourth objective of policy should be to increase the equality of distribution of the national income. This objective can be obtained partly by means of the extension of social services, financed by taxation, but cannot be fully achieved until the state obtains ownership of a considerable amount of capital wealth in order that the interest, profits and rents of such wealth may be more evenly distributed among the members of the community. It is suggested that this objective should come fourth not because it is the least important objective, but for the two following reasons.

(a) The objectives mentioned in §§ 1 to 3 are designed to increase the national income that is to be divided. They can be attained without diminishing the income of any class and indeed their achievement will increase the income of every class; they can therefore be brought about with the minimum amount of political opposition. It seems undesirable to start upon a redistribution of income, until measures have been taken to ensure that the income to be distributed is as large as possible. (b) The attainment of greater equality is almost bound to come after the attainment of the previous objectives. For it is not possible to extend fully the social services financed by taxation until measures have been taken to ensure that the income to be taxed is as large as possible. Moreover some time is bound to elapse before the redistribution of wealth can be brought about by the use of income derived from nationally owned capital, since the purchase of this capital by raising a surplus of taxation to buy out existing owners must proceed for a number of years before a significant fund will be available for the purpose of redistributing the national income more equally.

The Causes of Unemployment

§ 5.   It is impossible in a short memorandum to do more than mention the main phenomena that are connected with prosperous times and with times of depression. During prosperous times the money demand for consumption goods and so the price at which consumption goods can be sold is high. Money costs are not equally high, since money wage-rates and other costs fixed in terms of money do not rise as quickly as money demand. In consequence producers have an incentive to produce a large output and employment is relatively full. Moreover industry is profitable and there are large openings for this reason for new and profitable investment in capital development. It is true that in prosperous times the rate of interest at which money can be borrowed is generally higher than the rate of interest in times of depression, but in spite of this the profitability of industry is so much greater in prosperous times that the borrowing of money for expenditure on new capital development is great. This means that there is an active demand for capital goods, which in turn means a large output and full employment in the industries producing capital goods. Finally this active demand for capital goods means that the producers of capital goods are receiving large incomes, which they can spend on consumption goods; and this in turn maintains that active demand for consumption goods, which was noted as the first phenomenon of prosperity.

§ 6.   In times of depression the opposite phenomena are to be observed. The money demand for consumption goods is small; this causes unemployment and reduced production of consumption goods. Moreover because the demand for consumption goods is low, the profitability of industry is small and there are few profitable opportunities for capital development. This is so in spite of the fact that interest rates are generally low in times of depression; profits are so depressed that low interest rates do not stimulate fresh capital development. The small demand for capital goods means that those engaged in the production of capital goods have small incomes and are therefore unable to spend much on consumption goods, which in turn explains in large measure the fact that the demand for consumption goods is abnormally low.

§ 7.   If this brief outline of the phenomena associated with prosperity and depression is correct, there are only two really efficient methods of curing depression. The first method is to cause an increase in the amount of money spent on capital development, which will directly increase output and employment in the industries producing capital goods and indirectly by increasing the incomes of those engaged in the production of capital goods will increase the demand for consumption goods and so increase employment in and the profitability of industries producing consumption goods. The second method is to increase the amount of money spent on consumption goods, which will directly increase employment in those industries and indirectly by making these industries more profitable and opening up new fields of profitable investment will stimulate the demand for capital goods and so employment in the industries producing capital goods. It is to be observed however that neither of these methods is of any use unless it is certain that the increased stream of money spent on capital goods or on consumption goods is a new stream of money and not a stream of money diverted from some other channel of expenditure. For instance, no increase in employment will occur if the government spends more on capital development or gives more to the unemployed to spend on consumption goods, if this money is raised in such a way as to restrict the expenditure of other classes on goods to a similar extent.

§ 8.   (a) Expenditure on capital development may be directly stimulated by the government, if it raises new or idle funds to spend directly on public works, the development of public utilities or the development of nationalised industries.

(b) Expenditure on capital goods by private enterprise can be stimulated and expenditure on capital development by public authorities can be greatly facilitated, if the rate of interest at which money can be borrowed can be reduced. Such reductions in interest rates can be brought about by banking policy, as will be explained in §§ 15 to 25 below.

(c) Measures can also be adopted by the government to provide new funds to create a new flow of money demand for expenditure on consumption goods. A measure designed to bring this about in a rather unorthodox but highly effective manner is discussed below in §§ 26 to 33.

A National Development Board

§ 9.   It should be one of the very first tasks of the government to set up a National Development Board, which would constitute the main planning department in the state. Its existence and the proper fulfilment of its function are perhaps the most essential requirements before the problem of unemployment can be properly solved. It is not the task of this memorandum to discuss the problems connected with its personnel, its relations with other organs of government, its legal powers, etc.; but too much emphasis cannot be laid upon the nature of the duties which it should perform.

§ 10. It would be the primary duty of the National Development Board to see that plans were made for capital development to be undertaken by the central government, by municipalities and local authorities, by public utility undertakings, by all industries nationalised by the state, and finally by any other important bodies over which the state had any significant degree of control. The National Development Board would thus be the central planning authority, so far as the planning of development by the central government was concerned, and would be responsible for seeing that other important bodies were planning their capital development for a considerable period ahead.

§ 11. The object of this measure of economic planning should be to enable expenditure on useful and profitable development to be speeded up as long as there is abnormal unemployment and to enable such development to be postponed if there is an abnormally strong demand for labour leading to a shortage of labour in a large number of industries. Below in §§ 15 to 33 methods are suggested whereby in the first place the rate of interest may be vigorously lowered as long as abnormal unemployment appears and quickly raised if an abnormally strong demand for labour develops, and whereby in the second place consumers' purchasing power may be directly increased if abnormal unemployment exists and diminished if an abnormal demand for labour develops. So long as these two further elements of policy are being adopted it is proposed that the plans for capital development of the National Development Board should be undertaken on the principles outlined in the following paragraph.

§ 12. (a) The National Development Board itself – in as far as it is directly responsible for the planning of development to be undertaken by the central government – and every municipality, public utility, and socialised industry should plan its capital development for some years (e.g. three to five years) ahead. It is not of course to be expected that the plans for the more distant years can be as detailed or as definite as those for the immediate future, and they would continually be subjected to detailed and even fundamental alteration.

(b) Every body should plan for its development on the assumption that there will be full normal employment and the full normal purchasing power that would exist if employment is full. For only if sufficient capital development is undertaken can full purchasing power be maintained. If therefore sufficient capital development is undertaken and if further the measures suggested in §§ 15 to 33 for the control of interest rates and the maintenance of consumers' purchasing power have been adopted, full consumers' purchasing power will in fact be maintained and this assumption will turn out to be correct.

(c) Assuming that full consumers' purchasing power is maintained, the amount of capital development that any body will find it desirable to undertake in any year will depend upon the rate of interest at which money can be borrowed. Thus a municipality which is considering the construction of a road which will cost £20,000 will add a burden of £1,000 a year to the rates in interest on the loan if the rate at which it borrows is 5%, but only £400 if the rate of interest is 2%. Or a railway may find it profitable to undertake the electrification of part of the line if it can borrow for this purpose at 4% and a much larger portion of the line if the rate of interest is only 3%. Every body in preparing its plans should indicate at what rates of interest the different parts of the plan would be worth undertaking. It is most important that the National Development Board should in this way be provided with alternative plans at different rates of interest, so that it can know how much development should be undertaken at 5% interest rates, how much more if the rate were only 4½%, how much more if the rate fell to 3% etc.

(d) If the principles outlined above were adopted, it would be possible to vary appropriately the amount of capital development undertaken in any one year if the rate of interest is caused to fall when the demand for labour was abnormally low and to rise if the demand for labour should become excessively strong by the measures outlined below in §§ 15 to 25. But there is a further method by which the amount of capital development undertaken in any one year can be varied. Thus it would be worth while spending £300,000,000 on the electrification of the railways if the rate of interest is not higher than 4%, if such expenditure would earn a 4% return; but it would still remain to decide whether £100,000,000 should be spent each year for three years or £60,000,000 each year for five years. Each body should be required to draw up its plans in such a way that the expenditure worth undertaking at any given rate of interest is as far as possible capable of being concentrated on one or a few years or spread over a number of years. The National Development Board should be informed of the extent to which such variations can be made, and will then be in a position to vary the amount of money spent on capital development to a very large extent.

§ 13. The National Development Board must also have some power over the financing of these schemes of development. In as far as municipalities and undertakings which are not nationalised are concerned, the schemes should normally be financed by borrowing in the market or from other funds in the control of these bodies. But the National Development Board should have considerable powers to enable it to determine how much or how little these different bodies shall spend from year to year on development planned on the above lines. In as far as development is to be undertaken or financed by the central government or by socialised undertakings, methods of raising the funds are outlined in §§ 34 to 41 below, when the central Budget is discussed.

§ 14. It will already be apparent that the National Development Board must have very considerable powers to require sufficient planning of the desired kind and to control the actual amount spent on development. The plans required are in their most perfect form of very considerable complexity and it will be some time before this Board can hope to develop its functions fully. In the first years of its existence the plans will necessarily be incomplete and will not cover sufficient years ahead, sufficient industries or be sufficiently developed to be easily adjusted to different interest rates or to different degrees of concentration over longer or shorter periods of time. But the government should spare no trouble in setting up this Board as soon as possible and developing its functions as quickly as possible. It is of the utmost importance that this should be done, and even if not fully developed the Board will soon acquire considerable knowledge of and control over the amount of capital development to be undertaken.

The Banks

§ 15.　It is through the policy of the banks that the rate of interest can be controlled. But before discussing the policy to be pursued it is necessary to outline the present position and powers of the banks in England. This outline can best be made by showing first the powers and functions of the Bank of England and secondly the powers and functions of the joint-stock banks.

§ 16.　The position of the Bank of England can best be illustrated by a study of a Bank Return. The following is the Bank Return for 13 March 1935:

Issue Department

	£		£
Notes Issued:		Government Debt	11,015,100
In Circulation	378,919,814	Government	
In Banking		Securities	246,124,625
Department	73,600,769	Other Securities	409,744
		Silver Coin	2,450,531
		Amount of Fiduciary	
		Issue	260,000,000
		Gold Coin and	
		Bullion	192,520,583
	452,520,583		452,520,583

Banking Department

	£		£
Proprietors'		Government	
Capital	14,553,000	Securities	84,771,044
Rest	3,699,961	Discounts and	
Public Deposits	8,446,526	Advances	5,705,897
Bankers' Deposits	108,372,856	Securities	10,910,193
Other Deposits	40,400,235	Notes	73,600,769
		Gold & Silver Coin	484,675
	175,472,578		175,472,578

It will be seen that the Bank is divided for purposes of accounting into the Issue Department, which is concerned simply with the issue of notes, and the Banking Department, which is concerned with the other activities of the Bank. The Bank is by law allowed to print and issue from the Issue Department an amount of notes equal to the par value of the gold stock held by the Bank (£192,520,583) plus a fixed amount of notes to the value of £260,000,000, which are backed by securities owned by the Bank. Part of this total note issue will be in circulation, i.e. in the tills of the other banks or in the hands of members of the public (£378,919,814), while the remainder (£73,600,769) will be held as an asset in the Banking Department and will form the cash reserve of the Banking Department of the Bank. In the Banking Department of the Bank the main liabilities are formed by (a) the amount owed to the owners of the Bank, i.e. the capital subscribed (£14,553,000) and the profits which have been made but not distributed in interest (£3,699,961), and (b) the liability of the Bank to those who have deposited money with it, which deposits will consist of the Public Deposits or the deposit account of the government (£8,446,526), Bankers' Deposits or the deposit account of the joint-stock banks (£108,372,856) and Other Deposits (£40,400,235). Against these liabilities the Bank will hold assets of equivalent value made up of (a) its reserve of cash, i.e. the notes issued by the Issue Department but not in circulation (£73,600,769), (b) securities owned by the Bank (£95,681,237) and (c) advances and bills which the Bank has bought or 'discounted' (£5,705,897).

§ 17.   The position of the joint-stock banks can also be illustrated best from a return of their accounts. The following is a statement for the month of February 1935 of the position of the ten clearing banks, which include the five important joint-stock banks, Barclays, Lloyds, the Midland, the Westminster and the National Provincial together with five other banks of much less importance.

Liabilities

	£
Capital paid up	74,310,000
Reserve fund	53,980,000
Deposits	1,954,089,000
Acceptances	117,919,000
Notes in circulation	1,339,000
Reduction of bank premises account	260,000
	2,201,897,000

Assets

Cash and balances with Bank of England	213,166,000
Balances with other banks	43,614,000
Items in transit	3,473,000
Money at call and short notice	126,985,000
Bills discounted	264,946,000
Investments	606,402,000

Advances to customers	755,653,000
Acceptances	117,919,000
Bank premises account	44,553,000
Investments in affiliated Banks	25,186,000
	2,201,897,000

Here again the main liabilities of the joint-stock banks are (a) the amount owed to the owners of the banks either in the form of capital subscribed (£74,310,000) or of undistributed profits (£53,980,000) and (b) the amount of money deposited with the banks by customers and owed to these customers (£1,954,089,000). The assets held against these liabilities will consist in (a) the cash reserves of the banks (£213,166,000) which will include the joint-stock banks' deposits with the Bank of England, since the joint-stock banks count these deposits as good as cash, as well as the actual notes and coin held in the banks' tills, (b) money at call or short notice (£126,985,000), i.e. money lent for short periods of time at low interest rates to discount houses, which borrow money for the purpose of buying bills, i.e. securities which are due to be repaid in a short period of time, (c) bills bought or discounted by the banks themselves (£264,946,000), (d) other securities bought by the banks (£606,402,000) and (e) advances or money lent direct by the banks to their customers (£755,653,000).

§ 18.   It is now possible to demonstrate the important fact that the banks have the technical power of controlling the volume of money by lending more or less or by buying or selling securities, and thereby have the power of controlling the rate of interest ruling in the market. If the joint-stock banks buy £1,000,000 worth of securities in the market, they can pay for this by giving the persons from whom they buy the securities deposits with the banks of £1,000,000. Or if they lend £1,000,000 in direct advances to their customers they can supply the money to these customers by crediting them with £1,000,000 more deposits. In either case, by increasing their assets either in the form of securities in which they have invested money or in the form of advances to customers, the banks can increase the total amount of deposits. Conversely, by selling securities or calling in loans which will be paid for from deposits, which can then be cancelled, the banks can decrease the total volume of deposits.

§ 19.   This control over the volume of deposits means also that the banks have the power of controlling the rate of interest. The banks can increase the amount of deposits by lending more to customers or by buying securities; but this they can only do by inducing their customers to borrow more or by inducing someone to sell securities for deposits, and in order to do this they must offer loans at lower rates of interest or must offer higher prices for securities. A rise in the price of securities means however a lower rate of interest, since if for example the price of 2½% Consols rises from £50 to £100 this is equivalent to a fall in the rate of interest on long-term government securities from 5% to 2½%. Conversely the banks can diminish the amount of money by calling in loans and lending less or by selling securities, which will involve a higher rate of interest on advances and a lower level of security prices and so a higher rate of interest on securities.

§ 20.   But the joint stock banks must keep a certain reserve of cash in the form of notes, coin or deposits with the Bank of England against their deposit liabilities, in order to ensure that they can cash any part of their deposit liabilities that are likely to be cashed at any time. Experience has shown in this country that if they keep 10% of their total deposit liabilities covered in this way they will always have a large enough reserve to meet any demands for cash, and the joint-stock banks in this country do always in fact keep a proportion of about 10% of their deposits covered by cash. In this case it is clear that it is variations in the cash reserves of the joint-stock banks which determine whether the joint-stock banks will expand or contract their deposit liabilities by buying or selling securities and so lowering or raising interest rates. If for example the joint-stock banks receive £1,000,000 more cash from any source they must purchase securities or lend more until their deposit liabilities have risen by £10,000,000, if they wish to maintain only 10% of their deposit liabilities covered by cash reserves.

§ 21.   There are two main reasons why the cash reserves of the joint-stock banks may vary. (a) In the first place people may deposit cash with the banks which they were previously holding in their pockets, or people may cash their deposits and withdraw cash from the banks into circulation. When the public deposits cash, the banks will have to lend more and buy securities to prevent their cash reserve ratio from rising above 10%; whereas if the public draws cash from the banks, the banks will have to lend less and sell securities to prevent their cash reserve ratio from falling below 10%. (b) But in the second place the Bank of England by buying or selling securities itself can cause the cash reserves of the joint-stock banks to rise or to fall. If the Bank of England buys £1,000,000 securities and the persons from whom the securities are bought deposit the money in the joint-stock banks, then the total effect on the accounts of the banks is that the Bank of England holds as an extra asset £1,000,000 more securities in the Banking Department, while its deposit liabilities to the joint-stock banks have risen by £1,000,000, and that the joint-stock banks have £1,000,000 more cash in the form of balances with the Bank of England, while at the same time their deposit liabilities have risen by £1,000,000. Conversely, if the Bank of England sells securities and the persons who buy these securities pay for them with money deposited with the joint-stock banks, the joint-stock banks will have to pay the Bank of England by allowing their cash balances at the Bank of England to be reduced. In this way the Bank of England by buying and selling securities can increase or decrease the cash balances of the joint-stock banks. If the joint-stock banks always maintain a 10% reserve of cash against their deposit liabilities, they in turn will have to buy securities or lend more, and so will lower interest rates, when the Bank of England buys securities; and they will sell securities and lend less and thus raise interest rates in order to preserve their 10% cash reserve ratio when the Bank of England restricts their reserves of cash by selling securities.

§ 22.   It has already been shown that in times of abnormally great unemployment new expenditure on capital development should be stimulated not only by planned expenditure on such development, which was discussed in §§ 9 to 13, but also by reductions in the rate of interest which make it easier to borrow money for these purposes. This is indeed the main objective of monetary policy. It follows therefore that the government must have control over the policy of the Bank of England in expanding and contracting the cash reserves of the joint-stock banks by buying and selling securities. It is therefore suggested that the Bank of England should be socialised and that the Bank of England should purchase securities and so cause rates of interest to be lowered as long as there is an abnormal volume of unemployment, and should sell securities and so cause interest rates to rise as soon as there is an abnormally strong demand for labour. This policy cannot be offset by any action of the joint-stock banks, unless the joint-stock banks vary the proportion between their deposit liabilities and their cash reserve ratio. If, however, the joint-stock banks do allow their cash reserves to increase or decrease without in consequence increasing or decreasing their deposit liabilities appropriately by buying or selling securities, they can offset the action of the Bank of England in buying or selling securities. It would not be essential to socialise the joint-stock banks so long as it could be ensured that they do not allow their cash reserve ratio to vary very greatly; this assurance might be obtained by simple agreement with these banks, since it is their normal practice to maintain fairly constant reserve ratios, or by legislation requiring the joint-stock banks to provide daily figures of their deposits and cash reserves and imposing heavy taxation on any bank which allowed its reserve ratio to exceed say 12% or fall below say 9% for more than a certain number of consecutive days.

§ 23.   It is essential that as soon as a slump starts the rate of interest should be brought down quickly and vigorously to enable the necessary new capital development to take place. This involves a revision of many popular and orthodox ideas about monetary policy. Much greater and more sudden variations in the rate of interest must be expected than have been usual in the past, if economic policy is going to be able successfully to maintain a high level of employment. A very great deal can be done not only by the actual policy adopted by the Bank of England but by public explanation of the object of this policy. The rate of interest on securities is apt always to approximate to the rate which people on the whole expect to be the rate ruling in the future. If people expect the rate of interest on securities to be 5% in the future, it will be difficult to lower the rate very much below this figure without enormous purchases of securities by the banks; for as soon as the price of securities rises so that the yield on them is appreciably below 5%, persons will sell any amount of securities to the banks in order to hold deposits instead in the expectation that yields will rise and security prices fall again in the near future, so that the securities can be bought back again at a profit. The Bank of England can meet difficulties of this kind to a large extent by making it quite clear what it is determined to achieve by its policy. Suppose for example that a slump has started: the Bank might state publicly and in unambiguous language that it was determined to reduce yields on securities from a 5% to a 3% basis quickly and rapidly, that it would almost certainly not allow yields to rise above 3% in the near future and might very likely determine to reduce yields still more if such action proved necessary to absorb labour, that it had the power to reduce interest rates by increasing the supply of money, that it would increase the supply of money however great the increase might have to be in order to achieve its object, and that this was practically the sole object of its present policy. Such a declaration would cause people to adjust their expectations about interest rates much more easily and would at least diminish the extent to which the banks would have to purchase securities to lower interest rates by a certain amount.

§ 24.   Finally there are two possible ways in which the freedom of the Bank of England itself may be restricted in the control of the amount of money and so of interest rates. (a) In the first place it may not be able to expand the amount of money and lower interest rates because it would lose gold, if the country were on the gold standard, or at any rate cause a very severe depreciation of the exchange rate with other countries. This difficulty is met below in §§ 42 to 60. (b) But secondly the Bank of England itself must maintain a cash reserve against its deposit liabilities, and it was seen that this reserve takes the form of notes issued from the Issue Department and not in circulation, but held as a reserve of cash in the Banking Department of the Bank. The Bank by buying securities will increase its deposit liabilities without increasing its own cash reserves and it may be impossible for it to go beyond a certain point in this direction with safety. The Bank must not be prevented by this consideration from expanding and contracting its deposit liabilities sufficiently to give it full control over the rate of interest. Certain alterations in the laws relating to the note issue are suggested in § 30 below, and these suggestions are devised to increase the note issue automatically when unemployment is abnormally great and to decrease the note issue automatically when the demand for labour is abnormally high. But if the suggestions of §§ 26 to 33 are not adopted, it is suggested that an upper limit of say £500,000,000 be set by law to the notes which the Bank of England may put into circulation and that this be the only law relating to the note issue. In this case the Issue Department and Banking Department of the Bank might be combined, and the Bank would always have as a possible cash reserve the difference between the £500,000,000 and the actual number of notes in circulation. It would then be in a position in almost any imaginable eventuality to concentrate its attention simply and solely on controlling the rate of interest by expanding or contracting the cash reserves of the joint-stock banks.

§ 25.   There is one further difficulty which may make it difficult for the banking system as a whole to reduce interest rates on advances and loans and on government securities to the fullest degree necessary during a slump. The banks are bound to incur considerable running expenses and can only meet those expenses by the difference between the yield which they earn on their assets and the interest which they pay on money deposited with them. If interest rates are reduced to a very low figure it might become impossible for the banks to meet these expenses.

Moreover, if the banks are properly pursuing the policy of buying securities during a slump, even if the price of securities is already high, and selling securities during a period of abnormally high demand for labour, even if their price is already low, the banks may be involved in some capital loss due to these transactions. These difficulties are to some extent, though by no means entirely, illusory. For in the first place, though the yield on securities may be abnormally low during a period of slump, yet if the banks in such a period have properly expanded the amount of money by purchasing a large volume of securities the fall in their income due to low yields on securities will be at least partly counterbalanced by the fact that they are earning this yield on a much larger number of securities and their expenses will certainly not increase in proportion to the increase in their holding of securities. And in the second place, during a period in which the banks are purchasing securities in order to raise their price and to lower interest rates, it is only during the last part of this period that the banks are purchasing securities at very high prices; at the beginning of such a period they will be purchasing securities at the low prices and high yields associated with the previous period of boom; and during a period in which the banks are selling securities to lower their price and to raise interest rates, the banks will at first be selling securities at high prices and only later selling securities at abnormally low prices. It is therefore by no means certain that they will on the whole be involved in serious capital losses due to these transactions. But if the banks are involved in serious difficulties in carrying out these operations they should be allowed and indeed encouraged by agreement among themselves to counterbalance these losses by reducing the rates which they pay on money deposited with them and even by levying instead bank charges on the money deposited with them. Thus if during a slump the action of the banks has caused interest rates on their assets to be so lowered that they cannot cover their costs, they should meet this in the first place by agreeing together to pay no rate of interest at all on deposits and then by levying charges if necessary on all money deposited with them. Such action may even cause people to buy securities with their deposits instead of wishing to keep money deposited with the banks and this will help in raising the price of securities and lowering interest rates. This policy can only lead to any difficulty if it should cause people to hold notes or cash instead of deposits and any bank charges levied on deposits should not be made heavy enough to cause people to cash their deposits on a large scale. If the banks cannot meet their expenses by these means then it would be better for the government to subsidise their costs on approved principles rather than that this difficulty should lead to an abandonment of the desired financial policy. But such an eventuality is probably a remote one.

The Unemployment Assistance Board

§ 26.   It has been pointed out above that during a slump there is a considerable fall in the amount spent on consumption goods and that this not only causes unemployment among those engaged in the production of consumption goods but also, by making industry less profitable, severely contracts the opportunities for profitable capital development. It is possible to attempt to cure unemployment simply by stimulating expenditure on capital development both by means of public expenditure on development and by a banking policy designed to reduce interest rates in order to stimulate capital development by private enterprise. However, the opportunities for such development will be unduly restricted so long as a slump causes consumers' expenditure to fall off, both because industry will be making abnormally low profits and also because the rents or money receipts which public authorities can expect to obtain from such developments as housing will be unduly low. The following proposals are designed, during a period in which abnormally great unemployment exists, both to maintain consumers' purchasing power and to provide automatically additional cash reserves for the joint-stock banks in order to enable them to purchase securities and to lower interest rates; these proposals are also equally designed to reduce consumers' purchasing power and to restrict the cash reserves of the banks automatically as soon as an abnormally strong demand for labour develops in order to prevent the excesses of a boom. It will be best first to outline the proposals, next to explain how they will operate and finally to meet certain criticisms which may be brought up against them.

§ 27. It is proposed that all the able-bodied unemployed should be brought under one scheme for unemployment benefit irrespective of the trades in which they are normally employed and that no distinction should be drawn between those who are still in insurance and those who are no longer qualified for insurance benefits. All unemployed should be under the charge of a single Unemployment Assistance Board. The benefits paid by the Board to those who are unemployed should be on a generous scale. They should not necessarily be much below the wage which the worker would obtain in employment, so long as the Labour Exchanges could be made to function efficiently in informing the unemployed of all available jobs. Naturally no man should be entitled to benefit who has refused to take a suitable job offered by the Labour Exchange. So long as the benefits are drawn up on a really generous scale there is little to be said against a Means Test principle, whereby the man with greater needs and smaller independent means gets more than one without such needs or with independent means. The existence or non-existence of a Means Test makes no fundamental difference to the scheme proposed in these paragraphs.

§ 28. There is in any modern state in which industrial progress and change is taking place almost bound to be some unemployment. For the demand for different commodities will be changing; and this together with inventions and other changes will be causing the demand for labour to be varying in different industries. For reasons of geographical location, specialised training and lack of knowledge of opportunities in different firms, industries and localities, it is bound to take some time for labour to shift or to be shifted to a new job when a previous job is lost; and this means that however well the labour market is organised there will almost always be some unemployment. We may call unemployment due to these reasons 'normal unemployment', and such unemployment will lose most of its disadvantages if the rates of unemployment assistance are on a generous scale.

§ 29.   It is proposed that in order to finance the unemployment assistance suggested in § 27 the volume of normal unemployment should be assessed. Contributions should then be levied from all workers employed and from all employers according to the number of workers which they employ, as in the existing Unemployment Insurance Scheme; but these contributions should be levied at such rates that they would raise just sufficient funds for the Unemployment Assistance Board to cover the expenditure on unemployment assistance, if there were only the 'normal' volume of unemployment. Thus if 5% of unemployment is considered normal, the contributions should be so arranged that these contributions, if paid in respect of 95% of the total employable population, would provide just sufficient to pay the proposed scale of benefits to 5% of the employable population. It is proposed that the state should make no contribution from the Budget to the funds of the Unemployment Assistance Board. When the volume of unemployment rises above 5% and the ordinary receipts of the Board are no longer sufficient to cover its payments of benefit, it is proposed that the difference should be financed by the use of new notes issued by the Bank of England from its Issue Department and covered by a non-interest bearing debt of the Unemployment Assistance Board to the Bank of England; this debt should certainly be guaranteed by the state. When on the other hand unemployment falls below 5%, the normal receipts of the Unemployment Assistance Board will be in excess of its payments of unemployment benefit, and the excess of its receipts should then be used to pay off with notes its debt to the Bank of England, which would in turn cancel the notes as they were paid into the Issue Department of the Bank of England in this manner.

§ 30.   If this proposal were adopted, it would be necessary to amend the laws relating to the note issue by the Bank of England. The present note issue of the Bank of England (13 March 1935) is £452,520,583, this sum being represented by the £260,000,000 fiduciary issue backed by securities plus £192,520,583 notes backed by gold. It is proposed therefore that the law regulating the note issue of the Bank should be emended so that the total note issue is fixed at a certain fixed sum (e.g. £450,000,000 which is about equal to the present note issue) plus the amount borrowed by the Unemployment Assistance Board on the principles outlined above; the fixed sum of £450,000,000 notes should be backed by gold or ordinary securities, while the remainder would be backed by the non-interest bearing debt of the Unemployment Assistance Board. If at any time the receipts of the Unemployment Assistance Board had for some time been in excess of its expenditure so that the total indebtedness of the Board to the Bank had been repaid, the note issue would have been reduced to £450,000,000. After that any further excess of receipts of the Unemployment Assistance Board over its expenditure would be used not to reduce the notes issued by the Bank but to accumulate a reserve of notes held by the Unemployment Assistance Board. These notes would thus equally well be drawn out of circulation and would be available, as soon as unemployment rose above the normal volume, to finance the difference between the receipts and the expenditure of the Board without increasing the note issue of the Bank.

§ 31.   The foregoing proposals are made to achieve two objects in times of slump and two objects in times of boom. In a time of slump it is desirable to maintain expenditure on consumption goods both directly to maintain employment in industries producing consumption goods and also thereby to maintain the existence of fields of profitable capital development. This object can best be achieved by giving the unemployed generous unemployment benefit and financing this benefit in such a manner that it does not reduce the purchasing power of other individuals in the community. If the funds for unemployment benefit are raised by taxation this is likely to reduce the expenditure of those paying the increased taxes at the same time that it maintains the expenditure of the unemployed. If the funds for this purpose are borrowed in the ordinary manner, there is a possibility that this borrowing will cause interest rates to be kept up at a higher level than is desirable to promote increased capital development to absorb the unemployed, and in any case such borrowing will cause a debt of the Unemployment Assistance Board to be piled up on which interest has to be paid in the future and such interest payments will require increased tax receipts of one kind or another for their payment. But the second object of the scheme proposed above is to provide automatically an increasing cash reserve for the joint-stock banks as long as there is excessive unemployment, in order that they may extend their loans, advances and investments so as to bring interest rates down to stimulate borrowing for purposes of capital development. If the funds for unemployment benefit are provided by taxation or by ordinary borrowing this will not be done; but if the foregoing proposals are adopted, so long as there is excessive unemployment, the new notes paid to the unemployed will as they are spent be paid into the banks by the firms receiving them. This will automatically cause the cash reserves of the joint-stock banks to be increasing, and so long as these banks maintain a 10% reserve of cash against their deposit liabilities, they will be expanding their advances and investments by nine times the amount of the new notes deposited with them. Thus the proposal will automatically cause that increase in purchases of securities by the banks which is required to reduce interest rates, and this will go on so long as there is unemployment in excess of 5%. Conversely in times of boom as more labour is employed the expenditure of labour will not be excessively increased, since the expenditure of wages will only take the place of the expenditure of the unemployment benefit, and this reduction of expenditure of unemployment benefit will not be offset by lower taxation. Moreover so long as the receipts of the Unemployment Assistance Board are in excess of its expenditure the difference will cause a drain of notes from circulation and from the cash reserves of the joint-stock banks. The banks will in these circumstances have to reduce their loans or sell securities equal to nine times the amount of cash drained from their reserves, and they will thus be causing interest rates to rise, so long as the excessive demand for labour continues.

§ 32.   It is necessary to meet the criticism that the above proposals will be of an inflationary nature and should for that reason be rejected. The experience of inflation of the kind caused in Germany after the war by an attempt on the part of the government to finance its ordinary expenditure by printing new notes is to be avoided at all costs, but it is maintained that the proposals outlined above cannot lead to similar results. There are very essential differences between the proposals made here and the attempt to finance an ordinary budget deficit by printing notes. So long as there are in existence large amounts of unemployed labour and capital it is most desirable that the total amount of money spent on goods should be increased, and so long as such unemployment exists increased expenditure on goods, while it will cause some rise in prices, will in the main cause an increase in the output of goods rather than a simple rise in the price of the existing output of goods. An increase in the total amount of money spent on goods is only to be avoided when there is no serious unemployment of labour and capital; for in those circumstances, since more cannot be produced, the increased money expenditure can only cause prices to rise and cannot cause an increased output to be sold at slightly higher prices. Indeed the case for increasing the total amount of money spent on goods during periods of serious unemployment can be put much more strongly when it is realised that it is only by such an increase in total money incomes and total money expenditure on goods that output has been increased and the unemployed have been absorbed into industry in the past. In the past such an increase in total money expenditure has been delayed until interest rates have slowly fallen and a large amount of capital needs to be replaced, and this has in the end caused an increase in the money demand for commodities and so some rise in prices and a considerable increase in employment and output. The measures outlined above are only designed to bring this about quickly as soon as a slump starts. As long therefore as serious unemployment exists no dangers can arise from increasing the total amount of money demand for commodities. Inflation of the money demand for goods can only become dangerous when there is full employment, so that further increases in money demand can only lead to progressive rises in the price of goods. But it is in this respect that the foregoing proposals must be sharply distinguished from any attempt on the part of a government to finance an ordinary budget deficit by inflationary measures. For if a government has a permanent budget deficit which it attempts to finance by printing more paper money, such a method of finance must lead to progressive and inflationary price rises as soon as all factors of production are employed, so that the increased money demand can no longer lead to increased output of commodities. But so long as the ordinary Budget of the government is balanced and so long as the public authorities are only borrowing in the ordinary way for purposes of capital development, the measures outlined above cannot be dangerous. For as soon as there is only a normal volume of unemployment, i.e. just so soon as it is impossible for an increase in money demand to lead to increased production rather than to a rise in prices, the issue of new notes will automatically cease, since the receipts of the Unemployment Assistance Board will balance its expenditure; and indeed, if there were any further increase in the money demand for commodities leading to a further fall in unemployment, the measures proposed would cause a strong deflationary movement to develop, since the excess of receipts of the Board over its expenditure would automatically be used to diminish the volume of notes in circulation. Such proposals therefore are simply designed to maintain and increase money purchasing power, as long as serious unemployment exists and as long as such action can cause output and employment to increase; and provided that the rest of the government's Budget is conducted on orthodox lines, these proposals will cause equally strong deflationary measures as soon as the money demand for commodities and so for labour becomes excessively great. These proposals cannot therefore lead to dangerous inflation.

§ 33. These proposals have been put forward in their final form. If they are started when the volume of unemployment is not greatly in excess of 5% or whatever is determined to be the 'normal' volume of unemployment, there is no reason why they should be modified; the benefits can be determined on the most generous lines and the contributions from workers and employers calculated to make the receipts and expenditure of the Unemployment Assistance Board balance with 5% unemployment. If however there is a much greater volume of unemployment at the time when this scheme is started, there is a good deal to be said for approaching the final scheme by stages. If for example there were 20% unemployment, then if the scheme was started in its final form, there would be an issue of new notes started and an amount which would finance the whole of the new and generous benefits for three-quarters of the unemployed. This might cause too rapid an expansion of the note issue and too rapid an expansion of bank investments and loans, which could not be expected to lead to an ordered and controlled expansion of capital development. By making the contributions and benefits balance first of all for a 15% volume of unemployment – which could be done by maintaining part of the contributions from the ordinary tax receipts of the government or by not raising the rates of benefit to their most generous scale immediately – the volume of unemployment could be reduced more slowly from 20% to 15% of the employable population. When this point was reached, the scales of benefit might be raised or the state's contribution lowered so that the contributions and benefits balanced for a 10% volume of unemployment, and when unemployment had been reduced to this figure the scheme might be altered to its final form. By some such measures the very quick expansion of cash reserves, which would be caused by instituting the scheme for the first time in its final form during a period of very heavy unemployment, might be avoided and a slower but more ordered advance towards full employment attained. But once unemployment had fallen to a 5% level the full scheme should be maintained in order to provide very strong inflationary tendencies so soon as the demand for labour fell below the normal and very strong deflationary tendencies so soon as the demand for labour rose above the normal.

The Budget

§ 34.   Budgetary policy can be discussed from any of three aspects. It will be the object of the Labour Government to use its budgetary policy to aid it in attaining its objectives of obtaining full employment, of socialising different industries and of providing for greater equality. Budgetary policy is discussed in this section from these different points of view.

§ 35.   If the policy already outlined in previous sections is adopted the government will be presented with two important budgetary problems. In the first place it will be committed to planning through its National Development Board for considerable expenditure on capital development to be undertaken by the state, though it is to be observed that if this expenditure is planned on the lines suggested in § 12 and if the rate of interest is being lowered so long as abnormal unemployment exists, a large part of this expenditure will earn a yield as high as the rate of interest at which the state borrows for the expenditure. But in the second place the state will have lost all responsibility for the provision of funds for unemployment benefit and it will have done this at the same time that it has redeemed its pledges to raise to generous levels the scale of unemployment benefit. Moreover if the items of policy already discussed are efficiently and properly carried out, the state will not only have no unemployment benefit to meet from the Budget but by causing a rise in incomes and a general recovery will have increased the yields of its existing taxes considerably. It is for this reason that the primary object of policy should be to promote recovery by the means already suggested: for by so doing the government will automatically eliminate its expenditure on unemployment and increase its tax receipts.

§ 36.   It is proposed that the Budget should immediately be divided into two accounts, a Revenue Budget and a Capital Budget. The Revenue Budget would show on the one side all the ordinary tax receipts and all the profit or interest received from state-run concerns such as the Post Office or any other socialised industry, and on the other side all the ordinary government state expenditure such as interest on the existing national debt or on other bonds issued by way of compensation for the socialisation of property, as well as expenditure on defence and the cost of social services. The Capital Budget would show the total amount spent by the state on capital development or in subsidies to municipalities or other bodies for capital development, the amount advanced by the state to socialised undertakings for capital development and the amount spent by the state on the redemption of the national debt. The receipts of the Capital Budget would consist of amounts borrowed by the state, any surplus of income over expenditure in the Revenue Budget and the proceeds of any special levy on capital or any special death duties, which it was thought proper to allocate specifically to capital development or to the redemption of debt.

§ 37.   If the government successfully promotes recovery and provides full employment it should obtain a surplus of £100,000,000 in the Revenue Budget. It can use this surplus partly to increase expenditure on such services as education, pensions, etc., partly to lower indirect taxes which press hardest on the poorer sections of the community and partly to provide a surplus for the Capital Budget. It is suggested that the government should not in its first years of office very appreciably raise the rates of taxation on income or on capital, but should concentrate on increasing its tax revenue by means of ensuring that its recovery programme as outlined above is successful. For high rates of taxation are likely to cause a sense of insecurity among those controlling industries privately owned, and thus the incentive to invest in new fixed capital goods by private enterprise will be diminished if high rates of taxation are imposed. So long therefore as the government does not control through its National Development Board sufficient fields of investment in new capital equipment to ensure the success of its unemployment policy, rates of taxation should not be appreciably raised.

§ 38.   The Government should provide from its Capital Budget the funds necessary for those objects of capital development which have been planned by the National Development Board and which are to be financed by the central Government. These expenditures will consist either of funds necessary to finance capital development directly undertaken by the state or by those in charge of socialised industries or else subsidies paid to municipalities and public utilities controlled by public bodies for certain approved plans of capital development. These expenditures should in the first years be financed partly by the surplus from the Revenue Budget which will be contributed to the Capital Budget and for the rest by borrowing in the market in the normal manner.

§ 39.   It will be the policy of the Government to socialise certain major industries. The principles upon which the choice of industries to be socialised should be made and upon which socialised industries should be run are discussed in more detail in a later section (§§ 61 to 83). Here however it is necessary to discuss certain aspects of the financing of such undertakings. It is most important that full compensation should be paid upon the socialisation of undertakings in private ownership for the reason that unless this is done there will be very little incentive for private owners in other industries, which are likely to be socialised in the future, to undertake the capital development which would otherwise be profitable in those industries. For if owners expect socialisation of their capital to take place without full compensation they will have every incentive not to develop that capital, since they expect not to receive the full benefits of such capital development if and when it is taken over by the state. If however capital development for this reason diminishes greatly in the major industries of the country, it will be impossible for the government successfully to prosecute its unemployment policy by stimulating investment through its National Development Board. If however full compensation is expected, these difficulties will be avoided. Socialisation of industry will therefore bring no direct relief to the Budget. Industries should be socialised by means of the issue of government bonds to the owners bearing interest which fully compensates the income reasonably to be expected from the concerns which are socialised. The effect of this upon the Budget will be to increase in the Revenue Budget the amount spent in interest on debt while at the same time the income of the Revenue Budget from the profits of socialised industries will increase by a roughly similar amount.

§ 40.   As certain major industries are socialised, however, the control of the National Development Board over the volume of capital development can be increased. For socialised industries will be required to plan their capital development ahead with reference to the different rates of interest which different blocks of development will yield and also in a manner which allows the maximum freedom to the National Development Board to spread such development over a few or many years. In fact one of the major objects to be achieved by socialisation will be to give the government control over the volume of capital development through the National Development Board. If then the government concentrates on its unemployment policy as outlined above and on the socialisation of certain major industries, it should in a few years have caused a large degree of recovery and have obtained considerable control over investment for capital development. It will then be in a position to develop its budgetary policy on different lines.

§ 41.   As soon as the government has developed the foregoing parts of its policy to ensure that it has sufficient control to prevent serious unemployment, it will be in a position to turn its attention for the first time seriously to the problem of providing for a greater equality in the distribution of the national income. To some extent it can at this point simply by raising the rates of income tax develop expenditure further on the social services by such projects as making health insurance non-contributory, by lowering the age for old age pensions, by extending educational facilities, by providing family allowances, etc.; for higher taxation will no longer have such serious dangers as before. But the only certain way in which a much greater degree of equality can be achieved is by the state obtaining ownership of the national debt and the debt which it has issued in compensation for the socialisation of private undertakings or by obtaining ownership of further forms of property such as the land. For by so doing the state will be able to receive the interest, profit or rent from this capital and property without paying interest on compensation debt to the previous owners. It is at this point that certain specific taxes on all forms of privately owned capital such as the Rignano Duties or the levy on capital proposed in the 'Memorandum on Budgetary Considerations' Policy No. 276, February 1935 [by Colin Clark, in Meade Papers 2/7 and published as *A Socialist Budget*, New Fabian Research Bureau pamphlet no. 22, May 1935] should be imposed. These taxes can be specifically allotted to the Capital Budget and the rates of such duties or levies can be raised as the state obtains greater and greater control over the economic system on the lines suggested above. These duties together with the surplus from the Revenue Budget can then be used to finance the government's expenditure from the Capital Budget and should provide a considerable surplus in the Capital Budget to be used to reduce the capital sum of the debt of the state to private individuals. By these means the interest which has to be paid on the debt from the Revenue Budget can be reduced, while the whole of the new income derived from any capital development undertaken by the state will now accrue as an income to the Revenue Budget. The increased surplus of the Revenue Budget can then be allocated partly for the purposes of developing those services which provide for greater equality and partly as a further income for the Capital Budget. By these means the position will gradually be reached in which the state has a very large income from state property in the Revenue Budget and no expenditure on interest in the Revenue Budget, and at this point it will be possible to allocate part of this income as a social dividend to be distributed from the Revenue Budget on any desired principle of equality, and part as a surplus to be paid as an income to the Capital Budget for further capital development. As this stage is reached the government will, by paying a smaller or larger part of this sum as a social dividend to the members of the community, be able to control the amount of the national income spent on consumption and the amount allocated to capital development. When even at very low interest rates very little development is profitable, a large proportion can be paid out as a social dividend; whereas if new and profitable fields of development appear a much larger part can be apportioned to the Capital Budget for this capital development.

The Foreign Exchanges

§ 42. If the internal financial policy outlined above is adopted, it is essential that the foreign exchange rates with other countries should not be rigidly fixed. Let us suppose that there is a slump in other important countries, so that the price level and money incomes in other countries are falling. If in these circumstances English prices and money incomes are being maintained by the internal policy suggested above, the volume as well as the value of English exports will fall off in consequence of the fall in foreign prices and incomes, and the volume of English imports will rise in consequence of the fall in foreign prices. To meet this situation it will be necessary either to abandon the internal policy and to allow English prices and incomes to fall as foreign prices and incomes fall, or clsc to allow thc pound to depreciate in the exchange market sufficiently to offset the fall in foreign prices and incomes; for if the amount of foreign currency which can be bought for a pound is allowed to diminish, this will prevent the price of foreign imports from falling in this country and will allow the price of our exports in foreign markets to fall as foreign prices fall. Conversely, if there is a boom in other important countries and foreign prices and incomes are rising quickly, while the internal policy in England is preventing a similar rise in English prices and incomes, our imports will fall and our exports increase. To offset this, either the internal policy must be abandoned and English prices and incomes must be allowed to rise as foreign prices and incomes rise, or else the value of the pound in terms of foreign currencies must be allowed to increase to prevent the domestic price of our imports from rising as foreign prices rise and to allow the price of our exports in foreign markets to rise as foreign prices rise.

§ 43. The position is of course fundamentally different if other countries are pursuing internal policies similar to the policy pursued by this country. If certain other important countries are preserving a high level of employment by internal measures similar to those outlined above and designed to maintain high and relatively constant prices and money incomes, then the reasons given in the previous paragraph for being unwilling to stabilise the exchange rates with those countries do not exist. It will of course be very much easier for the government to prosecute its internal policy with success, if other countries are doing the same and the exchange problems discussed in the previous paragraph are avoided. It should therefore be one of the major objects of the government to achieve international agreements in economic policy and the principles of such international co-operation are discussed below in §§ 55 to 60. But even if such co-operation is achieved, it will still be undesirable to fix exchange rates rigidly with other countries for more than a limited period at a time. There are many reasons why this is so, but one example will illustrate the point. Let us suppose that the productivity of American industry were increasing at a more rapid rate than that of English industry; then if both countries were pursuing an internal policy designed to maintain a high level of employment at a constant money wage-rate, American money costs and prices would be falling more quickly than money costs and prices in England; if Americans produced commodities which competed with English commodities, the consequence again would be a fall in English exports and a rise in English imports. To offset this England would again be faced with the alternative either of causing a fall in English prices and money incomes, which would mean the abandonment of her internal policy, or else of allowing the pound to depreciate in terms of dollars to offset the more rapid fall in American prices. It may therefore be concluded that if international co-operation in the matter of internal policy is not achieved, exchange rates between the pound and foreign currencies must certainly not be stabilised, and further that even if such co-operation can be achieved, exchange rates should not be rigidly fixed for more than a limited period and that the rates at which they are stabilised should be open to revision if fundamental changes in the balance of trade take place.

§ 44. While rigidly fixed exchange rates are undesirable, to leave the exchange rates completely free to find their own level is probably also undesirable. For purchase and sale of foreign currencies for the purpose of importing and exporting commodities do not comprise all the factors which determine the exchanges; freedom to purchase foreign currencies for the purpose of lending money abroad rather than at home raises certain very important problems. Let us suppose that the government has stated unambiguously its intention to pursue an internal policy designed on the lines suggested above to increase the volume of employment to a normal level and that other important countries have not the same internal policy. Then there will for two very definite reasons be a great incentive for foreigners who own money invested in England or deposited in England to remove these funds, and for English people and institutions with property to lend their money abroad rather than at home. (a) In the first place people will realise well that in these circumstances for the reasons discussed above the government can only achieve its end if it allows the pound to depreciate. If the pound is expected to depreciate, people will sell pounds and buy foreign currencies at once in order to be able to sell foreign currencies again and to buy pounds when the depreciation of the pound has taken place. Thus if the rate of exchange is £1 to $4 and people expect that the government is pursuing a policy which will cause the exchange to depreciate to £1 to $2, so long as that depreciation has not taken place people will expect that a considerable profit is to be made by buying dollars with pounds in order to buy pounds with dollars in the future at the cheaper price. It follows that there will be speculative sales of English money and purchases of foreign currencies until the value of the pound has depreciated to a value near that which is expected to rule in the future. But this rate of exchange may be one which is not really justified by the circumstances; vague rumours and unfounded suspicions that the government's internal policy is likely to cause an uncontrolled inflation may cause the pound to depreciate in value from $4 to $2, when in fact a depreciation from $4 to $3·50 would be sufficient to offset any rise in prices and incomes which the government will bring about by its internal policy. Such speculative movements may therefore cause the value of the pound to depreciate and so the price of English imports to rise to a degree out of all proportion to the rise in English money prices and incomes actually brought about by the government. (b) But there will be a second reason why owners of English property may wish to lend much larger sums abroad. Part of the government's policy at home will consist in reducing rates of interest so long as there is an abnormal volume of unemployment at home; but if other countries are not at the same time lowering interest rates, there will be a strong incentive to lend money abroad rather than at home in order to obtain the higher yields abroad, and this incentive to lend a large amount abroad will continue so long as interest rates in England are kept very appreciably below those in other countries.

§ 45.   In a period when there is a boom in other countries and the policy in England is to prevent a boom in prices and incomes and to maintain high interest rates, the opposite influences will be felt. Persons will expect an appreciation of the pound; and both for this reason and because interest rates are being kept high in England, large amounts of money will be transferred from foreign countries to England. It is to be observed that international co-operation by which many important countries are adopting similar internal policies will largely prevent these exchange difficulties since such co-operation would remove the major reasons for large movements of capital from one currency to another. But so long as this country alone is adopting the type of internal policy outlined above the movement of capital from this country or into this country will present important exchange problems.

§ 46.   It would be possible for the government to allow complete freedom in the exchange rates between the pound and foreign currencies in spite of the possibility of large variations in the amount of money lent abroad. Such a policy would however have serious disadvantages. If people lend a very large amount to foreign countries because interest rates are low in this country and because a depreciation of the pound is expected, this foreign lending can only be financed if English imports fall and English exports increase. As people purchase foreign currencies in order to lend more abroad, this will cause the pound to depreciate in value; this depreciation in the pound will cause the price of our imports to rise in England and will thus reduce English imports, while it will cause the price of English exports to fall in foreign markets and so cause English exports to rise. And the exchange rate will have to depreciate until English exports are just sufficiently stimulated and English imports just sufficiently restricted to enable people to lend abroad that amount which they wish to lend abroad. Thus with a given level of prices of English goods at home and of foreign goods in foreign countries, a rate of exchange of £1 to $4 might be sufficient to allow people to lend £100,000,000 a year abroad; whereas a rate of exchange of £1 to $3 might be required to allow people to lend £200,000,000 a year abroad. A large increase in the amount lent abroad together with that degree of exchange depreciation which is necessary to enable that sum to be lent abroad will involve two grave disadvantages. (a) In the first place such a policy is likely to make the slump in foreign countries worse than it would otherwise be. A depreciation of the pound which simply offsets a rise in English prices and money incomes cannot harm other countries, since it simply prevents the rise in English prices and money incomes from causing an increase in English purchases of foreign goods and from causing a rise in the price of English goods in foreign markets. But if the exchange depreciation goes further than this and causes such a rise in English import prices that England buys less foreign goods and actually causes a fall in the price of English goods in foreign markets, then the foreign countries will be able to sell less to England and foreign industries will be less able than before to compete with goods produced in England. Such a change during a world slump may greatly intensify the difficulties in other countries, and so react unfavourably on the position in this country. (b) But secondly, quite apart from these effects on other countries, the result of an exchange depreciation which more than offsets any rise in English prices and incomes and any fall in foreign prices and incomes may be very undesirable from the purely English point of view. For it means that the price in pounds of English imports will rise out of all proportion to the rise in the price of goods produced in England and out of all proportion to the rise in English money incomes. In other words England would be paying a much higher price for imports, while obtaining only a slightly higher price for goods produced in England, and she would therefore be obtaining her imports on much worse terms in exchange for her own goods. As this country depends for a large part of the essentials of life upon imports it is desirable to prevent a large increase in foreign lending from causing such a depreciation of the pound that there is a large rise in the price of imported essentials of life which is unaccompanied by so large a rise in English money incomes.

§ 47. It will be seen then that as long as it is impossible to get co-operation among nations in their internal financial policies there is a strong case for the government to take control of the volume of foreign lending. The Government through some appropriate body must decide how much it is desirable shall be lent abroad each year. It is impossible to give any rule-of-thumb principles by which this decision should be governed; but the following are the main considerations which should be borne in mind:

(a) The extent to which a higher return can be earned on investment abroad rather than in England.

(b) The extent to which, if there is no alteration in the internal financial policy and in the existing rate of exchange with other countries, an excess of exports and other current receipts of foreign currencies will automatically be generated. This will show what funds there are available for lending abroad, if there is no change in the existing financial policy.

(c) The extent to which it would be necessary, while maintaining the internal financial policy unchanged, to depreciate the pound to raise the price of imports and to lower the price of exports in foreign markets sufficiently to increase the funds available for foreign lending by a given amount. This will give some indication of the cost involved in any increase in foreign lending.

(d) The extent to which the borrowing country in each case is borrowing for a productive use. In this connection it must be clearly realised that if the loan is a loan and not a gift, and if repayment of the loan and of interest on it is going to be demanded, the borrowing country must be using the loan in a productive manner which is likely to strengthen its position in the competitive markets of the world. If this is not the case, ultimate repayment is unlikely to materialise, and the attempt to repay by the borrowing country will cause very great economic difficulties and suffering in that country. In this connection it should always be remembered that where it is a question of maintaining a large volume of foreign lending with a low exchange rate or a small volume of foreign lending with a high exchange rate, the low exchange rate will damage other countries' export trade by making our goods cheaper in foreign markets, while a high exchange will make it easier for other countries to export. If therefore this country wishes to aid other countries in a time of depression, it can probably do more good by lending little to, but buying more from other countries, rather than by lending more and allowing its exchange to depreciate further, thereby competing more strongly with other countries in the export market and buying less from them.

(e) Any relevant political or other non-economic factors involved in lending abroad to particular countries or for particular purposes.

§ 48. If it is decided that a case has been made out for the complete control of foreign lending, it is next necessary to determine by what mechanisms this control can be exercised. It is of course relatively easy to control the issue of new securities on the London capital market on the part of foreign borrowers, if the government has set up a National Development Board, whose sanction would be necessary for any new issue. This control is already exercised unofficially to a large extent by the Bank of England. But this does not give the government the requisite control over foreign lending. For it remains possible for individuals and institutions to buy foreign currency or deposits in foreign banks or existing foreign securities with English money without check. Such purchases can only be effectively controlled if the government can control all purchases of foreign money, so that it is enabled to allow or disallow purchases according as they are made for approved purposes or not.

§ 49. By means of the institution of the Exchange Equalisation Account the Treasury has already obtained some degree of control over the exchanges, but this control is at present exercised by means of offsetting the movement of funds from one currency to another rather than by preventing such movements. The Exchange Equalisation Account is permitted to borrow by the sale of Treasury Bills up to a figure of £350,000,000. If foreigners are lending to England and are for this purpose buying pounds, the appreciation of the pound which would be caused by this can be prevented by the Exchange Equalisation Account, if the Account sells Treasury Bills for pounds and with these pounds buys foreign currencies at the same time that foreigners are buying pounds. Similarly if people wish to move pounds from England to foreign currencies, the consequent depreciation of the pound can be prevented if the Exchange Equalisation Account at the same time buys pounds with the foreign currencies which it has obtained through its previous transactions. But this method of control is very narrowly limited. For the Exchange Equalisation Account cannot prevent people from lending abroad; it can only offset this by purchasing pounds with the foreign currencies which it has previously purchased. If it is faced with a large and continuous increase in foreign lending it will be bound as soon as it has used up all its previous purchases of foreign money to let the increased foreign lending have its full effect in causing the pound to depreciate.

§ 50. The only certain method of controlling the amount of foreign lending is to monopolise the purchase and sale of foreign currencies in the hands of some appropriate public body, and to give this body the power of refusing to sell more than a certain amount of foreign currencies for pounds for the purpose of lending abroad. It is suggested that it should be made illegal to purchase or sell foreign currencies for pounds except through (e.g.) the Exchange Equalisation Account. Such a measure would require the close co-operation of the joint-stock banks and other financial institutions; it would not necessarily follow that these bodies should be socialised, but it should be made clear that the government would do so if they refused to co-operate in this part of the government's financial policy. It is proposed then that all purchase and sale of foreign currencies should be monopolised in the hands of the Exchange Equalisation Account, which will start operations with a certain holding of foreign money and a certain holding of English funds. The Account will then state rates of exchange at which it will purchase and sell foreign currencies and will allow all such purchases and sales for the import and export of commodities and for other approved purposes such as normal purchases for tourist expenditure, payment of interest on debts, etc. Having fixed certain rates of exchange it will be selling pounds for foreign money to finance English exports and selling foreign money for pounds to finance imports. The excess of its receipts of foreign money over its sales of foreign money will show how much is available for foreign lending. If this surplus available for foreign lending is less than has been expected, it can either depreciate the pound and offer to sell pounds at a lower price in terms of foreign money thereby stimulating English exports and making imports more expensive in order to obtain a larger surplus for foreign lending, or else the amount of foreign lending, for which plans have been made, must be curtailed. This decision must be made on the principles enumerated in § 47. At first the rates of exchange fixed by the Account must be open to daily or even hourly revision; but as soon as some measure of internal stability has been achieved and the foreign demand for English goods has been fully forecasted the rates of exchange with different currencies might be open to much less frequent revision. Certain proposals for temporary stabilisation of exchange rates in co-operation with other nations are discussed below in §§ 55 to 60.

§ 51.   Besides the passing of legislation requiring that all purchases and sales of foreign money should be made through the Exchange Equalisation Account and besides the assurance of the co-operation of or, failing that, control of other financial institutions required to make this law effective, certain other measures will be necessary to make this control of foreign lending effective. There are certain ways in which persons in this country may obtain ownership of foreign money to lend abroad, which do not entail the purchase of foreign money with English money. There are two important classes of transaction of this kind. In the first place English exporters may obtain foreign money in payment of the goods which they have exported, and instead of purchasing pounds with these funds may invest them directly in foreign countries. And in the second place persons who already own property of one kind or another in foreign countries may use the income from this property which they receive in foreign money for the purpose of direct reinvestment in foreign countries rather than for the purchase of pounds. The government must therefore pass legislation requiring those who receive income in foreign money for exports or as interest on foreign property to sell these foreign moneys for pounds to the Exchange Equalisation Account at the current rate of exchange fixed by the Account. It is probable that the income tax authorities already have sufficient knowledge of the holding of foreign securities in order to give the government the ability to see that this source of income is sold for pounds, and that the customs authorities could with comparative ease collect the necessary information about exports to see that exporters exchanged the proceeds of their sale of exports for English money.

§ 52.   It is suggested that, while complete control of foreign lending is desirable for the reasons given above, persons should be left free to exchange foreign money for English money or English money for foreign money without any restriction for the purposes of importing and exporting commodities. The object of foreign trade is to obtain imported goods in exchange for home-produced goods, whenever it is possible to obtain a greater amount of these goods by importing them than could have been obtained had the factors of production been withdrawn from the production of the exported goods and set to the production at home of the imported goods. This result is achieved if home-made goods are sold abroad whenever the price obtainable in the foreign market is, when converted into pounds at the ruling rate of exchange, not lower than the cost of production, and if all goods are allowed to flow in whenever the price at which they are offered by the foreigner, when converted into pounds at the ruling rate of exchange, is lower than the cost of producing the same goods at home. The exchange rate will be fixed as we have seen at that level at which, while full employment is achieved at home by means of the internal policy described above, the value of exports minus the value of imports plus the net receipts of income from abroad from such sources as interest on past foreign investments, debts, etc. is just equal to the amount which it is considered desirable to lend abroad.

§ 53.   In order therefore that the full advantages of international trade should be achieved three conditions must be fulfilled.

(a) There must be complete freedom of purchase and sale of foreign money at the ruling rate of exchange for the purposes of financing imports and exports.

(b) A system of costing must be adopted in all socialised industries, which will show as clearly as can be done the money cost of the factors of production required to produce the goods produced by these undertakings. This problem is discussed below at length in §§ 63 to 78. Each socialised undertaking must sell in the export market as much as it can without loss at this cost and at the current rate of exchange, and must import raw materials whenever it can obtain them cheaper in pounds by importing them than by buying them at home. If this principle is adopted each socialised industry·can arrange through appropriate mechanism for its own marketing.

(c) All import tariffs, quotas, prohibitions, etc. should be removed. This cannot perhaps be done at once, but the principles upon which this should be done in order to obtain similar reductions by other countries are discussed below in §§ 59 and 60.

It is perhaps worth while to point out that such a free trade policy will no longer cause unemployment, since the internal policy outlined above will be achieving full employment; and so long as further rises in English money demand for commodities are necessary to give full employment, the exchange rate will be allowed to depreciate, to cause the prices of imported goods to rise as English prices rise and to prevent the prices of English goods in foreign markets from rising as English prices rise. In so far therefore as the movement towards free trade takes place and causes English imports to rise in excess of English exports, the exchange rate will be allowed to depreciate to stop off part of the rise in imports and to stimulate exports.

§ 54.   It may be well at this point to summarise the principles upon which the exchange policy should be based.

(a) In no circumstances should foreign exchange difficulties lead to an abandonment of the internal policy designed to give full employment.

(b) If sufficient co-operation with other nations cannot be achieved so that the major countries are undertaking similar internal policies, the government should control the volume of foreign lending. This should be done by monopolising in one institution (e.g. the Exchange Equalisation Account) all purchase and sale of foreign money and by taking powers to see that exporters and others receiving income from abroad sell the foreign money so obtained to the Account at the current rate of exchange.

(c) The Exchange Equalisation Account should then fix rates of exchange and allow complete freedom of such purchases and sales for the financing of imports and exports and ordinary approved objects. The amount which it actually allows people to lend abroad will be equated simply to the excess sales of foreign money over the purchase of foreign money for these approved purposes.

(d) If the amount lent abroad is not the same as that which it was planned should be lent abroad, either the amount planned to be lent abroad or the rate of exchange should be revised, and this choice should be determined by the considerations enumerated in § 47.

(e) All socialised concerns should be instructed to sell abroad all that they can so long as the price they can get is as high as their cost of production, and to purchase from abroad when it is cheaper to do so.

(f) There should be progressive elimination of tariffs, import quotas and prohibitions, any undesirable increase in the excess of imports over exports to be offset by a change in the rates of exchange fixed by the Exchange Equalisation Account.

International Co-operation

§ 55. The refusal to stabilise rates of exchange with other currencies permanently does not preclude the possibility of very important measures of economic co-operation with other countries. Indeed the measures of economic policy so far discussed will be very much easier to carry out if international co-operation can be achieved. Emphasis should however be laid on co-operation with other nations in the determination of internal policies. For, if booms and slumps within individual countries can be eliminated by these means, by far the greater amount both of the undesirability of fixed exchange rates and of the difficulties of obtaining more nearly stabilised exchange rates will be removed. Moreover, a large part of the reasons for variations in the amount of foreign lending will be removed, and the need for control of foreign lending and the difficulty of achieving such control will be greatly diminished.

§ 56. In as far as co-operation with other nations in internal policy can be achieved, the possibility arises of stabilising temporarily the rates of exchange with the currencies of those countries. For there will no longer be violent changes in the value of exports and imports due to sudden changes in prices and incomes in these countries, nor will there be the incentive for sudden and large variations in the volume of foreign lending due to speculative movement of funds from one currency to another or to large discrepancies between the rates of interest in different countries. In as far therefore as a group of countries co-operate with this country in devising internal policies similar to that which this country adopts, the rate of exchange with the currencies of that country might be temporarily fixed. Such rates could be maintained if the Exchange Equalisation Account in this country and similar bodies or central banks in other countries bought and sold the currencies of these countries at fixed exchange rates.

§ 57.   These rates of exchange though temporarily fixed might require revision from time to time. In the event of fundamental changes in productive technique or in demand in different countries leading to large changes in the balance of commodity trade of one of these countries with the others, the rate of exchange between that country and the others would need to be appropriately adjusted. One important principle in adjusting these exchange rates should be observed. Any country which found it difficult to obtain a sufficient excess of exports over imports to finance its current obligations in (e.g.) interest on debt to be paid to other countries should be aided by the authorities of the other countries in achieving that measure of exchange depreciation sufficient to allow it to generate a favourable balance to meet these obligations. No international co-operation in arranging the rates at which the exchanges should be stabilised can succeed unless the principle is fully recognised that creditor countries will allow and indeed stimulate an excess of imports by means of which they can receive payment of these debts; and to do this the creditor countries must fix rates of exchange sufficiently appreciated in terms of the debtor countries' currencies to enable this to be done. On the other hand the principle should be equally clearly recognised that in the event of a slump in one country that country must rely mainly on internal expansion to obtain recovery and must not be allowed to depreciate its exchange rate in order to cheapen its exports and cut off its imports in an attempt to achieve recovery at the expense of the industries of other countries by obtaining a large increase in the excess of its exports over its imports.

§ 58.   During a slump certain countries, either because they have interest on debt to meet which is fixed in terms of money or else because they rely mainly on the export of commodities, such as wheat, the price of which slumps much more than the price of other commodities, will be in much greater exchange difficulties than other creditor countries exporting other types of commodity. These exchange difficulties are one of the major causes of the imposition of tariffs, quotas, prohibitions and exchange restrictions in these countries. It should be a clear principle of co-operation among nations in their internal policies that the countries in a relatively strong exchange position should be the first to undertake expansive monetary policies at home without a depreciation of their exchanges sufficient completely to offset the rise in their prices and incomes, and moreover that in the reduction of tariffs the countries in a relatively strong exchange position should reduce their tariffs sooner and to a larger extent than those in a weaker exchange position. Such action will increase their imports without increasing their exports to a similar degree, will enable the countries in a weak exchange position to obtain foreign money to meet their obligations by an excess of exports over imports, will therefore promote recovery in these countries as well and enable them in turn to remove their import tariffs, quotas, prohibitions, exchange restrictions, etc.

§ 59.   Besides trying to obtain co-operation with as many other nations as possible in devising appropriate internal policies and in fixing temporarily exchange rates with these countries on the principles outlined above, the government should also try to obtain agreements among nations for the reduction of tariffs and the elimination of import quotas and prohibitions. It has been argued above in §§ 52 and 53 that the government should in any case itself adopt a free trade principle and apply this principle to the operation of its own socialised industries. If however agreement with other countries to lower tariffs cannot be obtained, such a movement towards free trade should probably be postponed until the internal policy of the government and the exchange problems connected with it have been solved. For internal expansion in this country alone is likely to lead to a severe strain on the exchanges, part of which will be met by a control of foreign lending and part by a controlled depreciation of the exchange rate sufficient to offset the rise in English prices and money incomes. If at the same time English tariffs and import quotas were removed without a similar lowering of tariffs in other countries this would intensify the exchange problem, since it would be a further cause contributing to a rise in imports unaccompanied by an expansion in exports. In this case it would probably be best to make sure that the internal policy was successfully achieved, that the exchange problems raised by that policy were solved and that the exchanges were controlled, before embarking on unilateral lowering of tariffs which would entail further exchange depreciation. When this point is reached, there should be a progressive movement towards free trade by this country together with the appropriate degree of controlled exchange depreciation, if agreement with other countries to lower their tariffs at the same time cannot be achieved.

§ 60.   If however agreements can be reached with other countries to lower their tariffs simultaneously with reductions in English tariffs, this additional exchange problem does not arise or at any rate does not arise in so extreme a form, since English exports will be stimulated by the reduction of other tariffs as English imports are stimulated by the reduction of English tariffs. Moreover as this country now possesses tariffs with which to bargain it is worth while investigating their use as a means of obtaining reciprocal tariff reductions from other countries. The use of tariffs as weapons to achieve tariff reductions by other countries has been greatly hindered by the existence of Most-Favoured-Nation clauses in commercial agreements. By the terms of this clause, which exists in all English commercial agreements, each nation promises that it will not impose duties on imports from the other at a higher rate than those which it imposes on similar imports from any other country. If two nations which have signed commercial agreements with other nations containing this clause attempt to agree to reciprocal tariff reductions on the goods of the other nation, each nation is obliged to give to all the other nations any tariff reduction which it is giving to the single nation with which it is bargaining. Thus each of the two nations is obliged to give reductions in tariffs on imports from all other nations in return for a reduction by one nation alone in the duties imposed on its exports. It is for this reason that the bilateral agreements to reduce tariffs are so difficult to achieve. It is proposed therefore that the government should attempt in the first place to obtain tariff reductions by means of a general agreement among all or a large number of nations. If this attempt fails the government should seriously consider the possibility of an agreement among any nations which desire to reduce tariffs to form a 'low-tariff' group of nations and to modify appropriately the Most-Favoured-Nation clause in commercial treaties with other nations. An agreement might be formed between three or four nations to form a 'low-tariff' group in which no nation would levy any tariff of more than (e.g.) 10% nor impose any quotas or prohibitions on the goods imported from any other member of the 'low-tariff' group of nations. In this case the Most-Favoured-Nation clause should be re-interpreted in commercial agreements with other nations outside the 'low-tariff' group to mean that the country in the 'low-tariff' group would not impose higher duties on the imports from the nation in question than it levied on the imports of any other nation outside the 'low-tariff' group. By such means tariffs might properly be used as a means of obtaining reciprocal tariff reductions. At the same time it should of course remain free to any other nation in the world to join the 'low-tariff' group simply by agreeing to the conditions of membership of that group.

The Socialisation of Industry

§ 61.   It is necessary to realise quite clearly what are the advantages which it is hoped to gain by socialisation, in order to decide upon the principles upon which industries should be selected for socialisation and the principles upon which socialised undertakings should be operated. There are four main arguments in favour of state control and planning of industry. (a) It is argued that the socialisation and planning of industry will help to cure the problem of unemployment. (b) It is stated that planning of industry for the purpose of satisfying wants rather than for the purpose of making profits will lead to a better satisfaction of consumers' needs. (c) Socialisation is supported on the grounds that it will lead to a more efficient method of production and will eliminate many of the wasteful methods of competition. (d) Finally social ownership of capital is advocated as a means of removing inequalities in the distribution of income. Problems of socialisation will be discussed in the following paragraphs from each of these four points of view.

Socialisation and Unemployment

§ 62.   It was argued above in §§ 9 to 14 that in order to cure unemployment the state must plan and control a large amount of the capital development undertaken in the community. There is already some control over the volume of capital development (i.e. by the government, by municipalities and by public utilities already controlled by public bodies), which the state would exercise without further socialisation of industry. This may prove sufficient fully to control the unemployment situation; but if it should prove insufficient one of the major objects of socialisation will be to achieve a larger measure of control over and planning of the capital development of the community on the lines suggested in §§ 9 to 14.

Socialisation and the Efficient Service of Consumers' Needs

§ 63.   The second and third arguments in favour of socialisation, which were noted in § 61, were that the consumers' needs could best be met if industries were directly planned for this purpose and that socialised industry by eliminating the wastes of competition could produce more efficiently. These two arguments are very closely connected and it is best to treat them together. These two claims are however precisely the claims which can be advanced with most justification in favour of competition; the claims made in favour of a competitive system under these two heads will therefore be investigated in order to emphasise certain fundamental principles which should govern the choice of industries to be socialised and the operation of socialised concerns.

§ 64.   If there are a very large number of competing producers and purchasers, so that no single person can affect the price of any commodity by selling or buying more or less of it, and if further labour and the other factors of production are free and have the requisite knowledge to go into those occupations where they can obtain the highest reward, then free competition will bring about the most efficient use of the resources of the community for the satisfaction of consumers' needs. For in such circumstances producers will always employ more of any of the factors of production, e.g. labour, so long as the price at which they can sell the additional output due to employing more labour is greater than the cost of employing more labour, i.e. greater than the wage. In these conditions each factor of production will be paid in each occupation an amount equivalent to the price which consumers offer for the additional output due to employing the last unit of that factor in that occupation. These are however the conditions in which the desires of consumers will be best satisfied by the resources which are at the disposal of the community, and also they are just the conditions in which it will be impossible for the community, with a given amount of resources, to produce more of one commodity without producing less of another.

§ 65.   If consumers are purchasing commodities in a free competitive market, the prices which they are offering for different commodities will measure the degree to which they desire to have more of each of the different commodities. The price of the output of factors of production in each occupation will therefore measure the extent to which consumers desire the output due to the employment of additional factors of production in each occupation, and since each factor of production will in competition be offered a wage equal to the price paid by consumers for the output of that factor in each occupation, the factors will automatically in perfectly competitive conditions be attracted to those industries in which the value to the consumers of the addition to the output due to their employment is greatest.

§ 66.   A perfectly competitive system will also lead to a situation in which it will be impossible to shift factors of production from one use to another so as to increase the output of one commodity without restricting the output of any other commodity, and in this sense will ensure that the physical output obtained from the employment of a given amount of factors of production is as large as possible. It may be that, by shifting some labour from the production of one commodity to the production of a second and at the same time shifting some capital in the opposite direction from the production of the second to the production of the first commodity, the output of one commodity could be increased without any diminution in the output of the other. This would be the case if the productivity of capital was higher in relation to the productivity of labour in the production of the first commodity than it was in the production of the second commodity; for the output of both commodities might be increased if capital shifted to those industries in which its relative productivity were higher and labour shifted to the industries in which its relative productivity were higher. But since in a perfectly competitive system the factors of production will be paid amounts which correspond to their productivity, there would be an automatic attraction for more capital to be employed in those industries in which its relative productivity were higher and for more labour to be employed where its relative productivity were higher; and in this way perfect competition would bring it about that the physical output of the community which can be obtained from the employment of a given amount of resources is as great as possible and in all industries the most productive proportions between the different factors of production would be achieved.

§ 67.   The foregoing analysis has attempted to demonstrate two real advantages which perfectly free competition would bring about. But in the actual world there is not in many industries perfectly free competition even when there is no state interference. It is just because there is not and cannot be such perfect competition that there are strong arguments for socialisation to eliminate the wastes of.competition and to provide a better service of consumers' needs. There are two main reasons why such perfect competition cannot be expected in the real world. (a) There are many industries in which the most efficient unit of production must be on a very large scale, so that for this reason the absence of government interference will not lead to a large number of competing producers, no one of which has power to control the price of the product in the market, but rather to a single or at the most to a few large producers, each one of which can appreciably raise the price offered for the commodity by restricting his supply. Such undertakings are exemplified by the railways or the generation of electric power; to build an efficient railway or electric generating station a very large investment of capital and so the sale of a large output is required to produce at a low cost. For this reason it is impossible that a large number of competing railways or electric stations should serve a district and that no one of them should have any power of controlling the price at which transport or electric current is sold. (b) Secondly in many industries, while there may be a large number of competing producers, each producer may be producing· a slightly different product or supplying a slightly different market. In this case again it will not be true, although there may be a very large number of producers, that no producer can appreciably affect the price offered for his product by producing more or less. For example, there may be a very large number of firms producing tinned fruit, but each may be producing a slightly different quality with a different name and brand, which attracts a different group of purchasers to each firm. Though there are a large number of them, each firm will know that to sell more it must reduce its price considerably to invade its competitors' markets; for since the articles are branded and slightly different, a single producer cannot attract consumers readily from his competitors by offering his product at a very slightly lower price.

§ 68.   It is also not true in the real world that individual producers cannot affect the price of the factors of production, e.g. the wage-rate or the price of raw materials, by hiring or buying more or less of them. If there is only one large employer of labour of a certain kind or in a certain district, this employer of labour may be able to force the wage-rate down by employing less labour and putting some men out of work and may be unwilling to employ more labour, although the price of the product of that labour is greater than the wage-rate he has to pay, because he may realise that if he employs more labour he will have to pay a higher wage-rate to all the labour which he is already employing. In conditions in which there is not perfect competition between producers in the markets in which they sell their products and in the markets in which they purchase or hire their factors of production, it will no longer be true that each factor of production will be paid an amount corresponding to the price of the extra product due to its employment. In order to make as large a profit as possible, producers will always hire more of any factor so long as the addition to their cost by so doing is less than the addition to their money receipts obtained by the sale of the extra product. But when a producer in order to sell more has to accept a lower price for his output he will no longer add to his receipts the price of that extra product, but only an amount equal to the price of the extra product minus the reduction in price on all the output which he is already selling, since such a reduction in price is necessary to sell the increased output. Nor will he add to his costs simply the wage of the extra labour employed, but an amount equal to the wage of the extra labour plus the additional wage which he has to pay to all the labour which he is already employing, since the increase in his demand for labour may oblige him to offer a higher wage-rate all round. In these circumstances then the reward paid to a factor may for these two reasons be less than the price which the consumer offers for the extra product of that factor.

§ 69.   In these circumstances then neither of the two fundamental advantages of perfect competition will necessarily be achieved. For if a perfectly competitive industry is compared with an imperfectly competitive industry, in the first labour will be employed up to the point at which the price of its extra product is no greater than the wage of labour, whereas in the imperfectly competitive industry labour will be employed only up to a point at which the price paid by consumers for the extra product of labour is considerably in excess of the wage of labour. And in these circumstances the community would clearly be better off if some of the factors of production were shifted from the perfectly competitive to the imperfectly competitive industry. Moreover, if we compare a perfectly competitive industry with one in which employers can employ more capital without very much affecting the price of capital goods or the rate of interest at which they can borrow but would have to offer a considerably higher wage-rate to employ more labour, it would in these circumstances be possible to increase the total physical output by shifting labour from the perfectly competitive to the second industry and capital from the second industry to the perfectly competitive industry. For in the first industry the productivities of capital and labour will be in proportion to the price of capital and labour, while in the second the productivity of labour will be higher in relation to the productivity of capital, simply because producers will be unwilling to use much labour with their capital in the second industry for fear that they will thereby have to pay a higher wage on all the labour which they are employing. So it will happen that by using more labour to capital in this second industry and less labour to capital in the first industry the physical output of both industries could be increased.

§ 70.   It is worth while pointing out some of the other ways in which these wastes of imperfect competition will show themselves. (a) If there were perfect competition in the markets for the product of any industry there would be no expenditure on wasteful competitive advertisement. For if producers could extend their markets by a very small reduction in price no one of them would waste money on trying to increase the demand for his product. A wheat farmer who does not think that he alone can affect the market price for wheat does not spend money on attracting demand from his competitors; it is the producer of a branded article selling in an imperfect market who undertakes such expenditure. (b) Perfect competition would also bring it about that the output of each firm was of the most efficient size. For if any producer by producing more could reduce his costs and yet would not himself affect the market price for the commodity by selling more, producers would extend their output so long as they were not producing on a sufficient scale to produce at a minimum cost; and thus competition would concentrate the output of any industry on just that number of firms which enabled each firm to be producing at the lowest possible costs. But where the market is imperfect and each firm realises that it would have to lower its selling price or spend more on advertisement in order to sell more, no firm may have an incentive to expand its output, although all firms are producing below capacity. (c) Similarly in perfect competition efficient firms with lower costs will tend to drive out inefficient firms with higher costs, since any firm which is producing at a cost below the market price will expand; and as all the efficient firms expand together the market price will be lowered and the inefficient will be driven out as they can no longer cover their costs. But if the efficient firms must lower their prices far below those of the inefficient firms or must spend a lot on advertisement to invade the markets of the inefficient, the output may not automatically be concentrated on the efficient firms, since they might lose more by the costs of invading the markets of the inefficient than they would gain by gaining those markets. (d) Similarly the specialisation of particular firms on lines of output in which they are most efficient would automatically be brought about in perfect competition where no one firm has any cost in selling its particular product, but will not necessarily automatically occur where there is not such a perfect market. (e) The elimination of wasteful transport costs would also be brought about automatically with perfect competition, since if one firm in the north is selling in the south and one in the south is selling in the north, each will gain by selling in the nearer market. But if the goods are branded and the firm in the north must considerably lower its price to the consumers in the north who are buying from the firm in the south, in order to attract them from that firm, the reduction in selling price may more than outweigh the cost of transport of the goods to the south to its previous market.

§ 71. The previous theoretical paragraphs provide most important principles both for the choice of industries which are to be socialised and also for the operation of socialised industries, in order to ensure that the needs of consumers shall be most efficiently satisfied by the resources at the disposal of the community. It is, as has been shown, in those industries in which there is least perfect competition that there is greatest need for state control of industry. If it could be provided that in every occupation each factor of production were offered a reward equal to the price offered by consumers for the extra product of that factor and the factors of production were moved to those industries in which the price offered for their services were greatest, the resources of the community would be most efficiently used. The government should therefore in its choice of industries to be socialised choose those industries in which there is the widest discrepancy between the price paid to factors of production and the price offered by consumers for the extra product of the factors. These conditions will be present, as has been shown, where there are technical reasons why the industry in question must be made up of a few large-scale producers (e.g. railways and electricity), or where there is a large expenditure on competitive advertisement, or where the absence of state intervention is not automatically leading to the concentration of output on the most efficient plants or the operation of plants at their capacity output or the diminution of wasteful cross-transport charges or the specialisation of firms on the line of product for which each is most suited. In order to achieve the most efficient utilisation of the community's resources these industries should be socialised in the order in which these wastes of competition are most evident, but there is no reason at all on these grounds to socialise industries in which competition is fairly complete and these phenomena do not appear to any large degree.

§ 72. It is now necessary to discuss the principles on which socialised industries should be planned and operated. It has been argued that the resources of the community will be most efficiently used in the service of consumers' needs, (a) if factors of production are moved from one industry to another or from one firm to another so long as the loss of output caused in the first industry is of less value to consumers than the gain in output in the second industry, and (b) if factors of production are used in such proportions with each other in the different industries and different firms that it would be impossible by using (e.g.) more capital to labour in one industry and more labour to capital in another to increase the output of one industry without decreasing the output of the other industry. Socialised and planned industry to be efficient must obviously conform to these two simple rules, but there are broadly speaking two possible methods of attempting to carry out these principles. It is possible to set up a general planning commission, which will allocate the factors of production to be used by the boards of management of different socialised industries, and which will attempt to solve the problem by posing to itself the questions: 'Can we by restricting this output and increasing that, i.e. by moving factors of production from this industry to that, cause consumers to be better off?' and 'Can we by shifting one factor in this direction and another factor in that direction cause this output to be increased without diminishing that output?' Alternatively the problem can be solved if the three following conditions are fulfilled: (a) if consumers are left free to compete in the expenditure of their incomes for different products and so to settle the prices at which different commodities will sell; (b) if the boards of management of each socialised concern determine the technical problems of each concern, i.e. how much more they could produce if they had a little more labour of a given grade or a little more machinery of a given type or a little more land of a given quality or a little more of a certain type of raw material, and always offer a price for each of these factors which is equal to the price which consumers will pay for the additional output of each factor; and (c) if the factors themselves are always allocated to those occupations in which the price so offered for them is highest. For the prices which consumers offer for goods will measure the extent to which they would desire a little more of each product and the factors will be used in those occupations in which the value of their products to the consumers are greatest.

§ 73. Now it is often considered that the choice between these two methods is unimportant and that direct control and planning is the more obvious and straightforward method. This view is however entirely false. There are very considerable advantages to be gained from the second method of retaining free consumers' prices and of instructing those in charge of each socialised concern to offer prices for the factors of production on the lines indicated above. In the first place the second method can be run side by side with unsocialised competitive industry to obtain the best results. For if certain fairly perfectly competitive occupations are left unsocialised, in these industries the factors will, as has been shown, automatically be offered rewards which correspond to the value of their product to the consumers. In these circumstances therefore there will be a most efficient use of the community's resources, if factors are allowed to go into unsocialised industry as opposed to socialised industry so long as the prices offered to those factors by unsocialised competitive industries is higher than the prices offered for their services by socialised industries on the lines indicated above; and *vice versa* factors should properly be drawn from unsocialised competitive industries to socialised industries if the prices offered by socialised industries determined on these principles are higher than those offered by unsocialised industries. But in the second place – and this is by far the most important consideration – the task of a general planning commission which was unaided by free consumers' prices and by the prices offered for factors of production by different concerns and fixed on the foregoing principles would be the reverse of straightforward and would indeed be incapable of solution. If there were only two factors of production and only two commodities which could be produced, the task of the planning commission might be relatively simple. They might reasonably hope by using their judgement or by enquiry of consumers' representatives to be able to determine whether, by shifting factors from producing A to producing B, the consumers would be better off by having so much more B and so much less A; and similarly they might reasonably hope by consulting the technicians in each industry to find out whether they could by shifting labour from A to B and machinery from B to A produce more A without producing less B. But the planning commission will in fact be dealing with thousands of different products and scores of different factors of production, i.e. labour of different grades, machinery of different types, raw materials of different types and land of different qualities and different situations. It would be an impossible problem to decide first of all whether it would be possible to produce 10% more A, 5% less B, 15% less C, 20% more D and 3% more E by a given re-allocation of resources, or alternatively 5% more A, 5% more B, 10% more C, 2% less D and 30% less E, and then to decide whether the consumers would be best off as they were, with the first re-arrangement, with the second re-arrangement or with any of the thousand and one other re-arrangements which would be possible. Further, no amount of consultations with engineers and technicians will enable them to make sure that it is not possible by shifting a little of this raw material from A to B, and little of this land from B to C, or little of this grade of labour from C to A and of this machinery from C to E, and a little of this raw material from D to E and some of this land from E to A to increase the output of A without changing the output of any other product. It is clearly an impossible task. But the use of free consumers' prices, the offer of prices to factors of production equal to the price paid by consumers for the extra product of that factor in each occupation and the allocation of factors of production to those occupations which offer this highest price for their services will in fact achieve the seemingly impossible result.

§ 74. The recommendations made above in §§ 52 and 53 that there should be a progressive movement towards free trade and that socialised industries should adopt a system of costing and sell abroad whenever at the current rate of exchange they could thereby obtain a price higher than their cost and and should buy raw materials from abroad whenever it was cheaper to do so are only an extension of the arguments of the previous paragraphs. Socialised industries should each work out the extra cost in payments to different factors of production which would be entailed by producing a little more output, and should produce that little more so long as the costs are below the price which they can receive for the sale of that output. It has been argued that the adoption of this principle will achieve the best distribution of the resources among different industries at home. Now it will pay the community to produce for export and to import goods in return so long as it could obtain more of the imported goods by so doing than it would obtain if some of the factors were shifted from the export industries to produce at home the imported commodities. But if the principles of costing and pricing of commodities suggested above and the principles of free export and import are adopted, the best allocation of resources will be obtained. For the factors of production will be paid sums equal to the price of the product due to the employment of these factors; and if their price is higher in export industries than in industries producing at home goods which might be imported, this must mean that the product of the factors in the export industries is at the ruling prices worth more imported goods than can be produced at home by these factors. In these circumstances therefore the community will be better off if the factors of production are moved from the industries producing for the home market, in which the rewards offered to the factors are lower, to the export industries, in which the rewards offered to the factors are higher. Conversely if the value of the product of factors of production is higher in industries producing goods at home which might be imported than it is in the industries producing export goods, this will mean – so long as there is a free import of goods – that at ruling prices the product of the factors in the export industries will not purchase so much of the imported goods as can be produced with those factors at home; and in this case it is proper that the factors should be shifted from the export industries, in which the price offered for their services is lower, to the industries producing for the home market, in which the rewards offered to factors of production are higher.

§ 75.   It must however be clearly recognised that, if the principles of pricing and costing outlined above are adopted, this may mean that a number of concerns do not sell at a price sufficient to cover their total costs. It has been proposed above that socialised concerns should sell their products at prices which are just equal to the cost of the additional amounts of the factors necessary to produce an extra unit of output. In the case of industries which necessitate a very large investment in fixed capital this price may well be below the average cost of producing the commodity. Thus in the case of the railways, in which there must in any case be a certain fixed equipment of embankments, tunnels, lines, stations, etc., the cost of the additional labour, capital, raw materials, etc. which is necessary to produce an extra amount of transport facilities may be very much less than the average cost of providing those facilities; for to cover the total costs the cost of the whole fixed equipment must be spread over the whole of the transport facilities undertaken, whereas the cost of providing an extra amount of transport facilities by means of making a fuller use of the existing equipment may be very small. But it has been argued above that the best results will only be obtained if those in charge of the industry charge prices which just correspond to the cost of the additional factors of production required to produce the last unit of output. If this principle is observed, these industries will not obtain from the sale of their products sufficient to pay all the factors the prices which are being charged for those factors of production.

§ 76.   This problem can easily be met as soon as a considerable amount of property has been socialised by the state. All the earnings on the capital employed by the socialised concern will be paid into the Revenue Account of the Budget as suggested in §39. But industries which cannot cover their total costs for the reasons indicated in the previous paragraph will pay into the Revenue Budget less than the current rate of interest on their capital equipment. Thus if the rate of interest is 5% every concern will be instructed to borrow more from the Capital Budget so long as the price which consumers will pay for the extra output due to the investment in more capital in the concern is sufficient to earn more than a 5% yield on that investment; but at the same time the concern in question may actually only be earning 3% on an average on its capital for the reasons stated in the previous paragraph. In this case the industry will borrow more so long as the price of the additional output is sufficient to earn the current rate of interest on that investment, but it will pay into the Revenue Budget only that amount of profit, rent, etc. which it is actually earning on the average on its capital. If it is actually not receiving enough from the sale of its product to cover the cost of its raw materials and labour, then this industry will have to be subsidised from the Revenue Budget to that extent, instead of paying some interest on profit into the Revenue Budget. But this is unlikely to happen except in rare cases in which there is a very large discrepancy between the cost of producing one more unit of output with a given equipment and the average cost of producing the whole output.

§ 77.   While this problem is not therefore difficult to solve when socialisation and social ownership of property is relatively far advanced, it may raise difficulties in a transitional period. For it has been suggested above in §39 that it is most necessary in the event of socialisation of any concern to give existing owners compensation which will make up fully for the income which they were deriving from the concerns before socialisation, in order not to create unemployment by diminishing the incentive to invest in new capital in unsocialised industries. But in the case of industries which for technical reasons of the kind under discussion must take the form of single large-scale concerns, in which the cost of adding a unit of output is considerably below the average cost of producing that output, private owners will be in a monopolistic position and will certainly be earning a rate on their capital which is as high as the existing rate of interest, whereas it will be the policy of the industry when socialised to sell the product at a much lower price, which is no higher than the cost of producing an additional unit of output. Thus to compensate the owners fully bonds paying 5% on the value of the concern's capital may be issued to the past owners, whereas it would be the policy of the socialised concern if it adopted the principles outlined above to lower the price to the cost of producing an extra unit of output and so to sell more and use more factors in the industry, so that the socialised industry might contribute to the state Budget an income only equal to 3% on the capital of the concern. If this policy were adopted at once many socialised concerns might contribute to the Revenue Budget considerably less than was being paid out of the Revenue Budget as interest on the compensation bonds.

§ 78. The best solution of this difficulty would seem to be not immediately to extend the employment of factors in these industries to the fullest extent justified by the principles discussed in this section. It has been suggested above in §41 that, after the state has cured unemployment and has obtained sufficient control over the community's capital development, heavy taxes may be imposed in order to buy out the owners of compensation bonds. As these bonds are bought up and the interest to be paid from the Revenue Budget is reduced, so gradually the principles of pricing and costing may be introduced into those industries in which the price charged would on these principles be considerably below the price previously charged.

Socialisation and Equality

§ 79. The last of the objects to be achieved by socialisation, which were noted in §61, was a more equal distribution of income. This problem has already been discussed at some length in §41. In order to gain control of the volume of capital development or in order to obtain control over industries in order to eliminate the wastes of competition, social ownership or control is necessary; and these objects are not hindered by paying full compensation to the owners. But in as far as the objects of socialisation are to achieve greater equality, this payment of compensation is a great hindrance. In order to achieve equality the compensation bonds must be bought up by the state out of the proceeds of taxation, so that the income earned from socialised industries may go to the state for distribution in a more equal manner without having to be used to meet the interest on compensation bonds. It is worth while noticing that the social control of industries to eliminate the wastes of competition and the social ownership of property in order to obtain the income from property for more equal distribution do not go together. Thus it is possible for the state to run the railways but to go on paying the previous owners interest equal to their previous income from the railways; on the other hand it is possible for the state to buy up agricultural land to obtain the rents from such land without farming the land through state bodies, but to continue to hire out the land to tenant farmers as private landlords did before. Thus the attainment of control of industry to eliminate the wastes of competition and the attainment of ownership of the income from property by buying up state debt or other forms of property out of the proceeds of taxation need not go together. In its final form a socialist state may well own more property than it itself manages through its own boards and servants or it may well manage more property through public boards than it owns unencumbered with compensation bonds. This simply depends upon the degree to which it finds it must go in the one direction to eliminate the wastes of competition and in the other direction to get the desired distribution of income.

§ 80.   In devising its policy to achieve greater equality the state should observe the principle that labour is paid in wages an amount no greater than the value of the additional product of labour in each occupation. It is quite possible to get a greater equality of income in socialised industry by paying much higher wage-rates and so having little over in profit to contribute to the Revenue Budget of the state. But in this case the wage-rate paid will no longer be equal to the value of the additional product of labour nor will the rate of interest to be earned on additional investment in machinery correspond to the value of the additional product due to that investment. In these circumstances the prices of factors of production and of the products themselves can no longer in any way be used to determine the most efficient use of the factors of production for the service of consumers' needs on the lines suggested above; for as has been seen it is only if the prices of the factors of production are made equal in every occupation to the price of the extra product due to the use of a little more of that factor and if the factors move into those occupations in which the price is highest that the community's resources will be most effectively used. It is proposed therefore that while socialised industries should be run on these lines, a greater equality of distribution should be obtained not by a simple raising of wages at the expense of profit in socialised industries but by the use of this profit, which will accrue to the state, for the payment of pensions, allowances or a national dividend out of the Revenue Budget on the lines suggested in §41.

Socialisation. Summary and Conclusions

§ 81.   It is perhaps worth while summarising the different conclusions which have been reached as to the principles upon which the government's socialisation policy should be based.

(a) The socialisation of industry will aid the state in planning through the National Development Board the amount of capital development to be undertaken. Every socialised industry should be required to plan its development ahead on the lines indicated in §12, i.e. with reference to different rates of interest and allowing the utmost margin for the concentration of capital expenditure over few or many years.

(b) Full compensation should be paid to all existing owners in order during the transitional period not to remove the incentive for private owners to undertake capital development of property which has not yet been socialised.

(c) In the choice of industries to be socialised those undertakings should be selected in which competition is least perfect. Imperfection of competition can be judged by the degree to which the uncontrolled competitive industry wastes money on competitive advertisement, fails to concentrate output on the most efficient firms, fails to concentrate output on a small enough number of firms to cause the plants to be operated at full capacity, fails to eliminate wasteful cross-transport charges or fails to cause particular plants to specialise on the line of produce for which they are most fitted, or finally by the degree to which for technical reasons the industry must be in the nature of a monopoly.

(d) The boards of management set up over any socialised concern should be instructed to sell the product freely in the market at prices which correspond to the cost of producing the last unit of output. These boards should further be instructed to work out the extent to which an additional amount of each factor would add to the product and should offer payments to the factors which are equal to the price at which these additional products can be sold.

(e) The boards of management should also be instructed to sell their products abroad whenever they could get a price higher than the cost worked out on these principles and to buy their raw materials from abroad whenever it was cheaper for them to do so.

(f) The profit, interest and rent from the socialised industry should be paid to the Revenue Budget of the state and the socialised industry should borrow for the capital development which it found profitable to undertake through the National Development Board from the Capital Budget of the state.

(g) The price at which the products of socialised industry are sold, being equated to the cost of adding the last unit of output to the total product, might not serve to cover the average cost of production of the output, if there is included in average cost the market rate of interest to be earned on the value of the socialised property. Nevertheless in principle the price charged should in these circumstances be lower than the average cost, which would simply mean that the contribution of the socialised industry to the Revenue Budget might be less than the market rate of interest on the value of the capital of the socialised concern. The full operation of this principle might however be postponed in the case of an industry in which the price charged on the above principles would be so low that the industry would fail to earn a very large part of the income which would have to be paid out of the Revenue Budget as interest on compensation bonds; but the full operation of this principle should not be postponed beyond the time necessary to redeem these bonds from the proceeds of taxation.

(h) Such principles of socialisation are aimed at making industry fully efficient; they will not achieve equality, since the income from socialised industry accruing to the state will be offset by interest to be paid on compensation bonds. In order to achieve equality, heavy taxation should be imposed as soon as the state has sufficient control over the volume of capital development, the banking system and the foreign exchanges to prevent the recrudescence of serious unemployment, and the proceeds of these taxes should be allocated to buying out the existing owners of national debt of all kinds. The saving of interest on the Revenue Budget so achieved can then be used partly to finance capital development out of the Capital Budget and partly as a method of extending the equality of incomes first by the development of social services and later by the distribution of a social dividend. This use of the funds is preferable to a simple rise in wage payments which will lead to a smaller contribution of profit from socialised industry to the Revenue Budget, since this latter method would spoil the use of wage-rates, interest rates and prices in general to indicate the best use of the community's resources.

§ 82.   In order to achieve the most efficient use of the community's resources it is not only necessary that each factor should be offered a payment equal to the value to the consumer of the extra product due to the use of that factor in each occupation, but it is also necessary that the factors should move into those occupations in which the reward offered is highest. In this connection the state has important functions to fulfil in regard to all the factors but especially in regard to labour. The state must provide that labour is able to move from less well paid to better paid occupations through a really efficient system of Labour Exchanges and though the provision of facilities for training men for new occupations and for movement of men from one district to another. The trade unions in any particular occupation should not restrict the entry of new labour into the better-paid occupations, although such a movement will lower the wage paid in the better-paid and raise that paid in the lower-paid occupations. There should however be no difficulty in this matter if the Labour Government is properly achieving greater equality between the classes by the means outlined above.

§ 83.   The acceptance of these principles does not remove the necessity for economic planning. It has already been pointed out that the state must arrange for the planned control of capital development, of banking policy, of exchange rates and of the volume of foreign lending. Further the management of each socialised undertaking must plan its capital development ahead and must determine how much to produce and how much of each factor must be employed. Insistence has however been laid on the fact that all economic planning should be undertaken on certain definite principles of pricing and costing in order to achieve the best results. However, in order that any concern should determine whether it is proper on these principles for it to produce more or to employ more of certain factors of production, the body in charge of that concern must decide what is going to happen in the future to the price of its product and to the price of the factors of production; unless this judgement is made it is impossible to decide whether (e.g.) investment in a certain machine will in fact earn 5% or only 2% when it is installed. One of the major tasks therefore of these bodies will be to make accurate and scientific forecasts of the future in order to be able to approximate more closely to reality in attempting to carry out the principles of pricing and costing outlined above. Besides the planning departments which will naturally be attached to each individual public board, a control commission should be set up, whose task it would be to foretell as accurately as possible the probable future changes in population, in supplies of different factors and different products and so the future movements of wage-rates, interest rates, exchange rates, and prices of important products. Such a commission would be of the utmost help in aiding the different executive bodies discussed above to carry out successfully the principles of economic policy stated above.

A Supreme Economic Authority

§ 84. It must already be evident that some central body will be necessary with the ultimate power of deciding upon the policy to be pursued by the different bodies suggested in the previous sections. The National Development Board, the Minister in charge of the Budget, the Bank of England, the Controller of the Exchange Equalisation Account and the different boards of management of socialised industries will all be undertaking executive decisions in the economic sphere. But these decisions must affect each other very closely. Thus the decision how much shall be lent abroad, the decision what rate of exchange shall be fixed, the decision how much the rate of interest shall be lowered, the decision how much to speed up expenditure on capital development, the decision how much of any surplus in the Revenue Budget should be allocated to the Capital Budget, – all these and many other important decisions are intimately connected with one another, as the argument of the previous pages has attempted to show. A correlated and harmonious economic policy can be divided to suit changing conditions on the lines suggested in this memorandum, but that this may be so some single authority is required with the ultimate power of deciding what are the broad lines of policy can be devised to suit changing conditions on the lines suggested in suggested that a Supreme Economic Authority be set up, taking the form perhaps of a committee of four or five cabinet ministers with the aid of experts in every field, to make these ultimate decisions and that all the economic bodies in social control such as the National Development Board, the Bank of England, the Exchange Equalisation Account, the Treasury, the boards of management of socialised industries be responsible to this Supreme Economic Authority. This Authority would not interfere in detail with the policy of these other bodies, nor would it prevent them from working for themselves on the principles outlined above; but it would be the task of such an authority to see that the main policies of each particular body fitted harmoniously into the general economic policy suitable at each particular time.

5

A Simplified Model of
Mr Keynes' System

From The Review of Economic Studies, *vol. 4 (1937), pp. 98–107. An earlier version of this paper was presented to the Sixth European Conference of the Econometric Society in Oxford on 26 September 1936.*

The object of this article is to construct a simple model of the economic system discussed in Mr Keynes' *The General Theory of Employment, Interest and Money*, in order to illustrate:

- (i)   the conditions necessary for equilibrium;
- (ii) the conditions necessary for stability of equilibrium; and
- (iii) the effect on employment of changes in certain variables.

To simplify the exposition the following assumptions are made:

- (1)   There is a closed economy.
- (2)   There is perfect competition, so that every price is equal to the marginal cost of production.
- (3)   Two industries are examined – one producing goods for consumption and the other producing durable capital goods.
- (4)   The short-period elasticity of supply of capital goods is the same as that of consumption goods.
- (5)   In each of these industries the wage of labour is the only prime cost.
- (6)   Fixed capital equipment, which is assumed to last for ever, is the only other factor of production. In consequence, the total expenditure of money on consumption goods *plus* total expenditure on newly constructed capital goods is equal to the national income, which is distributed between wage-earners and the owners of fixed capital equipment.
- (7)   We shall deal only with short-period equilibrium. The short period is defined as the period of time in which the ratio between the output of new capital goods and the existing stock of capital goods is small, so that we can neglect changes in the stock of capital goods. It is, however, assumed that, within this short period, (a) producers have time to adjust their output until the marginal prime cost is equal to the price of the product, and to

adjust the rate at which they expand their capital equipment until the rate of interest is equal to the marginal efficiency of capital, and (b) all individuals have time to adjust appropriately their expenditure and their savings in consequence of any change in their incomes.[1]

I   The Conditions for Equilibrium

Our first task is to examine the conditions in which the system will be in equilibrium. The following eight conditions determine the position of short-period equilibrium:

(1) The price of a unit of capital goods equals its marginal prime cost.

(2) Similarly, the price of a unit of consumption goods equals its marginal prime cost.

(3) Total income equals the amount received for the sale of newly produced capital goods *plus* the amount received for the sale of consumption goods.

(4) Total income equals total profits *plus* the amount paid out in wages.

(5) The total volume of employment equals employment in producing capital goods *plus* employment in producing consumption goods.

(6) The amount spent on consumption goods is determined by the size of the national income. We shall suppose that, with a given propensity to consume, people always spend a constant proportion of their income on consumption. This satisfies Mr Keynes' psychological law that out of an increase in real income people spend part on consumption and save part, although it is a simple and special case of that law.

(7) The rate of interest equals the marginal efficiency of capital. We shall suppose that the same yield is expected in each future year on a unit of capital installed now and that this expected yield depends solely upon the profits being made at present in industry – a rise in present profits causing some rise in the yield expected in future years. The expected annual yield divided by the current cost price of a unit of capital goods is the rate at which we must discount the future annual yields to make the present value of a unit of capital equal to its present supply price; and in equilibrium this must equal the current rate of interest.

(8) The supply of money equals the demand for money, which is determined (a) by the volume of monetary transactions to be financed,

---

[1] Without any fundamental change in the method of analysis we could make allowances for foreign trade, imperfect competition, raw material and depreciation costs, etc. But to modify assumption (7) might involve far-reaching changes in method. If, for example, the time-lag between a change in income and the consequent change in demand for consumption goods were longer than the period in which changes in the size of the capital stock are negligible, we should be obliged to relate expenditure in any one short period to conditions existing in a previous short period. We should be obliged to relate certain terms by means of time-lags to other terms at an earlier time, and to write the stock of capital at any one point of time as the sum of outputs of capital goods over previous periods of time. But if we assume that these time-lags are short, we can postulate a given stock of capital, and suppose that the system finds an equilibrium before this stock can alter significantly.

and (b) by the rate of interest ruling in the market. We suppose that the total amount of money can be divided into two parts: (a) the amount of money held to finance business transactions, which bears a constant ratio to the money income of the community, and (b) an amount of 'idle' money held to satisfy the precautionary and speculative motives for liquidity. A rise in the rate of interest causes people to shift from 'idle' money to non-liquid assets; and to simplify our model we shall suppose that the ratio between the value of non-liquid assets held and the amount of 'idle' money held is a function of the rate of interest.

By means of these eight relationships we can show[2] that the volume of employment is determined for every given supply of money, for every given money wage-rate, and for every given proportion of income saved.[3]

II The Conditions for Stability of Equilibrium

The system is in short-period equilibrium when these eight relationships are satisfied. But is this equilibrium stable? Suppose that the money wage-rate and the proportion of income saved remain constant, but that there is an accidental increase in total expenditure on commodities, accompanied by the appropriate increases in output of capital and consumption goods. This will have two effects: (a) It will increase incomes and so the amount which people desire to save. (b) It will also cause profits to rise and thus cause the expectation of profit to increase, and this will increase the incentive to borrow money for investment. If a chance rise in incomes increases the incentive to save more than the incentive to invest, then the system is in stable equilibrium; for, if incomes rose, people would wish to save a larger increment of income than they wished to invest, so that incomes would fall again to their previous equilibrium level. If a chance rise in incomes increased the incentive to invest more than the incentive to save, incomes would continue to grow, until some entirely new position of short-period equilibrium were reached. In this case equilibrium is unstable.

In order to test the conditions in which equilibrium is stable, we must distinguish between two possible banking policies. The banks may (i) keep the rate of interest constant, or (ii) keep the amount of money constant.

(i) If the former policy is adopted the amount of money must be increased as the volume of business activity increases, so as to maintain a constant ratio between the value of non-liquid assets and the amount of 'idle money', so that with a given liquidity preference function the rate of interest will be unchanged. Equilibrium will be stable on this assumption

---

[2] See Appendix, §§ 1 and 2.
[3] If we suppose that the money wage-rate would fall so long as any labour were unemployed, the system cannot be in equilibrium without full employment. In this case the money wage-rate is no longer given, but the equilibrium volume of employment is now a given quantity – namely, the given volume of labour seeking employment. In this case the eight relationships would determine the money wage-rate in terms of the supply of money, the volume of labour to be employed and the proportion of income saved.

if the eight relationships show that with a constant money wage-rate and a constant proportion of income saved a fall in the rate of interest is necessary to preserve equilibrium when employment increases. For this means that unless the rate of interest falls any chance increase in incomes, profits, and employment would stimulate investment less than savings, so that any such expansion is impossible to maintain. But if the eight relationships show that a rise in the rate of interest is necessary to preserve equilibrium as employment increases, this means that a chance increase in incomes, profits, and employment would stimulate investment more than savings, so that some discouragement of investment by a rise in the rate of interest would be necessary to preserve equilibrium. Or, in other words, with a constant rate of interest equilibrium would be unstable.

It will be shown[4] that, on the assumption that the banks keep the rate of interest constant, equilibrium is stable or unstable according as $\pi \lessgtr 1 - l$, when $(1-l)$ measures the proportion of the national income which goes to profits and π measures the elasticity of expected future yields to changes in the present profitability of industry.[5] Since less than the whole national income must go to profits, we can conclude that equilibrium cannot be stable if a 1 per cent rise in present profits causes a 1 per cent or greater rise in the expectation of profits; and we may add that equilibrium is the more likely to be stable (a) the less sensitive are expected profits to changes in present profits, and (b) the larger the proportion of the national income which goes to profits.

(ii) If the banks keep the amount of money constant, the condition for stability of equilibrium is less severe. As before, any chance increase in incomes and expenditure, in addition to causing an increase in savings, will also stimulate investment by raising the present profitability of industry and so the yields expected in the future. But in this case the increased volume of business activity will leave less of the given stock of money to be held in excess of the requirements to finance current transactions. The ratio between the value of non-liquid property and the amount of 'idle money' will increase, which will cause the rate of interest to rise. This in itself will diminish the incentive to invest, so that there is less probability that the incentive to invest will increase more than the incentive to save in consequence of any chance increase in total incomes.

When the banks keep the amount of money constant, equilibrium is stable, if the eight equilibrium relationships discussed above show that, with a constant money wage-rate and a constant proportion of income saved, the supply of money must increase in order to preserve equilibrium as employment increases. This means that conditions are such that, unless the rate of interest is kept down by an increased supply of money, the incentive to save would grow more rapidly than the incentive to invest, so that an expansion would be impossible. If, however, the eight equilibrium relationships show that the supply of money must be

---

[4] See Appendix, § 4.
[5] If, for example, a 1 per cent rise in present profits causes a 2 per cent rise in expected profits, then $\pi = 2$.

diminished in order to preserve equilibrium as employment rises, then equilibrium is unstable with a constant supply of money. For in this case a chance expansion of employment and incomes would increase the incentive to invest so much more than the incentive to save, that an actual diminution in the supply of money would be required to raise interest rates sufficiently to maintain equilibrium.

It will be shown[6] that equilibrium in this case is stable or unstable according as

$$\pi \lessgtr (1-l) \left(1 + \frac{1 + \eta[1-m]}{m\lambda} \right)$$

where η is the short-period elasticity of supply of goods in general, m is the proportion of the total stock of money which is held idle to satisfy the speculative motives for liquidity and λ is the elasticity of the liquidity preference schedule, i.e. the percentage increase in the ratio between the value of non-liquid assets and the value of 'idle' money divided by the percentage rise in the rate of interest necessary to cause this shift to non-liquid assets. With the assumption that the banks kept the rate of interest constant, we found that equilibrium would be stable if $\pi < 1 - l$. It follows that if equilibrium would be stable with a constant rate of interest, it will certainly be stable with a constant supply of money; whereas equilibrium may be stable with a constant supply of money in conditions in which it would not be stable with a constant rate of interest. We conclude that equilibrium is the more likely to be stable (i) the smaller are π, l, m, and λ, and (ii) the greater is η.

It is of course possible that in the real world the system is unstable. But in what follows we shall assume that equilibrium is stable, since it is not possible to discuss the effect of given changes on the volume of employment if any small jerk to the system may start it off in one direction or the other in search of a completely new equilibrium.

III The Effect of Changes in Certain Variables on the Short-Period Demand for Labour

We can now examine the effect on employment of (1) a reduction in interest rates, (2) an increase in the total supply of money, (3) a reduction in money wage-rates, and (4) a reduction in the proportion of income saved.

(1) We suppose that the money wage-rate and the proportion of income saved are constant, and that the banks reduce the rate of interest by a certain proportion and then keep it constant at this new level. We wish to evaluate ε_i, the elasticity of demand for labour in terms of the rate of interest. It can be shown[7] that

$$\varepsilon_i = -\eta . \frac{1-l}{l} . \frac{1}{1-l-\pi} .$$

[6] See Appendix, §5.
[7] See Appendix, § 4.

If equilibrium is to be stable when the banks first lower and then stabilise the rate of interest, ε_i must be <0; for we have already argued that for equilibrium to be stable with a constant rate of interest conditions must be such that an increase in employment cannot take place without a fall in the rate of interest. If equilibrium is stable, a reduction in interest rates will therefore increase employment, and will be more effective in doing so (i) the greater is η, and (ii) the greater is π. If the short-period elasticity of supply of goods is large, a given rise in expenditure will cause a large increase in output and employment. If the sensitiveness of expected profits to changes in present profits is large, a given rise in profits will cause a large rise in expected yields, which will help to stimulate investment and so expenditure still further.

(2) We now suppose that the money wage-rate and the proportion of income saved are constant, but that the banks increase the total supply of money by a certain proportion and then keep it constant at this new figure. We wish to evaluate ε_M, the elasticity of demand for labour in terms of the supply of money. It can be shown that[8]

$$\varepsilon_M = \eta \ \frac{1-l}{l} \cdot \frac{1}{(1-l)\,(1+\eta[1-m]+m\lambda)-m\lambda\pi}.$$

For equilibrium to be stable when the banks first increase and then stabilise the supply of money, ε_M must be <0; for we have already argued that for equilibrium to be stable with a constant supply of money, conditions must be such that an increase in employment must be accompanied by an increase in the supply of money. We conclude, therefore, that, if equilibrium is stable, an increase in the supply of money will increase employment, and that it will be more effective in doing so (i) the greater is η, (ii) the greater is π, (iii) the smaller is λ, and (iv) the smaller is m. If the short-period elasticity of supply of goods is large, a given increase in expenditure will cause a large increase in employment; if the sensitiveness of expected profits to changes in present profits is large, a given increase in present profits will cause a large increase in investment expenditure; if people's willingness to shift from non-liquid assets to 'idle' money is only slightly increased by a fall in the rate of interest, a given proportionate increase in the supply of 'idle' money must be accompanied by a large fall in interest rates, and will therefore greatly stimulate investment; if the amount of money held 'idle' is a small proportion of the total holding of money, a given increase in the total supply of money will represent a large proportionate increase in the supply of 'idle' money, and so, with a given liquidity preference elasticity, will cause a large fall in interest rates.

(3) Our next object is to examine the effect on employment of a given reduction in money wage-rates, on the assumption that the proportion of income saved and the total supply of money are constant. For this purpose we wish to evaluate ε_w, the elasticity of demand for labour in

---

[8] See Appendix, §5.

terms of the money wage-rate. It will be shown[9] that $\varepsilon_w = -\varepsilon_M$ $(1-m\lambda[\pi-1])$ where ε_M has the value given above.

It is to be observed that if $\pi = 1$, $\varepsilon_w = -\varepsilon_M$. This is what we should expect. Suppose that there were a 10 per cent reduction in all money wage-rates combined with a 10 per cent reduction in the supply of money. Then *if* output and employment remained unchanged, the marginal prime cost and so the price of all commodities would fall by 10 per cent in view of the 10 per cent fall in the money wage-rate; and in consequence all money incomes would fall by 10 per cent. Ten per cent less money would be required to finance current transactions, and, as the total supply of money is also reduced by 10 per cent, the supply of 'idle' money would also have fallen by 10 per cent. But since the price of capital goods would have fallen by 10 per cent, the ratio between the value of non-liquid assets and the amount of 'idle' money would be unchanged, so that with a given liquidity preference schedule the rate of interest would be unchanged. Money savings would have fallen by 10 per cent because of the 10 per cent fall in money incomes. Money investment would also have fallen by 10 per cent if expected profits had fallen by 10 per cent; for the rate of interest being unchanged, and the supply price of capital goods and the expected money yield on them having fallen by 10 per cent, there would be no incentive to change the value of *real* investment, so that the money value of investment would have fallen in the same ratio as the price of capital goods. If $\pi = 1$, expected profits would in fact have fallen by 10 per cent; for the output of goods being constant and the price of goods and of the factor labour having fallen by 10 per cent, present money profits would have fallen by 10 per cent; and, if $\pi = 1$, this would have caused expected yields to be 10 per cent lower. In other words, the system would be in equilibrium with the same volume of output and employment, if $\pi = 1$ and there were a 10 per cent reduction in both the money wage-rate and the total supply of money. A 10 per cent reduction in the money wage-rate without any reduction in the supply of money may therefore be expected to have the same effect as a 10 per cent increase in the supply of money without any change in the money wage-rate. We should therefore expect that, if $\pi = 1$, a given reduction in money wage-rates will have the same effect in increasing employment as an equal proportionate increase in the supply of money.

If, however, π is < 1, a 10 per cent fall in the present profitability of industry causes expected future yields to fall by less than 10 per cent. In this case a 10 per cent reduction in money wage-rates, as it tends to reduce both the present money supply price of capital goods and the present money yields on capital, tends to increase the ratio between expected profits and the supply price of capital goods, and so to encourage real investment. In this case, therefore, a given reduction in money wage-rates is more effective in increasing employment than an equal proportionate increase in the supply of money. Conversely, if π is > 1, the fall in expected money yields is more than in proportion to the present fall in

[9] See Appendix, §6.

money profits and money costs; and a reduction in the money wage-rate tends, therefore, to lower the marginal efficiency of capital.

(4) Finally we can examine the effect on employment of a change in the proportion of income saved, on the assumption that the money wage-rate and the supply of money are constant. We wish to evaluate ε_s, the elasticity of demand for labour in terms of the proportion of income saved. It can be shown[10] that

$$\varepsilon_s = - \frac{(1+\lambda)m}{1+\eta} \cdot \varepsilon_M$$

where ε_M has the value given above (p. 84). As we have already argued, if equilibrium is to be stable in this case in which the supply of money is constant, ε_M must be >0; ε_s is therefore <0, so that a decrease in the proportion of income saved will cause an increase in employment.

This is what we should expect. A fall in the proportion of income saved will increase expenditure on consumption; and there will therefore be an increase in total expenditure and in employment, unless investment falls by as much as consumption increases. But investment will fall only if there is a rise in the rate of interest, and the rate of interest will rise only if there is a decrease in the supply of 'idle' money. But, with a given total supply of money, the supply of 'idle' money will decrease only if there is an increase in total expenditure, causing an increased demand for money to finance current transactions. The rate of interest cannot, therefore, rise sufficiently to diminish investment by as much as expenditure on consumption has increased.

Mathematical Appendix

§ 1. On the seven assumptions stated on p. 79 we can construct eight equations corresponding to the eight relationships discussed on pp. 80–1.

The price of a unit of capital goods equals its marginal prime cost, or

$$p_x = w \frac{dN_x}{dx}, \tag{1}$$

where p_x equals the price of a unit of capital goods, w equals the money wage-rate and N_x equals the volume of employment in capital goods industries. Since labour is the only prime factor of production, $\frac{dN_x}{dx}$ equals the marginal labour cost and $w\frac{dN_x}{dx}$ equals the marginal prime cost.

Similarly, for consumption goods

$$p_y = w \frac{dN_y}{dy}, \tag{2}$$

[10] See Appendix, § 7.

where p_y equals the price of a unit of consumption goods and N_y equals the volume of employment in consumption goods industries.

Total income equals the amount spent on newly produced capital goods plus the amount spent on consumption goods, or

$$I = xp_x + yp_y, \tag{3}$$

where I equals income, x equals output of capital goods, and y equals output of consumption goods.

Total income equals profits plus wages, or

$$I = P + wN, \tag{4}$$

where P equals profits received and N equals total employment.

Total employment equals employment in capital goods plus employment in consumption goods industries, or

$$N = N_x + N_y. \tag{5}$$

Amount spent on consumption equals a constant proportion of income, or $yp_y = (1-s)I$, where s is the proportion of income saved. From (3) it follows that

$$xp_x = sI. \tag{6}$$

The rate of interest equals the marginal efficiency of capital, or

$$i = \frac{E(P)}{p_x}, \tag{7}$$

where i equals the rate of interest and $E(P)$ equals the yield in each future year on a unit of capital goods installed now at a price p_x.

The ratio between the value of non-liquid assets and the amount of 'idle' money is a function of the rate of interest, or

$$\frac{p_x K}{M - kI} = L(i) \tag{8}$$

where K equals the constant stock of capital goods in existence, so that $p_x K$ equals the value of existing non-liquid assets. If M equals the total supply of money and k equals the proportion of income which people wish to hold in money at any moment of time to finance current transactions, kI equals the amount of money held for business purposes and $M-kI$ equals the amount of 'idle' money available to satisfy the speculative and precautionary motives for liquidity.

§ 2.   In these eight equations we have eight unknowns:[11]

$$x, y, p_x, p_y, I, P, i, \text{ and } N,$$

two constants

$$k \text{ and } K,$$

and three independent variables:

$$M, w, \text{ and } s,$$

so that the volume of employment, N, is determined in terms of the supply of money, the money wage-rate and the proportion of income saved.

§ 3.   If we differentiate each of the equations (1) to (8), allowing the eight unknowns and the three independent variables to vary, we obtain the following equations:

From (1) $\dfrac{dp_x}{p_x} = \dfrac{dw}{w} + \dfrac{d_x}{x} \cdot \dfrac{1}{\eta},$ (1a)

where η = the short-period elasticity of supply of capital goods = the proportionate increase in output divided by the proportionate rise in marginal labour cost

$$= \frac{dx}{x} \div \frac{d\left(\dfrac{dN_x}{dx}\right)}{\dfrac{dN_x}{dx}}.$$

From (2) $\dfrac{dp_y}{p_y} = \dfrac{dw}{w} + \dfrac{dy}{y} \cdot \dfrac{1}{\eta},$ (2a)

where η = the short-period elasticity of supply of consumption goods, which we assume (*vide* assumption 4) to be the same as the short-period elasticity of supply of capital goods.

From (3) $\dfrac{dI}{I} = s\left(\dfrac{dp_x}{p_x} + \dfrac{dx}{x}\right) + (1-s)\left(\dfrac{dp_y}{p_y} + \dfrac{dy}{y}\right),$ (3a)

where s = the proportion of income saved = $\dfrac{xp_x}{I}$.

---

[11] If we count N_x and N_y as well as x and y among the unknowns, we have two additional equations, $N_x = \varphi(x)$ and $N_y = \psi(y)$, since N_x depends solely on x and N_y solely on y.

From (4) $\quad \dfrac{dI}{I} = (1-l)\dfrac{dP}{P} + l\left(\dfrac{dw}{w} + \dfrac{dN}{N}\right),$ (4a)

where l = the proportion of total income which goes to wages $= \dfrac{wN}{I}$.

From (5) $\quad \dfrac{dN}{N} = \dfrac{s}{l}\cdot\dfrac{dx}{x} + \dfrac{l-s}{l}\cdot\dfrac{dy}{y}$ (5a)

for $\quad \dfrac{s}{l}\cdot\dfrac{dx}{x} = \dfrac{xp_x}{wN}\cdot\dfrac{dx}{x} = \dfrac{xw\dfrac{dN_x}{dx}}{wN}\cdot\dfrac{dx}{x} = \dfrac{dN_x}{N}, \text{ and similarly} \dfrac{l-s}{l}\cdot\dfrac{dy}{y} = \dfrac{dN_y}{N}.$

From (6) $\quad \dfrac{ds}{s} + \dfrac{dI}{I} = \dfrac{dp_x}{p_x} + \dfrac{dx}{x}.$ (6a)

From (7) $\quad \dfrac{di}{i} + \dfrac{dp_x}{p_x} = \pi\dfrac{dP}{P},$ (7a)

where $\pi = \dfrac{P}{E(P)}\cdot\dfrac{dE(P)}{dP}$ = the percentage rise in expected profits divided by the percentage rise in present profits which causes the rise in expected profits.

From (8) $\quad m\lambda\dfrac{di}{i} = m\dfrac{dp_x}{p_x} - \dfrac{dM}{M} + (1-m)\dfrac{dI}{I},$ (8a)

where $m = \dfrac{M-kI}{M}$ = the ratio of 'idle' money to the total supply of money

and $\lambda = \dfrac{i}{L(i)}\cdot\dfrac{dL(i)}{di}$ = the percentage rise in the ratio between the value of non-liquid assets and the amount of 'idle' money divided by the percentage rise in the rate of interest which causes this shift from 'idle' money to non-liquid assets.

§ 4.   If w and s are constant, we can eliminate $\dfrac{dx}{x}, \dfrac{dy}{y}, \dfrac{dp_x}{p_x}, \dfrac{dp_y}{p_y}, \dfrac{dI}{I}$ and $\dfrac{dP}{P}$ from equations (1a) to (7a), and we obtain

$$\varepsilon_i = -\eta\cdot\dfrac{1-l}{l}\cdot\dfrac{1}{1-l-\pi},$$ (9)

where $\varepsilon_i = \dfrac{i}{N}\cdot\dfrac{dN}{di}$. This expresses the elasticity of demand for labour in terms of the rate of interest. We have argued in the text (p. 82) that equilibrium will be stable or unstable when the banks stabilise the rate of interest, according as $\dfrac{di}{dN} \lessgtr 0$. It follows from (9) that equilibrium will be stable or unstable in these conditions according as $\pi \lessgtr 1-l$.

§ 5. Assuming again that w and s are constant, we can eliminate $\dfrac{dx}{x}, \dfrac{dy}{y}, \dfrac{dp_x}{p_x}, \dfrac{dp_y}{p_y}, \dfrac{dI}{I}, \dfrac{dP}{P}$ and $\dfrac{di}{i}$ from equations (1a) to (8a) and we obtain

$$\varepsilon_M = \eta. \ \frac{1-l}{l} \cdot \frac{1}{(1-l)\,(1+\eta[1-m]+m\lambda)-m\lambda\pi} , \tag{10}$$

where $\varepsilon_M = \dfrac{M}{N} \cdot \dfrac{dN}{dM}$, which expresses the elasticity of demand for labour in terms of the supply of money. We have argued in the text (p. 82) that, when with a constant wage-rate and a constant proportion of income saved the banks stabilise the supply of money, equilibrium will be stable or unstable according as $\dfrac{dM}{dN} \lessgtr 0$, i.e. from (10) according as

$$\pi \lessgtr (1-l) \ \left(1 + \frac{1+\eta[1-m]}{m\lambda}\right).$$

§ 6. Assuming next that s and M are constant, we can eliminate $\dfrac{dx}{x}, \dfrac{dy}{y}, \dfrac{dp_x}{p_x}, \dfrac{dp_y}{p_y}, \dfrac{dI}{I}, \dfrac{dP}{P}$ and $\dfrac{di}{i}$ from equations (1a) to (8a) and we obtain

$$\varepsilon_w = -\varepsilon_M \,(1-m\lambda[\pi-1]) , \tag{11}$$

where ε_M has the value given in (10), and $\varepsilon_w = \dfrac{w}{N} \cdot \dfrac{dN}{dw} =$ the elasticity of demand for labour in terms of the money wage-rate.

§ 7. Assuming now that w and M are constant, but that there is some change in the proportion of income which people decide to save, we can eliminate $\dfrac{dx}{x}, \dfrac{dy}{y}, \dfrac{dp_x}{p_x}, \dfrac{dp_y}{p_y}, \dfrac{dI}{I}, \dfrac{dP}{P}$ and $\dfrac{di}{i}$ from equations (1a) to (8a) and we obtain

$$\varepsilon_s = - \ \frac{(1+\lambda)m}{1+\eta} \cdot \varepsilon_M , \tag{12}$$

where ε_M has the value given in (10), and $\varepsilon_s = \dfrac{s}{N} \cdot \dfrac{dN}{ds} =$ the elasticity of demand for labour in terms of the proportion of income saved.

6

Summary of Replies to Questions on Effects of Interest Rates

This famous paper, prepared by James Meade and P. W. S. Andrews, is better known in the abbreviated form in which it was reprinted in T. Wilson and P. W. S. Andrews (eds), Oxford Studies in the Price Mechanism *(Oxford: Clarendon Press, 1951), pp. 27–31. The original version, which appeared in* Oxford Economic Papers, *vol. 1 (1938), pp. 14–31, is reproduced here.*

The following paper summarises the answers given by business men to the Oxford Economists' Research Group regarding the influence of the rate of interest. The business men consulted numbered 37, and included manufacturers in a wide range of industries (covering both capital and consumers' goods), merchants, and financial institutions. We have also had the benefit of the advice of an accountant and of two American Professors, one of Business Administration and the other of Accounting.

Before each meeting a questionnaire was sent out to give a general idea of the questions to be asked. The questions dealing with the effects of the rate of interest and with related matters were as follows:

1. Is the rate at which you can borrow from the bank an important consideration to you? Has an alteration in the bank rate ever had a material direct influence in inducing you to expand or to contract your activities?

2. Have you ever increased your stocks of raw materials on account of a fall in the bank rate?

3. Is the long-term rate of interest an important factor in regard to policies of capital extension?

4. Do you ever postpone, or speed up, extensions or renewals of plant because you expect the costs of building or the price of machinery to rise or fall?

5. Does it ever happen that the existence of large undistributed profits induces businesses to embark on capital extensions which they would not have undertaken otherwise?

   Conversely, does the desire to maintain dividends out of reserve during a depression, or to maintain a liquid position, sometimes act as an influence leading to the postponement of plant renewals or desirable capital extensions?

These questions were supplemented in discussion by many others, and the following matters were thus considered:

1. The effect of short-term interest rates and of the banks' lending policy on investment in fixed plant or in stocks.
2. The effect of long-term interest rates on investment in fixed plant.
3. The effect of expected price changes on investment in stocks.
4. The effect of expected changes in constructional costs on investment in fixed plant.
5. The effect of the state of demand for the product on investment in fixed plant.
6. The effect of abundance or scarcity of liquid resources on investment in fixed plant.

The following section gives the information extracted from each business man under each of the six heads. To avoid disclosing identities, those who gave us information are classified in the following groups and referred to by numbers within the groups.

      I.   Consumption goods industries.
     II.   Textiles.
    III.   Capital goods industries.
     IV.   Transport.
      V.   Retail trade.
     VI.   Finance.
    VII.   Building.
   VIII.   Merchants.
     IX.   Accountants
      X.   American Professors.

1 The effect of short-term interest rates and of the banks' lending policy on investment in fixed plant or in stocks

I.1.   Changes in the bank rate may affect fortunes but never policy.

I.2.   Short-term rates of interest important to business but doubtful if they really affect policy.

I.3.   Bank rate not decisive and probably not important. No material effect save upon carrying of raw materials; but in this respect it did affect actual policy. Would not increase their stocks of raw material just because of a fall in bank rate. Changes in interest rate *might* affect middlemen much more in his line of business, but he did not know. Would take into account the psychological effect of a substantial rise in bank rate. Psychological effect was a fact even if it had no economic justification. House building, electrification schemes, and speculations on the Stock Exchange quickly affected by bank rate, not the working manufacturer.

I.4.   Bank rate not a consideration, but the willingness of banks to lend may be. Willingness of banks to lend on a given security has varied much. Never increase stocks because of a fall in bank rate.

I.5.   Bank rate would not affect them.

I.6.   A change in bank rate might affect their decision to purchase machines. They buy stocks as they need them and have no spare money with which to speculate.

I.7.   Rate of interest of no importance in buying for stock.

I.9.   Bank rate has no effect on investment.

I.10.   Changes in rate of interest would have no effect.

I.11.   Do not borrow from the bank so that bank rate does not affect their stocks. Low bank rate certainly good for trade as it is a sign of confidence.

I.12.   The bank rate is completely unimportant. Thought that importance of banks as suppliers of working capital to business had been greatly overestimated. Has never increased stocks on account of a fall in the bank rate.

II.1.   Not influenced by interest rates in purchasing speculative stocks. Imagines that short-term rates would only influence business dealing in raw materials in which there is a very narrow margin.

II.2.   Stocks not increased on account of fall in bank rate.

II.3.   Does not borrow from banks. Always hedges purchases of raw materials and rate of interest would not affect them.

II.4.   His firm has always had all the money it needed and the rate at which it could borrow never influenced decisions. Business men do not consider bank rate.

II.7.   Bank rate of no importance.

III.1.   Bank rate would not affect stocks. Do not borrow from banks.

III.2.   Bank rate not very important, as the effect of changes is small in comparison with the profit margin. Bank rate would not affect stocks.

III.4.   Bank rate does not affect their policy and affects stocks very little.

III.5.   Bank rate has practically no effect. Have not increased stocks on account of fall in bank rate.

III.6.   Bank charges are too small a factor in comparison with other costs to be themselves decisive in any case. Never buy raw materials because of changes in bank rate.

III.7.   Bank rate of no importance, does not affect stocks.

III.8.   Bank rate has no effect.

IV.1.   Would never increase stocks because of a fall in interest rates.

V.1.   Normal changes in the bank rate would not affect size of overdraft or policy in matters of expansion.

V.2.   Have not increased stocks because of a fall in interest rates.

VI.1.   Banks almost entirely passive in expansion or contraction of advances except in conditions of extreme stringency. Banks grant advances against gilt-edged collateral more or less automatically, unless either the resources of the bank are fully engaged, or the purpose of the loan is suspected of being highly speculative or one which should be financed by increase in capital of the business.

VII.1.   Short-money rates are not important except in so far as a low bank rate lowers the return on gilt-edged and forces insurance companies to invest in buildings, etc.

VIII.1.   A change of from, say, 2 to 6 per cent in bank rate might be important, but normal changes have a very small effect. Merchants do not finance their purchases so largely by means of bank overdrafts as formerly. Bank rate is important mainly as a weather guide. A speculator buying stocks for short-period changes in price might, because of his small margin, be affected by changes in the rate, but the volume of stocks is not important here.
    VIII.2.   The influence of the bank rate is almost entirely psychological. A large proportion of a merchant's costs is constant, and a fall in the bank rate can be only a mild stimulant.

IX.1.   Short-term rates will not have much effect on the carrying of stocks. They may affect the method of financing extensions, but they will not affect the decision whether to extend or not.

X.2.   Bank rate does not affect expansions, but banks change their lending policy, and this is an important factor. Stocks not increased because of a fall in bank rate.

2   The effect of long-term interest rates on investment in fixed plant

I.1.   When pressed, admitted that in principle long-term rates might affect investment, but was extremely sceptical.
    I.2.   Interest is included in costs of new plant, but do not worry about it because obsolescence is so much more important. Fall in interest rates would never make a difference to putting in new machinery. Long-term rates important to firms owning land and buildings but not to ordinary manufacturing business. Thought at first that one company was led to cultivate the market for a new product because of low interest rates, but then decided that this was due entirely to the energy of their management. Sceptical whether conversion scheme had made firms willing to launch out; temperament of management was decisive; if sanguine, management would go ahead in any case.
    I.3.   When considering whether to scrap existing plant they demand that 25 per cent should be shown on a new plant in addition to interest, depreciation, and maintenance. Long-term rate rarely a decisive factor in a business like theirs.

I.4.   Long-term rates not a consideration determining capital extensions directly. Fall in long-term rates might have indirect effects. For example, he wishes to settle a certain income on various persons and this has induced him to stay in business and expand in order to earn and save the necessary sum. Low interest rates had an adverse effect on his customers who are *rentiers*, and *rise* in rates would be a factor making him push ahead with his shops.

I.5.   Long-term rate too small to be significant. Ratio of fixed capital to turnover is very small. Suggested that rate of interest might be significant in determining a change from labour to machine methods and instanced a recent installation of some accounting machinery; but when asked whether bank rate or long-term rate was used in costing machinery he took up telephone to inquire and was informed that they had not used any rate, but had assumed merely that the machinery must be written off in four years.

I.7.   At present time new works are being built; the time was propitious for three reasons; (i) expanding trade, (ii) low rate of interest, and (iii) low building costs: (i) alone is sufficient; (ii) alone is not sufficient; (i) and (ii) is a powerful incentive.

I.8.   Always had plenty of money for extensions without borrowing.

I.9.   Long-term rates have no effect on investment.

I.10.   Changes in rate of interest would have no effect.

I.11.   Long-term rate does not affect their extensions, which they finance themselves.

I.12.   The long-term rate of interest is quite unimportant. They extend or renew plant when the condition of the market for their goods makes it seem desirable. They always keep enough money available to take advantage of opportunities as they arise.

II.1.   They would not take long-term rates into account in deciding on extensions.

II.2.   Long-term rates should be important in determining extensions, but in fact other considerations usually prove decisive. In 1920 stopped construction because of high interest rates then prevailing; on being questioned, added that high construction costs were also important in this decision. In general new plant is either needed or not needed and factors such as interest and building costs are secondary.

II.3.   They have never considered the long-term rate of interest.

II.5.   Reduction in rate of interest from 4 to 2½ per cent, say, would make a considerable difference and would be taken into account in considering possible plant extensions. Wages, however, are *much* more important.

II.7.   Long-term rates of no importance.

III.1.   Being a private concern they refrain from paying a dividend if they want money for extensions. Long-term rate has not affected extensions in the business. Uncertainty of the saving effected by extension, and of course of trade, is so great that a small change in interest rates is negligible.

III.2.　Probably public companies more affected by long-term rates than his business.

III.4.　Long-term rate has never been important factor in extensions in his experience.

III.5.　Long-term rate has little or no effect on extensions, which are financed from profits retained in the business.

III.7.　Long-term rate has no direct effect.

III.8.　Long-term rate has practically no effect on extension.

IV.1.　High rates over a long period would make a difference. Considered, however, that the price level of capital goods is more important than the rate of interest. The rate of interest is a very indirect influence in most businesses.

V.2.　Are affected by movements in general interest rates. While interest rates have been low they have raised as much capital as they could and have been encouraged to expand. Changes of 1 to 2 per cent are very important. Interest rates are more important in retailing than in manufacture because rent expenses are so much higher in the former. Considered that interest rates ought to be important for all businesses.

VI.2.　Obvious that low interest rates are a help to industry, particularly building and municipal enterprises, but their importance has been exaggerated. In industry as a whole it is the state of the capital market that matters rather than the rate of interest.

VI.3.　On the whole, trade conditions which make expansion desirable are accompanied by conditions favourable to new issues. Most companies would raise capital if they needed it, even if interest rates were high, provided that they saw that the capital would be remunerative. Cheap money works slowly; leads first to conversions of debentures and by improving the return on share capital optimism spreads and new issues commence. Impossible to trace exact effects, but no doubt cheap money has considerable effect. Clearing up process in depression attributed to greater liquidity and therefore greater readiness to go ahead. Low interest rates by raising the value of gilt-edged securities help to improve liquidity. This question of liquidity and of clearing up process is very important.

VI.4.　Important effect of low long-term rate of interest originating from the low bank rate was the increase in liquidity that it gave to firms by increasing value of holdings of securities. Banks would be influenced in their lending policy for new expansions by the state of liquidity of each particular firm. Low bank rate also causes issuing-houses to become more active in finding business and to encourage the making of new issues.

VII.1.　A low interest rate by reducing costs makes it possible to tap the lower-grade house market, but it is not possible to define any close relation. Factory building is mainly influenced by trade prospects and not by costs or the rate of interest.

VII.2.　Changes in interest rates might have some effect on demand for dwelling-houses through their influence on rents; but did not think this influence very important. Did not think fall from 6 to 4½ per cent in rate on building-society advances was a major influence in the recent building boom. Interest rates have even less effect on the demand for industrial building, since, if trade is good, firms will be able to afford rising building costs, etc.

IX.1.   Other factors, state of demand and general state of trade, are so important that the long-term rate of interest will have little effect on decisions whether to extend or not. A good business never has difficulty in getting new capital save in abnormal times.

X.1.   Amortisation dwarfs the interest rate. Conversion of debt to lower rate of interest increases amount available for dividends and therefore increases the propensity to take risks.

3   The effect of expected price changes on investment in stocks

I.2.   A firm would increase stocks if it expected a rise in price and could not buy forward.
   I.3.   Might increase stocks because prices are attractive.
   I.4.   Stocks vary from time to time on expectation of price changes or changes in difficulty of purchase.
   I.8.   Sometimes buy copper for stock when they think it cheap. Rate of interest of no importance in buying for stock; only factor considered is expectation of price changes.
   I.12.   They do not buy their raw material speculatively. When there is a danger of not being able to get supplies (as, for instance, when a large armament programme is started) they take care to safeguard themselves by coming to agreements with suppliers.

II.1.   If raw materials become cheaper they may buy for years ahead. They buy when raw material prices are low enough to suit the predetermined selling price of the product.

III.1.   Expectation of a rise in price would affect their stocks.
   III.6.   Possible to make arrangements to buy materials forward without actually paying for them when price changes are expected.

V.2.   They do buy ahead when they expect prices to rise.

VIII.1.   The nearer a merchant is to the primary product, the more will he be influenced by expected changes of price. Merchants dealing with primary commodities frequently speculate through futures markets.
   VIII.2.   When a merchant's sales are increasing he usually likes to increase the stocks he carries; and increasing sales are usually associated

with rising prices. Apart from this, a merchant will buy speculatively when he is convinced that prices are too low.

IX.1.   Price is a very important factor. Thought that most business men do speculate in stocks. Every wise manufacturer increases his stock because of an expectation of a rise in price. The fear that deliveries may be difficult in the future is always important.

4   The effect of expected changes in constructional costs on investment in fixed plant

I.3.   Do not postpone or speed up plant extensions because of expectations of changes in the costs of installations.

I.4.   Building costs are important in determining capital extensions. They would speed up on account of low prices. They might even postpone, e.g. if they heard that the price of steel had doubled.

I.5.   Would not speed up or postpone extensions because of building costs. Might speed up in expectation that they would not get orders executed later.

I.6.   Does not think that changes in building costs would materially affect expansion plans.

I.7.   At present time new works are being built; the time is propitious for three reasons; (i) expanding trade, (ii) low interest rates, and (iii) low building costs: (i) alone is sufficient reason; (ii) alone is not sufficient; (i) plus (ii) is a powerful incentive.

I.8.   Virtually never speed up extensions because of expectations of price changes. Of opinion that this should be done; but the firm dominated by a personality averse to all capital expenditure. Recently they tried to put an order for machinery for delivery over three years; but since the makers reserved the right to put the price up after one year they put the three years' orders into one year.

I.9.   Never speed up or postpone extensions because of expected changes in cost.

I.10.   Changes in cost would not influence extensions. Prospect of rising prices *might* lead them to decide on extensions rather more quickly.

I.11.   Do not work out a long-period budget; but of course use their judgement in particular cases.

I.12.   Would not speed up or postpone extensions or renewals to plant because of expected changes in costs of building or the price of machinery. They extend their plant or renew it when the condition of the market for their product makes it appear desirable for them to do so.

II.1.   Might build plant in bad times because building prices are low, but did not wish to exaggerate this feature of policy.

II.2.   In 1920 stopped construction because of high interest rates then prevailing; on being questioned added that high construction costs were also important in this decision. 1920 was the only instance of cost of construction affecting extensions. In general new plant is either needed or not needed, and factors such as interest and building costs are secondary.

II.3. Speeding up or postponement of extensions because of expected changes in cost has not arisen in his time.

II.4. Expectation of changes in cost never enters into consideration of extensions or renewals.

II.7. Expectation of changes in cost is a matter which would be discussed at a board meeting, but other factors almost certain to prove decisive.

III.1. Expectations of price changes unimportant. Decisions to expand dependent entirely upon prestige of new works, extra savings, and upon having the necessary money available.

III.2. Do not speed up or postpone extensions because of expected price changes.

III.4. Do not speed up or postpone in expectation of price changes.

III.5. Try to look ahead so as not to be inconvenienced by delay in obtaining new plant. Prices usually increase with demand, and they are therefore well served by their present policy.

III.6. Both postpone and speed up extensions because of expected price changes.

III.7. Do postpone and speed up extensions because of expected price changes.

III.8. Market elasticity of demand for his product is very small and state of activity of trade is the determining factor. Expected changes in price are certainly a factor inducing the postponement or speeding up of renewals and extensions.

IV.1. Price level of capital goods is more important than rate of interest in connection with capital developments. Certainly would postpone or speed up extensions because of expectations of price change.

V.1. Speeding up or postponement of plant expansion because of expected price changes is not relevant in their case.

V.2. On the whole do not speed up or postpone extensions in expectation of price changes because expansion is limited by necessity of training staff and by their capital.

VII.1. Factory building is mainly influenced by trade prospects and not by costs or the rate of interest.

VII.2. If good profits are expected, increased costs do not matter much. If trade is good, firms will be able to afford rising building costs anyway. The speculative building of offices and factories might be affected.

IX.1. It is quite common when costs are high to defer the erection of buildings. It is less common to speed up extensions in expectation of a rise in costs, since it is possible to fix the contracts at current prices. Building costs have more importance than the costs of borrowing.

X.1. Firms do not usually speed up or postpone in expectation of price changes.

5 The effect of state of demand for the product on investment in fixed plant

I.4. You have to be courageous to expand when you are doing badly. Would postpone extensions owing to any change imparting uncertainty (e.g. departure from gold). In this case would deal with expanding business by temporary extensions. What makes most businesses extend is the fact that they cannot meet competition except by having a bigger scale of operations.

I.7. At present time new works are being built; the time is propitious for three reasons; (i) expanding trade, (ii) low interest rates, and (iii) low building costs: (i) alone is sufficient reason; (ii) alone is not sufficient; (i) plus (ii) is a powerful incentive.

I.8. Always had plenty of money for extensions without borrowing. Only factor considered is the state of the demand.

I.9. Do not embark on extensions except under pressure of demand.

I.12. They always keep enough money available to take advantage of opportunities as they arise, and they extend or renew plant when the condition of the market makes it appear desirable to do so.

II.2. In general new plant is either needed or not needed, and factors such as building costs and interest are secondary.

III.4. Extensions governed entirely by demand.

III.5. Capital extensions should be the result of a careful forecast of future demands. It does not matter very much whether money comes from undistributed profits, bank loan, or public loan, if the policy is sound and the extensions can pay cost of finance and make a profit.

III.6. Thinks present conditions artificial and that there will be another slump 1939–40, and therefore avoids extravagant capital extensions. State of trade is most important factor in connection with capital extensions.

III.8. Market elasticity of demand for his product is small and state of trade activity is the determining factor. Main factor in extensions is expected return on capital or a quicker turnover.

VII.1. Factory building is mainly influenced by trade prospects.

VII.2. Costs and interest rates have even less effect on the demand for industrial building than on that for houses, since if trade is good firms will be able to afford rising building costs, etc.

IX.1. Considers the state of demand for the product as very important in its effects on the investment in fixed plant. The current pressure of orders, the current profit margin, expectations regarding the future state of the market for the product will be the factors determining whether a business wishes to make an investment. It is after considering these that the business will decide whether to extend or not.

6   The effect of abundance or scarcity of liquid resources on investment in fixed plant

I.1.   Existence of surplus funds would emphatically not induce extensions which would otherwise not be undertaken.

I.2.   Existence of surplus funds would rarely if ever induce extensions. The opposite is frequently true, however.

I.3.   Existence of large undistributed profits would not induce them to expand. In a well-managed business postponement of plant renewals or extensions would not be affected by desire to maintain dividends or a liquid position.

I.4.   In the case of a *bad* business large undistributed profits would induce extensions, and this is a most frequent cause of ruin.

I.5.   Existence of undistributed profits would not affect extensions for which they have elaborate planning ahead. Questioned, he admitted that existence of capital in hand might lead to effort to expand. Expansion might be held up for lack of money inside firm.

I.6.   Existence of undistributed profits would certainly induce capital extensions.

I.7.   Existence of large undistributed profits facilitates rather than induces extensions. Desire to maintain a liquid position undoubtedly may influence postponement of extensions.

I.8.   Have had liquid resources for many years, but have never undertaken extensions except when urgently required. Desire to maintain dividends has definitely caused postponement of extensions, although this may be due to the fact that personality dominating the firm is averse to all capital expenditure.

I.10.   Changes in cost would not influence extensions; the main influence is the amount of liquid resources available. Amount of liquid resources would certainly induce extensions. Desire to maintain dividends or liquid position would not cause postponement of extensions.

I.11.   Business with large undistributed profits has a rational inducement to expand and can afford to take risks; more willing to undertake new ventures when you have 'plenty in the carry forward'. Scarcely conceivable that a firm should feel that it could not undertake a renewal or extension because it wanted to pay a dividend. Development of a business has first claim on cash resources.

I.12.   The existence of large undistributed profits may induce some firms to look around for something to do with the money. This is not the case with them. They extend or renew plant when the condition of the market makes it seem desirable. They always keep enough money available to take advantage of opportunities as they arise.

II.1.   May use undistributed profits to build more warehouses and to extend plant. But they never do this simply because the money is there.

II.2.   Undoubtedly some business men are moved by consideration of the absence or presence of liquid resources in determining extensions.

II.3.   Existence of liquid resources might perhaps induce extensions. Desire to maintain dividends might cause postponement of extensions or renewals.

II.4.   Existence of liquid reserves sometimes, but not often, induces extensions. Lack of liquid resources may more frequently lead to their postponement.

II.7.   Liquid resources sometimes do induce extensions. Lack of liquid resources probably less important factor in postponing extensions or renewals.

III.1.   Decision to expand affected greatly by consideration whether money is available or not.

III.2.   He thought that existence of liquid resources would induce extensions, but not often during bad trade; he believed it very common that lack of resources postponed extensions or renewals, but had no personal experience as he had never wanted money.

III.4.   Could not think of any example in which liquid resources induce extension. They would certainly not postpone renewals and probably not extensions for lack of liquid resources. Postponement might occur in private business, and certainly would in a public company which had over-distributed during good trade and then found itself in a nasty cash position during the depression.

III.5.   Depends on the company whether the desire to maintain dividends or a liquid position acts as an influence leading to postponement of renewals or extensions.

III.6.   Their reserves are not liquid, and so they have no experience of liquid reserves causing extensions. Dividend considerations would not be allowed to interfere with extensions and renewals.

III.7.   Large liquid resources may induce, and small liquid resources may discourage, extensions and renewals.

III.8.   Large undistributed profits would perhaps make them look upon extensions with a more favourable eye. Plant renewals might be postponed for lack of liquid resources, but it would be unwise to do so.

IV.1.   In private business existence of liquid reserves would induce extensions. In big business extension would be considered on its merits. In smaller firms absence of funds might prevent extension.

V.2.   Extensions may be induced by liquid resources and postponed in order to pay dividends, but it is a bad policy.

VI.3.   In discussing the effects of cheap money it was stated that the clearing up process in depression led to greater liquidity and therefore to greater readiness to go ahead. Low interest rates by increasing the value of gilt-edged securities helped to improve liquidity. This question of liquidity and of clearing up the ground is very important.

VI.4.   Low long-term rate of interest increases liquidity of firms by increasing value of securities. Banks would be influenced in their lending policy for new expansions by state of liquidity of particular firm.

IX.1.   Before making an extension, a business man will ask whether he has the money, will look at his cash position and the strength of his balance sheet. A sound business with a lot of idle capital might undertake extensions in order to employ the cash, but one must distinguish the business in a strong balance-sheet position from that which has a strong cash position because of bad trade. At the same time, a good business never has difficulty in getting new capital, save in abnormal times.

X.1.   The making of large profits rather than the existence of undistributed profits is the important thing, but the latter will increase the tendency to take risks.

Summary of Replies

The broad effect of the foregoing opinions may be summarised as follows:
   1.   There is almost universal agreement that short-term rates of interest do not directly affect investment either in stocks or in fixed capital. The reason usually given for this is either that the business does not borrow from the bank or else that the effect of changes in the rate is too small in comparison with the profit margin to make any difference. There are three exceptions to this. I.6 states that bank rate might affect the decision to purchase machines, but implies that it would not affect stocks. I.3 says that bank rate would affect the carrying of stocks, but admits that stocks would not be increased solely because of a fall in bank rate. VIII.1, whilst denying that the rate had any importance for merchants in general, thought that it might affect the policy of the speculative merchant who is buying stocks for small changes in price, and pointed out that the volume of stocks held by this type is not heavy. On the other hand, several business men took the view that the psychological effects of a change in bank rate are important, arguing that there is a tendency to regard such changes as analogous to a weather report, and as indications of the probable trend of trade. Merchants tended to stress this influence. Some witnesses, moreover, asserted that the willingness of the banks to lend, as distinct from the rate charged, was an important consideration, and that this was liable to vary.
   2.   The majority deny that the long-term rate of interest affects investment directly, although some indicate that it is of some importance to them. I.5 stated that it might affect the installation of labour-saving machinery, although the subsequent course of the interview suggests that it had not in fact done so. I.7 and II.2 suggest that it is a contributory cause in deciding upon investment. II.5, IV.1, V.2, and VI.2 suggest that it is of some importance; IV.1 emphasising the importance of low rates if they persist for some time, and V.2 emphasising the importance of interest rates to retailers to whom rent expenses are peculiarly important. I.2, while denying that it is of importance to him, suggested that it would be

important to firms owning land and buildings. VII.1 and 2 thought that the rate might have some effect on the demand for dwelling-houses, but tended to deny that it could have an important effect. They both deny that factory building is influenced either by costs or by the rate of interest, and both gave as the reason, that if trade is good increased costs do not matter. The majority who deny its importance give as their reasons either that they do not need to borrow for extensions or that it is too small an element in comparison with depreciation, obsolescence, or the uncertainty of the market for the product.

There is, however, some evidence that a fall in long-term rates would have favourable indirect effects. VI.3 emphasises the fact that this, by raising the price of gilt-edged securities, increases the liquidity of a business and that this is very important in affecting the readiness to go ahead. This point should be considered in connection with the replies analysed under (6) above, from which it will be seen that a large number of entrepreneurs stated that the willingness to go ahead would be affected by the presence of liquid resources. X.1 emphasises the importance of a slightly different effect, namely that the conversion of fixed debt to a lower rate of interest increases the willingness to take risks.

We have evidence, then, that in ordinary manufacturing business the long-term rate of interest is of some, though very limited, direct importance in affecting investment. It seems that the indirect effects in increasing the resources of the business readily available for the finance of development may be of considerably greater importance. The builders, also, while admitting that the rate of interest, especially if very high or very low, might have some effect, tended to deny its importance. We have had evidence from VII.1 and VI.4 that a fall in interest rates may have some effect in inducing large corporate investors to undertake greater risks, for example, construction of buildings for themselves as investments.

3. A considerable number of businesses seem to relate their purchases of raw materials to expected changes in their price or to expected difficulties in obtaining delivery. Although this is not a universal practice, and is denied by some entrepreneurs, we may at least conclude that it is of considerable importance.

4. There seems to be a great divergence of practice in the matter of considering the price of capital construction in deciding whether to embark on capital construction or not. This difference ranges from denials that it is ever of importance to assertions that it is a very important consideration. A sufficient number, however, state that they do take expected changes in cost of construction into account for us to be able to conclude that this is an important factor when we are considering industrial investment as a whole.

5. There is considerable divergence of practice among the business men as to whether the presence or absence of liquid resources induces or discourages investment and renewals. Those who asserted that the presence of liquid resources induced extensions and renewals were more numerous than those who denied this; and those who asserted that the absence of liquid resources discouraged extensions and renewals were

again more numerous than those who denied this. But those two majorities are not composed of the same entrepreneurs. There is certainly sufficient evidence for us to conclude that the presence or absence of liquid resources is a consideration of some importance in this connection.

It was stated by I.11 that the presence of large liquid resources gave a rational inducement for extensions, as they could then afford to take more risks, and the answer of X.1 bears out this contention. It was suggested by IV.1 that the presence or absence of liquid resources is of more importance in this connection to small private businesses than to large public companies.

7

Financial Aspects of War Economy

When Richard Stone met Meade in the summer of 1940, Meade 'was engaged in drawing up plans for . . . a survey [of the national economy] in the form of a complicated system of balancing tables'. On this foundation Meade and Stone prepared the official national income estimates for the UK published first in the White Paper, An Analysis of the Sources of War Finance and an Estimate of the National Income and Expenditure in 1938 and 1940 *(Cmd 6261), in April 1941. Meade's original paper is printed here, without the second appendix which listed the statistical data needed to fill in the tables (Richard Stone, 'The use and development of national income and expenditure estimates', in D. N. Chester, ed.,* Lessons of the British War Economy, *Cambridge: Cambridge University Press, 1951, pp. 83–101; Meade Papers 3/1 and file T230/96, Public Record Office). It is followed by three published papers by Meade and Stone, one also with David Champernowne, in which they presented their war-time national income estimates and the principles and problems of their construction.*

The following are notes on the method of analysing the financial aspects of the war economy and on the statistical data which would be useful for this analysis. Sections I, II and III of this note together with the Tables A to I of Appendix I are designed to discuss the purposes and the logical methods of this financial analysis. Appendix II contains a list of the figures which would be necessary to carry out this analysis. It will not be possible to obtain all the desired statistical data; and for the preparation of any final document reliance will have to be placed upon the limited amount of data actually available. The scheme of analysis is, however, presented in its complete form for two purposes: to illustrate the method of analysis to be adopted and to ensure that no relevant data which are in fact available are inadvertently overlooked.

The analysis of war finance can be divided, broadly speaking, into three main divisions. The first (discussed in Section I and Tables A to D) is concerned with the 'ultimate sources' from which the necessary sums can be raised (e.g. from taxation, personal and institutional savings, the sale of assets abroad, etc.). The second (discussed in Section II and Tables E to I) is concerned with the monetary and banking problems (or alternatively the problems of 'liquidity') which are involved in this financing of war expenditure.

A simple illustration may suffice at this point to draw a rough distinction between these two types of problem. An increase in personal savings out of a given level of personal incomes, by reducing expenditure upon consumption goods, will release labour, equipment and raw materials from the production of such goods; these released factors can be absorbed into the war effort by means of increased expenditure from the Budget for war purposes; and the finance of this increased defence expenditure can be raised by Government borrowing of the increased personal savings. In this sense, personal savings provide one 'ultimate source' of war finance. But the form in which individuals wish to hold their increased savings raises a further set of monetary problems. If the increased savings are used directly by the savers for the purchase of Government securities, the Government has merely to issue new securities to these persons to obtain the finance for its defence expenditure; if, on the other hand, the savers wish to accumulate additional deposits out of their increased savings, the Government must issue securities of a kind which the banks will be willing to hold as an asset against the additional bank deposits created to satisfy the savers' desire for liquid funds. Thus, in addition to finding 'ultimate sources' for the finance of its expenditure, the Government must adopt a debt policy, and the banks must adopt a monetary policy, appropriate to the 'liquidity' desires of the market.

The third main division of the financial aspects of war economy is concerned with the extent to which an inflation of money incomes should be permitted and the way in which such an inflation will manifest itself.

I The 'Ultimate Sources' for the Finance of Government Expenditure

For the purpose of analysing the 'ultimate sources' of Government finance it is necessary to estimate the magnitude of certain national 'income and outlay' figures. These figures are shown in Table D. It is to be observed that the terms included in these tables are so defined that the sum of the 'income' items in the left-hand column is necessarily equal to the sum of the 'outlay' items in the right-hand column in each table. Thus, for example, in Table A, items in the left-hand column merely enumerate the revenue accruing to individuals in any period of time, while the items in the right-hand column represent an exhaustive list of the different ways in which this revenue is used in the same period of time.

From an examination of Tables A to D it can be seen that the following are the 'ultimate sources' from which an increase in defence expenditure can be financed:–

(i)   *A decline in Public Expenditure for Civil Purposes.* It is clear from Table B that an economy of this kind releases funds for public expenditure on defence.

(ii) *An increase in Tax Revenue other than from Death Duties.* From Table B it is clear that an increase in such taxes would serve to

finance an increase in public expenditure on defence. It might
appear also from this table that an increase in Death Duties
would have the same effect; but Table D draws attention to the
fact that the sale of assets from the estates of deceased persons
mops up part of the savings of the individuals or the institutions
which purchase these assets, and does not therefore represent an
independent 'ultimate source' for the finance of defence expenditure.

(iii)   *A decline in Private Expenditure on new investment in fixed
capital, on maintenance and replacement of fixed capital, or on
stocks.* Table D illustrates the fact that such a decline releases
existing savings for the finance of a greater Public Deficit.

(iv)   *An increase in Personal Savings,* as shown in item (1) of Table D,
will enable the Government to find the finance for an increased
Public Deficit.

(v)   *An increase in Gross Institutional Savings,* as specified in item (2)
of Table D, also enables the Government to raise additional
sums by borrowing.

(vi)   *An increase in the Surplus of extra-budgetary Public Funds* (item
(3) of Table D) may be used directly by the Government to cover
an increased deficit, and

(vii)   *An increase in the Unfavourable Balance of Payments* (item (4) of
Table D) must be financed by the sale of gold or of foreign assets,
or by the accumulation of additional balances by foreigners in the
United Kingdom, and these sums may all be used, directly or
indirectly, to finance an increased deficit.

It must be remembered that the different items in Table D are so
defined that 'Savings' must necessarily be equal to 'Investment'. It might,
therefore, appear from the table that no problem really exists in finding
'ultimate sources' for the finance of the Public Deficit, no matter how
large that deficit may be; for since the two sides of the account in Table D
must by definition balance, the Public Deficit must always be covered
from one source or another. This is in fact true, provided that there is no
objection to an unlimited inflation of the money value of the national
income. An increase in money expenditure on defence tends to inflate
money incomes. This rise in money incomes will itself increase the yield
of taxation, the surplus of certain extra-budgetary funds, and the size of
the money flow of institutional and personal savings. In certain circumstances the speed with which the inflation is proceeding will itself
fundamentally change the contribution from these sources; for individuals and institutions may save money not only because they have
planned to save a larger amount out of their increased incomes, but also
because some period of time elapses between an unexpected increase in
incomes and the consequent increase in expenditure upon consumption
which will eventually result from this increase in incomes. In the interval
the increase in incomes is wholly saved.

The problem of finding the 'ultimate sources' for the finance of the
deficit must, therefore, be posed in the following way. A decision must be

taken as to the extent to which an inflation of money incomes should be permitted – a decision which in present conditions must be based chiefly upon considerations of the social and political effects of inflation, and upon the degree to which real scarcities of labour, equipment and raw materials exist. (See Section III below.) Having set a limit to the degree of inflation which is to be permitted, an attempt can be made to assess the change in the various figures in Table D which this degree of inflation would automatically bring about. If these changes would make 'Savings' greater than 'Investment', then the permitted degree of inflation is more than sufficient to finance the planned expenditure on defence. If, on the other hand, 'Savings' would still be less than 'Investment', either the actual degree of inflation must be expected to exceed the permitted level, or else other steps must be taken so to manipulate the other items in Table D, that 'Savings' are again equated to 'Investment' at the permitted degree of inflation.

Some indication may be given of the types of manipulation which may be undertaken to achieve this object. Rates of taxation may be raised; personal savings may be increased by patriotic appeals, by the provision of attractive incentives to savings or by compulsion; various measures may be taken directly to restrict consumption in ways which may be expected to lead to increased savings, or to restrict private investment in such a way as to release funds to finance the Public Deficit; or it may be decided to finance a larger value of imports by realising foreign assets more rapidly. It is as a guide to the effectiveness of different measures of this kind that Tables A to D should prove useful.

There remains, however, one further type of policy to be discussed. Monetary policy, which is discussed below in Section II, may itself affect the 'ultimate sources' of Government finance. In the analysis of this section it has been tacitly assumed merely that the debt policy of the Government and the monetary policy of the banking system are in combination such as not to be inconsistent with the maintenance of the level of money incomes within the permitted degree of inflation; or, in other words, it has been assumed that the supply of assets of various types by the Government, and of cash and deposits by the banks, has been such as to suit the 'liquidity preferences' of the market, as they develop in response to changes in income within the permitted limit of inflation, to changes in the political and military situation, and to changes in the various economic and social policies adopted by the Government.

But certain types of monetary policy may directly affect the 'ultimate sources' of Government finance; for example, a refusal on the part of the banks to grant advances for certain purposes might lead to a decrease in private investment. Moreover, the 'liquidity' position of individuals and institutions may directly affect their expenditure on consumption or on private investment. For example, it is probable that in recent weeks the public has desired to hold a larger amount of cash and of deposit money. In the case of workers who have no considerable holdings of assets which can be sold for cash, the building up of an increased cash holding may have been financed by increased savings out of current incomes. It is possible, therefore, that this element of savings may prove to be merely a *temporary* contribution to the finance of the war which will cease as soon as sufficient cash balances have been accumulated; and indeed this might be followed by an actual dissaving on the part of the workers if a change in the situation removed the desire for extra liquidity. For these and similar reasons the desire for liquidity and the incentive to save may in certain conditions be intimately connected. For this and similar reasons it is not possible, even logically, to draw too sharp a distinction between the problems connected with finding the 'ultimate sources' for Government finance and the problems of monetary policy; and in practical application the two types of problem are intimately connected. The following section gives an outline of the way in which the monetary problems may be analysed.

II Problems of Government Debt and Monetary Policy

The fundamental problem of monetary policy is to provide assets of different kinds and of different degrees of liquidity in amounts which, according to the varying 'liquidity preferences' of the market, are appropriate to mop up the 'ultimate sources' of Government finance. In order to attempt to foresee the most appropriate forms in which these assets should be provided (through the types of asset issued to finance the deficit and through the types of funds provided by the banks) it is necessary to study the current changes which are taking place in the 'liquidity preferences' of different sections of the money and capital markets.

Tables E to I[1] are designed to illustrate the type of statistical information which would be required fully to analyse these current movements of liquidity. Each table comprises one part of the capital market; it states, in the left-hand column, the sources from which each section of the capital market may have obtained funds and, in the right-hand column, the way in which these funds have been used for investment in assets of varying degrees of liquidity. The terms in the tables are so defined that the sums of the left-hand and of the right-hand columns must be equal; for in each case the left-hand column is a statement of the sources of capital funds received in a given period and the right-hand column represents the ways in which these same funds were invested in the same period. Thus the left-hand column of Table E enumerates the sources from which individuals accumulate or receive capital funds[2] and the right-hand column indicates the types of assets which these individuals have chosen for the investment of these funds. There may, of course, be a net decrease in any one of the particular assets

[1] Careful attention should be paid to the note at the beginning of Appendix I, in order to understand the way in which both capital assets and the capital market have been divided for the construction of these tables.

[2] Death Duties and Legacies and Gifts by Individuals to Institutions must be deducted from these funds because the surrender of part of individuals' capital assets for these purposes will reduce by an equivalent amount the total funds of capital assets remaining in individuals' possession.

held by individuals with a correspondingly greater increase in another type of asset; and a movement of this kind would indicate a change in individuals' liquidity preference of a greater magnitude than can be satisfied by the choice of investments merely in respect of newly accrued capital assets.

Many interesting connections between the various items in these tables and in the preceding tables might be pointed out. Thus all the items appearing in the left-hand column of Table D must appear somewhere in one of the left-hand columns of Tables E to I, since all the 'Savings' in Table D represent capital accruals to Individuals, Institutions, Foreigners or Public Authorities. Similar connections exist between various items in Tables E to I. Thus, the total of New Issues of Private Securities (Table F, item 4) must be equal to the sums of the net increases of Private Securities held by Individuals (Table E, item 9), by Institutions (Table F, item 11), by Foreigners (Table G, item 7), by Public Authorities (Table H, item 11) and by Banks (Table I, item 4). But these connections must remain of academic interest in view of the evident impossibility of obtaining the necessary statistical data.

In fact it will probably be possible to obtain information – and that merely in an incomplete form – only for Tables H and I. But this information would in itself be of the greatest importance; for it would give a clear indication of some of the most important changes in liquidity preferences. If indications can be obtained of the extent to which individuals and institutions are showing a preference for deposit money and for short-term public securities, of the extent to which the banks have been absorbing assets of various types, and of the types of debt which the public authorities have been issuing to various sections of the market, a solid basis would exist for the discussion of changes in various liquidity preferences. These indications of recent changes can then be used to estimate the type of banking and debt policy which in the near future is likely best to meet the demands of the capital market.

A further indication of changing liquidity preferences can be obtained from a study of various interest rates. A hardening in the rate of interest demanded by lenders on one type of asset as opposed to the rate at which they are willing to accept another type of asset may be taken to indicate a decreased preference for the former as opposed to the latter type of asset.

III Prices, Employment and Output. The Mechanism of Inflation

If the 'ultimate sources' of Government finance, discussed in Section I, are not sufficient to cover the planned expenditure upon defence, an inflation of the national income must be expected. In this connection two problems arise: (a) the decision as to the degree of inflation which should be permitted and (b) the analysis of the way in which the inflation will present itself. If considerable increases in production were possible, through the absorption of unemployed resources or the fuller utilisation of existing resources, an inflation of total national expenditure might show itself in an increased turnover of goods without much rise in prices, wage-rates and costs. On the other hand, if there are considerable shortages of labour or materials of the kind which will be required for the expansion of munitions production or for the satisfaction of increased private expenditure, a further inflation will show itself in increased prices rather than in increased output. In particular the competition of employers (particularly in the case in which a 100% E.P.T. [Excess Profits Tax] removes the incentive for economy in business) will drive up wage-rates and in consequence costs and prices.

A full analysis of the financial aspects of war economy should, therefore, contain a study of the movements of employment, unemployment, wage-rates and prices in the main sectors of the economy. This will indicate the extent to which a further inflation may be expected to raise prices rather than output in these various sectors.

Appendix I   Tables Illustrating the Method of Analysis

Tables A to D illustrate national 'income and outlay' figures necessary to determine the 'ultimate sources' for the finance of Government expenditure.

Tables E to I illustrate changes in the 'liquidity position' of different sections of the economy in order to determine the debt policy which should be adopted by the Government and the monetary policy which should be adopted by the banking system.

In these tables the following definitions are used: Public Expenditure as opposed to Private Expenditure means expenditure directly financed by the National and Local Governments. Defence Expenditure as opposed to Civil Expenditure means expenditure incurred directly for the prosecution of the war.

For the purposes of Tables E to I the holders of assets are divided into the following five groups: (i) Individuals resident in the United Kingdom, (ii) United Kingdom Private Institutions (i.e. all firms, corporations, associations, etc., other than Banks as defined below and National and Local Governments), (iii) Foreign, Colonial or Dominions, individuals, institutions, and governments, (iv) United Kingdom National and Local Governments (including funds directly controlled by these governments), and (v) Banks including the Bank of England and the Clearing Banks. The assets held by these groups are divided into seven types: (i) Bank Notes, (ii) Bank Deposits, (iii) Gold and Foreign and Imperial Assets of all kinds, (iv) Short-term Public Securities, defined as short-term debt of National and Local Governments, (v) Long-term Public Securities, (vi) Bank Advances, and (vii) Private Securities, an omnibus group which must be defined as including all other forms of debt (i.e. Stock, and Shares, Mortgages, etc. of private institutions). Clearly it would be possible to extend this 'liquidity' analysis to any desired extent by further sub-division of these groups of assets and holders of assets.

Table A   *Personal Incomes and Outlay (£ million)*

Income	*Outlay*
1. Gross Personal Incomes (before deduction of taxes, rates and compulsory contributions paid out of personal incomes. Including transfer payments such as betting receipts; personal gifts; interest on National and Local Government Debt; cash benefits from insurance policies of all kinds, from National and Local Governments, from social insurance funds, from trade unions, clubs and Friendly societies; pensions)	2. Taxes, Rates and Compulsory Contributions paid out of personal incomes:– (a) Income Tax (paid by individuals) (b) Sur-Tax (g) Motor-Vehicle Duties on Private Vehicles (h) Rates on Private Dwellings (i) Workers' Contributions to Social Services 3. Retail Sales, excluding goods purchased by hire-purchase (classified according to main heads: Food, Other Groceries, Drink, Tobacco, Clothes, Boots and Shoes, Piece Goods, Furniture, Hardware, Drugs, and Fancy Goods, Sport and Travel Goods, Petrol and Oil, Cars and Cycles, Newspapers, Coal) 4. Hire-Purchase Payments for Durable Consumption Goods 5. Personal Services (classified according to main heads: Travel, Domestic Service, Entertainments, Betting, Hotels and Restaurants, Medicine, Postal Services, Religion, Laundry, Private Education, Undertaking, Gas, Electricity, Water, Rents and house repairs exclusive of rates, Garaging and Car Expenses other than Insurance and Taxation, Other Services) 6. Life Assurance Premiums (Ordinary and Industrial) 7. Other Fees, Insurance Premiums, Contributions etc. (Fees to Local Authorities, Fire, Accident, Burglary and Car Insurance, Contributions to Clubs, Trade Unions and Friendly Societies) 8. Personal Gifts 9. Personal Savings (classified according to the main forms of savings)

Table B *National and Local Government Budgets: Revenue and Expenditure (£ million)*

Revenue	*Expenditure*

1. Death Duties
2. Taxes paid out of personal incomes
3. Other Taxes
4. Rates
5. Trading Profits (including surplus of the Post Office)
6. Interest and Rent from Public Property
7. Other Revenue not from Loans
8. Public Deficit
	9. Public Expenditure on Defence
	10. Public Expenditure for Civil Purposes (excluding Sinking Funds)
	    (a) National (excluding grants-in-aid)
	    (b) Local

Table C *Balance of Payments (£ million)*

Receipts	*Expenditure*

1. Net Receipts from Services:–
    (a) Shipping
    (b) Interest on Capital
    (c) Financial Services
    (d) Other Services
2. Unfavourable Balance, financed by capital movements:–
    (a) Sale of Gold and Foreign Assets from Exchange Equalisation Account
    (b) Sale of Mobilised Foreign Securities
    (c) Net Accumulation of Funds in Clearing Accounts and 'Special' and 'Registered' Accounts
    (d) Net Accumulation of Dominions and Other Foreign Balances
	3. Excess of Value of Imports over the Value of Exports

Table D   *National Savings and Investment (£ million)*

Savings	Investment
1. Personal Savings (as in A9)	5. Public Deficit (as in B8)
2. Gross Institutional Savings	6. Death Duties (as in B1)
(a) Undistributed Profits of Trading Concerns	7. Private Expenditure on Gross Investment (including expenditure for replacement as a result of fire, burglary, accidents, etc.)
(b) Sums allocated to maintenance, replacement and depreciation reserves by Trading Concerns	
(c) Cash receipts of institutions from insurance claims in respect of fire, burglary, accidents, etc.	(a) New Investment in Fixed Capital
(d) Excess of hire-purchase payments over new commitments for durable consumption goods	(b) Maintenance and Replacement of Fixed Capital
(e) Life Assurance Companies' Surplus (i.e. receipts from interest, dividends and premiums *less* outgoings on benefits, interest, dividends and expenses)	(c) Additions to Stock
(f) Increase in accumulated funds of other institutions (e.g. Trade Unions, Friendly Societies, Insurance Offices other than for Life Assurance)	
3. Surplus of extra-budgetary Public Funds (excluding Exchange Equalisation Account, Post Office and Savings Bank Accounts; including Social Insurance Funds, and compulsory war-risks insurance funds)	
4. Unfavourable Balance of Payments (as in C2)	

Table E *Capital Account Showing Changes in Liquidity of Individuals (£ million)*

Sources of Funds	*Use of Funds*
1. Personal Savings (as in A9) 2. Surrender by Individuals of Mobilised Foreign Assets 3. Increase in Bank Advances to Individuals 4. *Deduct* Death Duties (as in B1) and Legacies and Gifts by Individuals to Institutions	5. Increase in Notes held by Individuals 6. Increase in Deposits held by Individuals 7. Increase in Short-Term Public Securities held by Individuals 8. Increase in Long-Term Public Securities held by Individuals 9. Increase in Private Securities held by Individuals

Table F *Capital Account Showing Changes in Liquidity of Private Institutions (£ million)*

Sources of Funds	*Use of Funds*
1. Gross Institutional Saving (as in D2) 2. Surrender by Institutions of Mobilised Foreign Assets 3. Gifts and Legacies from Individuals to Institutions 4. New Issues of Private Securities 5. Increase in Bank Advances to Private Institutions	6. Gross Private Investment (as in D7) 7. Increase in Notes held by Institutions 8. Increase in Deposits held by Institutions 9. Increase in Short-Term Public Securities held by Institutions 10. Increase in Long-Term Public Securities held by Institutions 11. Increase in Private Securities held by Institutions

Table G *Capital Account Showing Changes in Liquidity of Foreigners (£ million)*

Sources of Funds	*Use of Funds*
1. Net Accumulation of Sterling Funds by Dominions and Foreigners (as in C2, c and d) 2. Increase in Bank Advances to Foreigners	3. Increase in Notes held by Foreigners 4. Increase in Deposits held by Foreigners 5. Increase in Short-Term Public Securities held by Foreigners 6. Increase in Long-Term Public Securities held by Foreigners 7. Increase in Private Securities held by Foreigners

Table H *Capital Account Showing Changes in Liquidity of Public Authorities (£ million)*

Sources of Funds	Use of Funds
1. Surplus of extra-budgetary Funds (as in D3)	6. Public Deficit (as in B8)
2. Sale of Gold and Foreign Assets from Exchange Equalisation Account (as in C2.a)	7. Increase in Notes held by Public Authorities
	8. Increase in Deposits held by Public Authorities
3. Increase in Bank Advances to Public Authorities (i.e. Ways and Means Advances from Bank of England, Treasury Deposits from Clearing Banks, Bank Advances to Local Authorities)	9. Increase in Short-Term Public Securities held by Public Authorities
	10. Increase in Long-Term Public Securities held by Public Authorities
4. New Issues of Short-Term Public Securities	11. Increase in Private Securities held by Public Authorities
5. New Issues of Long-Term Public Securities	

Table I *Capital Account Showing Changes in Liquidity of Banking System*

(Combined Balance Sheet of Bank of England and Clearing Banks) (£ million)

Sources of Funds *(increase in liabilities)*	Use of Funds *(increase in assets)*
1. Increase in Notes held (a) by individuals (b) by private institutions (c) by foreigners (d) by public authorities	3. Increase in bank holdings of (a) Short-Term Public Securities (b) Long-Term Public Securities
2. Increase in Deposits held (a) by individuals (b) by private institutions (c) by foreigners (d) by public authorities	4. Increase in bank holdings of Private Securities *less* surrender by banks of mobilised foreign assets
	5. Increase in Bank Advances to (a) individuals (b) private institutions (c) foreigners (d) public authorities

8

The Construction of Tables of National Income, Expenditure, Savings and Investment

By J. E. Meade and Richard Stone, from The Economic Journal, *vol. 51 (1941), pp. 216–233*

I Introductory

The national income may be defined in a number of different ways. Differences in definitions, which are all too infrequently given with precision by writers on this subject, may lead to great confusion in economic discussion. It is the purpose of this paper to show that the construction of balance-sheets of national income and expenditure clears up some of these problems of definition and provides a powerful statistical instrument for the cross-checking of various methods of estimating the national income. Such tables may serve two further useful purposes. First, they make it possible for the statistician to provide estimates of the national income and expenditure in the various forms which are most useful to the economist for the elucidation of many economic problems. Secondly, if a form of tables of this kind could be generally accepted, international comparisons of national incomes would be greatly facilitated.

Tables A, B, C, D and E (pages 131–5 below) are suggested outlines of the fundamental tables which serve the dual purpose of presenting the estimates in a form which is of most interest to economists and which enables the maximum amount of statistical cross-checking.

II Table A

This table presents the basic material for a national income enquiry in three forms:–

(i) *The Net National Income at Factor Cost* measures the money value of the income produced by, and accruing to, the various factors of production in any period of time – e.g., the rent of land, profits of business enterprises, interest on capital and the earnings of labour.

Statistically for the United Kingdom, these estimates would be based principally upon income-tax statistics and upon statistics of the number of workers in employment and upon the average earnings of such workers.

(ii)   *The Net National Output at Factor Cost* measures the value added to the product in various branches of economic activity. Statistically, these estimates would be obtained primarily by the Census of Production method of estimating the net value added in various industries, together with supplementary information on such items as the net income from foreign investment.

(iii) *The Net National Expenditure at Factor Cost* measures the amount of the net national income (or output) which is used for various purposes – e.g., for personal consumption, for current Government purposes and for additions to the community's capital. Statistically, the estimates would be based mainly upon public finance figures (for items 16, 17 and 18), upon a large number of different quantity and price series (for items 15 and 19),[1] and upon figures of foreign trade and other foreign transactions (for item 20).[2]

If the terms in the three columns of Table A are properly defined, the three totals (items 5, 14 and 21) must balance. Columns I and II are in effect merely different ways of enumerating the incomes earned by the various factors of production – Land, Capital and Enterprise, and Labour. In column I these incomes are enumerated according to the factors which earn the income, and in column II according to the various industries in which they are earned. In column I items 1 and 2 include the income received by the Government from state-owned property and the net income received from abroad by the Government and by the owners of foreign investments. The latter source of income is included in item 13 of column II, and the former in the various other items of column II. Item 12 of column II includes the salaries of civil servants and the pay of the armed forces – i.e., the factor incomes earned in Government service, which will not be included in the other items of this column.

Column III of Table A enumerates the expenditures which give rise to the factor incomes enumerated in columns I and II. Thus income is generated by personal expenditure on consumption and by the Government demand for goods and services. One preliminary matter which needs explanation is the reason for the insertion of items 17 and 18 in column III of Table A. Income, output and expenditure (items 5, 14 and 21 of Table A) are estimated 'at factor cost' and not 'at market prices'. If we consider the production of any particular commodity (e.g., for personal consumption) we may measure either the income received by the factors of production from the sale of that product or the amount spent by consumers on that product. The former will be less than the

---

[1] For some items of personal consumption and of investment the Census of Production figures would, no doubt, have to be used, so that there would not be complete statistical independence between the estimates of national output and of national expenditure.

[2] Cf. Table D, page 134.

latter if a tax is levied on the purchase of the commodity; and it will exceed the latter if the state pays a subsidy on its production. In order, therefore, that national income and expenditure may balance, we may – as is done in Table A – subtract indirect taxes from, and add subsidies to, the market value of the goods and services bought, in which case national income, output and expenditure are measured 'at factor cost'. Alternatively, we may add indirect taxes to, and subtract subsidies from, the national income and the national output, in which case income, output and expenditure would be measured 'at market prices'.

Column III also enumerates various expenditures – on personal consumption (item 15), on goods and services currently consumed by the Government (item 16), and on additions to the domestic equipment of capital (item 19) – regardless of the fact that these goods and services may be produced at home or may be imported from abroad. But it is only expenditure on home-produced goods and services which generates the factor incomes enumerated in columns I and II. Item 20 of Table A makes the necessary adjustment.

From Table D it will be seen that Foreign Investment (item 20 of Table A) is equal to income generated by receipts from abroad less current expenditure abroad. By including item 20 we are therefore adding to the other expenditures enumerated in column III of Table A, the income generated by receipts from abroad (e.g., the sale of exports) and are deducting those current expenditures which are made abroad (e.g., the purchase of imports) and which do not therefore generate factor incomes at home.

Item 19 of Table A raises a number of difficulties of definition. In the first place, income, output and expenditure (items 5, 14 and 21 of Table A) have been defined as 'net'. Income is said to be reckoned 'net', and not 'gross', when deduction is made from the receipts of gross profits to allow for the depreciation, renewal, repair, etc., of capital equipment; and expenditure is reckoned 'net' when a similar deduction is made from gross investment. Income, output and expenditure may be reckoned 'gross' if profits (item 2) are estimated before deduction of these allowances, if the values added to the product in different industries (items 6–10) are estimated before deduction of the expenses which must be incurred to maintain the capital of each industry intact, and if home investment (item 19) is estimated in such a way as to measure gross rather than net expenditure on fixed capital goods (i.e., if item 19 (*b*) is omitted from column III of Table A).

The problem of estimating 'net' investment raises fundamental problems of definition of income. (*a*) Income may be defined in terms of money values in the following way. We may say that a man's money income in any period is equal to the money value of his consumption plus the increase in the money value of his capital assets. For the sum of these two is the amount which he could have spent on consumption *while maintaining the money value of his capital stock intact*. (*b*) On the other hand, a man's income may be defined as the value of his expenditure on consumption plus the value of any increase in the real amount of his capital assets. For the sum of these two is the amount he could have spent on consumption *while maintaining the real amount of his capital stock intact.*

(*a*) If the first principle is adopted, home and foreign investment (items 19 and 20 of Table A) must be measured in such a way as to record the *increase in the value* of domestic fixed capital, of domestic stocks and of foreign assets. Similarly, in columns I and II income from profits must be defined so as to include the appreciation in the money value of all these assets, as well as the accounting profit which remains after deducting from current receipts the current cost of replacing the physical assets which are used up or depreciated in the process of obtaining those current receipts.

(*b*) The adoption of the second principle means that home and foreign investment must be defined as the *value of the increase* in all real assets, and that profits must be defined as the accounting profit resulting from the difference between current receipts and the current cost of replacing all real factors of production used up in current production.

The inclusion of item 19 (*d*) in Table A needs some explanation. In the investment of savings, use is made of certain services – e.g., those of stockbrokers and lawyers. In so far as the cost of these services is reckoned as a current cost of production by any business which is investing funds, it will have been included as one of the factor costs which must be covered by the market prices of the goods produced by the business. In this case the value of the services in question will already have been covered by the market value of the goods and services enumerated in other items of column III of Table A. But in so far as these services are not so accounted for, they must be regarded as an item in the cost of providing new capital equipment for the community; and if expenditure on services of this kind were not separately enumerated, the sum of income-generating expenditures enumerated in column III of Table A would be incomplete.

III Table B

This table shows the form in which estimates may be presented of personal incomes and of the uses to which personal incomes may be put (i.e., through expenditure on different forms of consumption or through savings). The first column of Table B ('The Composition of Personal Incomes') illustrates the way in which an estimate of personal incomes may be derived from the Net National Income at Factor Cost (item 5 of Table A).

If we start with the Net National Income at Factor Cost, we must first (Table B, item 2) add transfer incomes paid by the state (such as interest on the national debt, unemployment allowances paid by the state to the unemployed, etc.). For in Table A these items of transfer income are excluded (i) from the national income (which records only the incomes earned by the factors of production for productive work done), (ii) from the national output (which records only the value of the net output of various productive industries), and (iii) from the national expenditure (which in item 16 of Table A excludes expenditure by the state of a purely transfer character).[3]

We must next (item 3 of Table B) deduct all direct taxes paid on income in order to obtain the sum of incomes after deduction of direct taxes. We must next deduct those elements of this total of tax-free incomes which are not paid over to persons – namely, (i) Government income from property or from trading profits (item 4 of Table B), which is not paid over to individuals but is used as a part of Government revenue to finance Government expenditure, and (ii) undistributed profits (item 5 of Table B), which represents elements of tax-free income obtained from profits or interest or rent, which are saved directly by companies without being paid to individuals.

We then obtain (item 6 of Table B) an estimate of the total of personal incomes after deduction of direct taxes. This sum can be divided (as in the second column of Table B) to show the distribution of the total of personal incomes between groups of income-recipients ranged according to the size of their incomes. It must also be equal (cf. the third column of Table B) to the sum of personal expenditures on various forms of consumption and personal savings.

The columns of Table B present the information about personal incomes in a way which should be of interest to economists. For it shows (*a*) the relations between the net national income and transfer incomes and personal incomes, (*b*) the distribution of personal incomes between income classes and (*c*) the way in which personal incomes are spent or saved. The total of personal incomes, its distribution among income classes, and personal expenditures on various types of goods or services are the raw material from which – with the supplementary aid of information about the prices of various groups of consumption goods and

---

[3] It may be thought that the balance of Table B will be upset if item 2 includes only transfer payments from the Government to individuals. For there are a number of other forms of transfer income. For example, a son may receive an allowance from his father, or a pauper may receive a transfer income from a charitable organisation. The balance of Table B is, however, preserved by excluding such transfers both from personal incomes and from personal consumption. In the case of a son's allowance, since the father's 'expenditure' in giving the money to his son is excluded from personal expenditure (item 9 of Table B), the balance is preserved by excluding the receipt of the son's allowance from item 2 of Table B. A similar problem arises in the case of betting gains. Expenditure on betting leads (i) to the receipt of income by those engaged in the betting industry and (ii) to the receipt of a transfer income by those who win bets. In columns I and II of Table A the incomes of those engaged in the betting industry will be recorded; and, against this, item 15 of Table A (and so item 9 of Table B) must include only that part of expenditure on betting which is not transferred to those who win bets. The balance of Table B is thus preserved by excluding from transfer incomes (item 2) the money obtained from betting gains. Receipts of transfer incomes from charitable institutions may be regarded – as in the case of a father's allowance to his son – as a transfer between individuals, provided that suitable definitions of income and expenditure are adopted in the case of such institutions. (This problem is dealt with at greater length below, cf. pages 128–31.)

services – personal demand functions and propensities to consume may best be analysed.

The columns in Table B may also serve as a statistical cross-check. The sources used for the estimates in column I (in addition to the sources used for item 1 of Table B, which is the same as item 5 of Table A) are certain public finance figures (for items 2, 3 and 4) and figures of business accounts (for item 5). If income-tax statistics and figures of wages are used to make estimates of column II of Table B, there is little statistical cross-check between the totals of column II and of column I, item 1 of which is largely based on the same material. But if estimates for column II could be obtained from sample family budget inquiries, an independent estimate of the total of personal incomes might be obtained. In column III of Table B still other data could be used for the estimates – for item 9 a large number of series of production, prices or sales of different goods and services, and for item 10 an enumeration of the increases in all the different types of asset (cash, securities, etc.) held by individuals.

IV   Table C

A third table may be constructed to illustrate the flow of savings. Savings may be made by persons (item 1 of Table C) or by businesses (item 2 of Table C); and they may be used either to finance investment (item 4 of Table C) or the excess of current expenditure over current revenue of the Government (item 5 of Table C). But while Table C presents information about savings and investment in a form which may be of interest to economists, it does not provide any additional statistical cross-checking; for if item 5 of Table C is properly defined, Table C is simply a re-arrangement of certain items of Tables A and B.

This fact can best be seen by means of Table B'. We know that item 5 of Table A should be equal to the sum of items 15, 16, 17, 18, 19 and 20 of Table A. In other words, item 1 in column I of Table B' is equal to the sum of items 7, 8, 9, 11 and 14 in column II of Table B'. The remaining items in column I of Table B' are identical with the remaining items in column II of Table B'; for example, item 2 of Table B' is the same as item 10 of Table B'.

But the items in column I of Table B' are the same as those in column I of Table B, which represents the composition of personal incomes after deduction of direct taxes. It follows, therefore, that column II of Table B' must measure the sum of personal consumption and personal savings, or that personal savings equals the sum of items 8, 9, 10, 11, 12, 13, 14 and 15 of Table B', or that

Personal Savings + Undistributed Profits − Investment = Current Government Expenditure on Goods and Services, Subsidies and Transfers − Government Revenue from Direct and Indirect Taxes and from Government Income.

The above equation is the same as the balance between the uses and sources of savings as shown in Table C, if the right-hand term of the above equation is defined as the Budget Deficit. Or in other words, if this definition of the Budget Deficit is adopted, Table C must be regarded merely as a re-arrangement of Tables A and B.

V   The Interpretation of Public Finance

The use of this definition of the Budget Deficit requires some explanation. In the first place, the Budget Deficit refers to the total transactions of all public authorities; and a combined statement of revenue and expenditure must be drawn up for (e.g.) the Central Government, the local authorities and various extra-budgetary public funds. All transfers between these various authorities must be excluded from both revenue and expenditure. For example, grants-in-aid paid by the Central Government to the local authorities must be excluded from Central Government expenditure and from local authorities' revenue; and state contributions to extra-budgetary funds for social insurance must be excluded from Central Government expenditure and from the revenue of extra-budgetary funds. When this is done a combined revenue and expenditure account of the following type may be drawn up:–

Combined Revenue and Expenditure Account of all Public Authorities

Revenue	*Expenditure*
(a) Direct Taxes, Fines and Gifts	(f) Transfer Payments to private sector of the economy
(b) Indirect Taxes	(g) Subsidies
(c) Government Income from property and profits of trading services	(h) Net Current Expenditure by the Government on Goods and Services: (i) Total expenditure on goods and services,
(d) Balance, or Budget Deficit	*less* (ii) Revenue from sale of goods and services to private sector of the economy,
	less (iii) Government purchase of capital assets
(e) Total Revenue	(i) Total Expenditure

It will be seen that this combined revenue and expenditure account gives a definition of the budget deficit which corresponds to that which is necessary for the balancing of Table C. Item (h) of the Combined Revenue and Expenditure Account corresponds to item 16 of Table A. This item excludes from Government expenditure on goods and services an amount equal to the revenue of the Government from the sale of goods and services to the private sector of the economy (e.g., sale of postage stamps, rent from municipally owned houses, etc.). For such expenditures (*e.g.*, the purchase of postage stamps by individuals or for business purposes) will already have appeared in Table A, column III, either directly as an element of personal expenditure (item 15 of Table A), or as an element in the business costs, and so in the market prices of other goods and services produced for sale to persons, to the Government, for domestic capital construction or for export (items 15, 16, 19 or 20 of Table A). Item (*h*) of the Combined Revenue and Expenditure Account must also exclude Government expenditure on goods and services for investment purposes (e.g., for the extension of post-office equipment or for the building of publicly owned dwelling-houses), in so far as these expenditures are included in Home Investment (item 19 of Table A).

There is, however, a certain degree of arbitrariness in deciding what items of Government expenditure should be regarded as investment expenditure. But the principles to be adopted for the purpose of balancing the tables are clear. If, for example, expenditure on roads and on battleships is excluded from current expenditure by the Government, then it must be included in home investment, and *vice versa*. The state may also spend money on taking over property from the private sector of the economy. It may, for example, buy land or other property from private-property owners or it may in war-time take over existing stocks of commodities from private owners. In these cases, if these expenditures are included in current Government expenditure on goods and services, home investment must be reduced by an amount equal to the net value of the property or stocks transferred from private to government ownership.[4]

The definitions of Indirect Taxes, Subsidies and Government Income from the profits of trading services (items (*b*), (*g*), and (*c*) of the Combined Revenue and Expenditure Account) also raise certain problems of definition. For example, a state monopoly may be so run as to make an abnormally large profit on the goods or services sold. If part of the price of the commodity is considered to be an indirect tax, then a similar amount must be excluded from the Government profit from trading services, with the result that items 2 and 18 of Table A will be correspondingly diminished (algebraically). If the Government runs a trading service at a loss in order – for social reasons – to sell the goods or service concerned at a low price, then this loss may *either* be deducted from Government income from profits *or* may be included in subsidies. In the latter case both items 2 and 17 of Table A will be greater than they would have been in the former case.

The distinction between direct taxes and indirect taxes also raises certain problems of definition. The fundamental distinction is a clear one. Tax payments which are not deducted from current receipts as a cost

---

[4] There is a certain lack of symmetry in column III of Table A. Current expenditure for personal consumption and for consumption of goods and services by the Government are shown separately (items 15 and 16). But investment (items 19 and 20) is divided between home and foreign investment and not, in addition, between investment financed by the Government and investment privately financed. It would, of course, be possible to divide total investment between privately financed investment and Government investment, if this were considered desirable for any economic purpose.

before determining incomes are direct taxes[5] (e.g., the Income Tax), while those which are deducted from current receipts from market sales before determining incomes (e.g., taxes on the sale of beer or tobacco) are indirect taxes. In certain cases (e.g., Excess Profits Tax), a tax which, for economic reasons, it is desired to treat as a Direct Tax, may be deducted from profits before determining income for income-tax purposes. In order to treat such taxes as Direct Taxes, in item 5 of Table A income must be reckoned before the deduction of such taxes, and they must be excluded from item 18 of Table A.

Stamp Duties may be regarded partly as Direct Taxes and partly as Indirect Taxes, or wholly as Indirect Taxes. Stamp Duties – such as stamps on cheques by businesses – are to be regarded as a business cost of production, and are deducted from current revenue to calculate income from profits. They are therefore to be regarded as Indirect Taxes. Duties such as stamps on cheques drawn by individuals for their personal expenditure may be regarded as Indirect Taxes if they are added to item 15 of Table A and regarded as an addition to the market price paid by individuals for their purchases. If, however, they are not added to the market price of consumption expenditure, they must be regarded as a Direct Tax paid out of individual's income. Stamp Duties on the transfer of property may be treated as an Indirect Tax if they are included in item 19 (*d*) of Table A, and are thus included in the 'market price' of the goods and services used for production of additions to capital assets. If, however, they are not so included, they must be treated as a Direct Tax which is paid by an investor whenever a purchase of property is made.

For certain purposes it may be convenient to divide Direct Taxes into two groups: (i) those 'paid out of income' (e.g., Income Tax and Sur-Tax), and (ii) those 'paid out of savings' (e.g., Death Duties). This division would affect Tables B and C. If in item 3 of Table B only 'direct taxes paid out of income' are deducted, then business savings (item 5 of Table B) and personal savings (item 10 of Table B) must together be increased by a similar amount, so as to represent savings inclusive of that part of savings which is used to finance the payment of 'direct taxes paid out of savings'. For example, personal savings would be reckoned as the increase in capital assets held by individuals, before deduction of the amount of assets taken away from them by the state in payment of Death Duties, as property passed from one owner to another as a result of death. In Table C a new item – 'direct taxes paid out of savings' – would have to be added to column II, since the Government would absorb part of the savings of individuals as now defined, through the capital assets which it took over from them in the form of Death Duties.

It may also be useful to draw a distinction between (i) payments of direct taxes in any period and (ii) accruing liabilities to tax payments in that period. This distinction is of economic importance, if there is any

---

[5] It is convenient throughout the Tables to treat such payments as gifts to the Government and fines paid to the Government, which are not deducted as an expense chargeable against income and which do not represent expenditure by persons on the purchase of goods and services, as Direct Taxes. A separate category for such payments could, of course, be devised if it were thought desirable.

considerable time-lag between the earning of income and the date when tax is paid on it and if the total of incomes and rates of taxation are rising or falling. The current liability of taxpayers to pay taxes out of their current incomes at current rates of tax will be considerably in excess of the actual amount of tax being currently paid, if these tax payments have been assessed on lower past incomes and at a lower rate of tax than the current rate of tax. If item 3 of Table B shows current liabilities to direct taxation, as opposed to current payments of direct taxes, then items 5 and 10 of Table B must be shown as institutional and personal savings after deduction not only of current payments of direct taxes but also of the excess of current liabilities to, over current payments of, direct taxes. In other words, savings will now be shown as the net amount of income which is free to be saved after putting aside all that is necessary to meet the current liability to direct taxation. In Table C a balancing figure must be included, and the current Budget Deficit must be reduced by an amount equal to the excess of current liabilities to, over current payments of, direct taxes. A comparison both of the Budget Deficit and of Savings before and after making this adjustment is of interest in any period of rapid fluctuation of the national income or of rates of taxation.

VI   Table D

This table shows how Foreign Investment is equal to the excess of current receipts from abroad over current expenditure abroad, and it also provides a statistical cross-check of the calculation of Foreign Investment (for item 20 of Table A). The principle of the balance of this table is self-explanatory. The sum of the increases in different foreign assets (item 4 of Table D) must be equal to the excess of current receipts of funds from abroad over current expenditure of funds abroad; for it is only through such an excess that a net sum of foreign funds may be acquired for investment abroad.

VII   Table E

From Tables A and D a table may be obtained which shows Home Investment as equal to the excess of income generated by expenditure at home over current expenditure at home. If we subtract (algebraically) items 17 and 18 of Table A from columns I and III of Table A, we obtain figures of Net National Income and Net National Expenditure at Market Prices (as opposed to Income and Expenditure at Factor Cost).[6] If we then deduct column I of Table D from column I of Table A and column II of Table D from column III of Table A, we obtain Table E. Item 1 of Table E is the difference between the total Net National Income at Market Prices and that part of it which is due (e.g., through the sale of exports) to payments received from abroad. Item 3 of Table E is the

---

[6] See pages 119–20 above.

difference between current National Expenditure at Market Prices and that part of it which is spent abroad (e.g., in the purchase of imports). The difference between these two (item 4 of Table E) is equal to expenditure on capital development at home.

VIII   Methods of Ensuring the Balance in Table A

In the preceding paragraphs and the accompanying tables an outline has been given of the main problems of definition which must be solved in order to ensure that the tables balance. There are, however, a thousand and one small problems of definition which arise in attempting to measure the individual items in the different tables. It is impossible to treat all these minor definitional problems at length; but the sort of problems which arise and the way in which they may be solved can be illustrated by means of an example.

We may consider the problem of treating the revenue and expenditure of hospitals in such a way that the balance between columns I and III of Table A is preserved. In the economic system as a whole a host of transactions are taking place which either involve the payment of money from one owner to another or may be imagined to be accompanied by such a money transaction.[7] Some of these payments of money (e.g., the purchase of consumption goods) will be recorded as part of the Net National Expenditure in column III of Table A (N.N.E.). Some of these receipts of money (e.g., the payment of wages) will be recorded as part of the Net National Income in column I of Table A (N.N.I.). Any one transaction (e.g., the transfer payment of an allowance by a father to his son) may be recorded neither as N.N.E. nor as N.N.I. A transaction (e.g., the payment of wages in a productive business) may be such that its payment is not recorded as N.N.E. but its receipt is recorded as N.N.I. Another transaction (e.g., the purchase of imported consumption goods) may be such that its payment is recorded as N.N.E. but its receipt is not recorded as N.N.I. The principle to be adopted is that as money flows round in different transactions of payments and receipts it shall be recorded alternately as N.N.E. and N.N.I. and not twice running as N.N.E. or twice running as N.N.I.

We may apply this principle to a combined revenue and expenditure account of all voluntary hospitals. Such a combined account may be presumed to contain the following items:

---

[7] An example of this latter type of transaction is the payment to (e.g.) domestic servants of part of their income in kind (e.g., in food and lodging) by their employers. If we wish to record their wages in item 4 of Table A as inclusive of their money wages and of their wages in kind, we may imagine that the employer pays to the domestic servant the whole of this wage in money, and that the domestic servant then purchases from the employer the food and lodging provided in kind. In order to preserve the balance between columns I and III of Table A, if the whole of the wages of domestic servants is included in item 4 the whole of it must also be included in item 15 as personal expenditure on domestic services.

Revenue		Expenditure	
	Transaction last re-corded as:		*Transaction next re-corded as:*
(*a*) Gifts from individuals	N.N.I.	(*f*) Food, drugs, etc., purchased	N.N.E.
(*b*) Gifts from businesses	N.N.I.	(*g*) Salaries, wages, etc.	N.N.E.
(*c*) Net income from property	N.N.I.	(*h*) Repairs and maintenance	N.N.E.
(*d*) Fees for medical services performed	N.N.I.	(*i*) Balance, being sums saved or accumu-lated by hospitals	N.N.E.
(*e*) Government grants	N.N.I. or – N.N.E.		

We must examine each item of hospitals' revenue to see whether each item when it has been received was last recorded as N.N.I. or N.N.E., and we must examine each item of hospitals' expenditure to see whether it is next recorded as N.N.I. or N.N.E.

If definitions are adopted of such a kind that the whole of the revenue and expenditure is *either* first recorded as N.N.I. and then as N.N.E., *or* first recorded as N.N.E. and then as N.N.I., the treatment is such as to preserve a proper balance between columns I and III of Table A.

(*a*)   Gifts from individuals are paid out of individuals' incomes, and the incomes from which they are paid are recorded in Table A as a part of N.N.I. So long as gifts from individuals to hospitals are not recorded in item 15 of Table A as an element of personal expenditure, this item of revenue is recorded in Table A as N.N.I.

(*b*)   Gifts from businesses are paid out of profits, which are recorded in Table A as a part of N.N.I. Since the payment of a gift from a business to a hospital is not recorded in N.N.E. in Table A, this item may also be marked N.N.I.

(*c*)   Net income from property. This item is included in item 1 or 2 of Table A, and may therefore be marked as N.N.I.

(*d*)   Fees for medical services are paid out of income (N.N.I.). If they are not recorded as an item of personal expenditure[8] in item 15 of Table A, this item must also be marked as N.N.I.

(*e*)   Government grants. If Government expenditure on grants to hospitals were included in item 16 of Table A, this item would need to be marked as N.N.E. But if we exclude this item of Government expenditure from item 16 of Table A and treat it as a transfer payment to the private sector of the economy, we must consider the sources from which the necessary revenue was raised to transfer to hospitals. If it were raised by direct taxes, from Government income

[8] They should not be recorded as an item of personal expenditure, if – as is suggested below – items (*f*), (*g*) and (*h*) which represent the actual purchases of goods and services for medical purposes are so recorded.

or from borrowing, it would come out of income (N.N.I.). If it were raised by indirect taxation it would be recorded in item 18 of Table A as −N.N.E., which for balancing purposes is equivalent to N.N.I.

(*f*), (*g*) and (*h*). These current expenditures by hospitals may be recorded as N.N.E., if they are added to item 15 of Table A as an item of personal expenditure.

(*i*) Savings of hospitals. This item, in so far as it represents expenditure by hospitals on investment in (e.g.) hospital buildings, is recorded in item 19 of Table A as Home Investment (N.N.E.). If the savings are lent to other borrowers, it is not recorded directly as investment in Table A; but the expenditure of these savings by the borrowers will be so recorded (N.N.E.).

IX The Division of the Economy into Government, Business and Personal Sectors

In the above paragraphs and the accompanying tables the economy has been divided into three sectors – Government, business and persons; and the interrelations between the income, expenditure and savings of these three parts of the economy have been examined. It would appear that this division leaves no room for the transactions of various institutions – such as clubs, charities, trade unions, etc. – which are neither Government institutions nor business institutions. In order to avoid unprofitable complications of the tables which would arise if an attempt were made to introduce a fourth sector, it is convenient to treat such institutions merely as a channel through which persons receive and spend income. The way in which this may be done is best shown by taking one such institution as an example.

We can illustrate the method by taking again the treatment of the revenue and expenditure of voluntary hospitals. All the items of hospitals' revenue (in the revenue and expenditure account of hospitals shown on page 129 above) may be treated as being recorded in personal incomes in column I of Table B, and all the items of hospitals' expenditure may be treated as being recorded in personal expenditure or savings in column III of Table B.

(*a*) and (*d*). Gifts from individuals and fees paid by individuals are paid out of the total of individual incomes included in item 6 of Table B.

(*b*) The profits from which gifts are paid by businesses to hospitals are recorded as an element of item 1 of Table B; and provided that they are not deducted in undistributed profits (item 5 of Table B), this item will also be recorded as an element of personal incomes in item 6 of Table B.

(*c*) The income from property of hospitals is recorded in item 1 of Table B; and since it is not deducted in items 3, 4 or 5 of Table B, it remains in the total of personal incomes (item 6 of Table B).

(*e*) Government grants to hospitals, being treated as an item of Government transfer expenditure, will appear in item 2 of Table B, and therefore in the total of personal incomes (item 6 of Table B).

(f), (g) and (h).   These expenditures must be recorded as elements of personal consumption (item 9 of Table B).

(i)   Savings through hospitals must then be recorded as an item of personal savings, and the increase in the various assets held by hospitals must be included in the increase in assets held by individuals for the purpose of calculating item 10 of Table B.

We are, in fact, by these means regarding gifts from businesses, grants from the Government and the income obtained from property owned by hospitals as supplements to personal incomes, which enable individuals to purchase medical services or to save through the medium of hospitals.

Table A

I *Net National Income at Factor Cost*	II *Net National Output at Factor Cost*	III *Net National Expenditure at Factor Cost*

1. Rents
2. Profits and Interest
3. Salaries
4. Wages
	6. Net output of agriculture
	7. Net output of mining
	8. Net output of manufacturing
	9. Net output of transport
	10. Net output of distribution
	11. Net value of personal services
	12. Net value of government services
	13. Net income from abroad. (cf. Table D, item 1 (d) and (e))
		15. Personal Consumption at Market Prices
		16. Current Government Expenditure on Goods and Services
		17. Government subsidies
		18. *Less* Indirect taxes
		19. Home Investment:
		    (a) Gross Home Investment in Fixed Capital
		    (b) *Less* Depreciation, Renewals, Repairs, etc.
		    (c) Home Investment in stocks
		    (d) Costs involved in transfer of property
		20. Foreign Investment

5. Total Net National Income at Factor Cost	14. Total Net National Output at Factor Cost	21. Total Net National Expenditure at Factor Cost

Table B

I *Composition of Personal Incomes*	II *Distribution of Personal Incomes*	III *Personal Consumption and Savings*

1. Net National Income at Factor Cost (Table A, item 5)
2. Transfer Incomes from the State
3. *Less* Direct Taxes
4. *Less* Government Income
5. *Less* Undistributed Profits
	7. Personal Incomes:
	  (*a*) Gross Personal Incomes below £200 per head per annum
	  Less Direct Taxes on above incomes
	  (*b*) Gross Personal Incomes £200–£500 per head per annum
	  Less Direct Taxes on above incomes etc.
		9. Personal Consumption at Market Prices (Table A, item 15):
		  (*a*) Food, Drink and Tobacco
		  (*b*) Rent and rates
		  (*c*) Clothing
		  (*d*) Travel etc.
		
		10. Personal Savings:
		  (*a*) Net increase in cash held by individuals
		  (*b*) Net increase in securities held by individuals
		  (*c*) Net increase in other assets held by individuals

6. Personal Incomes after deduction of direct taxes	8. Personal Incomes after deduction of direct taxes	11. Personal Consumption and Savings

Table B′

	I *Personal Incomes*			II *Personal Consumption and Savings*	
		Cross-reference to other items			*Cross-reference to other items*
1.	Net National Income at Factor Cost	Table A, item 5	7.	Personal consumption	Table A, item 15
2.	Transfer Incomes from the State	Table B, item 2	8.	Current Government Expenditure on Goods and Services	Table A, item 16
3.	*Less* Direct taxes	Table B, item 3			
4.	*Less* Government Income	Table B, item 4	9.	Government subsidies	Table A, item 17
5.	*Less* Undistributed Profits	Table B, item 5	10.	Government transfer expenditure	Table B, item 2
			11.	*Less* Indirect taxes	Table A, item 18
			12.	*Less* Direct taxes	Table B, item 3
			13.	*Less* Government Income	Table B, item 4
			14.	Home and Foreign Investment	Table A, items 19 and 20
			15.	*Less* Undistributed Profits	Table B, item 5
6.	Personal Incomes after deduction of direct taxes	Table B, item 6	16.	Personal Consumption and Savings	Table B, item 11

Table C

	I *Sources of Savings*		II *Uses of Savings*
1.	Personal Savings	4.	Home and Foreign Investment
2.	Undistributed Profits	5.	Budget Deficit
3.	Total Savings	6.	Total Savings

Table D

I *Income Generated by Receipts from Abroad*	II *Current Expenditure and Investment Abroad*
1. Income generated by Receipts from Abroad: (*a*) Value of home-produced exports (*b*) Value of export of services (e.g., shipping, finance, etc.) (*c*) Receipts from foreign tourists (*d*) Net Income from foreign property (*e*) Net Government Receipts from Abroad	3. Current Expenditure Abroad: (*a*) Value of retained imports (*b*) Value of imported services (*c*) Expenditure abroad by tourists 4. Foreign Investment: (*a*) Net increase in holding of gold (*b*) Increase in holding of foreign money *Less* Increase in domestic money held by foreigners (*c*) Increase in holding of foreign securities and other assets *Less* Increase in domestic securities and other assets held by foreigners
2. Income Generated by Receipts from Abroad	5. Total Current Expenditure and Investment Abroad

Table E

I *Income Generated by Expenditure at Home*		II *Current Expenditure and Investment at Home*	
	Cross-reference to other items		*Cross-reference to other items*
1. Income generated by Expenditure at Home:		3. Current Expenditure at Home:	
(*a*) Net National Income at Market Prices	Table A, item 5, *less* items 17 and 18	(*a*) Personal Consumption and Current Government Expenditure on Goods and Services	Table A, items 15 and 16
Less	*Less*	*Less*	*Less*
(*b*) Income generated by receipts from abroad	Table D, item 2	(*b*) Current expenditure abroad	Table D, item 3
		4. Home Investment:	Table A, items 19 and 20, *less* Table D, item 4
		(*a*) Net increase in domestic fixed capital	
		(*b*) Net increase in domestic stocks	
		(*c*) Costs involved in transfer of property	
2. Total Income generated by Expenditure at Home		5. Current Expenditure and Investment at Home	

9

The Precision of National
Income Estimates

By Richard Stone, D. G. Champernowne and J. E. Meade, from The
Review of Economic Studies, *vol. 9 (1942), pp. 111–124. (The
appendix, which reproduced Tables A, B and D of the previous article,
is omitted.)*

I Introductory

The purpose of this paper is to consider to what extent the statistical
precision of estimates of the national income, national expenditure, etc.,
can be improved through the use of balancing tables of the type discussed
in an earlier article entitled 'The Construction of Tables of National
Income, Expenditure, Savings and Investment' [Chapter 8 above].
Throughout the present article references are made to the various tables
set out (on pages 131–5) at the end of that article. Those tables, which set
out the logical relationships between different economic quantities,
should enable us by a series of cross-checks to improve the statistical
precision of the various estimates. Thus in Table A independent
estimates may be made of the national income, national output and
national expenditure. If they are properly defined, their values should be
equal; and the comparison of independent estimates of each of these
values should therefore provide a powerful check on their accuracy. Such
checks can be further elaborated. For example the net national income as
modified in item 6 of Table B should, after deduction of personal
consumption (item 9 of Table B) be equal to personal savings (item 10 of
Table B), for which an independent estimate may be made. This
operation should provide a further cross-check of all the estimates of the
various economic quantities measured in Tables A and B. Our present
purpose is, therefore, to examine how all the logical cross-checks
between various items in the tables may best be used to improve the
statistical precision of these items.

It will be assumed in what follows that agreement has been reached on
the nature of the estimates we wish to make, that the logical questions of
definition have been settled, and that the practical work of measurement
has been done. In particular we shall consider the scheme which was
elaborated in the earlier article, but the results will be presented in a

general form so that they can be applied to the more elaborate constructions which further research will undoubtedly bring forth.

II The Underlying Concepts

Let us suppose in the first place that we have succeeded in estimating independently the national income, output and expenditure and that we cannot distinguish between the precisions with which each has been measured. In such a case we should be justified in taking the unweighted arithmetic mean of the three measurements as the best estimate of each of the terms of the identity. On the other hand we may have good reason to believe that one of the estimates is much more reliable than the other two. It would be reasonable to give it a larger weight in arriving at the average value of the three identical terms. We must therefore consider the principles on which these weights are to be allotted.

If it could be assumed that we knew how to measure the standard errors of our three estimates the answer would be simple; the weights we should use would be the reciprocals of the squares of these standard errors. The solution so obtained would give the minimum possible value of the sum of the squares of the standardised errors. Also, in cases where the error distributions are normal this solution would satisfy the criterion of maximum likelihood. In general, however, it will not be possible in what follows to measure the standard errors in the ordinary way and we shall have to resort to setting margins of error, which will be denoted by ζ, such that they are the best estimates we can make of parameters analogous to standard errors. Accordingly they must be thought of not in terms of a particular method of measurement but as limits which, however calculated, aim at providing information as to the precision of the estimates and as being so chosen that the chances are believed to be roughly two to one that truth lies within them. Each may be thought of as the standard deviation of the hypothetical distribution[1] of all possible independent estimates of an element. The errors which give rise to this distribution may be either logical or statistical in character. The first source of error is important since we are concerned with the probability that our estimate attains the true value of what we should have measured had our definitions been faultless. In practice they may not be, so that our tables would not balance even if our measurements were perfect.

The preceding paragraph shows clearly the limitation of the method here proposed when judged from the standpoint of ordinary statistical practice. Its main defence, however, is a simple one. In adjusting the observations it would always be possible to give each the same weight as the others, leading to the unweighted arithmetic mean in the case discussed above and to more complicated expressions in other cases. By this means it would always be possible to balance the tables and to arrive at a set of consistent estimates. There is no doubt, however, that such a

---

[1] In cases where this distribution is markedly skew or bimodal, the above method of estimating the standard deviation will be especially rough.

method would waste a good deal of information available to the investigator. It is not possible to work for long on material of this kind without forming some idea of the reliability of the estimates that go into making the final totals. Some of these estimates will be accounting figures, for the geographical area required, of some element defined precisely as it should be; and they must for all practical purposes be considered accurate. Others will be production figures which are accurately known – because the commodity in question is subject to tax and illicit trade is generally recognised to be of negligible importance – multiplied by a price index which may well be accurate to the nearest farthing in a shilling. Still other cases will occur in which both prices and quantities are no more than guesses based perhaps upon a partial investigation relating to a single part of the country or on the results of a census now ten years out of date. Manifestly it would be absurd to give the same weight to all such measurements even though their precision cannot be estimated by the usual statistical methods.

In most of the applications which follow the argument would not be affected if each ζ were changed in the same proportion to, say, $k\zeta$. In these cases it does not matter if one investigator is more sanguine than another provided that he is equally sanguine about all his estimates. He would still make the best estimates possible with the information available and would increase their precision. All the way through however he would overestimate their accuracy just as a more cautious observer would underestimate it.

If sets of identities have a number of terms, and these terms are built up of elements some of which are common, we can construct equations between the elements which, apart from errors, will be exactly satisfied. The central problem is how to obtain the best estimates of the elements in these equations. A preliminary question is: what are the most economical units in which to group the elements? It would always be possible to write each equation out in full so as to include every element as a separate term. The mere arithmetical labour of solving the final equations however would be enormous. It is essential therefore that the number of terms should be kept reasonably small.[2]

There are two limits imposed on any attempt to combine the elements so as to form a certain minimum number of combinations: first, a logical

---

[2] The use of the terms 'elements' and 'combinations' or 'units' in what follows may be illustrated from Table A at the end of the article. The 'elements' are the underlying statistical atoms from which the table is constructed. Thus a statistical series of, say, the amount of coal sold for domestic consumption may have been used as one 'element' in estimating larger 'units' or 'combinations of elements' such as the total of personal expenditure (item 15 of Table A). These 'units' may in turn be used to form larger aggregates; for example, the total of net national expenditure (item 21 of Table A) is formed by a particular grouping of a number of 'units' such as total personal expenditure, Government expenditure on goods, services and subsidies, etc. These larger aggregates form the terms of certain logical identities; for we know that, if properly defined and measured, national income ≡ national output ≡ national expenditure. These identities may be written out as equations whose terms are either the basic statistical 'elements' or, more conveniently, 'units' obtained by appropriate combination of these 'elements'.

limit, and secondly, and more narrowly, a statistical limit. Beyond these the process must not be carried.

The logical limit is set by combining the elements up to the point where none of the elements combined appears separately elsewhere. Thus, all the elements in personal consumption may appear as one combination since in no table does one of them appear without all the others. On the other hand the elements in net investment cannot form less than two combinations since, while home and foreign investment are combined in Table A, foreign investment appears alone in Table D. This restriction would of course no longer apply if we were unable to make independent estimates of both foreign investment and the balance of payments, i.e. if we were unable to construct Table D.

The statistical limit prevents the combination process being carried to the logical limit for the reason that if two elements, appearing in different logical combinations, are not statistically independent it is impossible to assign them individual margins of error, since the error of their sum is greater by a common factor than it would be if they were independent. Thus suppose that part of our information on personal savings in Table B, column III is derived from the same source as that used for column II (e.g. from a family budget enquiry); then three, and not two, combinations are necessary to cover items 7 and 10 of Table B. These are the part of items 7 and 10 which has a common statistical source and the statistically independent parts of these two items.

An extension of this restriction on the process of combining elements occurs where they are no longer considered as one dimensional and have one or more dimensions in common. Thus both the wages bill (item 4 of table A) and net investment (item 19(a) of Table A) may have as components the numbers employed in the building industry. In one case, however, this figure will be multiplied by average earnings to form part of the wages bill and in the second by gross output per head to form the gross output of the building industry. The average earnings and gross output may be completely independent but the two estimates of employment will be the same. Hence the errors in the estimates of the wages bill and net investment will be correlated and a separate treatment will be required. We shall discuss this subject on pages 146–8 below.

A combination is constituted by a single element or an aggregate of elements combined according to the immediately preceding rules. Combinations are therefore logically and statistically independent, and the improvement in our knowledge from studying the tables comes about as a result of one combination appearing in more than one table (i.e. in more than one equation). The information gained from one table restricts the probable value of that combination in another table, and so a value that might have seemed reasonable in the light of a smaller number of equations can be rejected. These combinations are the smallest and most economical units with which we can operate, and will be termed units in what follows.

III The Adjustment of the Observations

We shall begin with a very simple case where we have no other information than three estimates of the value of an identity; for example the three columns of Table A, calculated in such a way that each estimate may be treated as a single unit.

Let us write a_1, a_2, a_3 for the three estimates; $\zeta_1, \zeta_2, \zeta_3$ for their margins of error; and $\varepsilon_1, \varepsilon_2, \varepsilon_3$ for the discrepancies between the best estimate we can obtain and each of the a's. For $1/\zeta^2$ write π.

We then have:

$$a_1 - a_2 + \varepsilon_2 - \varepsilon_1 = 0 \tag{1}$$

$$a_1 - a_3 + \varepsilon_3 - \varepsilon_1 = 0 \tag{2}$$

As we have three unknowns we require a third equation to determine their value. This equation must express our willingness to alter each a so as to balance the table, and must depend on the margins of error and the amount of discrepancy between the estimates. We must choose those values $\varepsilon_1, \varepsilon_2, \varepsilon_3$ out of a field e_1, e_2, e_3 which, subject to (1) and (2), make:

$$\pi_1\varepsilon_1{}^2 + \pi_2\varepsilon_2{}^2 + \pi_3\varepsilon_3{}^2$$

the minimum value of:

$$\pi_1 e_1{}^2 + \pi_2 e_2{}^2 + \pi_3 e_3{}^2 = \omega, \text{ say}$$

with respect to the field e_1, e_2, e_3.

Noting that for these values of $\varepsilon_1, \varepsilon_2, \varepsilon_3$:

$$\frac{de_2}{de_1} = \frac{de_3}{de_1} = 1$$

it can be seen that this minimisation condition yields the third equation:

$$\frac{d\omega}{de_1} = 2\pi_1\varepsilon_1 + 2\pi_2\varepsilon_2 + 2\pi_3\varepsilon_3 = 0. \tag{3}$$

Dividing by 2 and substituting from (1) and (2) we obtain:

$$\varepsilon_1 = \frac{\pi_2\,(a_1 - a_2) + \pi_3\,(a_1 - a_3)}{\pi_1 + \pi_2 + \pi_3}. \tag{4}$$

Writing A for the best estimate we can make of the identity on the information available, we have:

$$A = \frac{\pi_1 a_1 + \pi_2 a_2 + \pi_3 a_3}{\pi_1 + \pi_2 + \pi_3} = \frac{\Sigma(\pi a)}{\Sigma\pi}, \tag{5}$$

which expresses A as a weighted average of the a's with π's as weights. If in this context we may follow R. A. Fisher in calling the reciprocal of the variance 'the amount of information', then (5) expresses the fact that our best estimate is an average of the a's each weighted by the amount of information it contains.

Using the notation employed above, it is well known that the variance of the above weighted average may be written $\dfrac{\Sigma(\pi^2 \zeta^2)}{(\Sigma\pi)^2}$ whence, since $\pi = 1/\zeta^2$, we have:

$$\zeta_A = \frac{1}{\sqrt{\Sigma\pi}} = \frac{\zeta_1 \zeta_2 \zeta_3}{\sqrt{\zeta_1^2 \zeta_2^2 + \zeta_1^2 \zeta_3^2 + \zeta_2^2 \zeta_3^2}}. \tag{6}$$

At this stage it can be seen that if ζ_1 is the smallest of the ζ's, then $\zeta_A < \zeta_1$. The result depends however on the assumption that we know accurately the proportion of $\Sigma\pi$ attributable to each of the π's. We can see this by writing A in the form $\Sigma\left(\dfrac{\pi_j a_j}{\Sigma\pi_j}\right)$ and noting that $\Sigma\left(\dfrac{\pi_j}{\Sigma\pi_j}\right) = 1$ so that any overestimate of one $\dfrac{\pi_j}{\Sigma\pi_j}$ involves a corresponding under-estimate in the remainder. Under these conditions the square of the margin of error of each term in the above sum is, correct to the second order of small quantities:

$$p_j^2 \zeta_{a_j}^2 + \varepsilon_j^2 \zeta_{p_j}^2,$$

where $p_j \equiv \pi_j/\Sigma\pi_j$.

From this it follows that the square of the margin of error of A is:

$$\zeta_A^2 = \Sigma(p_j^2 \zeta_{a_j}^2 + \varepsilon_j^2 \zeta_{p_j}^2)$$

$$= \frac{1}{\Sigma\pi_j} + \Sigma(\varepsilon_j^2 \zeta_{p_j}^2). \tag{7}$$

While it is in general unlikely that $\Sigma(\varepsilon_j^2 \zeta_{p_j}^2)$ will have a large influence on ζ_A^2, this analysis shows that there is some danger of overestimating the precision of the revised estimates by assuming that the p_j are known without error.

The method so far developed in this section can be applied to more complicated cases by combining or adding the estimates. Let us suppose that a_1 and a_2 have the same meaning as above, but that a_3, the net national expenditure, is made up of two parts. The first, a_4, is equal to personal expenditure plus Government expenditure on goods and services plus net home investment plus subsidies minus indirect taxes. The second is either foreign investment, a_5, or the balance of payments, a_6.[3] We thus have apart from discrepancies:

$$a_1 = a_2 = a_4 + a_5 = a_4 + a_6.$$

We may now combine a_1 and a_2 to give an estimate which we will call a_7. Then it is clear, since $\zeta_A^2 = 1/(\pi_1 + \pi_2)$ for A derived from a_1 and a_2, that:

$$\pi_7 = \pi_1 + \pi_2. \tag{8}$$

Similarly, we may combine a_5 and a_6 to give a_8, in which case:

$$\pi_8 = \pi_5 + \pi_6.$$

Finally, we may add a_4 to a_8 to give a_9. Then:

$$\pi_9 = \frac{1}{\zeta_4^2 + \zeta_8^2} = \frac{\pi_4 \, \pi_8}{\pi_4 + \pi_8}. \tag{9}$$

We now have:

$$
\begin{aligned}
\varepsilon_1 &= \frac{\pi_7 (a_1 - a_7) + \pi_9 (a_1 - a_9)}{\pi_7 + \pi_9} \\[2mm]
&= \frac{\pi_2 (a_1 - a_2) + \dfrac{\pi_4 \pi_5 (a_1 - a_4 - a_5) + \pi_4 \pi_6 (a_1 - a_4 - a_6)}{\pi_4 + \pi_5 + \pi_6}}{\pi_1 + \pi_2 + \dfrac{\pi_4 (\pi_5 + \pi_6)}{\pi_4 + \pi_5 + \pi_6}}
\end{aligned}
\tag{10}
$$

$$
\begin{aligned}
A &= \frac{\pi_7 a_7 + \pi_9 a_9}{\pi_7 + \pi_9} \\[2mm]
&= \frac{\pi_1 a_1 + \pi_2 a_2 + \dfrac{\pi_4 \pi_5 (a_4 + a_5) + \pi_4 \pi_6 (a_4 + a_6)}{\pi_4 + \pi_5 + \pi_6}}{\pi_1 + \pi_2 + \dfrac{\pi_4 (\pi_5 + \pi_6)}{\pi_4 + \pi_5 + \pi_6}}
\end{aligned}
\tag{11}
$$

and, assuming the p_j are accurately known:

$$
\zeta_A = \frac{1}{\sqrt{\pi_7 + \pi_9}} = \frac{1}{\sqrt{\pi_1 + \pi_2 + \dfrac{\pi_4 (\pi_5 + \pi_6)}{\pi_4 + \pi_5 + \pi_6}}}. \tag{12}
$$

---

[3] a_5 and a_6 are assumed to be estimated independently. a_5 corresponds to a direct estimate (from figures of changes in foreign capital assets and liabilities) of item 4 in Table D. a_6 corresponds to the difference between items 1 and 2 in Table D.

Similarly if we are interested in a_4 we shall again have to form a_7 and a_8 and then subtract a_8 from a_7 to form a_{10}. We then have for our best estimate of a_4 and its margin of error:

$$A' = \frac{\pi_4 a_4 + \pi_{10} a_{10}}{\pi_4 + \pi_{10}} \tag{13}$$

$$= \frac{\pi_4 a_4 + \dfrac{(\pi_5 + \pi_6)(\pi_1 a_1 + \pi_2 a_2) - (\pi_1 + \pi_2)(\pi_5 a_5 + \pi_6 a_6)}{\pi_1 + \pi_2 + \pi_5 + \pi_6}}{\pi_4 + \dfrac{(\pi_1 + \pi_2)(\pi_5 + \pi_6)}{\pi_1 + \pi_2 + \pi_5 + \pi_6}}$$

and, assuming the p_j are accurately known:

$$\zeta_{A'} = \frac{1}{\sqrt{\pi_4 + \pi_{10}}} \tag{14}$$

i.e. the reciprocal of the square root of the denominator of the expression for A'.

Finally, if we write A'' for the best estimate of foreign investment $\equiv$ the balance of payments, we have, writing a_{11} for $a_7 - a_4$:

$$A'' = \frac{\pi_8 a_8 + \pi_{11} a_{11}}{\pi_8 + \pi_{11}} \tag{15}$$

$$= \frac{\pi_5 a_5 + \pi_6 a_6 + \dfrac{\pi_1 \pi_4 (a_1 - a_4) + \pi_2 \pi_4 (a_2 - a_4)}{\pi_1 + \pi_2 + \pi_4}}{\pi_5 + \pi_6 + \dfrac{(\pi_1 + \pi_2) \pi_4}{\pi_1 + \pi_2 + \pi_4}}$$

and, assuming the p_j are accurately known:

$$\zeta_{A''} = \frac{1}{\sqrt{\pi_8 + \pi_{11}}} \tag{16}$$

These expressions for A'' are naturally similar to those given for A.

The analysis so far leaves us in the position of having adjusted each unit, taking into account all the other units and the relationships implicit in the tables. For many purposes it may be necessary to revise in the same way the elements from which each unit was built up. This can be done by apportioning the difference between the original and adjusted values of the units in proportion to the variances of the elements, i.e. in proportion to the ζ^2. This may be seen as follows.

Writing $\varepsilon_1, \varepsilon_2 \ldots \varepsilon_n$ for the difference between the original and revised values of the elements in a particular unit and E for the amount by which that unit has been revised we have:

$$\varepsilon_1 + \varepsilon_2 + \ldots + \varepsilon_n = E. \tag{17}$$

The minimisation condition given earlier requires in this case that subject to (17):

$$\pi_1 \varepsilon_1^2 + \pi_2 \varepsilon_2^2 + \ldots + \pi_n \varepsilon_n^2$$

should be the minimum value of:

$$\pi_1 e_1^2 + \pi_2 e_2^2 + \ldots + \pi_n e_n^2$$

with respect to the e's.

This will be satisfied if:

$$\pi_1 \varepsilon_1 = \pi_2 \varepsilon_2 = \ldots = \pi_n \varepsilon_n = \lambda, \text{ say} \tag{18}$$

that is if:

$$\varepsilon_1 = \lambda \zeta_1^2, \ \varepsilon_2 = \lambda \zeta_2^2 \ldots \varepsilon_n = \lambda \zeta_n^2$$

where:

$$\lambda = \frac{E}{\Sigma \zeta^2}.$$

The methods described so far should be used wherever they can be applied. In practice it is never necessary for the expressions to become complicated since no step involves more than the combination or addition of units. Cases arise however where this simple method breaks down and it is necessary to resort to the more general solution set out below. This solution will be required only where we are unable to reduce our logical equations to a form wherein no two equations have two or more units in common.

Suppose we have n estimates a_j. We wish to form revised estimates:

$$A_j = a_j - \varepsilon_j \qquad j = 1, 2 \ldots n \tag{19}$$

to satisfy m logical equations of the form:

$$\sum_j c_{ij} A_j = 0 \qquad i = 1, 2 \ldots m$$

or:

$$\sum_j c_{ij} \varepsilon_j = \sum_j c_{ij} a_j = E_i, \text{ say} \tag{20}$$

(the c_{ij} being known coefficients usually 0 or 1) and the minimisation condition that, subject to (20), $\Sigma(\pi_j\varepsilon_j{}^2)$ should be the minimum value of $\Sigma\,(\pi_j e_j{}^2)$ with respect to the e_j.

The determination of the values of ε_j which satisfy this condition subject to (20) is an example of the use of the method of undetermined multipliers[4] as was the problem set out in (17) and (18) above. The steps in this solution are as follows.

The minimisation condition may be expressed in the form:

$$\left\| \begin{array}{c} \pi_j\varepsilon_j \\[1em] c_{ij} \end{array} \right\| = 0, \tag{21}$$

which may be expanded in the form:

$$\sum_j c_{k_j}\varepsilon_j = 0 \qquad k = m+1, m+2\ldots n \tag{22}$$

where c_{k_j} are functions of the π_j and of the coefficients c_{ij} of equations (20).

These $n - m$ equations together with the m formally similar equations (20) give us n equations in the n unknowns $\varepsilon_1, \varepsilon_2 \ldots \varepsilon_n$. These equations are:

$$\sum_j c_{ij} = E_i \qquad \begin{array}{l} m \text{ equations} \\ i = 1, 2 \ldots m \end{array}$$

$$\sum_j c_{kj}\varepsilon_j = 0 \qquad \begin{array}{l} n - m \text{ equations} \\ k = m+1, m+2 \ldots n \end{array}$$

We thus obtain:

$$\varepsilon_1 = \frac{\left| \begin{array}{ccccc} E_i & c_{i_2} & c_{i_3} & \cdots & c_{in} \\ 0 & c_{k_2} & c_{k_3} & \cdots & c_{kn} \end{array} \right| \quad \begin{array}{l} m \text{ rows} : i = 1, 2 \ldots m \\ n - m \text{ rows} : k = m+1, m+2 \ldots n \end{array}}{C} = \frac{C_1}{C}, \text{ say}$$

---

[4] For an account of the method of least squares see E. T. Whittaker and G. Robinson, *The Calculus of Observations* (London: Blackie & Son, 2nd edition, 1932), Chapter IX; and for an exposition of the method of undetermined multipliers, see David Brunt, *The Combination of Observations* (Cambridge: Cambridge University Press, 2nd edition, 1931), Chapter VII.

$$\varepsilon_2 = \frac{\begin{vmatrix} c_{i_1} & E_i & c_{i_3} & \cdots & c_{in} \\ c_{k_1} & 0 & c_{k_3} & \cdots & c_{kn} \end{vmatrix}}{C} = \frac{C_2}{C}, \text{ say}$$

$$\vdots$$

$$\varepsilon_n = \frac{\begin{vmatrix} c_{i_1} & c_{i_2} & \cdots & c_{i\,(n-1)} & E_i \\ c_{k_1} & c_{k_2} & \cdots & c_{k\,(n-1)} & 0 \end{vmatrix}}{C} = \frac{C_n}{C}, \text{ say} \tag{23}$$

where:

$$C \equiv \begin{vmatrix} c_{ij} \\ c_{kj} \end{vmatrix} = \begin{vmatrix} c_{11} & \cdots & c_{1n} \\ \vdots & & \vdots \\ c_{n_1} & \cdots & c_{nn} \end{vmatrix} \tag{24}$$

By expanding the determinant in the expression (23) for ε_j we can transform it into:

$$\varepsilon_j = \frac{\sum\limits_s G_{js} a_s}{C} \qquad s = 1, 2 \ldots n \tag{25}$$

where the G_{js} are the appropriate linear functions of the minors of the determinant C_j.

From this we obtain as the variance of the revised estimate A_j:

$$\frac{\sum\limits_s G_{js} \zeta_s^2}{C} = \zeta_j'^2, \text{ say} \tag{26}$$

so that:

$$\zeta_j' = \sqrt{\frac{\sum\limits_s G_{js} \zeta^2}{C}} \tag{27}$$

where ζ_j' is the margin of error of the revised estimate A_j.

The final problem which we shall consider in this section is the treatment of elements which have a common factor. Thus an estimate of the wages bill may be based, so far as the building industry is concerned, on an estimate of the number employed in that industry multiplied by their average earnings. Let us denote these factors by α and β. Again, in estimating net investment, we may require to estimate the gross output of the building industry. This may be done by multiplying the number employed, α, by the gross output per head, say, γ. It is evident that the errors in any estimates we may make of these elements, say ab and ag, will be correlated. Accordingly, we shall overestimate the precision of any estimate containing both *ab* and *ag* if we neglect this correlation. We can avoid the difficulty by proceeding as follows.

Let us suppose that we have a number of estimates $a_1, a_2 \ldots a_n$ of α; $b_1, b_2, \ldots b_m$ of β; and $g_1, g_2 \ldots g_k$ of γ. We may apply the following method, which will be developed in terms of the *a*'s and *b*'s, to each of the pair of estimates involving the *a*'s.

Let us write:

$$\alpha\beta = C + D + E$$

where:

$$C = a\beta$$
$$D = (\alpha - a)\,b$$
$$E = (\alpha - a)\,(\beta - b)$$

and *a* and *b* are the weighted averages:

$$\frac{\Sigma\pi_{a_j} a_j}{\Sigma\pi_{a_j}} \qquad j = 1, 2 \ldots n$$

and

$$\frac{\Sigma\pi_{b_i} b_i}{\Sigma\pi_{b_i}} \qquad i = 1, 2 \ldots m$$

We may then take as estimates of *C*:

$$c_1 = ab_1, c_2 = ab_2 \ldots c_m = ab_m$$

and of *D*:

$$d_1 = (a_1 - a)\,b, d_2 = (a_2 - a)\,b \ldots d_n = (a_n - a)\,b$$

and of *E*:

$$e = 0.$$

The squares of the precisions are then:

$$\pi_{c_1} = \frac{\pi_{b_1}}{a^2}, \text{etc.}$$

$$\pi_{d_1} = \frac{\pi_{a_1}}{b^2}, \text{etc.}$$

and as an approximation:

$$\pi_e = \infty$$

In the frequently occurring case where we have only one estimate a of α and one estimate b of β, we have the following simple result:

$$c = a\,b \qquad\qquad \pi_c = \frac{\pi_b}{a^2}$$

$$d = 0 \qquad\qquad \pi_d = \frac{\pi_a}{b^2}$$

$$e = 0 \qquad\qquad \pi_e = \infty\,.$$

The second pair α and γ, with α in common, may be treated in the same way, thus giving rise to estimates c', d', e'. The combined precisions will then be appropriate in view of the lack of independence of $c + d$ and $c' + d'$. It is evident that e and e' can be omitted.

IV Example: Progressive Adjustment of a Set of Observations

Suppose we have for the equations: national income (a_1) = national output (a_2) = national expenditure other than foreign investment (a_4) + foreign investment (a_5)[5] = national expenditure other than foreign investment (a_4) + the favourable balance of payments on current account (a_6), the following estimates:

$$a_1 = a_2 = 4000$$
$$a_4 = 3900$$
$$a_5 = 100$$
$$a_6 = 200$$

Provided that we can attach margins of error to these estimates it is clear that a certain amount of preliminary testing can be done. For example, if we found that $\zeta_5 = \zeta_6 = 10$, and if we had a high degree of confidence in these margins of error, then it would be most unlikely that both a_5 and a_6 were correctly defined and it would be reasonable to examine their construction critically for some error of logical treatment or misunderstanding of the figures used. If this examination left us confident of the methods employed and of the treatment of the statistical material, then it would be unlikely that this material was as accurate as we had supposed it to be. This analysis assumes that we have succeeded in assessing the ζ's correctly; if we had really overestimated or underesti-

---

[5] a_5 is assumed to be estimated from the net change in overseas assets and a_6 from the difference between current receipts and payments from and to overseas countries.

mated the ζ's by a constant proportion, it is obvious that the treatment proposed would be valueless.

Let us suppose next that we have no knowledge that enables us to distinguish between the margins of error of the five independent estimates. We can then adjust the estimates by assuming that $\pi_1 = \pi_2 = \pi_4 = \pi_5 = \pi_6 = 1$ and using equations (11), (13) and (15). Writing a' for the adjusted values we obtain:

$$a_1' = a_2' = 4012.5$$
$$a_4' = 3875$$
$$a_5' = a_6' = 137.5$$

These adjustments will not be affected as long as we retain the assumption of the equality of the π's. It is evident however that each π is most unlikely to be unity, and this can be seen as follows.

χ^2 may be regarded as the sum of the squares of the standardised residuals or, in the notation here adopted, $\Sigma(\pi\varepsilon^2)$. We thus have:

$$\chi^2 = 2 \times 12.5^2 + 25^2 + 37.5^2 + 62.5^2 = 6250.$$

So high a value of χ^2 with three degrees of freedom is extremely improbable. If we wish to see what value of $\pi = \pi_1 = \pi_2 = \pi_4 = \pi_5 = \pi_6$ would lead to acceptable results, we may replace 6250 by n, the number of degrees of freedom, and solve for π. Tables of χ^2 show that with n degrees of freedom the value of χ^2 will exceed n about as often as not. This balance becomes more perfect the larger is n.

Putting $\chi^2 = 3$ in place of 6250, we obtain:

$$\pi = \frac{\chi^2}{\Sigma\varepsilon^2} = \frac{3}{6250} = 0.00048$$

whence $\zeta = 46$ approximately.

This provides us with a reasonable value for the margin of error of the estimates on the assumptions adopted so far, and one which is consistent with observation.

We may next suppose that we can form a more accurate estimate of each of the π's. Let their values be:

$$\pi_1 = \pi_2 = \pi_4 = \pi_5 = 0.0004 \quad \text{or} \quad \zeta_1 = \zeta_2 = \zeta_4 = \zeta_5 = 50$$
$$\pi_6 = 0.0025 \qquad\qquad\qquad \zeta_6 = 20$$

Again on the assumption that there is no error in the proportions $\pi_j/\Sigma\pi_j$ we can easily adjust the observations by using equations (11), (13) and (15). Writing A for these adjusted values we obtain:

$$A_1 = A_2 = 4026.4$$
$$A_4 = 3847.5$$
$$A_5 = A_6 = 178.9$$

Considering these to be the true values, χ^2 works out at 5.288 for the original estimates ($a_1 = a_2 = 4000$, $a_4 = 3900$, $a_5 = 100$, $a_6 = 200$), so that, with $n = 3$, $0.1 < P < 0.2$; thus our estimates of the margins of error do not appear significantly small in comparison with the discrepancies between the observed and 'true' values.

On the same assumptions we can calculate the margins of error of the A's. Writing Z for these adjusted values and Π for the corresponding precisions, we obtain:

$$Z_1 = Z_2 = 29 \qquad \Pi_1 = \Pi_2 = 0.00118$$
$$Z_4 = 31 \qquad \Pi_4 = 0.00104$$
$$Z_5 = Z_6 = 18 \qquad \Pi_5 = \Pi_6 = 0.00308$$

It will be seen that these values show a considerable gain in accuracy as a result of the adjustment. The apparent gain however overstates the true position since it is based on the assumption that the margin of error of each $p_j = \pi_j/\Sigma\pi_j$ is zero. The fact that this is unlikely to be the case must now be taken into account. To do this we require estimates of the margins of error of the p_j. Each ζp_j will in nearly all cases be both less than p_j and less than $1 - p_j$. Hence by putting each ζp_j equal to p_j or $1 - p_j$ (whichever is the less) we shall certainly not understate the influence of these margins of error. On this basis we obtain:

$$A_1' = A_2' = 4025.6 \qquad Z_1' = Z_2' = 37 \qquad \Pi_1' = \Pi_2' = 0.00073$$

$$A_4' = 3848.8 \qquad Z_4' = 41 \qquad \Pi_4' = 0.00061$$

$$A_5' = A_6' = 176.8 \qquad Z_5' = Z_6' = 22 \qquad \Pi_5' = \Pi_6' = 0.00210$$

In this example the adjustment does not appreciably affect our original estimates of the A's. But it does show that the neglect of the uncertainty in our estimates of the p_j may have led us to underestimate the margins of error of our final estimates by as much as 25 per cent.

V   Conclusions

This paper represents an attempt to solve a practical problem: given consistently defined estimates of national income, expenditure, savings, investment, etc., how are we to use all the information that they contain to improve the original estimates and assess the accuracy of the finally adjusted values. Seeing how difficult it is to make the original estimates and how useful it is to have a complete set that is consistent, it would be manifestly absurd to disregard information contained in the inter-relations of the variables.

What we have done is to give an account of a public method which certainly does not eliminate all private elements of intuition. The subjective factor of interpretative judgement was fully described at an early stage. It would have been pleasing if this could have disappeared altogether, but the data do not permit of such an intellectual purification. This being so, it would be silly to object that nothing is gained by going through the discipline of these calculations on the ground that our last state is not much better than our first. It is decidedly preferable to adopt a method which minimises the 'intuitive element' and which makes our thinking as independent of inspired guesswork as possible.

We may sum up therefore by saying that we have tried to develop the following:

(1) A method for setting out systematically and reducing to a minimum number of units the elements derived from observation.

(2) A method for adjusting these estimates, each of which is subject to error, based essentially on the theory of least squares and its application to conditional observations. We have tried to deal with this in as general a way as possible though we have also indicated a simpler method which can be applied to many practical cases. The crucial point of this analysis is the application of the concept of standard errors – or margins of error as they have here been called – to estimates the variances of whose error curves cannot in general be measured though they can be assessed.

(3) A method for obtaining a measure of the increase in accuracy in our estimates of the units due to using the information contained in the interrelations of the variables.

(4) A method for deciding whether or not the order of magnitude of margins of error is reasonable.

10

National Income and Expenditure

By J. E. Meade and Richard Stone. Meade and Stone's pamphlet was first published by Oxford University Press in 1944. The fifth and subsequent editions were written by Richard and Giovanna Stone (London: Bowes & Bowes, 1961–1977).

I Introduction

There was published last April for the fourth year in succession an official paper containing estimates of the national income and expenditure.[1] At first sight this White Paper with its elaborate tables of figures may appear too formidable and complicated a document to repay the attention of the uninitiated. Yet, as the Chancellor of the Exchequer has shown in recent Budget speeches, these estimates of national income and expenditure have formed one of the chief bases in the formulation of the general lines of the community's economic and financial policy in war-time. Such estimates show, for example, how rapidly the total income of the community is rising or falling; how that income is divided among wages, salaries, profits, rent, etc.; how income is spent, paid in taxes or saved by individuals; how national expenditure is divided among such objects as expenditure on personal consumption, expenditure for government purposes, expenditure for new capital equipment in this country or the acquisition of capital abroad. These figures cover, in fact, all the broad aspects of the whole community's housekeeping; and it is for this reason probable that they will continue to play an important part in the post-war world. The citizen who wishes to understand the central economic problems of the war-time or of the post-war economy must have some knowledge of these figures.

II What is the National Income?

What then *is* the national income? We all know, broadly, what we mean by an individual's income. He may receive it as a wage or a salary from his work, as a profit from his business, as interest or rent from his physical property, or from his ownership of securities such as government debt, or

[1] An Analysis of the Sources of War Finance and Estimates of the National Income and Expenditure in the Years 1938 to 1943, Cmd 6520, April 1944.

as an old-age pension or unemployment benefit from the state or from a public fund. Is the national income merely the sum of all the personal incomes of all the private individuals in the community?

Let us be clear from the outset that there are many admissible ways of defining the national income, and that there is nothing absolutely right or wrong about any of these definitions. The national income must be measured according to the definition which is most suitable for the particular purpose in view. The essential thing is to realise that there are many ways of defining the national income, to make sure exactly how it is defined in each case, and to choose the most suitable definition for any particular purpose. For example, if we wish to consider a problem concerning the way in which private individuals as a whole use their incomes for personal consumption, for tax payments, or for saving, we shall want to consider a national income which is just simply the sum of personal incomes. This total of all personal incomes, which we will call 'personal income before tax', amounted in the United Kingdom in 1943 to £7,708 million.

But there are some elements of income which never get distributed to individuals at all. Chief among these, in most modern communities, are the undistributed profits of business firms and corporations, and the direct taxes levied on business profits. Such concerns make a profit; but only a part of this profit is distributed in dividends to the individual owners of the concern; the rest is either paid in taxation to the state or is saved directly by the concern and used for the extension of the concern's capital equipment or for the building up of its reserves of securities and cash. For certain purposes it is useful to define the national income in such a way as to include these undistributed profits as well as the total of personal income. For example, they are liable to taxation as well as the profits and other forms of income which are distributed to individuals. If we wish, therefore, to consider the rates of taxation which are necessary to raise a given revenue for the state, we must consider as our basic national income for taxation purposes personal income before tax *plus* undistributed profits (or impersonal private income before tax). This we will call 'private income before tax'. In 1943 impersonal private income before tax amounted to £995 million, so that private income before tax was £8,703 million.

For the consideration of personal habits of saving and spending, including the payment of taxes of all kinds, we are concerned with personal income before tax; for the consideration of tax revenue we are concerned with private income before tax. But there is yet another fundamental purpose for which we may wish to make use of estimates of the national income. The national income may be so defined that it measures the total money value of all the goods and services produced by the community in a given period of time. For, if we exclude from our income concept all receipts that do not accrue from the production of goods or services, and if we include all receipts that do so accrue, we shall have a measure of the value of the output of all goods and services. Such a concept is, clearly, fundamental. If we wish to study potential standards of living in the community, we must interest ourselves precisely in this;

for standards of living can be maintained only from the community's output of goods and services; or if we wish to study fluctuations in economic activity and in unemployment, the basic problem is to discover what has happened, or is likely to happen, to the community's total output of goods and services.

How does the private income before tax differ from the total of all income received from the production of goods and services? In the first place, it covers a large range of incomes – called transfer payments – which represent not payments for the production of goods and services, but transfers of income through the medium of the state or a similar public body from one set of individuals to another. The two main classes of transfer payments in this country are interest paid on the national debt and social security payments – such as unemployment benefit and old-age pensions – which are financed by levying taxes or compulsory contributions from those in work or below a certain age to make income payments to those out of work or above a certain age. This form of income, which amounted to £628 million in 1943, must be excluded, if we wish to estimate the total income received in wages, salaries, profits, interest and rent for the production of goods and services. Second, private income before tax does not cover income from property owned by the state. Rent accruing to local authorities from municipally owned houses or the profit accruing to the state or to local authorities from the operation of the Post Office or other publicly owned services, are examples of such income. It is not included in private income before tax since it accrues neither to private individuals nor to private business concerns; it is paid directly to the public authority concerned and can be used to finance some part of that public authority's expenditure. Nevertheless, since it is received from the production of goods and services, income from property owned by the state, amounting to £97 million in 1943, must be included in any estimate of the total national income accruing from the production of goods and services. Such an estimate is, therefore, derived from the estimate of private income before tax by subtracting all transfer payments and by adding government income from property. The resulting estimate is called the 'net national income at factor cost'. For 1943 it is estimated at £8,172 million.

It is necessary to explain why the national income, when defined in this way so as to estimate the total income accruing from the current production of goods and services, is said to be at factor cost. The phrase *at factor cost* is to be contrasted with the phrase *at market prices*. Factor cost represents what producers receive for the sale of their products, and market price what consumers pay for them. The difference between the two is the net amount of indirect taxes or similar charges which the state skims off the market value before it gets through to the producers. Indirect taxes are taxes, such as excise duty on beer and tobacco, which are levied on the sale of goods and services; they are, therefore, included in the market price which the consumer pays for the goods or services, but do not accrue as an income to the factors of production – labour, enterprise, capital, and land – which produce the goods or services in question. Thus, when the consumer pays a market price of 2s 4d for twenty cigarettes, approximately 1s 8½d goes in an indirect tax to the Exchequer and 7½d is left over to be paid in wages, profits, rent, etc., to the producers or salesmen of cigarettes and the materials which enter into them. At market prices the packet of cigarettes is worth 2s 4d; but it contains a factor cost of only 7½d. The net national income at factor cost enumerates the income actually received by the factors of production for the current production of goods and services. If we want to estimate the total market value of the goods and services produced, we must add the total of indirect taxes to the net national income at factor cost. On the other hand, subsidies, which raise the income of producers above the amount paid by consumers, must be subtracted. The resulting estimate is called the net national income at market prices. In 1943 the net excess of indirect taxes over subsidies was £1,283 million and the net national income at market prices was £9,455 million.

But why are these estimates said to be net? The difference between *net* national income and *gross* national income depends upon the treatment of depreciation allowances and other similar charges necessary to make good and to replace capital equipment as it wears out. A company's profit may be said to be reckoned gross if it is calculated without making any deduction for the maintenance of the company's capital assets, and to be reckoned net when allowance has been made for such a deduction. In the net national income (whether at factor cost or at market prices) profits are reckoned net of depreciation allowances, etc.; and the total of such depreciation allowances, amounting to some £400 million in 1943, must be added in order to obtain an estimate of the gross national income whether at factor cost or at market prices.

The relationships between these different estimates of national income are illustrated in Table I on page 156 by means of figures for the United Kingdom and for the United States of America.[2] The main purpose of this table which illustrates five possible meanings of the term national income is to show that there are many possible ways of defining the national income, and that it is important to choose for the purpose in hand the most suitable definition. Above all, it is necessary to know, when one discusses an estimate of the national income, what that estimate does or does not include. The use of national income estimates will often darken rather than enlighten public discussion until these precautions are observed.

But the table already illustrates the interesting information which may be obtained from a careful consideration of national income estimates. — How much more important transfer payments are in the United Kingdom (with its heavy burden of national debt and its well-developed social services) than in the United States; in 1943 transfer payments represented

---

[2] The official estimates for the United States, published by the US Department of Commerce, are not computed on precisely the same basis as the estimates for this country. For the purpose of comparison, therefore, it has been necessary to rearrange the American figures so as to achieve as much comparability as possible. While this comparison is not thought to be misleading it has been necessary to round off the American figures to the nearest US $500 million. Undue importance should not be attached to a close comparison of minor component items.

Table I   *Various Definitions of National Income*

		United Kingdom £,000,000		United States $000,000,000	
		1938	1943	1938	1943
1	*Personal income before tax*	4,779	7,708	68½	145½
	plus Undistributed profits before tax	259	995	½	20
2	*Private income before tax*	5,038	8,703	69	165½
	less Transfer payments	−478	−628	−3½	−5½
	plus Government income from property	44	97	—	—
3	*Net national income at factor cost*	4,604	8,172	65½	160
	plus Indirect taxes and similar levies net of subsidies	621	1,283	8½	15
4	*Net national income at market prices*	5,225	9,455	74	175
	plus Allowances for maintenance, depreciation, etc.	340	400	7	10
5	*Gross national income at market prices*	5,565	9,855	81	185

as much as 7 per cent of private income before tax in the United Kingdom, while they represented only 3 per cent of private income before tax in the United States. — How relatively unimportant government income from property is in both these countries; the balance would presumably be very different if one could obtain comparable figures for a country such as the USSR where the greater part of property is communally owned. — Between 1938 and 1943, as a result partly of higher prices, and partly of increased economic activity due to the demands of war, the net national income at factor cost in current money terms rose by 77 per cent in the United Kingdom and by 144 per cent in the United States; the greater rate of increase in the United States illustrates the fact that in 1938 the American economy was slack and depressed, and had much greater possibilities of expansion than the British. — What an important role indirect taxes play in the economies of both countries; in 1943 it appears that, on the average over all goods and services, no less than 14 per cent of the market price went in indirect taxes in the United Kingdom, while the corresponding proportion in the United States was 8½ per cent.

Here are a few of the observations and problems immediately suggested by estimates of total national income for two countries for two years. Sooner or later we should obtain comparable estimates for a large number of countries for a number of consecutive years; these estimates in turn are capable of being broken down in great detail – personal income, for example, being divided among different income groups to show the inequalities of income distribution, and the net national income at factor cost being divided among the main sources of income to show the varying distribution of income between wages, salaries, profits, interest and rent. In addition to this we have still to analyse the whole field of national and of personal expenditure. We are as yet only at the threshold of the subject. When these figures have been fully explored on a comparable basis for many countries over many years, we shall be equipped with a statistical description of the world's economy, incomparably more informative than anything that has hitherto been contemplated.

III National Outlay and National Expenditure

The preceding paragraphs have been devoted to a description of the various meanings of the term national income and to estimates of the national incomes of the United Kingdom and the United States of America. National income is concerned with the earnings or current receipts acquired by individuals or institutions. But in addition to income there are two other fundamental ideas to be described and estimated – namely outlay and expenditure.

Outlay describes how the recipients of income dispose of that income. For example, each individual in the course of a year must dispose of all his income for that year in three main ways: – he can spend part of it on goods and services for consumption, he can pay part of it over to the state in taxation, and he can save the remainder of it. Thus there corresponds to personal income before tax a personal outlay taking the form of personal consumption, personal tax payments and personal saving.

But for certain purposes we are interested to know, not how people dispose of their incomes, but from what source they earn that income. Income is itself generated by some form of expenditure. Thus, the income earned in wages, salaries, profits, interest, and rent for the production of goods and services is derived from the sale of such goods and services – or, in other words, from the expenditure of the purchasers of those goods and services.

It is not possible here to develop this subject by setting out and analysing all the possible definitions of national outlay and of national expenditure. We will consider, by way of illustration, only one of the more important definitions of national outlay and one of the more important definitions of national expenditure – namely (i) personal outlay (corresponding to personal income before tax) and (ii) net national expenditure at factor cost (corresponding to net national income at factor cost).

IV Personal Outlay and Personal Income before Tax

Table II (on page 159) illustrates for the United Kingdom and the United States the composition of personal income and the outlay from this income either on personal consumption, tax payments, or saving. For the United Kingdom, comparable estimates are unfortunately not yet available for years before 1938; but a comparison of 1938 with 1943 is interesting in that it reveals the changes that have been brought about by the development of a war economy. For the United States, on the other hand, comparable estimates go back to 1929; and the years shown in the table are chosen so as to illustrate the effect of the great depression (between 1929 and 1933), the recovery from this depression (between

1933 and 1937), and the developments in the American economy (between 1938 and 1943), which occurred during the phase of economic preparation for war, economic aid to the Allies and actual American belligerency.

It is unnecessary to comment in any very great detail on the constituent items of personal income before tax in the United Kingdom. Broadly speaking, personal income may be derived from three sources: – (i) from rent, royalties, interest, dividends, etc., accruing from property or from business interests; (ii) from wages and salaries, including in this context the pay and allowances of the armed forces, obtained from work; and (iii) from miscellaneous transfer payments of a social security character. These three sources are distinguished in Table II. The largest is the category of wages and salaries, and the smallest is that of social security transfer payments. In 1938 wages were appreciably less than twice as great as salaries; in 1943 they were appreciably more than twice as great as salaries. Personal income from rent, interest, profits, etc., constituted 33 per cent of total personal income in 1938, but only 27 per cent of total personal income in 1943. It must be remembered that all these personal incomes are measured before deduction of direct taxes which are payable by individuals (e.g. income tax, sur-tax and death duties), so that these percentages must not be taken to indicate the proportion of spendable income which is left to various classes of individuals for their enjoyment after the payment of taxes. If allowance were made for this fact, the proportion accruing to owners of property and similar interests in particular would be appreciably lower. On the other hand, it must also be remembered that these figures do not include undistributed profits or direct taxes (such as E.P.T. [Excess Profits Tax]) which are levied on profits before they are ever distributed to individuals. For this reason, the figures of personal receipts from rent, interest, profits, etc., fall appreciably below the actual income accruing from land, capital and property in general before it is reduced by taxation or by being 'ploughed back into the business'.

In the course of the war (or rather between 1938 and 1943) personal income before tax in the United Kingdom rose by more than £2,900 million. This rise was due to the expansion of employment and of economic activity in general as a result of the demands of war, and to the rise in money wage-rates and other rates of remuneration which have occurred during the war. Small transfer payments in the aggregate have been little changed; for an appreciable increase in pension payments has been offset by the fall in payments in respect of unemployment and the relief of poverty which the economic activity of war has brought about. Income received by individuals from rent, interest, profits, etc., has increased by nearly 30 per cent or by some £450 million; and the operation of excess profits taxation has prevented what would otherwise have been a much greater increase. Salaries and wages including the income of the armed forces are up by almost 85 per cent or by about £2,450 million.

How has this increase of personal income reacted upon personal outlay? The lower half of Table II illustrates these developments. In

Table II   *Personal Income before Tax and Personal Outlay*

		United Kingdom £000,000		United States $000,000,000				
		1938	1943	1929	1933	1937	1938	1943
1	Net rent, royalties, interest (including national debt interest) and profits received by persons	1,594	2,059	32	17	26	22½	39½
2	Salaries, wages and other labour income (including the income of the armed forces)	2,907	5,361	52½	29½	47	43½	103
3	Other personal income (e.g. pensions, unemployment benefit, etc.)	278	288	½	1½	1½	2½	3
4	Personal income before tax	4,779	7,708	85	48	74½	68½	145½
5	Personal expenditure on consumption at market prices*	4,138	5,049	73	43½	64	60	92½
6	Direct taxes and similar levies paid by persons	472	1,169	3	2	4	4	20
7	Personal saving	169	1,490	9	2½	6½	4½	33
8	Personal outlay	4,779	7,708	85	48	74½	68½	145½

* This item includes the sums shown in item 28 of Table II of Cmd 6520 as well as those in items 27 and 29.

1938, 87 per cent of personal income was used for consumers' purchases of goods and services, 10 per cent for the payment of direct taxes, and only 3 per cent for personal saving. Increased taxation, the rationing of consumption goods, shop-shortages of unrationed goods, and the patriotic motives of the savings campaign have changed all this; and the private citizen in 1943 bought less consumption goods and services and thus saved productive resources and the financial and shipping facilities necessary for importation, releasing these resources for the essential needs of war. By 1943 the proportion of personal income devoted to consumers' purchases had fallen to 66 per cent, while the proportions devoted to the payment of taxes and to saving had risen to 15 per cent and to 19 per cent respectively. Another way of illustrating the same essential development is to say that of the £2,930 million of increase in personal income, £700 million went in increased direct taxes, £1,320 million was devoted to increased saving, and only £910 million was used for increased consumers' purchases. But even this does not fully represent the magnitude of the change-over to war. Many items of consumers' expenditure – drink, tobacco, entertainments, and the goods now subject to purchase tax – have had their prices deliberately raised by increased indirect taxes, as a means of raising revenue for the war effort. This has, in part, been offset by the payment of subsidies by the state to keep down the price of certain essentials; but when a balance between increased indirect taxes and subsidies is struck, there is found to be an increase of £460 million in net receipts of indirect taxes specifically on consumption goods and services. In addition, there are other indirect taxes falling on output generally which are largely met out of personal income. Thus, of the £2,930 million increase in personal income, less than £450 million represents increased expenditure on consumption goods at factor cost, while at least £1,160 million represents increased taxes (direct and indirect) and £1,320 million represents increased savings.

But, it may be argued, there should have been no increase at all in consumers' purchases. Rather, there should have been a reduction in such purchases, so that not only the whole increase of personal income might be devoted to the war effort, but something more might have been taken from the pre-war level of consumption for use for war purposes. This has of course happened – and on a considerable scale. The figures in Table II, it must be remembered, are figures of money expenditure; and when allowance has been made for the rise of money prices which took place between 1938 and 1943, as a result of increased costs of production (such as increased wage-rates), of increased prices of imported goods, and of increased indirect taxation, it seems that total real consumption fell by slightly more than 20 per cent in this period. For various reasons even this figure may underestimate the amount of belt-tightening which the ordinary civilian consumer has undergone. Thus, the figures do not allow fully for reductions in the quality of many consumption goods (such as the reduction in the size of the daily newspaper); they include all the forms of expenditure (such as for essential foodstuffs and the rent of existing houses) which either cannot be much reduced, or which it is pointless to reduce; and they cover a full allowance for the consumption of food, clothing, etc., by the armed forces, a form of consumption which constitutes an essential part of the war effort. Inessential personal consumption must have been cut by very much more than 20 per cent.

The following table (Table III on page 161) shows the way in which the total of personal consumption in the United Kingdom was distributed among the main heads of expenditure in 1938 and 1943.

One of the most striking features of this table is the very high proportion of total expenditure which is devoted to the primary necessaries of food, rent, etc., fuel and light, and clothing, even in years of peace; for example, in 1938 as much as 57 per cent of total personal expenditure was on these items, of which food is by far the largest. Another outstanding feature in the table is the very great increase in expenditure on drink and tobacco during the war, an increase which accounts for just over two-thirds of the increase in the total of personal consumption. This increase is not, of course, mainly due to the consumption of increased quantities of drink and tobacco, but to the greatly increased rates of indirect taxation. Of the total of £1,053 million

Table III* *Composition of Personal Expenditure on Consumption in the United Kingdom, 1938 and 1943 (£ million)*

	1938	1943
Food		
Household expenditure		
Bread and cereals, etc.	165	225
Meat, bacon, etc.	275	273
Fish, fresh and canned	43	35
Oils and fats	98	57
Sugar, preserves and confectionery	108	105
Dairy products	189	203
Fruit, fresh, canned and dried	79	35
Potatoes and vegetables	84	126
Beverages not included below	54	46
Other manufactured foods	33	37
Other personal expenditure	70	122
Beer, wines, spirits and other alcoholic beverages	268	565
Tobacco	174	488
Rents, rates, and water charges	491	510
Fuel and light	203	240
Other household goods	274	184
Clothing	447	447
Travel, including privately owned vehicles and their		
running expenses	289	227
Other services†	556	588
Other goods, including the income issued in kind to		
HM Forces and Auxiliary Services	238	536
Personal expenditure on consumption at current		
market prices	4,138	5,049

* This table is based on Table B, p. 5 of Cmd 6520 and the additional information contained in *Hansard* for May 26th and August 3rd, 1944.

† Including the sums shown in item 8, Table I, p. 19 of Cmd 6520.

spent in 1943 on this item, approximately two-thirds represented indirect taxation.

It has already been pointed out that between 1938 and 1943 the direct tax payments of persons rose by £700 million, while personal saving rose by £1,320 million. The distinction between direct taxes and saving may appear at first sight a perfectly clear and unequivocal one: direct taxes are the payments (such as income tax and sur-tax) which an individual must make to the state out of his income, while saving is the excess of an individual's income over his consumption and his direct tax payments, and represents the amount of money which, in the course of the year in question, he adds to his capital in the form of an increased cash holding, an increased bank deposit, or a purchase of savings certificates or other securities or capital assets. There are, however, two reasons why the distinction between direct taxes and saving is rather more blurred than this would suggest. In the first place, since the introduction of the system of income tax deferred credits, whereby a certain amount of present income tax payments are pledged by the government for post-war repayment to the individual tax-payers, the following question arises. Should the payments of this part of income tax be considered to be the payment of a direct tax or the accumulation of an additional (though compulsory) saving? The answer is, of course, arbitrary. For some purposes (e.g. if one is considering how much the individual is now required to pay over to the state), these payments should be regarded as direct taxes; for other purposes (e.g. if one wishes to consider what are the current additions to individuals' post-war accumulations of purchasing power), they are better treated as saving. In Table II they have, in fact, been treated as direct tax payments. The White Paper from which these figures were taken indicates that for 1943 the income tax payments due for repayment after the war amounted to £170 million.

Second, there is a more subtle overlap between direct taxes and saving. A clear distinction must be drawn between direct tax *liabilities* and direct tax *payments*. Direct tax payments are simply the payments of direct taxes which are actually handed over in the period in question to the tax collector. Direct tax liabilities, on the other hand, are the liabilities arising in the period in question in respect of the income earned in that period, for the payment of direct taxes at some future date. In a period – such as that between 1938 and 1943 – when money incomes were rising rapidly, these two quantities may diverge very considerably. For the actual tax payments being paid over now will have been assessed on the lower incomes of some previous period, with the result that current tax payments will be considerably lower than current tax liabilities. This is more than an academic point. The figure of direct taxes of £1,169 million for 1943, shown in Table II, represents tax payments actually made in 1943. Direct tax liabilities incurred in the course of that year were in fact some £1,250 million, i.e. some £80 million greater than the sums actually paid over to the tax collector in the course of the year. For this reason part of the £1,490 million of personal saving set aside in the course of the year, more than £80 million, was in effect a pledge against future tax payments and only the remainder (£1,407 million) really represented an unpledged addition to individuals' capital assets.

The right-hand part of Table II gives similar information for the United States of America. There is no room here to comment fully upon the developments which it shows in the war years between 1938 and 1943. The same broad movements are shown as in the case of the United Kingdom – an expansion of personal income as a result of the increased activity of a war economy, and a relative expansion of direct tax payments and of saving at the expense of personal consumption as a result of the diversion of resources to war purposes.

The American figures, however, enable us to make estimates of personal income and expenditure for the years before 1938, and in particular to cover the period (1929 to 1933) of the great depression and the period (1933 to 1937) of recovery from this depression. The movements of the American figures during this period are of more than just historical interest. They illustrate, in an extreme form, the sort of variations in economic activity which may take place in a peace-time economy.

Between 1929 and 1933 in current money terms personal income in the USA fell by no less than 44 per cent, from $85,000 million to $48,000 million. As a result of this collapse of consuming power, consumers' purchases of goods and services fell by 40 per cent (from $73,000 million to $43,500 million), direct personal taxes and similar payments fell by 33 per cent (from $3,000 million to $2,000 million) and personal saving fell by 72 per cent (from $9,000 million to $2,500 million). As Table II shows, there was subsequently a marked recovery of incomes and, in consequence, of consumers' purchases, tax payments, and saving between 1933 and 1937.

V   Net National Income and Expenditure at Factor Cost

In the preceding paragraphs, we have discussed changes in personal income and the reaction of such changes upon personal consumption, payments of personal taxes, and personal saving. In the remaining paragraphs we shall discuss the net national income at factor cost (i.e. the fundamental concept of the national income as representing the value of the community's net output of goods and services), and the way in which aggregate demand for, and expenditure upon, the community's goods and services generates this national income.

Table IV gives figures of the net national income, and of the net national expenditure at factor cost for the United Kingdom and the United States. It has already been explained (page 154 above) that the net national income at factor cost differs from the total of personal income in that (i) it excludes transfer payments (such as interest on the national debt and unemployment benefit) which individuals receive other than by way of a direct participation in the production of goods and services, and (ii) includes impersonal and public income (such as undistributed business profits or profits from state-owned enterprise) which accrue from the production of goods and services, but are not paid over to individual persons. Thus it represents all the earnings in the production of goods and services of the factors of production (such as labour, capital, or land) which are engaged in production. The first half of Table IV shows the total of this national income, divided among the earnings of the different factors of production, i.e. among the rent of land and buildings, the profits and interest of other forms of capital and business enterprise, the salaries of salaried workers, the wages of wage-earners, and the remuneration of members of the armed forces.

The total national income, defined in this way, has risen very substantially in the course of the war – from £4,604 million in 1938 to £8,172 million in 1943. This increase is due to two main factors – (i) the expansion of total economic activity which has come about as a result of increased hours of work, the reduction and virtual elimination of unemployment, the absorption of unoccupied persons (particularly women) into economic activity and the armed forces, and in general the greater effort put into war production, and (ii) the rise in money wage-rates and the rates of money pay of workers in general, and the rise

The Collected Papers of James Meade

Table IV   *Net National Income and Expenditure at Factor Cost*

	United Kingdom £000,000		United States $000,000,000				
	1938	1943	1929	1933	1937	1938	1943
1 Rent of land and buildings	380	384	34	12	25	22	57
2 Profits and interest	1,317	2,427					
3 Salaries	1,099	1,366					
4 Wages	1,728	2,909					
5 Pay and allowances of the armed forces	80	1,086	52½	29½	47	43½	103
6 Net national income at factor cost	4,604	8,172	86½	41½	72	65½	160
7 Personal expenditure on current goods and services at market prices	4,138	5,049	73	43½	64	60	92½
8 Expenditure by public authorities on goods and services	837	5,187	10	8½	13	13½	90½
9 Private net investment at home	305	−126	8½	−4½	3½	−½	−6
10 Net investment overseas	−55	−655	½	—	—	1	−2
Less							
11 Excess of indirect taxes and similar levies over subsidies	−621	−1,283	−5½	−6	−8½	−8½	−15
12 Net national expenditure at factor cost	4,604	8,172	86½	41½	72	65½	160

in money profits which has accompanied the insatiable demands which the war makes upon the community's limited resources of men, materials, and machines. An extremely rough and approximate idea of the relative importance of these two factors may be obtained by realising that, while money wage-rates have risen by 37 per cent between 1938 and 1943, the net national income at factor cost has risen by as much as 77 per cent. If the rise in money wage-rates was typical of the rise in rates of money reward which have accrued to all factors of production as a result of the increase in money values between 1938 and 1943, this would leave almost a 30 per cent rise in national income to be explained, not by increased rates of money pay, but by increased economic activity of one form or another. It must be remembered that a large part of this increase represents the expansion of the armed forces. The calculation is necessarily very rough because, for example, variations in their rates of remuneration are not reflected in the 37 per cent.

It is interesting to observe the typical pre-war distribution of the national income between rent, profits and interest, salaries, wages and the remuneration of the armed forces, and the effect which the development of the war economy has had upon this distribution. The following figures (Table V) show the proportion of the national income accruing to each of these classes in 1938 and 1943.

Table V *Percentage of Net National Income at Factor Cost Accruing to Various Factors of Production in the United Kingdom*

	1938	1943
	(per cent)	
Rent	8	5
Profits and interest	29	30
Salaries	24	17
Wages	37	35
Income of the armed forces	2	13
Total	100	100

Salaries and rent are in many cases more or less stabilised by contract or by convention (or in the case of rent by war-time legal restrictions), and they have therefore risen relatively little. Wages and profits, on the other hand, have increased rapidly as increased demand has brought more men and machines into active full-time employment, and as the rates of pay of wage-earners and of capital have been driven up by the high demand of war-time. It must be remembered, however, that the figures in Tables IV and V illustrate the payments to the various factors of production before deduction of direct taxation, and that a large part of increased profit has, in fact, been absorbed by excess profits taxation of 100 per cent of the rise in profits above the standard level.

It must always be remembered that the national income figures shown in the top half of Table IV are figures of money income. Variations in these figures do not, therefore, necessarily correspond to variations in total real income, since a rise or a fall in these figures may be explained in part at least by a corresponding rise or fall in prices. This is well illustrated by the pre-war figures of national income given for the United States in Table IV. Between 1929 and 1933, such was the decline in the general level of demand for goods and services in the United States, that the American national income (corresponding to the value of goods and services produced in the United States) fell by 52 per cent from $87,000 million to $41,500 million. A decline in aggregate buying on this scale naturally led not only to large-scale unemployment and a depressed level of economic activity, but also to a decline in prices. In fact, of the decline of rather more than one-half in the American national income in money terms during these years, approximately one-quarter may be explained by a fall in the general level of prices, leaving rather more than one-third to be explained by a reduction in output. In the United Kingdom, between 1929 and 1932 (the worst year of the depression in this country), the national income in money terms declined by only about 15 per cent, an amount not greatly in excess of the fall in prices, so that real income was only slightly diminished. In fact, what happened was mainly an interruption in the continued rise of real income which would otherwise have occurred.

The constituent elements of aggregate national expenditure are shown in the lower half of Table IV. These items enumerate all the elements of that demand for the community's goods and services which give rise to the income of the labour, enterprise, capital and land earned in their production. First, among these elements of demand may be placed consumers' expenditure on goods and services for personal consumption. A consumer's expenditure on bread or on a hair-cut represents so much income for the baker and wheat-farmer or for the barber and his suppliers. Second, expenditure by the central government, by local authorities or by other public authorities on communal services also gives rise to income; state payments to policemen or to soldiers provide the income of policemen and soldiers, and state payments in respect of police-stations or tanks give rise to income in the building industry or in the engineering shops. The figures given for expenditure by public authorities on goods and services, in Table IV, show the enormous influence which war expenditure by the state has had on this figure, which rose from £837 million in 1938 to £5,187 million in 1943. This figure does not include all state expenditure; for example it excludes expenditure on transfer payments (such as national debt interest, old-age pensions, etc.) which does not appear in the top half of Table IV as part of the income of the factors of production engaged in producing goods and services, and which, to preserve the balance of the table, must therefore be excluded from the total of national expenditure enumerated in the bottom half of the table.

The two items discussed in the previous paragraph – namely the consumption of goods and services by individuals and the consumption of goods and services by public authorities – normally constitute the two main sources of expenditure which generate the income of the producers of goods and services. But in addition to the demand for goods and services for private or public consumption, there may be a demand for goods and services for the purposes of adding to the capital equipment of the community. Item 9 in the lower half of Table IV, called net investment at home, makes room for this element of income-generating expenditure on goods and services. A typical example of such expenditure is the money which a business borrows and spends on machinery or building in order to extend its productive plant. It must, however, be realised that it is not all expenditure on machinery, building, etc., which must be included here, but only that part of such expenditure which is not covered by depreciation allowances to replace or repair existing capital equipment as it wears out or becomes obsolescent; in other words, we are dealing with net, and not with gross, home investment.

At first sight it might appear that, in order to preserve the balance between national expenditure and national income in Table IV, *all* expenditure on capital equipment should be included, regardless of whether it is for the replacement of existing equipment or for the further expansion of such equipment; for every demand for machinery generates income in the machinery-producing trades, regardless of the purpose for which the machinery is purchased. Nevertheless only the excess of expenditure on capital equipment over and above current depreciation allowances should be included in investment in item 9 of Table IV. The reason is that expenditure on personal consumption (item 7 of Table IV) and government expenditure on goods and services (item 8 of Table IV) cover the total cost of producing goods and services for these purposes; or, in other words, they already cover not only the wages, salaries, profits, etc., earned in producing these goods, but also the depreciation allowances put aside to make good the capital equipment of productive industry. These two items of national expenditure already, therefore, account for an amount of expenditure on capital goods, corresponding to the depreciation allowances set aside to cover the repair and replacement of existing capital equipment. Similarly, on the income side the earnings of those who repair or replace machinery are included, but the depreciation and similar allowances from which they are met are excluded from profits and rent.

We have now covered the first three items of net national expenditure at factor cost – personal consumption (item 7 of Table IV), expenditure on goods and services by public authorities (item 8 of Table IV) and expenditure on goods and services for net investment in new capital equipment at home (item 9 of Table IV). But two important adjustments must be made to the net national expenditure before it will balance the net national income at factor cost. In the first place, we have not yet made any allowance for overseas trade or similar economic transactions with countries abroad. The figures for personal and government expenditure and for net home investment include many forms of expenditure on imported goods and services; but the demand for foreign goods does not generate income at home, and we must therefore exclude all expenditure on imports from the bottom half of Table IV. On the other hand, the figures of national expenditure so far exclude all expenditure by foreigners on British exports of goods and services; and such expenditure must therefore be added to the national expenditure, since it – just like any other form of demand for British products – generates income in the United Kingdom. The net result is that we must add the net excess of exports over imports of goods and services, to the preceding items of national expenditure in the bottom half of Table IV. This is done in item 10 of Table IV, called net investment overseas. This item is so called because the net excess of current overseas receipts over current overseas payments measures the extent to which a country is adding to its net capital claims on other countries. Just as net investment at home measures the value of the additions to the country's capital equipment at home, so net investment overseas measures the extent of its additions to its net capital claims on other countries.

The final adjustment, which needs to be made, is to subtract (as is done in item 11 of Table IV) all items of indirect taxation and of similar charges from the preceding items of national expenditure. Reference has already been made above (pages 154–5) to the reasons why this has to be done. The previous items of national expenditure measure expenditure at current market prices. But not all of this generates income for the factors of production which produce the goods and services in question; for some part is skimmed off in indirect taxes, which are paid over to the state. Expenditure at market prices must, therefore, be reduced by the total of indirect taxes net of subsidies before it can be equated to the national income at factor cost which it generates.

We may turn now to the significant changes which occurred in the national expenditure between 1938 and 1943 as a result of the war. The outstanding feature is, as one would expect, the great increase in government expenditure on goods and services, from £837 million in 1938 to £5,187 million in 1943. This is an increase of no less than £4,350 million. How was this increase financed?

In real terms the war effort has been met in four essential ways: – (i) by increased employment and effort and technical innovations leading to a higher real output of goods and services, (ii) by restricting personal consumption of inessentials, (iii) by refraining from adding to the capital equipment of peace-time industries and occupations (e.g. by ceasing to build new dwelling houses), and by running down stocks of inessential capital equipment at home, (iv) by an excess of imports over exports of goods and services far larger than is normal in peace-time, financed by the sale of gold and foreign assets, i.e. by running down net capital claims on other countries. All these four movements are illustrated by the figures in Table IV. (i) The great increase in the net national income at factor cost between 1938 and 1943 (i.e. in the value of the community's aggregate output of goods and services) has already been discussed above (page 163). Here it may be recalled that between 1938 and 1943 real economic activity, apart from any rise in money prices, may have increased by as much as 30 per cent. (ii) The reduction in real consumption has already been discussed in an earlier connection (pages 158–9); here it is necessary only to recall that, although money expenditure on consumption at market prices has risen in these years, real consumption has probably been cut by at least 20 per cent, when account is taken not only of the rise in retail prices but also of the decline in the quality of some goods and services. (iii) The extent to which we have financed the war by living on our capital, both at home and abroad, is shown by the high negative figures of home and overseas investment for 1943 (items 9 and 10 of Table IV). The change from positive investment at home of £305 million in 1938 to negative investment, or disinvestment, at home of £126 million in 1943 meant that, so far as privately financed investment was concerned, we were financing the war effort to the extent of £305 million by refraining from adding to our stock of capital equipment at the 1938 rate and to the extent of £126 million by refraining from replacing our existing stock of capital equipment as it wore out. (iv) The high figure of disinvestment overseas of £655 million in 1943 shows that to this extent we had an excess of overseas payments for imports of goods and services, or for overseas costs of the war, over our receipts from the sale of goods and services and other current sources overseas. We were financing this excess of imports by realising gold or other overseas assets, or by incurring increased capital liabilities to overseas creditors.

The great change in the structure of our economy, due to the requirements of war expenditure, is illustrated by the following figures [Table VI] of the proportion of our net national income at factor cost (i.e. of our net productive effort) in 1938 and 1943 which was devoted to personal expenditure, government expenditure and net investment at home and overseas. The fact that the investment figure was highly negative in 1943 means, of course, that the total expenditure on the other two items was greater than 100 per cent of the total resources available from the currently produced national income, and that these resources had to be supplemented by the community drawing on its internal and external capital resources.

Table VI   *Percentage of Net National Income at Factor Cost Devoted to Various Items of National Expenditure. United Kingdom – 1938 and 1943**

	1938	1943
	(per cent)	
Personal expenditure	77	49
Government expenditure	18	60
Investment at home and overseas	5	−9
Total	100	100

* For the purpose of this table, the excess of indirect taxes over subsidies specifically on consumption goods and services is deducted from personal expenditure and the remainder is deducted *pro rata* from personal expenditure, government expenditure and investment at home and overseas.

The American figures of national expenditure given in the bottom half of Table IV for 1938 and 1943 may be compared with the British figures for the same period to show the experiences of the two economies in this period of war mobilisation. There is no space here to undertake this comparison, which must be left to the reader. The American figures of national expenditure for the great depression from 1929 to 1933, and for the subsequent recovery from 1933 to 1937, are also given in the bottom half of Table IV. They underline the large decline in home investment in new capital equipment in the United States during the depression, and they show how – with the fall in spendable income – there was an accompanying severe contraction in expenditure for personal consumption. Between 1929 and 1933, expenditure on personal consumption fell by 40 per cent and net home investment became negative. These figures illustrate the way in which national expenditure estimates might be used to analyse peace-time fluctuations in demand. The problems of policy raised by the need for greater economic stability are, however, another matter. All that statistical estimates of national income and expenditure can do is to increase our understanding of what is happening or is likely to happen to the various appropriate estimates of national expenditure and national income, so that policy may be formed with a truer appreciation of the real significance of economic events.

11

Internal Measures for the Prevention of General Unemployment

The Economic Section of the War Cabinet Offices began to consider problems of post-war reconstruction early in 1941; Meade wrote the first of a long series of memoranda on the subject in February. The following paper, the first of those of which Meade chose to retain a copy when he left the Section in 1947, is dated 8 July 1941. It was widely circulated outside the Section and was one of the first documents to be considered by the inter-departmental Committee on Post-war Internal Economic Problems, which began meeting in November 1941 (Meade Papers 3/2, Public Record Office T230/13 and 66, CAB87/54).

Introductory

1   In the work for post-war reconstruction the prevention of large-scale unemployment is of the greatest importance. It is an essential condition for any policy devised to raise general standards of living. It would remove the greatest single factor in causing social insecurity. It would further remove one of the main economic obstacles to the development of sound international relations; for widespread unemployment is an important factor in disturbing world peace, both directly through its repercussions on international economic relations and indirectly through the internal social and political unrest which it causes.

2   Unemployment takes many forms.
  (i)   There is an inevitable nucleus of temporarily unemployed persons who are passing from one job to another.
  (ii) In certain conditions there is likely to be a concentrated body of unemployment in special areas or special occupations due to a decline in particular industries which may result from changes in industrial technique or in the demand for particular products.
  (iii) But, in addition to this, there are from time to time, periods of general unemployment in which labour is unable to find work in the majority of occupations and industries. The world-wide depression which developed after 1929 affords a striking example of such general unemployment.

Unemployment of the first two types ((i) and (ii) above) requires special measures for its solution: the labour market must be so organised that employers seeking new hands are promptly brought into contact with workmen seeking employment; facilities must be made available for the transference and retraining of labour; and arrangements may be made for the localisation of new industrial enterprises as near as possible to the sources of unemployed labour. These problems will be very important in the immediate post-war period of reconstruction. For it will be necessary to transfer men and other economic resources from the armed forces and from munitions production to production for reconstruction and for civilian needs; and at a somewhat later date, it will be necessary to transfer resources from rehabilitating the damaged capital equipment of the country to more normal peace-time occupations. In order that these transfers may be carried out as smoothly as possible, care must be taken to ensure the greatest possible mobility of men and resources between different occupations.

3   This Memorandum is, however, confined to the problems of general unemployment of type (iii) above. That is to say, it is confined to a discussion of the ways in which the general level of demand for labour may be maintained at a height sufficient to absorb the unemployed into new occupations as quickly as they can be transferred to them. This also will be of great importance in the post-war period, in order to ensure that there are alternative jobs to which the men demobilised from the armed forces and from the munitions industries may be transferred, and, at a somewhat later stage, to ensure that there are alternative jobs awaiting those who have been engaged on the work of physical reconstruction of war-damaged property. It will remain of importance in the more normal subsequent years, in order to ensure that there are alternative jobs for men who become unemployed in any industries which decline because of changes in the technique of production or in the demand for various products. In short, the solution of the problem of general unemployment is a necessary condition for the successful reduction of other types of unemployment. For unless there is a high demand for labour over a wide range of expanding occupations, there will be no alternative field of employment for labour transferred from declining industries.

4   This Memorandum is confined to the internal aspects of economic and financial policy for the prevention of general unemployment. It is clear, however, that a successful solution of this problem depends upon the adoption of an appropriate external economic and financial policy. Some reference is made below (§ 25 to 28) to the way in which commercial and monetary relations with other countries will affect the success of our internal policy. A full discussion of these external problems would, however, raise a large number of controversial issues which are only in part relevant to the problem of unemployment; and for this reason it has been thought better to postpone their discussion to a subsequent paper.

Industrial Policy and Unemployment

5   General unemployment can be avoided only by maintaining the demands for goods and services in general at a sufficiently high level, in order that any decline in the demand for labour in particular occupations may be offset by a corresponding increase in the demand for goods and services of other kinds. But in order that a policy of this kind may be successful, it is necessary that industrial organisation and policy should be of a kind that will readily allow an expansion in the production of those goods and services for which demand increases. Whether a large number of industries are brought under public control or left under private management, industrial regulations of a restrictive character must be avoided. A few examples of such restrictive measures will serve to illustrate their effect. An industry may be regulated in such a way that restrictions are placed upon the entry of new firms into the industry, that the production of the existing firms is limited by quotas, or that new plant may not be installed in the industry; certain lines of agricultural production may be regulated in such a way as to limit the output of particular agricultural products; and trade unions, by limiting the number of apprentices in a given trade, may restrict output in that trade. The extension of such controls over a wider and wider field of industry makes it more and more difficult for unemployed labour and unemployed resources of every kind to find new employment. The trend of pre-war industrial policy was greatly to extend the range of such restrictive measures; and considerable pressure may be expected after the war by interested groups to maintain many of the war-time controls in order to extend such restrictions over a still wider field. Such a development would most seriously endanger the success of the measures suggested below for preventing general unemployment in the post-war period.

Fluctuations in General Trade Activity

6   Experience has shown that modern industrialised communities are liable to recurrent periods of decline in general trade activity, during which there is a large increase in general unemployment. Trade depressions have a number of features in common. There is a general decline in expenditure on new works of capital construction and, in consequence, a decline in incomes and in expenditure on goods for personal consumption; this generates a further decline in the demand for goods and services. Prices and profits fall, and unemployment grows throughout the economic system. Similarly, periods occur from time to time when an abnormally high level of expenditure upon capital construction inflates money incomes and the money demand for goods and services even beyond the point which is required to absorb the available productive resources. In such a period of excessive trade boom, prices and profits are unnecessarily inflated.

7   In the immediate post-war period demobilisation and reconstruction

will raise problems in many ways comparable with those of a more normal peace-time 'trade cycle'. On the one hand the reduction of government expenditure as the armed forces are demobilised and as the production of munitions is decreased will release labour and, by reducing the spendable incomes of those engaged in the armed forces and in the munitions industries, may threaten to lead to a vicious spiral of general trade depression. On the other hand, the desire immediately to spend money on rebuilding damaged property, on plant that has not been fully maintained during the war, on the reconstruction of depleted stocks, and – in the case of private individuals – on clothes, furniture, motor-cars and other durable consumption goods whose supply has been seriously restricted during the war, may lead to an immediate post-war reconstruction boom.

8   It is impossible to foretell with certainty how these factors will operate in the immediate post-war period; but it is probable that a considerable reconstruction boom will develop immediately after the war and that this will be followed by the threat of a serious depression. Such was the sequence of events after the war of 1914–18. After this war, as a result of the much more extensive character of war damage, there will be a much wider field for immediate post-war reconstruction; and at the same time demobilisation may well be delayed by the need to maintain large forces in Europe for some time after the war. For these reasons the immediate reconstruction boom may be more marked, and the subsequent threat of depression may more nearly coincide with the actual demobilisation of the armed forces and of the munitions industries than after the last war.

9   The work of physical reconstruction of buildings, industrial plant and shipping after the war may take a number of years. A considerable part of this work will be controlled and financed either directly by the state or from funds controlled by the state under War Damage Insurance or under the return of 20 per cent of Excess Profits Tax for the rehabilitation of industrial plant. The transition from this period of reconstruction to the more normal period, which will follow it, may threaten to lead to a serious depression of trade activity. As the need for expenditure on physical reconstruction is reduced, it will become necessary not only to transfer labour and other productive resources to alternative use for the production of different types of capital equipment or of additional supplies of consumers' goods, but also to stimulate the money demand for these new goods and services. Means must therefore be found:–

(a)   so to plan the physical reconstruction of war damaged property that expenditure on it tails off as gradually as possible,
(b)   to initiate new alternative forms of capital construction, and
(c)   to stimulate the demand for consumers' goods.

The measures by which this may be achieved are discussed in the following paragraphs (10–20).

The Maintenance of the General Demand for Labour

10   The measures which are appropriate for maintaining the general level of demand for goods and services, and so for labour, may be enumerated under the following heads:–

(a)   Banking policy
(b)   Investment policy
(c)   Consumption policy, and
(d)   Budgetary policy.

11   *Banking Policy*. The banking system can, by changing the terms upon which new funds may be borrowed, discourage new capital construction in times of excessive boom and encourage new capital construction in times of general depression. For this purpose the banks can raise or lower the rates of interest charged by them on advances and loans of various kinds. The market for other loans may also be influenced through the sale or purchase by the banks of securities in the capital market. A sale of securities by the banks reduces the amount of money available in the market, lowers the price of the securities sold, and thus raises the cost of borrowing funds in the capital market for new capital construction. Conversely, a purchase of securities by the banks increases the supply of money, raises security prices and reduces the cost of borrowing new funds for capital construction. There is general agreement among economists on these principles of banking policy; but some differences of opinion exist concerning the degree to which monetary policy will be effective if unaccompanied by other measures.

12   *Investment Policy*. In so far as the state can directly control works of capital construction, these should be reduced in times of boom and expanded in times of depression. Additional works of capital construction employ directly a certain number of workers in a period of general depression; but, in addition to this, the spending of the incomes of those engaged on the 'public works' maintains the demand for other goods and services and thus generally stimulates economic activity. The widest possible range of capital construction should be regulated on this principle by the Government. This involves in particular the regulation of capital expenditure by local authorities, by public utilities and by the railways. Between 1926 and 1937 expenditure on the construction and maintenance of fixed capital by the Central Government, the local authorities, the public utilities and the railways accounted for more than one-half of the total of such expenditure for the whole of Great Britain; and the proper planning and timing of this block of capital expenditure would, therefore, constitute a very powerful weapon of control over the total capital expenditure of the community. The adoption of this policy depends, therefore, primarily upon arrangements between the Central Government and the local authorities, public utilities and railways (a) of a financial character which will enable capital expenditure to be properly timed and (b) of an administrative character

which will enable plans of capital development to be prepared in advance with a view to obtaining the maximum amount of flexibility in the timing of their execution.

13   The control of the Central Government over the timing and planning of capital works might possibly be extended even beyond the range indicated in the previous paragraph. In particular, it may be possible for the Government in times of depression (a) to adopt measures to encourage capital investment by private enterprise and (b) to stimulate works of capital development in other areas of the world (such as the Colonial Empire) – works which would not otherwise be undertaken and which would lead to the employment at home of unemployed resources in the production of the necessary capital equipment.

14   This policy of timing expenditure on capital development in such a way as to even out general fluctuations in trade activity cannot succeed unless the projects of capital development are planned well ahead. Experience has shown the difficulty of improvising additional schemes of capital development during a depression; for time must be spent in making the neccesary plans, in obtaining control over the land needed for public works, and in initiating the desired expenditure. Success depends upon planning ahead the maximum number of schemes of development in such a way that flexibility is preserved in the actual dates at which the development will be undertaken. In this way a reserve of capital works may be built up against future periods of general depression.

15   The immediate post-war situation must be controlled by a proper planning and timing of the reconstruction of damaged property and of the rehabilitation of industrial equipment which has not been fully maintained during the war. This control should so work that, if there is an excessive reconstruction boom immediately after the war, the less essential projects of reconstruction can be postponed and the work thus spread over a longer period. In particular the payment of compensation for war-damaged property and the repayment of the 20 per cent of Excess Profits Tax for the reconstitution of industrial capital should be carefully controlled and timed with this object in view. The proper planning and timing of such reconstruction on the lines indicated above, involve, as in the case of the more normal works of capital construction discussed above (paragraph 12), financial and administrative arrangements between the Central Government on the one hand and local authorities, owners of private property and business concerns on the other hand, in order to ensure that the plans of rebuilding, etc. are worked out well in advance and that the actual expenditure is properly timed. The transition from the period of post-war capital reconstruction to that of more normal conditions will require careful planning, in such a way that, while expenditure on reconstruction is gradually reduced, new projects of capital development can be initiated and the demand for consumption goods can be stimulated.

16   *Consumption Policy*. Measures may be taken in a period of general depression directly to stimulate the demand for consumption goods, and in periods of excessive boom to restrain such demand. Those devices may take many forms:–

(a)   Purchases of consumption goods through hire-purchase finance might be controlled in such a way that they were made difficult in times of boom and made easy in times of depression. In the absence of such control, hire-purchase is liable to exaggerate trade fluctuations; for consumers are likely to engage in commitments in excess of their incomes in good times, and are then obliged to restrict their purchases in order to repay debt in bad times.

(b)   A direct stimulus to consumption in times of general unemployment may be provided through the reduction of direct taxes levied on income or of indirect taxes levied on the purchase of goods and services, or through the payment of direct money allowances by the state to consumers. Conversely, expenditure on consumption goods in times of excessive boom may be restrained through the raising of direct taxes on income or of indirect taxes on the purchase of goods and services.

(c)   If, as a result of the long-period development of the social services, it is decided to extend the scope of Government expenditure (e.g. by the introduction of a scheme of family allowances) these new schemes should be introduced at a time of slack trade (when it is desired to stimulate the demand for goods and services) rather than at a time of good trade.

(d)   For some time after the war it will be necessary to maintain a number of the war-time controls over the purchase of consumption goods – such as the schemes for the rationing of foodstuffs and clothing. For, so long as scarcities of raw materials and similar difficulties prevent the supply of these goods on a considerably larger scale, rationing will be required to ensure the continuation of an equitable distribution of the scarce supplies. Within limits it may be possible to time the relaxation and removal of these restrictions on consumption in such a way as to stimulate the demand for consumption goods when this is most required from the point of view of the unemployment position.

17   Deferred credits for income tax, as suggested in the recent Budget proposals [the Keynesian proposals of *How to Pay for the War* (London: Macmillan, 1940) incorporated in Sir Kingsley Wood's Budget of 7 April 1941], provide an example of financial action of the type suggested above (paragraph 16 (b)), since they are financed out of increased direct taxes payable in the war period of full employment and may be repaid in a post-war period of slack trade. Their repayment will, however, need to be carefully timed. It should be postponed, as far as possible, in any immediate post-war period of reconstruction boom, and should be concentrated in any subsequent period in which a general trade depression threatens the community. It is worth while considering whether a

scheme of this kind – involving the accumulation of deferred credits out of direct taxes in periods of active trade and their repayment to individuals in periods of depression – should not become a permanent feature of financial policy after the war.

18   *Budgetary Policy*. If the policies suggested above (paragraphs 12–17) are adopted, an increase in state expenditure and a reduction in revenue must be foreseen in periods of slack trade, and a reduction of expenditure and an increase in revenue in periods of good trade. In other words, debt must be incurred in years of depression; whereas in periods of active trade, when revenue is increased and state expenditure is contracted, debt must be repaid. The policy of preserving an annual balance of revenue and expenditure with a constant provision for debt redemption must give place to a policy of concentrating debt repayment in years of active trade.

19   The post-war problem of the national debt and of its repayment will, however, be a particularly serious one for a number of reasons.

(a)   At the close of the war the national debt will be much greater than before the war; and though war borrowing will probably be continued at the present relatively low rates of interest or even at still lower rates, there is bound to be a considerable increase in the total interest payable on the debt. The high rates of taxation needed to meet the interest on debt after the last war may have exerted a depressing influence on business enterprise and so have intensified the problem of general unemployment. For this reason it is desirable to repay the debt, if repayment can be financed in such a way as not itself to exert a seriously depressing influence.

(b)   There is no reason to believe that the repayment of debt arranged solely on the lines suggested in the previous paragraph will be sufficient. Indeed periods in which an excess of Government expenditure over revenue is desirable to reduce general unemployment may well be more frequent than periods of active trade in which debt may be repaid through an excess of revenue over expenditure. In other words, budgetary policy devised solely on the lines indicated in the previous paragraph might lead to a continued growth in the debt, which will already be inflated and which it will be desirable on other grounds to reduce.

(c)   In the post-war period there are certain special reasons for believing that public borrowing may have to continue for a number of years. During the period of physical reconstruction it is probable that a large part of the necessary capital expenditure will have not only to be controlled but also to be financed by the state; and further considerable sums of public expenditure of one kind or another may be required to ease the transition from a war-time to a peace-time economy. During this period public borrowing may prove inevitable. The later transition from physical reconstruction to a more normal peace-time economy may well require the initiation of new alternative forms of public capital development and of measures to stimulate the demand for consumers' goods and services. This second period of transition will again require heavy state expenditure and fairly low levels of taxation on income and on consumption, if a general depression is to be avoided.

20   There are certain methods by which this dilemma (between the need to reduce the burden of debt and the need to expand expenditure and to reduce taxation in order to stimulate trade activity) can be resolved.

(a)   In the first place, it is important that in the post-war period a deflation of money prices and of money incomes below the level ruling at the close of the war should be avoided as far as possible. For a deflation of money prices and of money incomes raises the real burden of the fixed national debt and necessitates higher rates of income tax on the reduced level of money incomes in order to meet the interest payable on it. Indeed, there is something to be said for the continuation of a moderately rising trend of prices and money incomes for some time after the war as a means of mitigating the burden of fixed debt (see paragaphs 21–22 below).

(b)   A capital levy at relatively high rates might be imposed on individuals' capital wealth – with suitable exemptions for small property and with suitably progressive rates of levy – in order to redeem, by one surgical operation, a large proportion of the outstanding national debt.

(c)   More generally, debt can be continuously redeemed out of revenue without threatening to cause general unemployment, if a form of tax can be found the imposition of which does not restrict expenditure on goods and services by the taxpayer. Such a tax is exemplified by a tax imposed on, and paid out of, individuals' capital assets. For, while a tax which is paid out of income reduces the demand for consumption goods and services, a tax which is paid out of personal holdings of capital assets does not reduce the demand for consumption goods; and if a proper banking policy is adopted (on the lines indicated in paragraph 11 above), conditions in the capital market can be kept easy, so that there are no financial obstacles to prevent industry from borrowing for expenditure on capital development. It is important, therefore, to discover what forms of taxation are most likely to satisfy these criteria, and to rely upon these taxes as far as is practicable for the raising of revenue.

The General Level of Prices

21   The measures suggested above (paragraphs 10–20) should serve to prevent violent fluctuations in the general level of demand for goods and services and so in the prices offered for such goods and services. The same instruments of control may be used, not only to prevent marked fluctuations in the price level, but also to determine the long-period trend

of money prices; for a somewhat more restrictive policy must be adopted over the average of good and bad years if a gradual deflation of prices rather than a gradual rise in the price level is desired.

22   A deflation of prices is liable to lead to serious unemployment, if the fall in selling prices is not accompanied by an equally rapid rise in productivity; for a fall in selling prices leads to an increased real burden on productive enterprise in the form of costs which are either fixed in money terms (as in the case of interest on debt) or are not capable of an easy or rapid downward revision as selling prices fall (as in the case of money wage-rates). For this reason, after the present war every effort should be made, by the means suggested in paragraphs 10–20 above, to prevent any serious deflation of the general level of prices. Indeed there is much to be said for the continuation of a moderate upward trend of prices in the years following the war. (See paragraph 20(a) above.)

Wages Policy and Unemployment

23   We do not advocate attempts to reduce general unemployment by variations in the general level of wage-rates. But in certain circumstances an adjustment of particular wage-rates may be useful as a means of reducing unemployment; for example, to allow wage-rates in depressed industries in a particular area to fall might help to stimulate new industrial activity in that area, or a reduction of wage-rates (as of other costs) in important constructional industries might, in certain circumstances, hasten the recovery of industry from depression.

24   There is, however, one way in which an unwise wage policy might seriously hinder the prevention of general unemployment. The underlying idea of the proposals made above (paragraphs 10–20) is that measures should be taken to increase the total money demand for goods and services whenever there is general unemployment. These measures will give rise to the danger of a vicious spiral of inflation, if widespread demands for increased wage-rates arise during a period in which considerable general unemployment still persists. For any attempt to expand the total demand for goods and services in a period of rapidly rising wage-rates would involve a continual inflation of money expenditure, money prices and money wage-rates. In fact, in order to prevent a runaway inflation, the attempt to reduce general unemployment would have to be abandoned. A wage policy which refrains from insisting upon rapidly rising wage-rates, except in so far as increases in productivity permit, is for this reason a necessary condition for a successful effort to prevent such unemployment.

International Economic Policy and Unemployment

25   An outstanding feature of trade fluctuations is the fact that they

usually occur more or less simultaneously in most of the economically developed nations. The world-wide character of the great depression after 1929 was a striking example of this fact. For this reason it is of importance that international action should be taken to control general fluctuations of trade activity. The most important countries should co-operate in the timing of national policies on the lines indicated above in paragraphs 10–20, designed to restrain the general level of monetary demand for goods and services in times of world-wide boom and to stimulate such demand in times of world-wide depression.

26   There are great difficulties in carrying out a national policy on the lines indicated in paragraphs 10 to 20 above in the absence of such international co-operation. If, in a period of world-wide depression, the United Kingdom alone attempted to maintain and expand the internal money demand for its goods and services, while other countries made no such attempt, the United Kingdom would endanger the balance of its commercial and financial relations with the rest of the world. The maintenance of incomes and prices in the United Kingdom combined with the fall of incomes and prices abroad would stimulate the British demand for imported goods, while the foreign demand for British exports declined. The payment made for the excess of imports would necessitate the loss of the United Kingdom's reserves of gold and of foreign exchange, unless measures were taken to offset the unfavourable balance of trade. Such measures might take the form of imposing special restrictions upon imports or of allowing the exchange value of sterling to depreciate.

27   For these reasons the adoption of purely national policies against trade depressions endangers any international agreements to remove import restrictions and to stabilise the exchange value of the different national currencies. Public opinion will almost certainly insist that a national policy of the kind necessary to diminish unemployment, should not be abandoned for the purpose of preserving international commercial and monetary agreements. It is, therefore, of the utmost importance to achieve international co-operation in the planning and timing of national monetary, budgetary and investment policies for the control of trade fluctuations. In default of effective international action on these lines, internal policy designed to prevent general unemployment must necessarily be less effective, and its prosecution would involve the adoption of national measures (either of exchange control, of exchange fluctuations or of restrictions on imports) to control the balance of payments.

28   In the immediate post-war period the United Kingdom together with a number of other countries will be faced with a strain upon its balance of payments with other countries. For the income from our overseas investments will have fallen as a result of the mobilisation and sale of a large part of our overseas assets, and our export trade will have fallen to a low level. At the same time it will be necessary to import considerable quantities of goods necessary for reconstruction, for the reconstitution of

depleted stocks and for the expansion of civilian production. The problem of bringing the United Kingdom balance of payments into adjustment will, for these reasons, require careful attention, and the solutions adopted must be such as not to impede the internal measures against unemployment suggested above. This particular problem lies outside the scope of the present memorandum.

Summary of Problems Requiring Further Investigation

29   The main problems of policy, which require further detailed study in order to apply the general principles of policy outlined above, are the following:-

(a)   The measures necessary to ensure an easy transference of labour between occupations, industries and regions (*paragraphs 2 and 3*).

(b)   The extent to which the forms of industrial control and organisation which are likely to exist after the war are open to the objections raised in *paragraph 5*.

(c)   The extent to which capital expenditure by the Central Government, the local authorities, public utilities and the railways can be planned and timed in the way suggested in *paragraphs 12–15* and the administrative and financial arrangements which would be necessary for this purpose.

(d)   The extent to which the Central Government should, and the means by which it could, influence the timing and planning of capital expenditure by private enterprise (*paragraph 13*).

(e)   The extent to which capital works in overseas territories (such as the Colonial Empire) could be planned on the same principle (*paragraph 13*).

(f)   The administrative and financial arrangements necessary to ensure that physical post-war reconstruction by local authorities, public utilities, private enterprise and property-owners in general is planned well in advance and is timed properly (*paragraph 15*).

(g)   The measures, if any, which are desirable and practicable to control hire-purchase in the way suggested in *paragraph 16(a)*.

(h)   The extent to which the lowering and raising of rates of taxation on income and on goods and services might be used as a means of controlling private expenditure on goods and services (*paragraph 16(b)*).

(i)   The possibility of introducing the system of deferred credits of income tax, proposed in the Budget of April 1941, or a similar scheme, as a permanent peace-time measure (*paragraph 17*).

(j)   The desirability and practicability of imposing a capital levy or of introducing other suitable forms of taxation for the repayment of the national debt (*paragraphs 20(b) and (c)*).

(k)   In addition to the above problems of internal policy, a further study should be undertaken of international economic policy and of the commercial and foreign exchange policy of this country from the point of view of their effect upon general unemployment (*paragraphs 25 to 28*).

12

Variations in the Rate of Social Security Contributions as a Means of Stabilising the Demand for Labour

Meade's proposals for post-war employment policy included measures for influencing consumption expenditure counter-cyclically, as in his Consumers' Credits and Unemployment *(London: Oxford University Press, 1938). The existence of the Beveridge Committee on Social Insurance and Allied Services in 1942 provided Meade with the opportunity to put forward a detailed scheme. This was submitted to the committee in his memorandum on 'The Economic Aspects of the Proposed Reforms of Social Security' (9 June 1942) and elaborated in the two following memoranda dated 21 July 1942 and 10 August 1942 (Meade Papers 3/2 and Public Record Office T230/101). As a result of intervention by Keynes and Sir Richard Hopkins (Permanent Secretary of the Treasury 1942–45), Meade's proposals did not appear in the Beveridge Report (Cmd 6404, November 1942) but as Appendix II of the White Paper on Employment Policy, Cmd 6527, in 1944 (see Public Record Office T230/102 and* The Collected Writings of John Maynard Keynes, *Vol. 27, London: Macmillan, 1980, Chapters 4 and 5).*

I The General Argument for the Scheme

1   It is generally agreed that in order to prevent widespread unemployment (other than an irreducible minimum of 'intermittent' unemployment or such unemployment as is caused by 'structural' maladjustments of industry), measures should be taken to stabilise at a high level the general level of money demand for goods and services. Measures must be devised to stimulate money demand during periods of general depression and to restrain demand during periods of excessive boom.

2   For this purpose various types of measure are possible. *Banking Policy* may be so designed as to create conditions of low interest rates and of plentiful monetary supplies in times of depression and to raise interest rates and restrict supplies of money in times of excessive boom. There are, however, narrow limits to the amount that one can hope to achieve by such a policy. Although it might always be possible with a sufficiently drastic upward movement of interest rates to damp down trade activity, a

policy of easy money alone is unlikely rapidly and promptly to restore the position during a depression.

3   It has frequently been suggested that there should be such a *Control of Public Investment* that expenditure on public works is so timed as to offset fluctuations in private capital expenditure. There can be little doubt that such a 'public works policy' should be adopted as part, at least, of the post-war mechanism for stabilisation. But it is doubtful whether alone it can suffice to prevent depressions. For it is by no means certain that a sufficient volume of public works expenditure can be readily varied in timing, and it is virtually certain that such expenditure cannot be very rapidly and promptly turned on and off in response to the needs of the general economic position.

4   For these reasons it is argued that these policies should be supplemented by a device or devices whereby consumers' expenditure may be promptly stimulated or restricted, and it is suggested that a *policy of lowering and raising rates of taxation* would serve this purpose. If individuals were taxed less heavily when a general depression threatened to develop, they would have additional tax-free income to spend and might thus be expected to offset a decline in the general level of demand. Conversely, an excessive rise in the general level of demand might be countered by a rise in tax rates.

5   If variations in taxation are to be an effective instrument of control for this purpose, one must operate by means of a tax which collects a considerable amount of revenue, and variations in which will effectively influence the general level of demand for goods and services or for labour. But it is not sufficient that the tax should be of a considerable size and should affect demand. It is the whole object of the proposal to find an instrument of control which is not only effective, but also operates promptly and rapidly in its effect. It is necessary, therefore, to select a form of taxation which can be promptly and rapidly adjusted.

6   There are not very many taxes which satisfy all of these criteria. The income tax, for example, while it would be suitable in many respects, can normally be varied only once a year at a particular time of the year and its alteration is not even then immediately effective. There is bound to be a considerable time-lag if the income tax were to be adjusted for the purpose of stabilising demand, even though the extension of deduction of tax at the source would enable adjustments to be made more rapidly than before. Moreover, if income-tax allowances are increased again after the war, it will no longer fall at all heavily on the large mass of wage-earners, but rather on those classes where expenditure is less likely to be quickly varied in response to a marginal change in tax-free income.

7   Employers' and employees' contributions to social insurance are, however, a compulsory levy which satisfy all these conditions. The employees' contribution is paid directly out of the weekly wage and is

thus likely effectively and promptly to influence wage-earners' expenditure. The employers' contribution is equivalent to a weekly tax on employment; and its variation should, therefore, affect the profit margin to be earned on the employment of additional labour. The effect of a variation in the employers' contribution upon the employment of labour may be less prompt and less certain than the effect of a change in the employees' contribution upon the demand for consumption goods; but nevertheless a reduction in the charge on employment in times of bad trade should prove a useful stimulus to producers. Both employers' and employees' contributions should administratively be capable of prompt variation. Moreover, as will be argued below (paragraphs 16–17), the total of post-war social security contributions is likely to be sufficiently large to make their variations a very significant weapon for the purpose of stabilisation.

8   The purpose of this note is, therefore, to suggest that the rate of employers' and employees' contributions to social insurance should, after the war, be adjusted upwards and downwards about an appropriate normal level, in such a way that abnormally low rates are levied during periods of trade depression and abnormally high rates if an inflationary situation develops.

9   Such variations will admittedly involve making heavier levies in times of boom on certain persons whose money incomes have not been increased as a result of the boom conditions, and whose real incomes may actually have been reduced as a result of a higher cost of living. This is a cost which must be borne in the case of practically any scheme which can be proposed for the stabilisation of *total* incomes by means of variations of taxation. It is a cost that will be well worth while paying for an effective stabilisation of total demand, provided that the legitimate interests of those with abnormally low wage-rates are protected. (See paragraph 20 below.)

II   The Criteria for Variations in the Rate of Contribution

10   The first question to be decided is the means by which the timing and the extent of variations in the rates of contribution should be judged. The ultimate object of schemes of this kind for the stabilisation of demand is to prevent general unemployment of economic resources, such as occurs from time to time during general depressions of trade activity. The first and most obvious procedure is to estimate the 'standard' percentage of unemployment among insured workers that must be ascribed either (a) to the minimum of workers that at any one time are likely to be out of work as they move from job to job or as their trade is seasonally slack, or (b) to far-reaching disturbance in the geographical or occupational distribution of labour which has resulted from structural changes in industry. We may call unemployment of these two sorts 'intermittent' and 'structural' unemployment respectively. It would then be ruled that as the percentage

of unemployment rose above this 'standard' figure, so – on a sliding scale – the rates of social security contributions should automatically be reduced below their 'norm'; and conversely rates of contribution would be raised above their 'norm' as the unemployment percentage fell below its 'standard'.

11   This criterion is not, however, quite so simple as it may at first sight appear. In the first place, the 'standard' level of unemployment is both difficult to measure and may be expected to vary from time to time. The amount of 'intermittent' unemployment may itself be reduced by a better organisation of the labour market, by improved facilities for labour transfer, and by a change in the relative importance of stable and of unstable occupations. The amount of 'structural' unemployment – caused by a wholesale contraction of markets for the products of particular industries – is in its very nature liable to change, and its duration is very greatly dependent upon the particular economic policies (e.g. of labour transfer or affecting the localisation of industry) which are adopted to meet it. In particular, the amounts of 'intermittent' and 'structural' unemployment will be greater during the structural readjustments necessary in the course of the immediate post-war transitional period than during subsequent and more settled years. It would clearly be necessary to have some mechanism whereby, in the light of experience, the sliding scale between the rate of contribution and the unemployment percentage could be revised.

12   It is possible, however, to raise a more far-reaching objection to the use of the unemployment index as an automatic criterion for variations in the rate of social security contributions. It may not be appropriate to attempt to expand employment by a general stimulation of demand in every case in which unemployment is greater than that which can be described as 'intermittent' and 'structural' in character. This will be so only if a moderate wages policy is adopted. But if money wage-rates and, in consequence, the price level began to move sharply upwards in spite of the existence of unemployment, it might be necessary to restrain the general level of money demand in order to prevent the development of a vicious spiral of inflation, even though unemployment remained above the level of 'intermittent' and 'structural' unemployment.

13   For this reason other indices besides that of the unemployment percentage are relevant for decisions about the need for expansive or restrictive economic and financial policies. Thus, if the money national income, the price level and wage-rates were all moving rapidly upwards, measures of financial restraint would be necessary, even if unemployment were not yet reduced to the minimum of 'intermittent' and 'structural' unemployment. In the formulation of general economic and financial policy (e.g. of the planning and timing of public works or of appropriate monetary and budgetary policy by the Treasury) there is no doubt that these other indices must be duly considered.

14   There is, however, reason for believing that, as far as variations in the rate of social security contributions are concerned, these other indices had best be disregarded. In the case of the social security fund, it will be desired to achieve a balance over an average of years between the receipts and contributions of the fund. If all the widest economic and financial issues are taken into account in determining the rate of contributions, there is no reason to believe that this balance will be achieved. But if a simple automatic sliding scale between rates of contribution and the unemployment percentage is chosen, *and if this sliding scale is adjusted from time to time with the sole object of achieving a balance in the fund over an average of years*, it is to be expected that any lack of balance of the fund will not accumulate progressively in the one direction or the other.

15   It is suggested, therefore, that the rates of contribution should be automatically varied inversely with variations in the unemployment percentage and that this sliding scale should be regularly considered for revision with the sole object of obtaining a balance of the fund over an average of years. If this arrangement were adopted, the scheme itself would be useful in providing a prompt stabilising device for helping to correct immediately and without delay any marked fluctuations in the total demand for labour. It would not, however, itself directly influence the general level of unemployment which existed over an average of good and bad years. This level would depend upon a variety of other factors; it would be reduced:-

(a)   by an improved organisation of the labour market;
(b)   by an increase in labour mobility;
(c)   by the adoption of a moderate wages policy which removed the danger that a high demand for labour would lead to a rapid inflation of money-wage costs and money prices, and
(d)   by the adoption over an average of good and bad years of a sufficiently expansive general monetary and financial policy.

For the determination of the broadest issues of financial and fiscal policies many indices would have to be considered; but for the social security fund the use of an automatic scale, so adjusted as to preserve a long-run balance of the fund, would appear to be the most appropriate method.

III   The Quantitative Importance of the Scheme

16   For purely illustrative purposes, a possible scheme is outlined in the Annex to this memorandum. That scheme is based upon a 'normal' contribution of 5s 0d a week (2s 6d by each employer and employee) which rises to a maximum of 7s 6d a week (3s 9d by each employer and employee) and falls to a minimum of 2s 6d a week (1s 3d by each employer and employee). On the assumption that with 8 per cent unemployment a 5s 0d contribution will produce a total of £230 millions of revenue, a variation in the unemployment percentage from just under 5 per cent to

just over 11 per cent would produce a variation of some £245 millions per annum in the revenue from contributions (or a variation of some £122½ millions per annum in the contributions levied from employers or from employees separately). Variations of this order of magnitude should be very significant as a stabilising device. A variation of over £120 millions in the net spendable wages of employees should have a considerable and prompt effect of the same order of magnitude in stimulating their demand for goods and services. The variation in the employers' contribution is equivalent to a change of over £120 millions in a tax on employment, and this should have some immediate effect (the magnitude of which is difficult to estimate) upon the demand for labour.

17   These primary effects will have secondary and tertiary repercussions. Additional expenditure by wage-earners on commodities generates income in the production of those commodities, and this leads to some further increase in expenditure and in incomes. An additional demand by employers for labour generates additional wage-incomes which lead to further increases in expenditure and in incomes. It has been estimated that in the pre-war economy a primary stimulus to the national income of this kind may lead to a total increase of the national income twice as great as the initial impulse itself. If this is so, the variation of employers' and employees' contributions combined of some £245 millions might well lead to a total variation of national income of some £350–£450 millions. This would represent some 5½ to 7 per cent of a post-war national income of £6,500 millions. According to Mr Colin Clark's estimate, the decline in the national income between 1929 (the best year before the great depression) and 1932 (the worst year of the great depression) was some 11½ per cent. This scheme might be hoped, therefore, to cope with a very appreciable part of the absolute decline of income that may be expected to occur even in a depression of great severity.

IV   Certain Detailed Problems

18   The scheme outlined in the Annex is put forward merely as an illustration of the sort of way in which the proposals made in this memorandum might be embodied into a practical scheme, if they were accepted in principle. This illustrative scheme may serve to focus attention on a number of important practical issues which will require solution, if the scheme is to work satisfactorily; but it is not claimed that the actual details of the illustrative scheme in the Annex could necessarily be applied without such modifications as may be required on administrative grounds. On such issues we do not feel competent to express an opinion.

19   In the first place, it will be necessary to decide whether the sliding scale suggested in paragraph 1 of the illustrative scheme is suitable. A preliminary examination of the movements in the unemployment percen-

tage between 1923 and 1938 suggests that, in order to avoid changes in the rate of social security contributions that are occasioned by purely random and erratic changes in unemployment, it would be wise to make changes in the rate of social security contributions depend upon intervals of not less than two points in the unemployment percentage. If intervals of this size were chosen, it would probably not be necessary to eliminate seasonal movements from the unemployment percentage, since the great majority of seasonal movements would fall within the two-point intervals of the unemployment percentage.

20   It has already been suggested (see paragraph 9 above) that special provisions may be necessary to safeguard the position of those wage-earners who are paid abnormally low wages. For an increase in the rate of employees' contribution from a 'norm' of 2s 6d to 3s 9d (such as might occur during a boom, according to the sliding scale suggested in the illustrative scheme) might impose an intolerable burden on those whose earnings are abnormally low. For this reason it is suggested in paragraph 2 of the illustrative scheme that – while the employer and employee should normally each bear one half of the total weekly contribution – in no case should the deduction from the employee's wage exceed, say, one twentieth of his total weekly earnings.

21   It is very possible that the administrative suggestions made in paragraph 5 of the illustrative scheme are inappropriate, or at least capable of great improvement by those who are technically competent to judge the issues involved. There is, however, one point which should be carefully remembered in considering the actual administrative problems which are involved in raising a levy which is capable of quarterly variations. It is important to avoid any scheme which will enable employers to speculate upon a rise or a fall in the rate of contribution. For they would be speculating on what was, in many cases, practically a certainty, and would, therefore, be in a very strong position to profit at the expense of the social security fund. It is most desirable to find a system which will compel employers to stamp each employee's card for each quarter with stamps of a value appropriate to that quarter.

22   Clause 6 of the illustrative scheme suggests that the state's contribution should be maintained at a fixed sum regardless of fluctuations in the rates of contribution of employers and employees. If this method of finance is adopted, the whole of the fluctuation will fall upon the reserves (or the debt) of the fund; and if there is any maladjustment of the sliding scale, the fund will stand to gain or to lose from any such error.

23   It may be argued that the social insurance fund should not fluctuate to such an extent and that it would lose its character as an insurance fund if it stood to gain or to lose by any chance mistake in estimating the appropriate sliding scale between rates of contributions and unemployment, even though the sliding scale were open to periodic revision in order to obtain a proper balance. Clause 6(a) illustrates a means by which

the state instead of the social security fund would have to meet the fluctuation by borrowing or by repayment of debt, and would have to stand the risk of gain or loss over a period of good and bad years if the sliding scale were not properly estimated.

24   For this purpose, the total weekly contribution (state, employers' and employees') which was considered necessary to balance the fund would be estimated – *e.g.* at 8*s* 8*d*. It would then be determined how much of this the state (*e.g.* 3*s* 8*d*) and how much employers and employees (*e.g.* 5*s* 0*d*) should be expected to contribute over an average of good and bad years. A sliding scale would then be introduced for employers' and employees' contributions such as was expected to provide 5*s* 0*d* on the average of good and bad years. The state would be required to provide a variable weekly contribution equal to the difference between 8*s* 8*d* and the current contribution from employers and employees. This arrangement would be open to periodic revision in the light of experience in order to adjust the sliding scale in such a way that in future years the desired division of contributions between the state and employers and employees might be more nearly approached.

Annex   An Illustrative Scheme

Note: The following scheme is outlined on the assumptions
(a)   that employers' and employees' contributions to social insurance are levied by a weekly stamp for each man employed and that one half of the cost of the stamp is deducted from the employee's wage,
(b)   that on the average the stamp is to cost 5*s* 0*d* and, at 8 per cent unemployment, will produce some £230 millions per annum in revenue, and
(c)   that the state contributions are to amount to some £170 millions per annum, which is equivalent to a weekly contribution per man employed of about 3*s* 8*d* (*i.e.* $^{170}/_{230} \times$ 5*s* 0*d*). See SIC (42) 33 [a memorandum by the Government Actuary on the finance of the Beveridge proposals], paragraphs 54 to 56. The following paragraphs will need revision in so far as these estimates are liable to be revised.

1   The weekly stamp to be affixed by the employer to each employee's social security card shall vary according to the unemployment percentage on the following sliding scale:-

Unemployment Percentage	Weekly Social Insurance Stamp
Less than 5 per cent	7*s* 6*d*
Between 5 and 7 per cent	6*s* 3*d*
Between 7 and 9 per cent	5*s* 0*d*
Between 9 and 11 per cent	3*s* 9*d*
More than 11 per cent	2*s* 6*d*

2   One half of the current cost of the social insurance stamp shall in each period be deducted by the employers from the employees' wages, except that no deduction from an employee's wage shall exceed an amount equal to 1s 0d in the £ of the weekly wage.

3   The sliding scale shall be considered for revision by the social insurance statutory committee at the end of the first three years during which it has been in operation, and thereafter at the end of each ten-year period. The revision shall be undertaken in the light of experience in order to determine that scale which is most likely to keep the social security fund in balance over a period of good and bad years, when allowance has been made for the amount of state contributions and of any other income of the fund.

4   The social insurance statutory committee shall announce at the end of each calendar quarter of the year the rate of contribution which will rule during the forthcoming calendar quarter on the basis of the sliding scale given in paragraph 1 (or as revised in accordance with paragraph 3). For the purpose of this sliding scale the unemployment percentage shall be the average of the unemployment percentages of the preceding three months.

5   Employers must fix to each employee's social insurance card, in respect of contributions payable during each quarter, insurance stamps of the value current during that quarter. Post Offices will buy back from employers any excess stock of stamps which employers may possess of an out-of-date denomination.

6   The state shall contribute to the social insurance fund a contribution of 3s 8d per week in respect of every employed person.

6(a)   (An alternative to paragraph 6.) The state shall contribute to the social insurance fund during each quarter a weekly contribution in respect of every employed person equal in value to the difference between 8s 8d and the rate of employers' and employees' weekly contribution current during that quarter.

13

The Effect on Employment of a Change in the Employer's Social Security Contribution

Meade wrote this analysis in response to a discussion of the previous paper by the members of the Economic Section on 7 August 1942 (Meade Papers 3/2 and Public Record Office T230/14 and 101).

1 We are agreed on the analysis of the effect of a change in the employee's contribution. A reduction will affect the amount of spendable income, and, in accordance with the marginal propensity to consume of the wage-earner, this will affect the demand for goods and services.

2 [J. M.] Fleming's argument about the effect of a change in the employer's contribution, as I see it, runs on familiar 'Keynesian' lines. He argues that its effect, like the effect of a change in the employee's contribution, will depend upon the marginal propensity to consume of the employee. As far as the employers are concerned, a reduction of their contribution by an amount equal to, say, 5% of the wage-rate, is equivalent to a reduction by 5% of the wage-rate. This reduction of costs will lead to a reduction of all marginal short-period costs by 5%. Prices will fall by 5%. All incomes, other than wages, will in consequence (in a closed economy) fall by 5%. While the wage-cost has fallen by 5%, the money wage received by the worker will not have fallen; but the 5% fall in the cost of living will have been equivalent to a 5% rise in real wages. The ultimate effect, in the absence of any changes in the rate of interest, will thus depend again upon the worker's *real* marginal propensity to consume, i.e. upon whether the fall in prices makes him save more or buy more goods and services.

3 [Lionel] Robbins asks: what is the mechanism by which this adjustment of all prices and costs takes place? The following is at least one possible process of adjustment. The reduction of employers' contributions represents a reduction of cost that enters into prime costs. Prices are gradually reduced as producers compete to put more on the market as a consequence of reduced costs. Producers also find that the prices of the capital goods and intermediate products, which they use, are being reduced by their suppliers for similar reasons. This process of adjustment

continues until the 5% reduction of wage-rates has – in a closed economy – spread over all prime costs.

4   This is not, however, to argue that all prices will in fact, even in a closed economy, actually fall by 5%. This would be so if the worker's marginal propensity to consume were zero, and there was in consequence no increase in effective demand, employment or output. In fact the gradual downward adjustment of prices will be accompanied by increased purchases by wage-earners as a result of the increased real incomes of wage-earners. This will prevent prices from falling as much as they could otherwise have done; output will increase, and, as a result, the marginal short-term productivity of prime factors will be somewhat lowered. But this would not modify Fleming's contention that the effect of a reduction in employee's contribution is essentially the same as that of a reduction in employer's contribution. The effect of both depends upon the marginal propensity to consume of wage-earners.

5   I confess that, in drafting paragraphs 7 and 17 of EC(S) (42) 18 Revise ['Variations in the rate of social security contributions as a means of stabilising the demand for labour', Chapter 12 above], I did not have these considerations properly in mind; and on consideration I now agree much more fully with Fleming than I admitted in our meeting on Friday August 7th. There are, however, in the real world a number of reasons for believing that a reduction in employer's contribution will differ in effect from a reduction in employee's contribution. In the following paragraphs I mention four such reasons.

6   (i) In the first place, we are in fact dealing with an open and not with a closed economy. Whereas a reduction in employee's contribution will do nothing to cheapen home production, a reduction in employer's contribution will do so. It will at any given foreign exchange rate and any given level of external prices stimulate exports and restrict imports. In so far as this factor is concerned, a reduction in employer's contribution will be more effective than a reduction in employee's contribution in stimulating employment. (It will increase our favourable balance of trade; and it might therefore, under Clearing Union principles [Keynes' plan, which was sent to the US Treasury in August 1942] require to be offset by an appreciation of our currency or by a depreciation of foreign currencies, if it should have so marked an effect as to put us in a 'surplus' position or other countries into a 'deficiency' position. But that is another matter).

7   (ii) So long as the policy of price subsidies to the cost of living is maintained for the purpose of stabilising that price index, variations in the rate of employer's (as opposed to employee's) contribution may be offset in part at least by variations in such subsidies. Thus, in so far as reduction of the employer's contribution is prevented from leading to a fall in the cost of living by a simultaneous reduction of price subsidies, there will be no increase in real wages, no increase in home effective demand and (in a closed economy) no increase in employment. This

extreme case is, however, unlikely to occur. For some prices outside the cost of living are likely to be allowed to decline; and, in so far as these are of importance, the normal increase in effective demand will occur.

8   (iii) The mechanism of the effect of a reduction in employer's contribution differs from that of the effect of a reduction in employee's contribution. For, while the latter acts directly through the increased spendable money income of the wage-earner, the former operates through a fall in prices. Such price reductions will be less prompt, and – in some cases – for conventional and institutional reasons may be really sluggish. In so far as the employer's contribution is reduced and his prices are not correspondingly lowered, the producer will have an additional profit margin. But this is unlikely for a considerable period to be distributed as a dividend and actually spent, and in any case the marginal propensity to consume from profits is low.

9   There may, moreover, be other short-run important effects of the change in the employer's contribution, which will occur in so far as prices are only slowly adjusted to the change in prime costs. Thus there will be a temporary increase in profits and in the rate of profit to be earned on investment, which will last as long as the fall in marginal prime costs is not accompanied by an equivalent reduction in prices.[1] This might conceivably set up a cycle of expansion caused by a temporary increase in investment which led to an increased demand for consumption goods which led to increased profits and so to a permanent justification of the temporarily increased rate of investment. This could, however, happen only if the position from which we started before the change in the employers' contribution was one of *unstable* equilibrium (i.e. one in which any fortuitous upward or downward impulse on investment would lead to an accumulative upward or downward movement of the whole system). It would be foolish to deny that a system which is prone to vast cyclical swings may never be in such an unstable position; but I doubt whether a reduction in employers' contribution could be relied upon to have any very serious effect of this kind.

10   It is possible also that, in so far as the adjustment of selling prices to a reduction in employer's contribution is sluggish, producers – since there is now an increased margin between prices and prime costs – may take on more labour in order to produce more. In other words, the process of adjustment, instead of taking the form of a reduced price – leading to increased demand for the product – leading to an increased demand for labour – leading in turn to increased incomes and expenditure and some partial restoration of selling prices, may take the form of an increased demand for labour – leading to increased output – leading to an increased

---

[1] This is additional to the increase in the rate of profit which will result ultimately from the increased demand for goods arising out of the increased real incomes of wage-earners. This latter stimulus to investment will take place (provided that the marginal propensity to consume of wage-earners is greater than zero) equally as a result of a reduced employer's or a reduced employee's contribution.

supply coming forward on the market to meet a somewhat increased demand – leading to some partial fall in selling prices. But whichever way the adjustment works, the result should be the same, unless the economy starts from a position of unstable equilibrium and the two different processes give different jerks to the system.

11   (iv) We come finally to the fact that, in part at least, the money wage-rate is linked to the cost of living. I suggest that the most realistic assumption to make is that the money wage-rate is a function of two variables – the cost of living and the volume of employment. It is certain that a rise in the cost of living will be followed – although only after some time and to a lesser proportionate extent – by some demands for increased money wages. Moreover, the lower is the volume of unemployment, the more likely is it that money wage claims will be advanced. If the money wage (i.e. the wage from which the employee's contribution must be deducted in order to arrive at the wage-earner's spendable income and to which the employer's contribution must be added in order to arrive at the producer's total wage cost) is in this partial way dependent upon the cost of living, then the effect of a change in employer's contribution will differ somewhat from that of a change in the employee's contribution. For while the latter operates through changes in the wage-earners' spendable incomes without any direct change in the cost of living or in the wage-rate, the former operates through a change in real wages brought about by the change in the cost of living which will react back upon the money wage-rate.

12   Thus a reduction in the employer's contribution will lead to a reduction in prices. This will lead to a reduction in the money wage-rate, which in turn will lead to a reduction in prices, and so on. Provided that this series is convergent (which it will be if the fall in money wage-rates is less than in proportion to the fall in the cost of living at each stage) we shall arrive at a new equilibrium, even without relying upon any increase in demand for labour and in employment to cause a rising tendency in money wage-rates. In these circumstances, in which the money wage-rate is partially dependent upon the cost of living and partially upon the volume of employment, it follows that any given fall in the cost of living in a depression will be accompanied by a smaller reduction in the money wage-rate, if it is also accompanied by a reduction in the rate of employer's contribution. For the reduction in employer's contribution will mean that at any given relation between prices and the money wage-rate there would be an increased demand for labour and, therefore, a higher money wage-rate. But it is difficult to say whether or not a depression will be accompanied in fact by larger or smaller fluctuations in the cost of living, as a result of adopting the policy of varying employers' contributions. On the one hand, the policy of varying

contributions will stabilise employment and effective demand,[2] and through stabilising employment it will tend to stabilise money wage-rates and so prices. On the other hand, there will be another element in prime cost and so in price (namely the employer's contribution), which will be more variable than before.

13 We can, however, say one thing with certainty. In so far as there is a series of lagged adjustments to be carried out between prices and wage-rates, because the change in employer's contribution acts upon the cost of living and, because the money wage-rate is partially dependent upon the cost of living, a change in employer's contribution will be less prompt in its effect than a change in employee's contribution. Thus compare a reduction of employee's contribution which gives a 5% increase in wage-earners' spendable incomes with a reduction of employer's contribution which corresponds to a 5% fall in the producer's wage-cost. The latter is first of all subject to the delays of price adjustment, which will slowly tend to lead to a 5% fall in the cost of living. But when the cost of living has fallen 5%, the money wage is in consequence reduced by, say 2½%, so that even yet real wages have not risen by 5%. Prices will in time fall by a further 2½% as a result of the 2½% decline in money wage-rates. But even now real wages will have risen by less than 5%, since money wages will now fall by, say, another 1¼% as a result of the 2½% fall in the cost of living. It is only at the end of this process that real wages will have risen by the fall of 5%.

14 I have my eye all the time on the draft of EC(S) (42) 18 Revise, from which this discussion started. I suggest something on the following lines to take the place of paragraph 7:-

'A reduction in the employee's contribution will promptly increase the weekly receipts of the wage-earner; and except in so far as the wage-earner saves this increase in his disposable income, it should lead to a prompt and effective increase in his demand for goods and services. In effect it is unlikely that the wage-earner will save, except temporarily, any very large part of the increase in his receipts; and thus at least after a moderate time-lag, there should be an increase in demand corresponding to the greater part of the reduction in the employee's contribution.

The effect of a reduction in the employer's contribution is rather more difficult to assess. It will represent a reduction in his costs of production, and in so far as this reduced cost works its way through to reduced selling prices it will help to expand the demand for his product both at home and in overseas markets. If a policy of stabilising the cost of living by the payment of price subsidies is in operation, some part of

---

[2] I take it that this statement will not be questioned. For the actual money wage-rate is irrelevant, while the tax margin between the money wage-rate and the price is relevant, to the 'Keynesian' determinant of employment in the short-run equilibrium position. I am, of course, in the above assuming that the series of price adjustments due to changes in price reacting on wages and so again on prices is a convergent one.

the increased effective demand for goods and services which might have been brought about by a fall in selling prices would be offset by a reduction in price subsidies. Moreover, the money wage-rate itself may be linked in part to the cost of living; and a change in the cost of living, brought about by a change in that element of cost which is represented by the employer's contribution, will thus itself lead to a change in wage-rates and so to further changes in prices. It is probable that the series of adjustments would somewhat delay the effect of a change in employers' contributions upon the effective demand for goods and services. It may therefore be concluded that a change in the employer's contribution will have a somewhat more delayed and uncertain effect than a corresponding change in the employee's contribution; but there is no reason to believe that the change in the margin between prices and costs which is represented by a change in employer's contribution will not ultimately have an effect comparable to that of a similar change in the employee's contribution.'

15   In paragraph 17 I would suggest some restatement of the quantitative effects of the scheme, on the following lines:-

'We should thus on the proposed scale of contributions be able to achieve a variation of some £240 millions in total contributions between years of good and bad trade; of which some £120 millions would represent changes in employees' and some £120 millions changes in employers' contributions. If we assume that some 80% of any increase in wage-earners' receipts will be spent, the variation of employees' contributions would give rise directly to a change of some £96 millions in wage-earners' expenditure. We must, however, take into account the secondary and tertiary repercussions of this increase in expenditure. For this increased demand for goods and services will give rise to increased output and employment and so to increased wages and profits and so to further increases in expenditure, and so on. There is some evidence that in the United Kingdom these repercussions are likely approximately to double the effect of the primary increase in expenditure. If this were so, the ultimate effect of a reduction of £120 millions in employees' contributions would be to increase the total national income by some £192 millions.

Reasons have been given above (see paragraph 2) for believing that the primary effect upon demand of a change in employers' contributions, while less certain and less prompt than that of a change in employees' contributions, may nevertheless well be of a comparable order of magnitude. If this is so, we should be justified in assuming that the combined effect upon the national income of the proposed scale of variations in employcr's and employee's contributions would amount to as much as £300 to £400 millions. . . . '

14

Maintenance of Full Employment

Meade wrote the first draft of what led eventually to the White Paper on Employment Policy (Cmd 6527, 1944) in March 1943 for the ministerial Reconstruction Priorities Committee established in January 1943. He revised it twice in the light of his colleagues' comments to produce the version printed below. Lionel Robbins, the Director of the Economic Section, redrafted it before it was circulated to the committee, for 'after all that he has had to put up with from us, it would have been a last indignity to ask J. E. M. to do this' (Meade Papers 3/2, Public Record Office T230/15 and 66–68, CAB87/12 and 13). The descriptive appendices A to D of Meade's paper have been omitted.

Introductory

1   This paper attempts to outline the means by which employment after the war may be maintained at a high level.

2   Part I analyses the nature of the problem. It is argued that the essential condition of success is to maintain the total national demand for goods and services, and that this policy of financial stabilisation must be accompanied by increased mobility of economic resources and by a moderate prices and wages policy.

3   Part II describes the methods by which these objectives may be achieved. First, international measures for the expansion of world demand and, secondly, national measures for the control of internal demand are outlined. Finally, the industrial and labour market conditions necessary to ensure success for a policy of full employment are discussed.

4   Part III outlines in more realistic terms the actual sequence of events which may be expected after the termination of hostilities; and emphasis is laid upon the special conditions which will rule in the immediate transitional period.

5   Part IV gives a summary of the points which require further investigation.

I   The Problem of Unemployment

(i)   Frictional Unemployment

6   'Full' employment after the war cannot mean no unemployment. The number of unemployed persons cannot be indefinitely maintained at the negligible level at which it is today in war-time. In peace-time there will always be some persons who are changing jobs or whose work is temporarily interrupted as a result of weather conditions, seasonal variations, or similar factors. In war-time this minimum residue of unemployment can be radically reduced, because of the totalitarian controls which the state uses in directing the labour force, and in controlling production and consumption. But if – as is assumed in this paper – state control will not be maintained on such an extensive scale after the war, some appreciable minimum of such frictional unemployment must be expected.

7   It is estimated (Appendix A) that in the inter-war years this type of unemployment alone accounted for about 4½ per cent of the insured population. Unemployment on this moderate scale should not cause undue hardship; for it consists largely of a continually changing body of men, any one of whom is unlikely to be out of work for any very prolonged period.

8   It is large-scale unemployment, in excess of this minimum, which constitutes the really serious problem. Such unemployment in the past has been due, in the main, to two causes: first, to structural maladjustments which have led to special pockets of unemployment in special areas or in special trades, and secondly to recurrent deficiencies in aggregate demand for goods and services below the level necessary to absorb the productive resources of the community.

(ii)   Structural Unemployment

9   The demand for one type of labour may decline for special reasons. Thus a shift of demand from coal to oil, or the opening up of new foreign sources of coal, or a change in technique which greatly increases the productivity of labour in coal-mining, would lead to a reduction in the demand for the services of coal-miners. For reasons such as these pockets of severe unemployment may develop in special industries and, thus, in special areas.

10   In the inter-war years unemployment, due to structural changes of this type, was of great importance. Thus, it is estimated (Appendix A) that structural unemployment in the inter-war period probably accounted for about 6 per cent of the insured population.

11   'Special' unemployment of this kind can be mitigated by a flexibility in wages policy which permits some reduction of wage-costs in depressed

areas or trades in comparison with the wage levels ruling in those parts of the national economy where activity is expanding. For in these circumstances the demand for the products of the depressed areas or trades will not decline so rapidly. But the problem of special unemployment cannot fundamentally be cured without an increase in the mobility of economic resources: labour and capital and enterprise must move to the industries and districts where labour can be most economically engaged. Any attempt to cure it solely by an expansion of total national expenditure might lead rather to an inflationary rise of prices in other industries.

12 Labour mobility from declining trades is itself greatly encouraged by an atmosphere of steady expansion in other trades. The history of the 'special' areas in the inter-war period would have been very different, if that period had been marked by a consistent and steady expansion of general economic activity elsewhere. The problem of finding work for the unemployed coal-miners of South Wales, for example, would certainly have been much easier if, throughout the inter-war period, there had been a consistently brisk demand for labour in the majority of other occupations and districts.

(iii) Depression Unemployment

13 The above paragraphs suggest that, while frictional unemployment alone in the inter-war period accounted for an unemployment percentage of about 4½ per cent, frictional and structural unemployment together accounted for an unemployment percentage of some 10 per cent. Yet in 1932, the worst year of the Great Depression, the unemployment percentage rose to no less than 22 per cent.

14 Such depression unemployment can only be prevented by avoiding the recurrent deficiencies in aggregate demand for goods and services which lead to such depressions. Moreover, the avoidance of such depressions is an essential prerequisite for the cure of structural unemployment, since it is only possible to deal successfully with such a problem in an atmosphere of general economic expansion in all the surrounding areas and trades which are not specially affected by the structural maladjustment. The maintenance of total national expenditure, and thus of total national income, must be the primary objective of any policy for the maintenance of full employment.

15 National incomes have fluctuated very severely in the past. The figures given in Appendix B show how great and widespread was the fall in national incomes of a large number of countries which resulted from the Great Depression after 1929.

16 Thus the national income of the United States fell by no less than 51 per cent in the three years between 1929 and 1932. The decline in the United Kingdom national income was much more moderate, being only 15 per cent in the same period. But the depression in this country

interrupted what might otherwise have been a steady and continuous rise of real income. This interruption was sufficient to cause the average number of insured unemployed in the United Kingdom to rise from 1.263 million in 1929 to 2.829 million in 1932, or from 10.4 per cent to 22.1 per cent of the insured population.

17   Fluctuations in demand which give rise to these troubles may take many forms. There may be a decline in the total amount of money borrowed and spent on capital development; a change in Government policy may lead to a decline in the demand for goods and services by public authorities; or a change in rates of taxation or in expenditure habits may affect the total amount of money spent by individuals on goods and services for personal consumption.

18   But however a reduction in demand may arise in the first instance, it is liable to have a cumulatively depressing effect, unless it is promptly and effectively offset. A decline in demand for capital equipment, for example, will lead to a decline in incomes earned in the production of such equipment; this in turn will lead to a decline in demand for goods and services for personal consumption; this in its turn will lead to a decline in the profitability of industry, and so to a further decline in the demand for new capital equipment; and so on.

19   For this reason it is a much more formidable task to halt a serious depression once it has started than it is to prevent a depression from starting. In the first case a sufficient stimulus must be exerted, not only to offset the initial cause of depression, whatever that may be, but also to counterbalance the cumulative process of deflation which will have set in. Early and prompt action will be doubly effective, but it will require constant and careful preparation.

20   Fluctuations in total demand may also arise from external events. In the case of the United Kingdom this is of special importance. A high proportion of our total national income in the past has been derived from the production of exports; and, in view of our continuing necessity to import essential raw materials and foodstuffs, this dependence on exports is bound to continue. A world depression (such as that which developed after 1929) contracts the purchasing power of our foreign customers; and thus reacts with peculiar severity upon our own economic activity. The importance of this factor is illustrated in Appendix C. In 1929 our export trade represented almost one fifth of our total national income. During the three years 1929 to 1932 the value of this important sector of our production declined by 50 per cent as the result of the general world depression.

21   The foregoing paragraphs may help to give some indication of the amount of unemployment for which we must be prepared after the war. If the level of frictional unemployment were the same as in the inter-war period, if the incidence of structural unemployment (which can never be

entirely avoided) were halved, and if we were successful in completely abolishing all depression unemployment, the unemployment percentage would be about 7½ per cent.

(iv) Profit Margins and Wage-Rates

22 No policy for the maintenance of total national demand can, however, be effective unless it is accompanied by appropriate policies for prices and wages. Increased demand for goods and services will lead to an expansion of production, only if prices are not raised excessively as demand increases. Increased demand for labour will lead to increased employment, only if it does not lead to an immoderate rise in money wage-rates.

23 Prices must therefore be kept at a moderate level in relation to costs. Whatever industrial structure is regarded as most appropriate, the essential problem from the point of view of maintaining full employment is to prevent the misuse of monopolistic power for the restriction of output and the raising of prices and of profit margins.

24 A moderate wages policy is equally essential. If an expansion of demand leads to rapidly rising money wage-rates and so to an inflation of costs and prices, the attempt to prevent unemployment by means of an expansion of the general level of total demand will sooner or later have to be abandoned. This condition does not, of course, mean that standards of living may not be improved through rising wage-rates as the productivity of labour is increased; through the redistribution of income by taxation; or through the increased purchasing power of the wage-earners which will result simply from a greater volume of employment at uninflated wage-rates. It does, however, imply the continuation of a moderate wages policy even in periods of active demand for labour.

II Methods of Solution

25 The maintenance of full employment will be a formidable task, and will require a readiness to try novel expedients. For it is a problem which has not yet been satisfactorily solved in any single country. To some extent the maintenance of full employment may conflict with other desirable objectives of social policy. For example, if this country were to cut itself off from foreign trade relations, it could avoid external disturbances – at the cost of widespread impoverishment. New inventions are also liable to create unemployment through the industrial reorganisations that they may make necessary; but economic progress is not to be banned on these grounds.

26 In other cases full employment may conflict with personal liberty. If the state maintained totalitarian controls over wages, prices, production and consumption, unemployment could no doubt be reduced to a very

low level. The following paragraphs are, however, written on the assumption that, for this country at least, a system must be devised which allows for a well-developed international commerce and a high degree of industrial flexibility and of personal liberty. There is, fortunately, little doubt that with an improvement in labour mobility and with moderate policies for wage-rates and profit margins, a policy of control over the level of total monetary demand will reduce unemployment to, and maintain it at, a level much lower than that which ruled during the inter-war period.

27　Various methods have been suggested in the past for the reduction of unemployment by removing persons from the labour market: e.g. by earlier retirement from work or by raising the school-leaving age. Other measures have been suggested for distributing the available amount of work over a larger number of persons: e.g. by the organisation of short-time work, by a general reduction of hours of work, or by the institution of longer or more frequent holidays. Many of these things are, no doubt, desirable on their own merits. But they should be judged on their own merits and not as means for diminishing unemployment. For it is a confession of failure to organise involuntary idleness. Steps should rather be taken to ensure that, so long as people prefer an increased real income of goods and services to increased leisure, the economic system works smoothly enough to employ people in this additional production.

(i)　International Action for the Maintenance of World Demand

28　It is particularly in the interest of this country to achieve an international economic settlement based upon the principle of steady expansion in world markets.

29　Certain proposals have already been put forward for this purpose. Suggestions have been made (RP(43)12 ['The International Regulation of Primary Products', 6 February 1943, Public Record Office CAB87/3]) for a wide-scale use of international buffer stock schemes for raw materials and foodstuffs. These schemes would be of great importance as an instrument for the stabilisation of world demand. They would not prevent the gradual adjustment of the prices of primary products to long-term changes in the conditions of supply or of demand; but they would prevent violent price collapses resulting from a general trade depression. When the prices of primary products, and thus the incomes of all those countries which specialised in their production, threatened seriously to decline, the international buffer stocks would inject new purchasing power into world markets by buying up these commodities for stock. In this way they would serve to prevent the intensification of world depressions which result from the fall of purchasing power in the countries producing primary products.

30　This method of international control has many advantages. It would work promptly as soon as a world depression threatened to start; for the purchase of commodities for stock would start automatically as soon as their prices began to decline. Moreover, the amount of additional world buying power which it would be possible to generate by the purchase of commodities for stock would be very appreciable.

31 But buffer stock control in itself would not be enough. For while it can prevent a depression in the industrialised countries from spreading to the primary producing countries and thus intensifying the difficulties of the industrialised countries themselves, it cannot offset any initial decline in economic activity in the industrialised countries themselves.

32 Buffer stock control might, perhaps, be supplemented by a scheme to influence the flow of international investment in long-term capital. One of the main tasks of any international investment board would be to promote expenditure on international development whenever the general level of world purchasing power was deficient.

33 There are serious difficulties in the way of such a policy of international public works. Control of international investment is an uncertain and untried expedient, on which it would be unwise to rely too heavily. Apart from this, it is in any case difficult promptly to advance or to postpone expenditure on projects for capital development, so as to offset fluctuations in world demand which may occur for other reasons. But there are two ways in which an international investment board might serve a useful purpose:

(i) Immediately after the war there will be a period in which world demand will outrun total world supplies; but it is possible that, at some subsequent time, a continuing stimulus to international investment might be useful to offset a persistent tendency towards conditions of slackness in trade activity.

(ii) Even though international investment could not be varied from year to year so as to offset fluctuations in world demand arising from other causes, it might at least be possible to avoid what has so often happened in the past – namely, an intensification of world depressions by a decline in such investment at a time when total world demand was itself declining.

34 The preceding paragraphs suggest that international buffer stocks and international investment for long-term capital development – even in combination – would need supplementation. Such supplementary action is to be found in measures for the maintenance of demand within each country.

35 These measures will themselves be discussed at some length in the following section (paragraphs 38–101). There are, however, great advantages to be gained from a close international co-ordination of such national policies. If in a period of world-wide depression this country were alone to adopt a policy of internal expansion, there would in

consequence be a rise in our demand for imports at a time when our export markets were contracting. This added difficulty to our balance of payments could be avoided if appropriate policies of internal expansion were adopted more or less simultaneously in the most important countries. Some international organisation for the co-ordination of national policies of expansion might be of use for this purpose.

36 For similar reasons, international mechanisms (such as those recently suggested in the Clearing Union and the Commercial Union [by J. M. Keynes and Meade respectively; for the latter see Volume III, Chapter 3]) which aid the adjustment of balances of payments will enable individual countries more freely to adopt internal policies to prevent large-scale unemployment.

37 Against an international background of the kind outlined above, the prospects of success for the internal policies discussed in the following section would be greatly improved. An international economic order based upon the above principles would ensure that no one country could take action (e.g. by an unnecessary depreciation of its currency or by an excessive increase of its protective devices) to provide employment for its own people merely at the expense of the demand for the products of its foreign competitors. On the other hand, each country would be freed from external preoccupations, so that it could take effective internal measures to promote the full employment of its people.

(ii) National Action for the Maintenance of Internal Demand

38 Any post-war policy of control over aggregate demand should be conducted in the light of the statistics of national income and expenditure which are now made available quarter by quarter. The following figures for the year 1938 (the last pre-war year) are reproduced for purposes of illustration.

		Net national income at market prices		Net national expenditure at market prices
		£ millions		£ millions
1	Rent	373	7 Personal	
2	Profits and interest	1,351	Expenditure on	
3	Salaries, etc.	1,081	Consumption	4,041
4	Wages, etc.	1,790	8 Expenditure by	
5	Indirect Taxes	630	Public Authorities on Goods and Services	833
			9 Home Investment	406
			10 Foreign Investment	−55
6	Total Net National Income	5,225	11 Total Net National Expenditure	5,225

39 Personal expenditure, expenditure by public authorities, and expenditure for the purpose of capital development at home or abroad – all these give rise to a demand for goods and services, in the production of which the national income is earned and labour is employed.

40 Figures of national income and expenditure may thus be used in planning ahead for full employment. The first step is to estimate how great the total national income must be in order to provide full employment to the available labour. Steps must then be taken so to control total national expenditure that this total is as great as, but no greater than, the national income necessary for the purpose of giving full employment.

41 It remains, however, to decide which of the various items of total national expenditure it is best to control for this purpose. Investment is the item which is most liable to fluctuate. This is only natural; for expenditure on capital equipment can more easily be postponed than expenditure on consumption, which in the absence of serious fluctuation in income is more likely to remain at an even flow year in year out. Foreign investment is, moreover, subject to various external disturbances.

42 It would clearly cause less disturbance to social policy and to standards of living, if it were possible to control total national expenditure by stabilising those particular items of expenditure which are most likely to fluctuate. This involves the control of investment. If it were possible to stabilise this most variable item, the main initiating cause of economic depressions would be removed.

43 There are, however, two reasons for believing that investment policy will not, in itself, suffice to maintain total national expenditure at the desired level. First, investment is not the only source of fluctuation. Personal expenditure on durable goods, such as motor-cars, is itself liable to considerable variation, and it may be necessary to exert an influence over such expenditure. Or, to take another example, Government expenditure may vary as a result of changes in social policy, and it may be desired to offset this by a change in personal expenditure rather than by a change in investment.

44 Secondly, one must consider not only what forms of expenditure one would like to control, but also what forms of expenditure can in fact be influenced to a sufficient extent and with sufficient rapidity to offset any initiating cause of instability.

45 Thus, foreign investment would remain liable to considerable variation even though the measures of international economic organisation discussed above (paragraphs 28–34) would greatly reduce any such variations; and being dependent so largely on external factors, foreign investment is not readily controllable. Home investment by private

enterprise, although it can be influenced, is not easily brought under direct state control; and there are difficulties in exercising a positive state control even over the capital expenditure of other public bodies such as local authorities. It may well be asking too much of an investment policy to try so to control public investment that, not only are the natural fluctuations in such investment itself evened out, but that it is actually made to fluctuate in such a way as to compensate for any initiating disturbances that may otherwise occur in private home investment, in foreign investment, in government expenditure or in personal expenditure.

46   But even if fluctuations of sufficient magnitude in home investment could be brought about to compensate for any possible variations in the other items of national expenditure, it would still be doubtful whether a control of investment alone would operate with sufficient rapidity. And yet rapidity of adjustment is essential. If, once a decline in total national expenditure is allowed to develop, it may lead at an alarming pace to a general depression of alarming dimensions. For a contraction of expenditure causes a contraction of incomes, a contraction of incomes leads in turn to a contraction of expenditure, and so on.

47   Personal expenditure on consumption may be easier to influence promptly than investment. Whereas investment requires a long period for the preparation of plans for capital development, personal expenditure on various goods of a luxury or semi-luxury character can be varied with little tedious forethought; and it probably will be so varied in response to a change in spendable incomes brought about by, for example, a change of tax policy. Thus, the control of personal expenditure by appropriate changes of tax policy is probably an essential supplement to an investment policy.

48   The above arguments suggest that a policy for the control of total national expenditure should be eclectic in character. Investment policy should undoubtedly play a prominent, perhaps the most prominent, part; but one must be prepared to supplement such policy by other means. Whether at any particular time it would be better to rely upon controls over investment or personal expenditure, or even upon a change in normal government expenditure or in foreign investment, as the best means of avoiding trouble, can only be judged on the merits of each case as it arises. In the paragraphs which follow there is a short discussion of the ways in which each of these main items of national expenditure might be influenced.

HOME INVESTMENT

49   Home investment (i.e. expenditure on internal capital development of all kinds) covers expenditure by public authorities on such works as house-building or road-building, as well as capital expenditure by private enterprise. It covers investment in working capital (i.e. in additions to

stocks of raw materials, of goods in process of manufacture, or of finished goods) as well as investment in fixed capital, such as plant and machinery.

50   It is essential, in order to achieve an effective policy for the proper planning and timing of investment, to obtain adequate statistics of investment of all kinds. The necessary statistics could be compiled as part of the present continuing investigation into National Income and Expenditure.

51   The first prerequisite of investment policy is an appropriate banking policy. The banking system by adjusting supplies of currency and the basis of monetary credit can control interest rates and influence the terms on which funds can be borrowed for long-term, as well as for short-term capital development.

52   It is doubtful whether banking policy alone is an effective method for controlling capital expenditure. A sufficiently drastic raising of interest rates might, perhaps, be relied upon to prevent an undesired inflation of total national expenditure; but in times of deepening depression, no practicable reduction in interest rates is likely to stimulate capital expenditure promptly enough to stave off a period of large-scale unemployment.

53   Banking policy should be regarded rather as providing an appropriate background for other methods of control over home investment. Thus, a general reduction of interest rates at a time when it is desired to stimulate home investment would remove any purely monetary obstacles in the way of increased capital expenditure. In particular, a persistent tendency to depression might be met by a lasting adjustment of interest rates to a new and lower level.

54   The state can exercise a direct control over capital development through the appropriate planning and timing of its own capital works. Such a policy should be extended to cover the planning and timing of capital works by all other bodies (e.g. local authorities, public utilities, railway authorities, etc.) over which the state can exercise the necessary control.

55   In the past, public investment has tended to decline at the same time as private investment. For, as a general depression develops and public revenue contracts, public authorities, like private businesses and private individuals, tend to restrict their expenditures. This intensifies general depression and the problem of unemployment. Thus, capital expenditure by the main public services (cf. Appendix D) fell during the Great Depression, from a peak of £181 millions in 1927 to £126 millions in 1934, and rose again during the general trade recovery to as much as £215 millions by 1937.

56   At the least, therefore, a public investment policy which succeeded

in stabilising such expenditure, would constitute a considerable advance on past experience. But one may hope for more than this. On the basis of the figures in Appendix D, it is suggested that, in the pre-war years, annual public investment might have been varied, by proper timing and planning, by, say, £100 millions between the highest and lowest annual rates of such expenditure.

57   A variation of £100 millions in such expenditure would have further repercussions; for the stimulation of incomes, caused by the expansion of public investment, would lead to a higher demand for goods for personal consumption, and this, in turn, would reduce losses and would stimulate the demand for capital equipment throughout industry. By a series of such repercussions a direct variation of £100 millions in public investment might have caused a variation of some £200 millions in total national expenditure, and so in total national income. A public investment policy which offset £200 millions of any variation in total national expenditure would be an important element in the control of a major depression; but it would not alone be sufficient to stabilise the national income which declined by as much as £600 millions between 1929 and 1932.

58   To ensure the success of a public investment policy, works of capital construction must be planned well in advance of their execution by all authorities, and these plans and other necessary preliminaries must be brought up to the point at which actual expenditure on the works can be started at need with the minimum of delay. Moreover, some central authority must be in a position to turn on or off the financial tap by means of which the authorities concerned receive the funds for financing their work; and by direction, by persuasion, or by financial inducement, it must be able not only to postpone the capital expenditure of the authorities concerned when the need arises, but also to speed up such expenditure when a general depression is otherwise expected to develop.

59   The control of private investment does not differ essentially from that of public investment. Although the control is looser and less direct, there are nevertheless certain ways in which the state can influence the timing of capital development by private enterprise. Thus, the continuation of control over new capital issues, combined with an appropriate monetary policy on the lines indicated above (paragraphs 51–53), might affect the timing of private capital development by affecting the ease with which funds can be raised for these purposes.

60   For a certain time after the war, as long as raw material and labour controls are continued, the state will be able to exert a direct influence over private capital works. If and when these controls are relaxed, it will be necessary to devise an alternative mechanism.

61   It might be possible to introduce a fiscal inducement for the planning and timing of private capital development. Specific tax privileges might

be given in respect of capital developments, provided that these were executed at times when it was desired to stimulate total national expenditure.

62 New enterprise may, after the war, be held back by difficulties of finding capital finance for new businesses. Obstacles of this kind might be removed by the institution of a Government Finance Corporation for the purpose of advancing capital to industry and, in particular, to new enterprise. Such an institution would not only help to raise the general level of new private investment, but would also give the state an additional means of influencing the planning and timing of such investment.

FOREIGN INVESTMENT

63 Total national expenditure can be stimulated by an increase in foreign investment as well as by an increase in home investment. This implies an increase in the excess of exports over imports of goods and services, combined with the lending abroad of the funds necessary to finance this excess of exports.

64 Immediately after the war this country will be faced with an excess of imports, which it will be necessary to correct by a very substantial expansion of exports. Such an increased expenditure on our exports, necessary on quite other grounds than the control of unemployment, will, in fact, lead to an increase in the total demand for our goods and services at a time when it would otherwise be desirable to restrain rather than to stimulate total national expenditure. It will thus intensify, rather than alleviate, the problem of stabilising the aggregate of such expenditure.

65 At a later date, however, when a deficiency of total national expenditure threatens to reappear, an even greater expansion of our export trade (particularly of machinery and similar engineering products) financed by the loan of funds for the development of overseas territories may provide important opportunities for employment in this country. This country is one of the richest in capital in relation to its population, and it would be appropriate in the long run that it should again develop a sufficient excess of exports to partake in positive foreign investment, for the development of backward territories and the provision of employment at home.

GOVERNMENT EXPENDITURE ON GOODS AND SERVICES

66 The public investment policy suggested above would mean that capital expenditure by the state was to some extent used as a means of control over total national expenditure. Current expenditure by the state (on defence, education, health, police, etc.) is not easily amenable to variation simply for the purpose of controlling total national expenditure; for it must be increased or diminished as part of a long-term social, political or economic policy. It may, however, occasionally be possible so

to time parts of such expenditure (e.g. the choice of periods at which new state services are introduced) that there is some tendency for it to be concentrated in periods of threatening trade depression.

67 From time to time there are likely to be appreciable variations in the general level of Government expenditure for non-economic reasons. The level of defence expenditure, for example, will be affected by international-al political requirements. It is important to take such variations into account in planning the level of other items of national expenditure. Thus, if at some future date a change of, say, £100 millions a year is foreseen in Government expenditure, an attempt should be made to influence investment or personal expenditure on consumption, so as to induce an equal change of £100 millions in the opposite direction in some other element of total national expenditure.

PERSONAL EXPENDITURE ON CONSUMPTION

68 During the war it has been necessary to restrict personal consumption in order to release economic resources for the war effort. This has been brought about by the savings campaign, by taxation, and by rationing and various other restrictive devices. For a short transitional post-war period – the problems of which are discussed at greater length in a subsequent section of this paper (paragraphs 102–115) – these restrictive measures will probably need to be continued; but as a more permanent feature of the post-war economy, we shall require more flexible means by which personal expenditure can be stimulated when unemployment threatens to reappear, as well as being restrained in times of incipient inflation.

69 Expenditure on such durable consumption goods is likely, in the absence of control, to intensify the problem, since purchasers can postpone their purchases in bad times and concentrate them in times of good trade. This element of instability is exaggerated by hire-purchase; for consumers can engage in commitments in excess of their incomes in good times, and are thereby obliged to restrict their purchases still more extensively in order to repay debt in bad times. Hire-purchase might, perhaps, be controlled in such a way as to deter new purchases in times of prosperity and to stimulate such purchases when there is a threat of unemployment. This might be done by appropriate variations in the terms of hire-purchase finance.

70 By far the most important weapon of control over personal expenditure is that of taxation. A rise in rates of taxation serves to restrain personal demand; a reduction of taxation stimulates it. A reduction in income tax increases the amount of tax-free income which consumers can spend. A reduction in the purchase tax or in other indirect taxes levied on consumption, by lowering the prices of the taxed commodities, increases the ability of purchasers to buy them. On these grounds the annual Budget in the future might be planned in such a way as to exert a direct influence over total national expenditure – by planning

for low rates of taxation and so for increased personal expenditure when trade depression threatens.

IMPLICATIONS FOR BUDGETARY POLICY

71   Many of the proposals made above involve an increase in Government expenditure and a reduction in Government revenue at times when it is necessary to stimulate general demand. If a stabilising policy of this kind is adopted, the Budget must be regarded as a balancing regulator of the national economy, pumping out purchasing power by increased expenditure and decreased revenue when trade depression threatens, and sucking it back by means of budget surpluses at other times.

72   Whether over a term of years the budget deficits would exceed the surpluses, or vice versa, it is impossible to say in advance. If the natural forces of economic development and expansion are sufficiently strong, at home and abroad, it may prove possible on balance to redeem the heavy legacy of national debt left by this and previous wars. If, on the other hand, these natural forces are inadequate, it may be difficult to maintain full employment without incurring an ever-mounting burden of Government debt. As time goes on, the service of this growing debt may create an ever more serious problem of transfer of income within the community: either taxes will have to be increased to levels damaging to enterprise, or else expenditure for socially desirable objects will have to be stinted.

73   It may be that the national debt will be reduced by the single surgical operation of a capital levy. Apart from this there are, however, certain lines of policy which, if vigorously pursued, will either obviate the necessity for an ever-expanding national debt or else greatly mitigate its effects.

(a)   Our chief hope for avoiding stagnation in world monetary demand lies in the long run in the development and equipment of backward and impoverished countries. This calls for the resumption of international investment on a large scale.

(b)   Steps may be taken to intensify private capital development at home by reducing interest rates to the lowest possible levels, and by so framing tax policy as to encourage private capital outlay and discourage the holding of idle money balances. The maintenance of private investment will be greatly facilitated if the general level of wages and prices, while avoiding any disturbing oscillations, can be kept on a slow and steady upward trend. Such policies as these will not merely help to sustain purchasing power without the necessity for constant government borrowing, but will also diminish the burden of the existing debt.

(c)   Taxes and state expenditure may be so applied as to encourage personal consumption expenditure and discourage saving. Measures to mitigate inequalities of income and wealth, such as progressive taxation and generous provision for social security, tend, as a by-product, to have a stimulating effect on consumption expenditure and employment.

THE NEED FOR PROMPT ACTION

74   Up to this point various suggestions have been made for planning ahead in such a way as to preserve an aggregate national demand sufficient to provide full employment. The general object of such planning would be to ensure that total national expenditure in the future would be on a scale adequate to provide full employment. But the actual decisions of policy would, of course, have to be based not only upon statistics of national income and expenditure, but upon all the statistical and other information upon which the best forecast could be made about the future trends of general trade activity. In addition to statistics of income, expenditure, employment and production, every effort should be made to collect information (e.g. as to the state of the order books of various industries) which would most directly show the probable future movements of expenditure, production and employment.

75   Even with the best information, however, such plans are bound from time to time to break down: an error may have been made in forecasting the needs of the future, or the action taken may have failed to restrain or to stimulate expenditure to the degree required. In such circumstances plans must be revised as quickly as possible, and fresh action taken.

76   But there will be an intervening period in which a depression may start to develop; and once the secondary repercussions of an incipient depression have been allowed to develop it will be doubly difficult to regain control over the situation. In addition, therefore, to the methods of forward planning of the total national expenditure which have been described above, it is important to find some prompt and possibly automatic device which will check the development of a depression, as soon as a decline in employment begins, and which will thus give a breathing space for the revision of the more normal plans for the control of national expenditure.

77   Such a device for rapidly offsetting the worst repercussions of a depression may be found in the scheme outlined in Appendix E, under which the amount of purchasing power in the hands of the public would be promptly and automatically adjusted by variations in social security contributions. The rate of such contributions would be automatically lowered if unemployment rose above a certain level. This rapid and automatic reduction in the charges levied from employers and employees should lead to a prompt and effective stimulation of demand.

78   In particular, a reduction in the employee's contribution will promptly increase the weekly receipts of the wage-earner; and except in so far as the wage-earner saves the increase in his disposable income, it should lead to a prompt and effective increase in his demand for goods and services. In effect, it is unlikely that the wage-earner will save, except

temporarily, any very large part of the increase in his receipts; and thus, at least after a moderate time-lag, there should be an increase in demand corresponding to the greater part of the reduction in the employee's contribution.

79 The scheme outlined in Appendix E suggests that the rate of social security contribution should be linked with the unemployment percentage, in such a way that contributions would be automatically raised in times of full employment and lowered in times of unemployment. It is suggested that, if both the employer's and the employee's contributions could be varied within limits from 1s 3d above to 1s 3d below the normal weekly rate of contribution, the combined effect might be to alter total annual national expenditure by as much as £300 millions. It should thus introduce a very substantial, as well as a very prompt, stabilising influence.

80 As an alternative method, a stabilising influence might be introduced by making deferred income tax credits a permanent feature of the economy. The repayment of such credits after the war should, in any case, be controlled – repayment being made at as slow a rate as possible as long as it is desired to restrain total national expenditure, and being speeded up as soon as it is desired to stimulate such expenditure.

81 In Appendix F a scheme is suggested whereby this principle might be perpetuated. Every year a certain part of each individual's income-tax payment would be credited to a deferred income tax credit; and the rate at which individuals were permitted to draw upon these credits for expenditure would be automatically regulated so as to be raised in times of unemployment and lowered in times of full employment. The figures given for the purpose of illustration in Appendix F suggest that it might be possible to introduce an important stabilising influence by this means.

(iii) Industrial and Labour Market Conditions

82 A policy of controlling total national expenditure will not prevent the reappearance of unemployment unless:

(i)   a high level of demand for goods and services leads to increased production and employment rather than to rising profit margins and wage-rates; and
(ii) there is a greater mobility of labour and capital.

PROFIT MARGINS AND WAGE-RATES

83 In some cases, moderate prices and profit margins may best be secured by promoting competitive conditions, so that new competing output is forthcoming as soon as a brisk demand for the product of the industry leads to any excessive rise of profit margins. The entry of new enterprise into profitable industries could be assisted by means of the finance corporation suggested in paragraph 62 above. Action would have

to be taken to deal with price-rings and similar organisations; and a change in the patent law might reduce the power of monopolies based upon exclusive patent rights.

84   In other cases, complete public ownership may be the appropriate remedy. In these cases, the expansion of output and the maintenance of moderate profit margins in response to increased demand should form the basis of public operation. Moreover, investment of new capital equipment in a publicly owned concern is directly controlled by a public authority and can therefore form an additional element in the state's public investment programme.

85   In yet other cases an intermediate solution may be preferred. Restriction of output may be prevented by subjecting an industry to a price control which prevents prices from being raised out of relation to costs of production. A particular form of such control would be the continuation of the production of 'Utility' goods whose prices and qualities were controlled, so that increased demand must lead to increased turnover rather than to increased profit margins.

86   Many different forms of industrial structure are compatible with the maintenance of full employment. The essential question is not whether the industrial structure is of the one form or the other, but whether in each case it is of a kind which ensures expansion of output rather than increased profit margins in response to increased demand.

87   There is no need to stress the necessity of a moderate wages policy in order to prevent a vicious spiral of inflationary rises in wage-costs and prices, instead of an expansion of employment, resulting from any expansion of total national expenditure. It is to be hoped that the moderate wages policy, which has been successfully maintained without specific state control during the active demand of war, may be continued unchanged into the full employment which it is hoped to provide in peace. But if it should not, it will be necessary to impose some limitation upon the rate at which wage-rates may be raised, unless it is preferred to abandon the objective of full employment.

MOBILITY OF ECONOMIC RESOURCES

88   So long as there is any economic progress, with improvement in the standard of living, there will be changes in the relative importance of different industries and occupations. In order to reduce unemployment in industries which are declining (as well as to make possible adequate expansion of those which are becoming of greater importance), there must be mobility of labour and capital.

89   The fact that new resources becoming available for the first time enter the expanding industries, while normal wastage from the declining industries is not made good, is sufficient to account for much of the

necessary change. In the case of capital, this is, of course, the main element; but in the case of labour, unless resources are to be left unemployed, there must be an additional transfer of workers from their present occupations to new kinds of employment. Moreover, if growing industries are situated in different regions from those which are declining, workers will also have to move geographically.

90 In the years between the wars, the decline of the staple industries caused heavy structural unemployment. This was, moreover, highly concentrated in certain regions, so that there was a depressed area as well as a depressed industries problem. These years, however, did not experience uninterrupted conditions of generally expanding demand on a scale adequate to offset the decline in the staple industries. If general demand had been maintained at a higher level, then it is likely that the problem would have been much less intractable. Movement from declining to expanding industries must depend upon the employment opportunities which are available in the prosperous industries; the maintenance of a high level of general demand, by means of the financial and other general measures already outlined, should, in the post-war period, provide such employment opportunities on a scale adequate to absorb the workers displaced from industries undergoing structural decline.

91 It is, however, important that the employment opportunities in the expanding industries should not be reduced by restrictive practices. Mobility may also be reduced if relative wage-rates between occupations and regions become too rigid. In so far as money wage-rates in the regions in which labour supplies are scarce are higher than in the regions in which labour is redundant, there is an incentive for labour to move to the higher-paid regions. At the same time there would be an incentive to expand production in the areas where wage costs are lower. The same is true of mobility between occupations.

92 If, therefore, the high level of general demand can be maintained, and restrictive practices are reduced to a minimum, the problem of structural unemployment should be less intractable than it was between the two wars. There is, however, one important factor which will tend to reduce mobility. As a result of the falling birth rate over the last few decades, the working population is coming to consist of a higher proportion of older people. Older people are naturally less mobile than the young, and, moreover, the less rapidly a population expands, the less is the scope for bringing about changes in the relative importance of different industries by redirecting the stream of new recruits, so that actual transfer of older workers from one occupation to another, with perhaps transfer from one region to another, becomes more necessary.

93 When conditions are favourable, i.e., when there are adequate employment opportunities in expanding industries, there will usually be considerable movement of workers without direct intervention by the

state. Such spontaneous movement, however, is hardly likely to be enough to remove all structural unemployment, and intervention by the state would be necessary to overcome the obstacles to movement. The problem would be largely one of devising appropriate administrative measures, such as the provision of training, of financial assistance for removal and the cost of lodgings, and of assistance in finding alternative accommodation. The extension of schemes such as those developed by the Ministry of Labour before the war, modified as necessary by subsequent experience, should go a long way to meet post-war needs.

94 The obstacles to transfer from one occupation to another can largely be resolved into the two questions of training and wages. Experience suggests that this is an appropriate field for the extension of state action. There are, however, limits to the numbers who could be trained over a given period. The problem of wages arises when a worker who is skilled in his old occupation has to enter a new industry as a trainee. This is again a problem which arose in the inter-war years, and, again, the experience then gained should provide the basis for post-war schemes. In such cases, for example, employment might be temporarily subsidised.

95 The problem of geographical transfer, which, when it is present, is almost invariably additional to occupational transfer, is more obstinate. The various costs of movement involved in such transfer can be relatively easily met by state action, as was done in all the pre-war schemes. Some of the problems raised in movement from one house to another were not, however, fully covered by such schemes. For example, it may be difficult for workers who own their own houses to dispose of them; others who are purchasing their houses through building societies may be unable to sell them at sums sufficient to meet the outstanding balance of the mortgages; in some cases again, workers have the advantage of living in houses at specially low rents in their old areas; and in all cases movement will be impeded unless alternative accommodation is readily available in the new areas.

96 In addition to these various costs, which can probably be overcome without too great difficulty, there are very important personal factors which may involve great resistance to transfer and which cannot be so readily overcome. Indeed, in some respects this is the crux of the problem, for those workers whose local and family ties are weakest will probably move on their own account, leaving, as subjects for state action, those whose ties are strongest and who are, therefore, most likely to resist inducements to transfer.

97 Because of the difficulties of transfer on a scale necessary to eliminate geographical unemployment, it is sometimes suggested that industry should be taken to the workers rather than the workers transfer to new areas. Control over the location of industry is, therefore, suggested as necessary, on the one hand by developing some diversification of industry in every area, to reduce the risk of intensely localised

unemployment in the future, and on the other as a means of avoiding large-scale transfer of workers from areas which have become depressed. There is, however, considerable divergence of view about the general desirability and extent of such control. One view is that the industrialist is in the best position to decide the most efficient site for his factory, so that to prevent, or even to restrict, his freedom of choice would result in increased costs of production, and perhaps prevent the establishment of the factory. At the other extreme, there is the view that complete control over location, by means, for example, of a system of licences, is necessary not only in order to assist the treatment of the problem of depressed areas, but also to prevent certain aberrations on the part of the industrialist, and to ensure that the location of industry as a whole is such as to give maximum social efficiency.

98   Both of these extreme views are open to strong criticism. It can be shown that in many cases the state, either consciously or unconsciously, already influences the choice of the industrialist. In so far as a new factory requires new public services, their provision by local authorities (accompanied by the de-rating of industrial premises and the increased subsidisation of local rates) means that the industrialist seldom meets the full costs of establishing such services. Thus it may be argued that if complete freedom of choice is to be left to the industrialist, he should have to bear all the costs incurred. Alternatively, if it is thought desirable on other grounds that industrial concerns should be relieved of a substantial part of the cost of local services, the state should see that this arrangement does not lead to an unnecessary duplication of social capital. Again, although there may be some cases in which a new industrial development is more or less tied to a particular site, in the large majority of cases there is some range of choice among sites of equal efficiency; thus, it may be argued that to leave the final choice to the industrialist is wrong, and that the state should intervene to decide which of the comparable sites should be adopted in the interests of maximum social advantage. Moreover, the fact that on general grounds wage-rates are not permitted to fall in depressed areas to the abnormally low levels to which they would otherwise be driven by the competition of large numbers of unemployed in the labour market removes a possible incentive for expanding employment in those areas; and it is arguable that this justifies state action to encourage employment in those areas. Finally, some control over industrial location is implied in the development of Town and Country Planning, which will, to some extent, restrict the areas into which new industries are free to go.

99   There are, however, considerable dangers in strict control and direction of industrial location. In some industries the differences in cost involved in different locations are of considerable importance, and for these it is unlikely that rational state control would give results appreciably different from those of free choice by the industrialist. Even where this is not the case, there are difficulties involved in the choice of which areas should be developed, or prevented from declining in

importance. Certain of the depressed areas were developed primarily for their coal or other natural resources. When the coal is worked out or no longer profitable to mine there is probably a case for the ordered withdrawal from these areas, unless there is strong reason to believe that they are suitable for general industrial purposes. It would clearly be unfortunate if the future pattern of industrial location should be fixed by events which occurred in the past and which are no longer relevant. Again, there are many political and administrative difficulties in the way of complete control; almost every new factory might become the subject of a political struggle between different areas. Moreover, if there were a general presumption that new industries would be directed into a depressed area, this would certainly act as an impediment to other kinds of necessary readjustment; one of the factors delaying readjustment in the inter-war years was the failure to realise that the staple industries of the depressed areas were unlikely to recover their former predominant position, and it is undesirable that such impediments should be strengthened.

100   For these various reasons, it seems clear that it is not possible to lay down a general principle that industries must be moved to the workers, any more than the converse that the workers must be moved to industry. Each case should be considered on its own merits. In some the state may well relieve structural unemployment by bringing industry to the area; in others, the best policy would be to use all the services of the state to secure a planned withdrawal from the area. In others it may be that the appropriate procedure would be to apply both kinds of remedy, transferring some labour away from the area, and providing employment for those who remain.

THE LABOUR CONTRACT

101   The maintenance of the general level of demand combined with an increased mobility of labour and capital should prevent the regrowth of mass unemployment after the war. It might be possible also to reduce the level of frictional unemployment to which reference has been made in paragraphs 6–8 above. If employers gave rather longer labour contracts, the amount of intermittent unemployment might be reduced; and employers might, for example, in certain trades produce for stock in slack periods instead of turning off labour temporarily. It is a matter for further consideration whether and, if so, by what means such a lengthening of labour contracts could be brought about.

III Immediate Post-war Problems

102   The preceding sections of this paper have been concerned with the problems of unemployment, which are likely to arise after the immediate post-war transition from war-time to a peace-time economy has been effected. The period of actual transition itself will present special problems.

103 Reasons have been given at length in another connection (RP(42)21 ['The Internal Economic Problems of the Post-War Transitional Period', 30 June 1942, Public Record Office CAB87/2]) for holding the belief that, for a time after the war, there is likely to be an excess of potential total national expenditure over the supplies of goods and services available on the market. This was so after the war of 1914–18 and this tendency will probably be more marked after this war.

104 In the first place, although there will be considerable reduction in Government expenditure, expenditure on the armed forces and on other services is likely to remain at a substantially higher level than it did last time.

105 Secondly, home investment by private enterprise for a time will be very high. Not only will normal arrears of maintenance and expansion of housing and of industrial plant and equipment need to be made good, but war damage to property of all kinds will require to be repaired. Stocks of working capital will, in many cases, need to be reconstituted.

106 Thirdly, individuals' demands for goods and services for personal consumption will be very insistent for a time. The severe restriction of purchases which has taken place during the war will mean that, for many durable or semi-durable goods – cars, wireless sets and clothing, for example – there will be a large pent-up demand, which will be reinforced by the potential expenditure of the post-war income tax credits and small savings which many persons will have to spend.

107 Fourthly, it is generally admitted that this country will have to take special measures to expand its export trade, not only to restore the pre-war position, but also to replace the loss of overseas income from such sources as foreign investments. The necessary export drive will require special measures to give priority to production for export; whatever may be the actual means adopted for this purpose, it will increase the total demand for home-produced goods and services.

108 The transitional period will, therefore, require measures of financial restraint. Savings will still need encouragement; tax rates will have to remain high; in some cases rationing or other limitations on the consumption of particular commodities will need to be continued; and restraining influences, by the allocation of raw materials or of labour, or by a system of licensing, will probably have to be exercised not only over building, but also over other forms of capital development.

109 At the same time, however, there may be a serious, though temporary, unemployment problem due to the dislocations caused by the process of rapid transition from war to peace. Many millions of men and women may need to find new jobs as a result of demobilisation from the armed forces, civil defence, and the munitions industries. They will not all be demobilised in the right place, nor will they all have the training

which will best fit them for their new peace-time tasks. Moreover, for a time, special bottlenecks in the form of acute shortages of key workers or specific raw materials or of special types of equipment may delay the full re-employment of all the demobilised labour.

110   For these reasons, special measures will be required to promote the occupational and geographical mobility of labour and to break down bottlenecks which may hold up the re-employment of labour in particular trades.

111   These short-period problems lie outside the scope of the present paper. But two points are directly relevant to the problem of longer-period unemployment. In the first place, the difference between the problems of unemployment in the immediate post-war transition and in subsequent years must be fully realised. If an attempt were made to cure immediate post-war dislocations by a general stimulation of total demand, the result would be merely a general inflation which would discredit the use of a proper policy for the more normal subsequent period.

112   But, secondly, the experience of the immediate post-war period will teach many lessons for the subsequent periods. Thus the need for the geographical and occupational mobility of labour will be a continuing one; and the mechanisms used in the transitional period for the placing and retraining of demobilised labour may serve permanently, with suitable modification, to promote labour transfer in subsequent periods.

113   Moreover, some of the measures of fiscal policy by which total demand will be restricted during the transitional period can also be used to stimulate expenditure in subsequent periods. As far as taxation is concerned, for example, the reverse of those fiscal measures which have been found most effective in restraining it.

114   The post-war building programme recently under discussion (cf. IEP(43)2 ['Report on the Economic Background of the Post-War Building and Constructional Programme', 14 January 1943, Public Record Office CAB87/57]) provides a good example of continuity between problems of the immediate post-war period and those of the more normal longer period. The building programme will at first require great restraint, while the supplies of materials and labour are being built up to meet an inflated demand; it will for a time continue at a high level; and it will then tend to decline. The period of restraint will give place to a period in which activity may need to be stimulated. But the problems of control will remain in many respects unchanged. For example, there will be a continuing need for labour mobility at first for a large-scale movement into building and later, possibly, for some net contraction of the labour supply; building will provide a good example of an industry in which, if a high level of demand is allowed to give rise to a rapid rise of prices and costs, output and employment may fail to expand adequately;

and it will be necessary throughout to maintain the greatest possible flexibility in the total building programme, so that activity can be speeded up or postponed as far as possible to meet the needs of the general stabilisation of total national expenditure.

115 This continuity of policy should apply to the whole field of home investment. Thus, after the war an attempt should be made to bring into relation with the available capital resources not only the building programme but also the other programmes of capital development. These programmes will at first be primarily for physical reconstruction, and the first concern will be to restrict them. But this period should merge without any sharp break into the more normal post-war period, when the main task will be to maintain capital development at a stable and high level.

IV Summary of Conclusions

(a) International Action for the Maintenance of World Demand

116 In addition to the proposals which have already been put forward for the control of the prices of primary products by means of international buffer stocks, and for monetary and commercial policies – through the proposed Clearing Union and Commercial Union – to aid in the adjustment of international balances of payments, it is suggested that there are two other forms of international action which require consideration:-

(i) Arrangements should be made for the control of international investment in such a way as to aid in the stabilisation of total world demand.

(ii) Some mechanism is required for the international co-operation of national policies for the maintenance of internal demand.

(b) The Control of Home Investment

117 A general influence over investment, both by public authorities and also by private enterprise, can be exercised by means of banking policy:-

(iii) Banking policy should be so controlled as to ensure a reduction in long-term as well as in short-term interest rates, and a general easing of monetary conditions, if a general stimulus to demand is required for the purpose of maintaining full employment.

118 Public investment should be properly timed. Such a policy raises a number of issues.

(iv)   All public investment must as far as possible be planned ahead and all other preliminary arrangements must be made well in advance, so that actual capital expenditure can be speeded up as promptly as possible when necessary.

(v)   It is necessary to determine how the central authority can best control the capital expenditure of the various authorities concerned, by direction or by financial inducement, in such a way as to speed up as well as to postpone capital construction.

(vi)   It is necessary to consider the methods by which public authorities' capital expenditure should be financed.

119   A number of means have been proposed by which investment by private enterprise might also be controlled:-

(vii)   A continuation of the control of new capital issues would help to control the timing of private investment.

(viii) There might be some system of relief of taxation on capital development that is properly planned and timed.

(ix)   A special Government Finance Corporation for the advancing of capital funds to industry and, in particular, to new enterprises might assist the control of private investment.

(c)   The Control of Personal Expenditure on Consumption

120   The control of personal expenditure on consumption will probably have to play a prominent part in any post-war control of total national expenditure:-

(x)   Hire-purchase finance might be so controlled as to restrain purchases in times of full employment and to stimulate them in times of threatening depression.

(xi)   Rates of taxation might be raised or lowered as a means of influencing private expenditure.

(d)   Budgetary Policy

121   The proposed policy for controlling total national expenditure involves the use of the Budget as a balancing instrument.

(xii)   Budgetary policy should be reviewed in the light of this principle, in particular to consider how the problem of the national debt can best be handled in a manner consistent with the policy for full employment.

(e)   Prompt Action for Offsetting Fluctuations

122   There is need for some scheme for the prompt offsetting of

economic fluctuations in order to nip in the bud any tendency for a general depression to develop. For this purpose:-

(xiii) Personal expenditure might be controlled by raising social security contributions in times of full employment, and lowering them in times of unemployment.

(xiv) Alternatively, such expenditure might be controlled by the continuation of a scheme for income tax deferred credits, the repayment of which would be timed so as to provide additional expenditure in times of unemployment.

(f) Prices, Profit Margins and Wage-Rates

123 In order that a policy of economic expansion may succeed, an inflation of prices, profit margins and wage-rates must be avoided. In this connection the following points need further investigation:-

(xv) The possibility of financing the entrance of new enterprise into profitable industries by means of the finance corporation suggested at (ix) above.

(xvi) The possibility of a change in the law which would reduce the power of monopolies based upon the exclusive use of patents.

(xvii) Means for dealing with price-rings or other industrial arrangements which tend to the restriction of output and the maintenance of prices and profit margins.

(xviii) The possibility of continuing the control of prices and qualities of standardised articles in order to promote a large output at low profit margins.

(xix) The price policy which should be adopted by public enterprise for any goods or services that may be so produced.

(xx) The continuation of a moderate wages policy is an essential condition for a policy for full employment.

(xxi) While a general reduction of money wage-rates is not suggested as a means for curing the problem of 'general' unemployment, some flexibility of wage-rates which allows wages to be higher in expanding than in contracting regions and occupations will aid in diminishing the problem of 'special' unemployment.

(g) The Mobility of Economic Resources

124 To prevent large-scale structural unemployment the mobility of labour and capital must be increased.

(xxii) Restrictive practices which hinder the entrance of new workers into expanding trades impede a policy for full employment.

(xxiii) Adequate facilities must be available for the retraining of labour.

(xxiv) Adequate financial assistance must be given to meet the costs of transfer from one area to another.

(xxv) The transfer of labour raises the problem of alternative housing accommodation.

(xxvi) It is a matter for consideration what steps should be taken to bring employment into specially depressed areas.

(h)   The Reduction of Frictional Unemployment

125 There are certain ways in which frictional unemployment may be reduced.

(xxvii) If it were possible to encourage longer-term labour contracts, the volume of frictional unemployment might be reduced.

(i)   Statistical and Other Information

126 In order that a policy for full employment may be operated effectively and promptly, an adequate body of statistical and other information must be available. There should be a general enquiry into the adequacy of existing statistical information for the purpose. In particular:-

(xxviii) Consideration should be given to the collection of that type of information (e.g. the state of producers' order books in different industries) which is most useful in forming a judgement on the probable *future* course of expenditure, production and employment.

(xxix) The statistics at present available for home investment are inadequate, and fuller estimates in this connection should be prepared as part of the present continuing enquiry into national income and expenditure.

(j)   Development of Administrative Machinery and Powers

127 No attention has been given in this paper to the new administrative arrangements or the new governmental powers which would be necessary to carry out the various suggestions made for the maintenance of full employment.

(xxx) An investigation is needed of the new administrative machinery or new governmental powers that would be required for carrying out the above suggestions.

Appendix E Variations in Social Security Contributions

I An Illustrative Scheme

1   The following scheme for variations of social security contributions is put forward as an illustration of the proposals made in paragraphs 76–79 of the main memorandum.

2   The following are the details of a possible scheme:-

(i)   The weekly stamp to be affixed by the employer to each employee's social security card shall vary according to the unemployment percentage on the following sliding scale:-

Unemployment Percentage	Weekly Social Insurance Stamp
Less than 5 per cent	10s 0d
Between 5 and 7 per cent	8s 9d
Between 7 and 9 per cent	7s 6d
Between 9 and 11 per cent	6s 3d
More than 11 per cent	5s 0d

(ii)   One half of the current cost of the social insurance stamp shall in each period be deducted by the employers from the employees' wages, except that no deduction from an employee's wages shall exceed 2s 0d from any wage payment not exceeding £2 or 1s 0d from any wage payment not exceeding £1.

(iii)   The sliding scale shall be considered for revision by the social insurance statutory committee at the end of the first three years during which it has been in operation, and thereafter at the end of each ten-year period. The revision shall be undertaken in the light of experience in order to determine that scale which is most likely to keep the social security fund in balance over a period of good and bad years, when allowance has been made for the amount of state contributions and of any other income of the fund.

(iv)   The social insurance statutory committee shall announce at the end of each calendar quarter of the year the rate of contribution which will rule during the forthcoming calendar quarter on the basis of the sliding scale given in paragraph (i) (or as revised in accordance with paragraph (iii). For the purpose of this sliding scale the unemployment percentage shall be the average of the unemployment percentages of the preceding three months.

(v)   Employers must fix to each employee's social insurance card, in respect of contributions payable during each quarter, insurance stamps of the value current during that quarter. Post Offices will buy back from employers any excess stocks of stamps which employers may possess of an out-of-date denomination.

II   The Quantitative Importance of the Scheme

3   In the illustrative scheme outlined in the preceding paragraph, it is suggested that employers' and employees' contributions should vary by as much as 5s 0d (*i.e.* from 10s 0d when the unemployment percentage was less than 5% to 5s 0d when the percentage had risen above 11%). This would mean that the employer's and the employee's contribution would each vary by 1s 3d above or below its normal level of 3s 9d. This would produce a variation of some £250 millions per annum in the revenue from contributions. Of this some £125 millions would represent changes in employees' and some £125 millions changes in employers' contributions. If we assume that about 80% of any increase in wage-earners' receipts will be spent, the variation of employees' contributions would give rise directly to a change of about £100 millions in wage-earners' demand for consumption goods and services. We must, however, take into account the further repercussions of this increase in expenditure. For this increased demand for goods and services will give rise to increased output and employment and so to increased wages and profits and so to further increases in demand for consumption goods and services, and so on. There is some evidence that in the United Kingdom these repercussions are likely approximately to double the effect of the primary increase in expenditure. If this were so, the ultimate effect of a reduction of £125 millions in employees' contributions would be to increase the total demand for consumption goods and services by some £200 millions.

4   The effect of a change in employer's contribution is less certain. It would probably be less prompt and smaller than that of a change in employee's contribution. If it were between a quarter and a half as effective, the combined effect upon the total demand for consumption goods and services of the proposed scale of variations in employer's and employee's contributions would amount to between £250 and £300 millions. This calculation is on the conservative side; for it does not make any allowance for the stimulus to the demand for capital goods which might be expected to result from the improvement in the demand for consumption goods, nor for the further repercussions of any such stimulus to the demand for capital goods.

5   These figures suggest that the proposed scheme would exert a very substantial stabilising influence on the national income. On the assumptions made in the preceding paragraphs an increase of the unemployment percentage by two points (e.g. from 7% to 9%) would lead to an automatic reduction of employers' and employee's contributions of some £60 millions a year which – after allowance for its direct and indirect repercussions – might lead to an increase in demand of some £75 millions a year. At the same time it may be roughly estimated that a 2 per cent decrease in employment after the war may itself reduce the national income by some £120 millions a year. If these calculations are correct it would follow that the proposed scheme would itself account for more

than one half of the general stabilising influence that must be exerted to offset fluctuations in employment and the national income. Whatever may be the uncertainties in these calculations it may at least be confidently concluded that the scheme is quantitatively of great significance.

III The Automatic Character of the Scheme

6 For the operation of the controls over the total national expenditure which are discussed in paragraphs 49–73 of the main memorandum (e.g. the planning of public investment and the formation of budgetary policy), it will be necessary to plan ahead from year to year. For these purposes no automatic criterion of action can be adopted. On the contrary, on the basis of information about movements in prices, production, employment, national income and the future prospects of various sections of the national economy, a judgement must be formed as to the prospects of an inflation or deflation of the general level of total national expenditure. On the basis of such judgement an 'arbitrary' decision must be taken about future policy.

7 If a suitable body could be found for the administration of such a scheme, it is arguable that alterations in the rate of social security contributions should similarly be determined 'arbitrarily' within certain limits. By such means all the relevant factors would be borne in mind; some purely fortuitous and temporary changes which may result from the best devised 'rule of thumb' sliding scale might be avoided; and the policy in this particular field could be co-ordinated with all the other aspects of economic and financial policy which may be adopted for the purpose of stabilisation.

8 On the other hand the peculiar virtue of the proposal for variations in social security contributions is that, acting as a stop-gap if the more general plans for stabilisation do not achieve the desired result, it will take effect with the greatest promptness as soon as unemployment does in fact actually rise or fall. For this purpose what is required is precisely an automatic link with the unemployment percentage.

9 There are, moreover, certain special arguments in favour of an automatic system. In the first place, a solution which left the determination of changes in such important levies as the social security contributions to the 'arbitrary' decision of a public body, however impartial, would raise very great political difficulties; and an automatic change of levy, on a scale pre-determined by Parliament, should avoid at least some of these difficulties. Secondly, in the case of the social security fund, it will be desired to achieve a balance over an average of years between the receipts and contributions of the fund. If all the widest economic and financial issues are taken into account in determining the rate of contributions, there is no reason to believe that this balance will be achieved. But if a simple automatic sliding scale between rates of

contribution and the unemployment percentage is chosen, and *if this sliding scale is adjusted from time to time with the sole object of achieving a balance in the fund over an average of years*, it is to be expected that any lack of balance of the fund will not accumulate progressively in the one direction or the other.

10   The dangers inherent in an automatic link between the percentage of unemployment and the level of social security contributions should be met by two provisions of the scheme outlined in paragraph 2:-

(i)   In the first place, an examination of the movements in the unemployment percentage between 1923 and 1938 suggests that, in order to avoid changes in the rate of social security contributions that are occasioned by purely random and erratic changes in unemployment, it would be wise to make changes in the rate of social security contributions depend upon intervals of not less than two points in the unemployment percentage. If intervals of this size were chosen, it would not be necessary to eliminate seasonal movements from the unemployment percentage, since the great majority of seasonal movements would fall well within the two-point intervals of the unemployment percentage. The intervals proposed in the sliding scale in paragraph 2(i) have been chosen with this object in view.

(ii)   Secondly, the provision made in paragraph 2(iii) for the periodic revision of the sliding scale should make it possible to adjust the scheme properly to long-period changes in the amount of 'structural' and similar unemployment which it would be inappropriate to attempt to remove solely by measures of financial expansion.

Appendix F   The Use of Income Tax Deferred Credits as a Stabilising Mechanism in Peace-time

1   The suggestion is made in this Appendix that the mechanism of income tax deferred credits with which taxpayers are becoming familiarised in war-time might be continued in peace-time for restraining or stimulating consumers' expenditure according as the situation required a restraining or stimulating influence.

2   It is assumed that a system can be continued whereby a certain amount of income tax (called the deferred credit) is credited annually to each income taxpayer. This may be on the present basis (i.e. the amount of income tax which is levied as a result of the reduction of allowances from one level to another); or it might quite simply be ruled that the first £x of income tax to which any individual was liable should be added to his deferred credit.

3   Each taxpayer would have a Deferred Credit Book in which his

deferred credits would be accumulated annually. Each quarter it would be announced how great was the maximum sum which each taxpayer could draw in cash in the course of that quarter at the Post Office from the accumulated sums in his Deferred Credit Book. This maximum would vary automatically on a fixed sliding scale according to the unemployment percentage ruling on the average of the preceding three months.

4   The following is a numerical example of the way in which the scheme might work. Assume 5 million income taxpayers paying to their deferred credits a total of £100 millions a year (i.e. an average annual deferred credit of £20 a head). Then the following might be an appropriate sliding scale:-

Unemployment percentage in preceding quarter	Maximum amount to be withdrawn in quarter by each taxpayer	Total amount withdrawable by 5 million taxpayers (annual rate)	Previous column less the £100 millions paid annually in income tax for the accumulation of deferred credits, i.e. net deflationary (−) or inflationary (+) influence of the scheme (annual rate)
	£	£m.	£m.
Less than 5%	0	0	−100
Between 5 and 7%	2½	50	− 50
Between 7 and 9%	5	100	0
Between 9 and 11%	7½	150	+ 50
More than 11%	10	200	+100

5   With this sliding scale, at 8 per cent unemployment the total of accumulated deferred credits which could be encashed (£100 million per annum) would be equal to the deferred credits being newly accumulated. At unemployment percentages lower than this the taxation levied for new deferred credits would be greater than current encashments of outstanding deferred credits; but at unemployment percentages greater than 8 per cent the scheme would have a net stimulating effect upon consumers' expenditure.

6   The scheme is likely to be less effective than that put forward in Appendix E for variations in social security contributions. In the first place, it will be effective only so long as taxpayers have an accumulation of deferred tax credits on which to draw; and for this reason its effectiveness would diminish as a depression continued. Secondly, permission to withdraw credits for expenditure is less likely to stimulate expenditure than the remission of a weekly charge on wage incomes.

7   Nevertheless, if the proposal made in Appendix E is for any reason

unacceptable, this scheme might provide an important alternative. In the example given in paragraph 4 the annual rate of withdrawal of accumulated credits might vary by as much as £200 millions. Even though the variations in total expenditure which the scheme would directly bring about would probably, for the reasons given in the preceding paragraph, be considerably less than this, yet the total resulting offset to the national income might be very substantial when account is taken of the secondary repercussions of any direct change in expenditure.

8   If the general idea of some such scheme were acceptable, it would be necessary to consider a number of questions arising out of the transition from the war-time position to a more normal peace-time economy.

(i)   During the immediate post-war transitional period, the unemployment percentage will not well indicate the need for a stimulation or restraint of expenditure. It is only at a somewhat later date that automatic use of such an index would become appropriate.

(ii)   During this transitional period it will no doubt be desirable as far as possible to restrain the encashment of existing deferred credits and to maintain high rates of taxation. Could the introduction of a permanent scheme be attractively dressed up in such a manner as to make this Spartan behaviour more palatable?

(iii)   There are certain commitments or expectations about the repayment of existing deferred credits and the readjustment of existing income-tax allowances. Can these be made compatible with the introduction of a permanent scheme?

15

Sir William Beveridge's
Full Employment in a Free Society
and the White Paper on Employment
Policy (Command 6527)

After the publication of the White Paper in May 1944 and of Beveridge's book in November (London: George Allen & Unwin, 1944), Meade wrote this commentary, dated 1 December 1944, which was circulated to ministers by Lord Woolton, Minister of Reconstruction 1943–45, early in 1945 (Public Record Office T230/16 and 69, Meade Papers 3/2 and Meade Diary, 14 January 1945).

I   The General Principles of Policy

1   In any comparison between Sir William Beveridge's book and the Government White Paper on Employment Policy the most striking feature is the great similarity in the general treatment of the problem in the two documents. In both cases the analysis of the problem and the policy suggested for its solution are essentially the same. Indeed, it may now be safely assumed that the principles of post-war employment policy are generally agreed among economists, political parties, officials and the general public. It requires no more than the vaguest memory of the inter-war years to realise what an important advance this fact marks.

2   Sir William Beveridge maintains that 'action against unemployment must be taken on three lines – of maintaining at all times adequate total outlay; of controlling the location of industry; of securing the organized mobility of labour. The first of these is the main attack; the others are subsidiary – mopping-up operations.' (Paragraph 31.) The White Paper on Employment Policy argues that 'a country will not suffer from mass unemployment so long as the total demand for its goods and services is maintained at a high level.' (second paragraph of the Foreword); and it goes on, in a later section, to explain that 'the Government propose to attack the problems of local unemployment (a) by so influencing the location of new enterprises as to diversify the industrial composition of areas which are particularly vulnerable to unemployment; (b) by removing obstacles to the transfer of workers from one area to another

and from one occupation to another; (c) by providing training facilities to fit workers from declining industries for jobs in expanding industries'.

3   The central and agreed intention is, therefore, to forecast and, as far as possible, to control the general level of total national expenditure in such a way as to maintain a steady and high demand for labour: such action, it is agreed, will prevent the recurrence of mass unemployment due to a general deficiency of buying throughout the economic system. But it is also agreed that specialised unemployment, due to declining demand for labour in particular occupations or in particular districts, even in conditions of a high general level of demand, may cause serious pockets of localised unemployment. For these reasons in both documents it is recognised that the central policy of maintaining aggregate demand at an adequate level should be supplemented by measures to encourage the occupational and geographical mobility of labour and by measures to encourage the development of industry in districts of high unemployment.

4   In both documents it is also recognised that the general policy must be made effective in conditions in which the consumers are, broadly speaking, free to choose what they will and what they will not buy, and workers are free to choose where they will work and what they will work at. In the White Paper this assumption of a 'free society' is not explicitly stated; but all the policies which it proposes are in fact based on such an assumption. In Sir William Beveridge's book this assumption is explicitly stated: 'The Report, as its title indicates, is not concerned simply with the problem of full employment. It is concerned with the . . . methods of achieving full employment . . . subject to the proviso that all essential citizen liberties are preserved' including 'freedom in choice of occupation; and freedom in management of a personal income'. (Paragraph 11.)

5   The above points cover the main principles of employment policy. But there are also some further consequential matters on which there is, in principle, agreement between Sir William Beveridge's book and the White Paper. In the first place, both documents make the point that the policy of maintaining a high and stable level of employment may be frustrated if a brisk demand for labour is followed by an immoderate and inflationary upward movement of wages. Sir William Beveridge asks: 'Under conditions of full employment can a rising spiral of wages and prices be prevented if collective bargaining, with the right to strike, remains absolutely free?' (paragraph 13); and the White Paper argues that 'if we are to operate with success a policy for maintaining a high and stable level of employment, it will be essential that employers and workers should exercise moderation in wage matters so that increased expenditure provided at the onset of depression may go to increase the volume of employment.' (Paragraph 49.)

6   Secondly, there is agreement that restrictive practices both by workers and by employers may impede the carrying out of a full

employment policy. Restrictive practices of workers' organisations by preventing new workers from entering the industries whose products are in high demand or by impeding workers in any industry from producing as much as they otherwise might, are recognised to be obstacles in the way of achieving the maximum level of employment at the highest possible standard of living. It is also recognised in both documents that agreements among producers to restrict output or to maintain prices might cause an expansion of demand to waste itself in increased prices and profits rather than to lead to increased output and employment. Sir William Beveridge writes that 'it is clear that if, with peace, industrial demarcations with all the restrictive tendencies and customs of the past return in full force, a policy of outlay for full employment, however vigorously it is pursued by the State, will fail to cure unemployment and may encounter difficulties in raising the general standard of living' (paragraph 234); and that 'the response of industries already strongly organized to the setting up of a demand for their services might take the form of endeavouring to exploit the demand by raising prices, rather than of meeting the demand by increased production. It is essential that a full employment policy should be protected against such risks of exploitation.' (Paragraph 294.) The White Paper expresses similar sentiments in saying that 'workers must examine their trade practices and customs to ensure that they do not constitute a serious impediment to an expansionist economy and so defeat the object of a full employment programme. Employers, too, must seek in larger output rather than higher prices the reward of enterprise and good management.' (Paragraph 54.)

7 In the third place, the policy for high employment adopted in both these documents does not depend either upon the maintenance of private enterprise or upon the socialisation of industry. The essential feature of the policy is so to control the total level of national expenditure that there is a sufficient, but not excessive, demand for the products of industry when industry is producing at a high and active level. It is the policy of ensuring that there is a market for what is produced when the labour resources of the community are actively employed; but the problem of finding a market for the product of any particular industry is the same, whether that industry be run under conditions of private enterprise or of public control. The Government White Paper, the product of a Coalition Government, naturally tacitly assumes that the question of socialisation versus private enterprise is left unbegged. Sir William Beveridge in his book expresses the assumption more explicitly when he writes: 'The basic proposals of this Report are neither socialism nor an alternative to socialism; they are required and will work under capitalism and under socialism alike, and whether the sector of industry conducted by private enterprise is large or is small.' (Paragraph 300.)

8 Finally, it is common ground between the White Paper and Sir William Beveridge's book that continuity in the principles of policy, whatever may be the changes in the political complexion of the government of the day, is a necessary condition for the effective carrying

out of an employment policy. Since the policy in question does not in general depend either upon the preservation of private enterprise or upon the extension of socialisation, such continuity of policy should prove possible. Effective and swift action in face of a depression will be possible only if there is nation-wide acceptance of the principles of employment policy. Sir William Beveridge makes this point when he writes that 'in a free society the governing authority is liable to be changed at short intervals by peaceful methods of organization and voting. There must be reasonable continuity of economic policy in spite of such changes of government.' (Paragraph 12.) The White Paper states that 'if action is to be taken quickly enough to have its full effect, the Government of the day must be able to rely on the support and co-operation of the public in applying the principles of an agreed national policy.' (Paragraph 86.)

II   The Target Level of Employment

9   When we move from the general principles discussed above to the detailed suggestions made in the two documents, there are a number of important differences of emphasis. The most important of these is the treatment of the target level of employment. As far as the Government White Paper is concerned, no definite numerical target is set. The only passage in which any numerical value is given to the future average level of unemployment is in Appendix 2 of the White Paper on 'Variation of Social Insurance Contributions'. Here, in order to illustrate the working of the scheme, a numerical example is given in which it is assumed that the average level of unemployment is forecast at 8%.

10   In other words, the Government White Paper adopts very sensibly a rather non-committal attitude on the degree to which it will be possible to reduce unemployment; and when, merely for the purposes of illustration, a numerical figure must be quoted, it makes a cautious estimate. In a public document with the authority of the Government behind it no other attitude could be responsibly taken. The whole employment policy is a novel one and the conditions which will rule after the war are uncertain; and in these circumstances it would be unwise to raise expectations which it might not prove possible to fulfill. For reasons which will be outlined in later paragraphs of this note, there are in fact great obstacles to be overcome before one can feel assured of the full success of an employment policy. It would certainly be unduly cautious not, in fact, to aim at something appreciably better than 8%; but publicly to commit the Government to a figure considerably lower than this might be unwise at this stage.

11   Sir William Beveridge, on the other hand, sets as his target an average unemployment percentage of 3%; and nails his colours to this mast.

12   It is to be observed that this average of 3% is only one-half of what

was probably the average level of unemployment in the years before 1914. Sir William Beveridge, who is perhaps the outstanding authority on this question, himself calculates that the most probable average rate of unemployment between 1883 and 1913 was 6%, as compared with an average rate of 14.2% between the two wars. In other words, Sir William Beveridge is assuming that employment policy should be so successful as to reduce unemployment to not much more than one-fifth of the inter-war level and to one-half of the level before the First World War.

13   This is obviously a very high target. It means not only the complete abolition of the inter-war mass unemployment; but a halving of the much more moderate unemployment that existed before that. It is, however, probable that the economic system has become less flexible since the pre-1914 period. Since the First World War there have been introduced many very desirable social reforms of a kind which are to be extended after this war through the improvement of the social services. In addition to any direct effect which such reforms may have in reducing the immediate pressure on the unemployed to find a new job, they may have even more important secondary effects in making the economic system rather more rigid. For example, so long as the unemployed and other persons in want are cared for by the state, trade unions and other monopolistic bodies dealing with the regulation of wages and conditions of entry into different occupations, in deciding upon the line of policy which they shall adopt, are tempted to pay more attention to the interests of their own members who are in work than to the desirability of finding extra employment for their own unemployed members or for other outsiders. And if the outsiders, when they are unemployed, are supported by the state, they in turn will have less incentive to break the labour monopoly.

14   Moreover, there is a profound change gradually coming over the labour market as a result of changes in the population structure of the country. In the years before the First World War the population was growing rapidly and the ratio of new juvenile entrants into each industry was accordingly high. Now the working population of the country is stabilised, and is likely soon actually to decline. The ratio of new entrants to the number of persons in each industry will be very much lower than before the First World War. This means that the economic system will be much more rigid and that it will be much more difficult to shift labour from one locality to another or from one occupation to another. In the first place, the young can move more rapidly than the old; and, secondly, it is much easier to change the relative importance of different industries by guiding new entrants into one industry rather than into another, than it is to take existing workers out of one industry and transfer them into another.

15   For all those reasons the problem of avoiding structural unemployment is likely to be more difficult than it was before the First World War. There are, of course, certain considerations to set against this. In the first

place, there was undoubtedly some unemployment before the First World War which was due to general deficiency of demand, and we may at least aim at improving on this. Secondly, before the First World War the labour market was unorganised and the employment exchanges did not even exist. We may hope, therefore, to avoid some measure of frictional unemployment by the better organisation of the labour market. But when all is said and done, it remains extremely sanguine to set as an absolute target a halving of the level of unemployment before the First World War.

16   When one comes to analyse the make-up of Sir William Beveridge's 3%, the difficulties of attaining so low an average level are equally apparent. The 3% is made up of three items:-

   (i)   Sir William Beveridge allows 1% for seasonal unemployment.
   (ii)   He allows another 1% for the margin for change of unemploy-
          ment incidental to progress, or, in other words, for the
          unavoidable minimum of temporary unemployment as men
          move from one job to another.
   (iii) Lastly, he allows another 1% of unemployment because this
          country depends largely on international trade which we cannot
          completely control so that we must allow for a certain measure
          of unplanned fluctuation and instability in the demand for our
          products.

17   As far as the allowance for seasonal unemployment is concerned, Sir William Beveridge writes: 'The actual amount of seasonal unemployment before the present war was estimated at about 2 per cent by Mr. Christopher Saunders, rather more in bad years and less in good years. The same study showed that there was much seasonal unemployment – the motor industry was a conspicuous illustration of this – for which there was neither justification nor need. With proper organization and under conditions of full employment there should be no difficulty in reducing seasonal unemployment to half its former figure, that is to say to 1 per cent.' (Paragraph 169.) This is the only reference to seasonal unemployment in Sir William's book; and we are left, therefore, to understand that the target level of unemployment is based upon the assumption that the seasonal element in unemployment is halved without the 429 pages of the book on full employment having given any indication of the way in which this result is to be achieved.

18   The other 2% unemployment for which Sir William allows in his target covers, as we have seen, merely the inevitable minimum of frictional unemployment and of unemployment which will result from inability to stabilise completely the foreign demand for our exports. In other words, it assumes that there is literally no unemployment on the average either of a structural character or resulting from a general deficiency in demand except in so far as inevitable instabilities in foreign trade may result in either of these two consequences. But since the

average of such structural unemployment and of unemployment resulting from a general deficiency of demand is to be zero, there must year in, year out be literally no unemployment of this character.

19   These are indeed extreme assumptions. Sir William Beveridge must be assuming that we can perfectly forecast the general level of total national expenditure which is necessary to give full employment without inflation, and that we have perfect and completely effective controls over all domestic items of national expenditure (including private investment), so that, having made our perfect forecast, we then achieve a perfect fit of future expenditure to the quantity which has been judged necessary. It is only on assumptions such as these that it is realistic to assume that year in, year out there will be literally no unemployment due to general deficiency of demand except in so far as the demand for our exports may vary.

20   It must, moreover, be assumed that those responsible for fixing wage-rates are so moderate that even with this unprecedented pressure of demand in the labour market, there are no occasions on which it might be judged necessary by the central authorities to moderate the pressure of general demand in order to prevent the development of an inflationary upward spiral of wage-rates. As will be seen later in these notes, Sir William Beveridge does not suggest any drastic action for controlling the upward movement of money wage-rates. It may be that at 6% unemployment, even 5% unemployment, it will prove possible without any rigid wage-stop to obtain such moderation (not only on the part of trade unions, but also on the part of the many employers who will be short of labour) as will be sufficient to prevent the general level of money wage-rates rising appreciably faster than the productivity of labour. But is it really right to assume that this will certainly be the case if year in, year out the unemployment percentage is not allowed to rise above 3%?

21   Moreover, the 3% target assumes that there is literally no structural unemployment except such as may result from uncontrollable fluctuations of foreign demand for our exports. Is this really a tenable assumption in an economy which, for the reasons given above, is in certain ways likely to be less flexible than in the past? It might perhaps be possible to achieve something approaching this result if the far-reaching war-time controls directing labour, consumers' expenditure and the localisation of industry were to be continued into peace. Any pockets of structural unemployment could then be absorbed by directing the workers to go somewhere else and produce something else; by directing producers to produce something else somewhere else; or by forcing consumers to take the products of the depressed locality or the depressed industry. But, as will be seen later in these notes, Sir William Beveridge does not propose such drastic action for the control of structural unemployment. Indeed, he goes out of his way to assert as one of the fundamental conditions of his proposals that the ordinary peace-time freedom of choice for workers and for consumers will be restored; and in

certain passages of his book he expressly recognises the fact that such freedoms of choice are bound to complicate the problem of curing unemployment. For example, in paragraphs 14 and 15 of his book he writes: 'Freedom in choice of occupations makes it harder to ensure that all men at all times are occupied productively. It makes it impossible to retain men forcibly in particular work or to drag them to it with a threat of imprisonment if they refuse to go. One assumption underlying this Report is that neither the Essential Work Order nor the powers of industrial direction, which have been found necessary in war, should be continued when the war is over. In Britain at peace the supply of labour cannot be adjusted by decree to the demand for labour; it can only be guided by economic motives. . . . Freedom in the management of a personal income complicates the problem of full employment from another side. If men cannot be forced to buy just what has been produced, this means that the demands for labour and its products cannot be fitted forcibly to the supply.'

22   In general, Sir William defines full employment as 'having always more vacant jobs than unemployed men' (paragraph 4.) It is, however, doubtful whether a definition of the target level of employment of this kind is essentially useful. For example, a considerable volume of unemployment might be concentrated in a particular locality; and for structural reasons it might not be possible immediately to transfer it to other employments; at the same time there might already be full employment in the rest of the country. An expansion in the general level of demand might merely cause an inflation in those parts of the country where employment was already full without absorbing any labour in the depressed locality. There would, therefore, be little point in any such action even if the number of unemployed in the depressed district was less than the number of unfilled vacancies in the rest of the country, so that on Sir William Beveridge's definition there was not yet 'full employment'.

23   For reasons of this sort, it is difficult scientifically to define full employment by relating the number of vacant jobs to the number of unemployed. What is required is a policy of general expansion in the level of aggregate national expenditure, so long as it is possible thereby to give greater employment without running into risks of inflationary upward movements of prices and wages, and to combine such action with special measures for transferring labour from special depressed localities and occupations, and for encouraging the localisation of new enterprises (so long as this can be done without undue economic cost) in the special depressed localities. By these means, consistently and vigorously applied, we may hope to reduce the average level of unemployment appreciably below the 14.2% of the inter-war years and, indeed, even appreciably below the 8% chosen for illustrative purposes in Appendix 2 of the White Paper on Employment Policy. But it would certainly be unwise for responsible authorities to adopt as a public target an average level of unemployment anything like as low as Sir William Beveridge's 3%.

III   Private Investment

24   It is clear from the very high target which Sir William Beveridge sets himself that literally no undesirable variation in the national expenditure is, in his opinion, to be allowed except in so far as some moderate instability in our exports is admitted to be inevitable.

25   This is a formidable undertaking. As is pointed out in the White Paper on Employment Policy (paragraph 47), there are two elements in the national expenditure, namely, private investment and the foreign balance, which are likely to fluctuate considerably and also, unfortunately, happen to be exceptionally difficult to control. Sir William Beveridge admits that there may be some undesirable fluctuation in the foreign balance through uncontrolled variations in our exports; but his target allows for literally no undesirable variations in total investment.

26   Such perfectionism would be, in any circumstances, hard to achieve; but Sir William Beveridge makes his task even more difficult. He rejects 'the view that public works should be kept on tap to be expanded or contracted to meet fluctuations which are allowed to continue in private investment at home' (paragraph 211). On the other hand, the White Paper, realising that the control of private investment is more difficult than the control of public investment, argues that 'for the purpose of maintaining general employment it is desirable that public investment should actually expand when private investment is declining and should contract in periods of boom' (paragraph 62.) Thus the White Paper sets itself the task of stabilising as far as possible the combined total of private and public investment, a task which, in all conscience, is likely to prove hard enough. Sir William Beveridge on the other hand, sets himself the still harder task of stabilising both private and public investment separately and, through the choice of a 3% unemployment target, he asserts that he can attain perfect success in this task.

27   Sir William Beveridge would, therefore, for his policy require much greater powers over private investment than would a Government which was carrying out the White Paper policy. Sir William Beveridge sets up a National Investment Board for the purpose of controlling investment and, in particular, for stabilising private investment. The setting up of such a Board is of course merely a matter of administrative machinery; and while such administrative questions are no doubt of extreme importance, the fundamental economic question is the nature of the powers which the central authority (whatever may be its administrative shape) will possess over private investment. From a reading of Sir William Beveridge's paragraph on the National Investment Board, it appears that it will have the following powers and functions:-

(i)   It is conceived as enlisting the support of private enterprise in planning and timing private investment.

(ii)   It is also conceived as influencing private investment through the provision of finance at a low rate of interest in appropriate cases.

(iii)   The National Investment Board will have some negative power in stopping or reducing by order proposed items of private investment.

28   In addition to this paragraph on the National Investment Board (paragraph 241) there are in other sections of the book two other allusions to the control of private investment.

(iv)   In paragraph 209(3) Sir William writes that the regulation of private business investment will take the form of taxation policy designed to stabilise investment so far as possible, but he does not give any details of the taxation policy which will be adopted for this purpose.

(v)   Finally, Sir William Beveridge argues that 'if the private owners of business undertakings . . . fail, with all the help of the State and in an expanding economy, to stabilize the process of investment, the private owners cannot for long be left in their ownership.' (Paragraph 300.) The sanction for inducing a particular private industry to co-operate with the state in planning ahead its investment is the threat of its socialisation if it fails to do so.

29   As for points (i) and (ii) above, the White Paper on Employment Policy (paragraphs 59 and 61) also envisages enlisting the co-operation of private enterprise in planning investment ahead and using the instrument of low interest rates to promote private investment. As for point (iv) above, the White Paper admits (paragraph 61) that certain fiscal measures for the control of private investment merit further consideration, although its emphasis is on the use of deferred [income] tax credits rather than on the use of tax policy itself.

30   There remain points (iii) and (v) above. In these respects Sir William Beveridge proposes more extensive controls over private investment than does the White Paper. The negative power (point (iii) above) to stop or reduce private investment by order, may be of some assistance in the control of private investment, although it is not likely to have any very substantial effect in preventing a serious decline in private investment if a general depression should threaten. As to point (v) above, namely the power to control private investment through the threat of socialisation, it is very questionable whether this power can be envisaged as giving a quick and sure control over the timing of private investment. It is one thing for Sir William Beveridge to argue that (assuming that we try to cure unemployment without the extensive socialisation of industry) we must, nevertheless, be prepared in the last resort to socialise if in fact it turns out that we cannot otherwise prevent fluctuations in total investment. It is quite another matter for Sir William Beveridge to argue that in fact we are going to succeed in stabilising private investment, by holding out the

threat of instantaneous socialisation for any industry which does not stabilise its investment. It is not impossible to imagine conditions in which such a method of control might be expected to cause disturbances in the behaviour of the private business man.

IV Thermostatic Control

31   The above paragraphs should have made it clear that perhaps the main difference of emphasis between Sir William Beveridge and the White Paper is the perfectionism of the former. Sir William Beveridge claims that we should be able to maintain the unemployment percentage as low as 3% year in year out, although this involves a perfect control over both public and private investment. The White Paper takes a rather less ambitious, but – as some would argue – more realistic, line in refusing to name so low a numerical target and admitting that unemployment may in fact appear from time to time, although (such is the intention) on a very much lower scale than in the inter-war period.

32   It is not, in fact, going to be at all easy to forecast what level of total national income will be required to maintain a high level of employment, nor to estimate in advance the degree to which, without special Government intervention, the sum of the individual items of national expenditure is likely to diverge from this desired level.

33   Yet even if perfection in such forecasting were possible, it would remain extremely difficult so to control the various items of national expenditure as to make the total add up to the desired magnitude. Exports, and so the foreign balance, are, by general agreement, not even mainly within our domestic control. Public investment, it must be remembered, is not merely, indeed not mainly, investment carried out by the Central Government: it comprises the capital expenditure of a large range of local authorities and other public bodies, control over which may be only one degree less difficult than in the case of private investment. As for this last item, it is abundantly clear that with the best will in the world, it will not be a simple matter for the state to bring within its certain control the future activities of private business men.

34   It was for this reason that the Government White Paper included the proposal for the automatic variation of social insurance contributions, a device which (paragraph 68) it compared to 'a thermostatic control'. The purpose of this device was to prevent any initial decline in total national expenditure (due to a lack of perfection in forecasting or in control) from starting off the familiar vicious spiral of declining expenditure leading to declining income and so to further declines in expenditure, until the whole economy was suffering from a general depression. If an initial decline in demand can be immediately and automatically prevented from leading to secondary declines in demand, enormous advances would have been achieved in the cure of unemployment. A breathing space would

have been gained for rectifying the initial mistake and the decline in any case could [not] attain the catastrophic dimensions of the past.

35   Sir William Beveridge, however, in his postscript on the Government's employment policy has little good to say for the White Paper proposal for a thermostatic control. He argues that 'the advantages are not very great; this device would, at highest, mitigate the secondary rather than the primary effects of fluctuation.' (Page 264.) This attitude is, of course, entirely consistent for a perfectionist who is never going to allow any undesirable fluctuation to take place either in private or in public investment, and is thereby going to maintain the unemployment percentage year in, year out at the unchanged level of 3%. Clearly, if the unemployment percentage is never going to vary at all, the whole idea of a thermostatic control becomes pointless.

V   The Problem of Internal Finance

36   Sir William Beveridge makes full use of the new technique of considering the national income and expenditure as a whole in order to decide whether the economy is threatened with a general inflationary or deflationary development, and of controlling accordingly the general level of national expenditure. The procedure in peace-time will presumably be: (1) to consider the total manpower that is likely to be available in the forthcoming period; (2) to consider the value of the total national income that this supply of manpower would produce if it were fully employed; (3) to estimate the likely level of the different items of national expenditure; (4) thereby to determine the probable inflationary or deflationary gap (i.e. the excess or deficiency of the estimated total of national expenditure over the target national income); and (5) to consider the measures to be taken to close this gap.

37   As Sir William Beveridge writes 'The Minister of National Finance has to take each year one cardinal decision: after estimating how much, assuming full employment and under the taxation which he proposes, private citizens may be expected to lay out that year on consumption and private investment, he must propose for that year public outlay sufficient, with this estimated private outlay, to employ the whole man-power of the country, that is to say sufficient to make the assumption of full employment come true. This cardinal decision involves a break with the two main principles which have governed the State Budgets of the past; first, that State expenditure should be kept down to the minimum necessary to meet inescapable needs; secondly, that State income and expenditure should balance each year.' (Paragraph 182.)

38   It is recognised by Sir William Beveridge that there are various ways in which this balance between the planned national expenditure and the target national income may be achieved. He makes special reference (paragraphs 191–196) to three main methods. These he calls:-

'Route I – Increase of public outlay, leaving rates of taxation unchanged.

Route II – Increase of public outlay, with all-round increase of taxation sufficient to balance public income and expenditure.

Route III – All-round reduction of rates of taxation, leaving public outlay unchanged.'

39 The method of Route I is the straightforward one of increased public expenditure (e.g. increased public investment) financed by borrowing. The increased public expenditure on goods and services gives direct employment; and since this increased demand is not financed from taxation which might simultaneously cut down the demand of taxpayers for other goods and services, it leads to a net addition in total national expenditure. This primary increase has secondary repercussions: that part of the increased income which is not itself either paid over to the state in taxation, spent on imports or saved will in turn lead to a secondary increase in demand for home produced goods and services; and so on, in a succession of increases in demand leading to increases of income.

40 But it is to be observed that this method (Route I) involves an increase in public expenditure without a corresponding increase in tax revenue, with the result that there is a budget deficit or, at the least, a reduction in any pre-existing budget surplus.

41 The method of Route II is to increase public expenditure on goods and services, but to finance this, not from borrowing, but by raising rates of taxation. It might at first sight be thought that in this case there would be no net increase in total national expenditure, since the increase in Government expenditure on goods and services would be accompanied by a simultaneous diminution in the expenditure of those who have to pay a great part of their income in taxation to the state. It is, however, unlikely that taxpayers will reduce their expenditure by the full amount of the increased taxation which they are called upon to pay, since some part of the increased tax payment is likely to be paid out of income that would otherwise have been saved. Thus some moderate net increase in national expenditure (equal to the amount of the additional tax payments which come out of private savings and not out of private expenditure) will in effect take place.

42 But, in order to achieve a given net increase in total national expenditure, very much larger increases in public expenditure must be contemplated if they are financed out of taxation than would be necessary if they were financed out of borrowing. The quantitative analysis of the probable effects of this 'Route II' method of stimulating demand (as made by Mr Kaldor in Appendix C of Sir William Beveridge's book) suggests that the increase in public expenditure which would in fact be required would be on so vast a scale that we may in fact rule this method out as a practical alternative.

43　There remains Route III. In this case an increase in net national expenditure is stimulated, not by an increase in Government expenditure on goods and services, but by a reduction in rates of taxation which, by leaving consumers with larger spendable incomes, would stimulate additional private demand. This method, like that of Route I, would, of course, involve a budget deficit or a reduction in any pre-existing budget surplus. In this they are similar. The difference between them lies in the choice between the stimulation of public expenditure and the stimulation of private expenditure as a means of curing general unemployment.

44　As a matter of realistic policy, it is probable that, if the community were threatened by serious general depression, some combination of Routes I and III would have to be employed. The planning and timing of public investment, in so far as it is practicable, would enable increases in public demand to be brought about in the manner of Route I. But if the threatening depression were severe, action on these lines might not prove sufficient. There are severe practical limits to the extent and the speed with which public investment can be increased on the outbreak of a depression; and any practicable increase in public investment might not in fact prove sufficient to fill the threatening deflationary gap.

45　If such a situation were to develop, public investment policy would need to be supplemented by reductions in rates of taxation or by some similar means (such as the repayment of deferred [income] tax credits) in order to stimulate private expenditure so as to fill the remaining part of the deflationary gap. Public investment requires careful planning ahead and involves difficult administrative problems of control in order that it may be used quickly and on an adequate scale; but private expenditure can probably be turned on and off fairly quickly and with little or no planning in advance.

46　The White Paper lays its main stress on the methods of Route I in those sections (paragraphs 62–66) which are devoted to the planning and timing of public investment. But reference is also made to the methods of Route II in paragraph 72 of the White Paper, where there is a discussion of fiscal measures for the control of private consumption.

47　The use of Routes I and III, however, whether singly or in combination, inevitably raises the problem of budget deficits. On this problem there is a very considerable difference of emphasis between Sir William Beveridge's book and the White Paper.

48　Sir William Beveridge lays down three rules for future budgetary policy. 'The first rule is that total outlay at all times must be sufficient for full employment. This is a categorical imperative, taking precedence over all other rules, and over-riding them if they are in conflict with it. The second rule is that, subject to this over-riding categorical imperative, outlay should be directed by regard to social priorities. The third rule is that subject both to the first and second rules, it is better to provide the means for outlay by taxing than by borrowing.' (Paragraph 197.) The second of Sir William's rules is irrelevant to the present issue, but he is quite unambiguous in the emphasis which he lays on rules one and three. In his opinion the rule that the state should ensure that total national expenditure is adequate takes absolute priority; and while it is admittedly preferable to do this without incurring a budget deficit, nevertheless the avoidance of a budget deficit should in no circumstances be permitted to stand in the way of a financial policy which will ensure a level of total national expenditure adequate to give full employment.

49   The White Paper on Employment Policy deals with this subject in paragraphs 74–79 of that paper. It does not take such an unambiguous line. Indeed, it has been criticised (perhaps with some justification) as being somewhat indefinite in its attitude. However this may be, it certainly does not give absolute priority to employment policy over the preservation of budget equilibrium. This is apparent from the following passage:- 'In controlling the situation, especially in the difficult years after the war, the Government will have equally in mind the need to maintain the national income, and the need for a policy of budgetary equilibrium such as will maintain the confidence in the future which is necessary for a healthy and enterprising industry.' (Paragraph 79.) It is not, however, clear what action is advocated if the preservation of national expenditure at the target level involves a financial policy which is incompatible with the avoidance of a budget deficit over an average of years.

50   One important point is common ground to the two documents. One passage in the White Paper suggests that some continuing increase in the national debt might perhaps be permissible in so far as the national income is growing (as a result, for example, of rising productivity). Thus the White Paper argues that 'proper limits on public borrowing also depend on the magnitude of the debt charge in relation to the rate of growth of the national income. In a country in which money income is increasing, the total debt can be allowed to increase by quite appreciable amounts without increasing the proportionate burden of the interest on that debt.' (paragraph 78.) In paragraphs 57 and 58 of Mr Kaldor's Appendix C to Sir William Beveridge's book, it is calculated that on certain assumptions the Government after the war 'could borrow an average annual amount of £250,000,000 without increasing the ratio of the annual interest burden to the national income above the level it will have reached at the end of the war'. As, however, Mr Kaldor expects expenditure by the Central Government on purposes other than the debt charge will rise much less rapidly than the national income, he estimates that 'the national debt could be allowed to expand at the average rate of no less than £775,000,000 per annum over the period 1948–70, without having to raise any new taxes for the maintenance of "budgetary equilibrium".' It is, of course, important to make sure that the arithmetical assumptions of Mr Kaldor's calculations are well founded,

but there can be no question that there is substance in the general line of his argument.

51   Nevertheless, there is the possibility of sharp conflict of policy which neither Sir William Beveridge nor the Government White Paper fully resolves. On the one hand, it is morally certain that the political demand for an effective employment policy will be such that central financial policy will have to be determined year by year, with the primary objective of reaching the target level of national expenditure and without any excessive concern over the immediate effects of such a policy upon the balance of the Budget. On the other hand, the White Paper is, of course, justified in taking the problem of a continuing budget deficit seriously. It is true that the interest on the national debt is merely a transfer of income from the taxpayer to the debt holder within the state, but such a transfer is not without its serious disadvantages. A high level of national debt interest in relation to the national income involves a high rate of national taxation before any revenue is available for other forms of state expenditure. High rates of national taxation are in themselves an evil (quite apart from any adverse effects which they may have upon the distribution of income) in that they may reduce the incentives of private individuals and private businesses to work, produce, take risks and undertake capital development.

52   Indeed, in the economic interests of the community it is desirable to devise an employment policy on lines which are compatible with the actual repayment of the already inflated national debt. Is it possible to find the means of reconciling these two apparently irreconcilable objectives – a financial policy that will invariably maintain national expenditure at the target level and a financial policy that will reduce the debt over the average of years?

53   A solution of the dilemma may perhaps be found on the following lines. In the interests of employment policy measures should be taken (on the lines of Routes I and II discussed above) to increase total public expenditure and, if necessary, to stimulate private expenditure through the reduction of taxation; and this should be done on any scale necessary to close the deflationary gap. That is to say, Sir William Beveridge's first rule for financial policy that 'total outlay at all times must be sufficient for full employment' would take absolute priority in the short run.

54   But, if it were considered that the long-run result of this policy would be to cause the continuation of a budget deficit over the average of years, or to reduce the average rate of repayment of the national debt to an undesirably low level, then special measures would be taken to enable the short-run policy of maintaining at all times a sufficient level of total national expenditure to be carried out with a more favourable balance between budgetary revenue and expenditure. The following are two forms of long-term policy which might have this effect:-

55   First, a long-term monetary policy might be adopted for further reductions in the rate of interest. The effect of this would be two-fold. It would reduce the interest burden on any given national debt and would thereby automatically diminish the proportion of the national income that would have to be raised in taxation to meet the charge on any given level of borrowing.

56   But it would also have the effect of stimulating both private and public investment. The interest element in the annual cost incurred by many forms of public investment represents a serious charge upon local rates, and in the case, for example, of municipal housing represents a very considerable proportion of the economic rent of the house. Reductions in interest rates should have a similar effect in making profitable schemes of development which were previously unprofitable. For these reasons a permanent reduction in the long-term rate of interest from a high to a low level is likely to raise the average level of annual capital expenditure by public authorities to a permanently higher figure.

57   The result of this would, therefore, be that in order to attain any given level of total national expenditure the Central Government would be required to face over the average of years a smaller budget deficit. Investment by private enterprise and by municipal authorities being greater, the Central Government will have less need to increase its own public expenditure or to stimulate private consumption by the reduction of taxation, in order to achieve any given level of national expenditure.

58   It has become fashionable in recent years to play down the long-run effect of a permanent reduction in the long-term rate of interest. In Sir William Beveridge's book, for example, there is reference in paragraph 241 to the possible stimulation of private investment through a low rate of interest; there is reference to the importance of the interest element in housing (paragraph 220); and there is a curt reference to the effect of a low rate of interest in encouraging outlay on capital goods in an appendix on the policy of cheap money (Appendix B, Section 4, paragraph 21). But when the main 'Routes to full employment' are under discussion no reference is made to the possible 'Route' of stimulating investment by reduced interest rates, although this remains one of the few fundamental measures by which a continuing policy for high employment may be combined with a long-term policy for the reduction of the national debt.

59   There is a second way in which in the long run an effective policy for high employment may be combined with a policy of debt reduction. Some reference to this method is, in fact, made in Appendix C of Sir William's book, where Mr Kaldor discusses a Route IV for the attainment of full employment.[1] This method consists in changing the structure of the tax system in such a way that a given level of taxation is paid more out of

[1] Sir William, however, disregards this method in the main text of his book, on the grounds that it presents extreme practical difficulties. (Page 345, Footnote 2.)

savings and less out of money which would otherwise have been spent on the consumption of goods and services. A change in the tax structure of this kind would, of course, stimulate private expenditure on goods and services without leading to any worsening of the balance between budgetary revenue and budgetary expenditure.

60   Mr Kaldor puts forward his suggestion in a very limited form. He considers only the effect of different forms of taxation upon the distribution of the national income. He suggests that if more taxation is levied from the rich (who are likely to save a relatively high proportion of their income) and correspondingly less taxation is levied on the poor (who save a smaller proportion of their income), the net effect will be to cause an increase in expenditure on goods and services for personal consumption and a reduction in savings, although the same total revenue is raised from the same total income. It is, no doubt, true that an increased progressiveness in the tax system of this kind will stimulate personal expenditure. This is an aspect of long-term budgetary policy which should receive proper emphasis.

61   Beyond a certain point, however, increased progressiveness in the tax structure may have serious effects upon the incentive of private enterprise to spend money on capital development. The inducement to undertake private investment, particularly if there are considerable risks involved, may be appreciably lessened if the rate of tax on high incomes becomes penal in its severity. On these grounds, and in view of the already highly progressive nature of the tax system, there are strict limits to the stimulation of total national expenditure which can be bought by this method.

62   But there is another type of change in the tax structure which may have the same favourable effects in stimulating private expenditure on consumption without having similar adverse effects upon private invest-ment. The tax structure may be changed, not so much in order to achieve a change in the distribution of income, but to give a direct advantage to those who are willing to undertake schemes of private investment or to spend their income on consumption as opposed to those who save it. For example, a very high rate of tax on undistributed business profits would give companies an incentive to distribute all the profits which they made to their shareholders. This would undoubtedly stimulate personal expenditure on consumption without any loss of tax revenue. If at the same time special tax privileges were granted in respect of business expenditure on capital developments, there would be a simultaneous inducement for private businesses to undertake private investment.

63   Alternatively, it might be useful to impose a substantial annual tax assessed on the capital value of individuals' property and simultaneously to reduce rates of income tax and sur-tax. It seems probable that an appreciably higher proportion of the capital tax than of the income tax would be paid out of savings, and that a capital tax would have an

appreciably smaller effect than an income tax in diminishing the incentive to undertake private investment.

64 To summarise, there may well be a conflict between Sir William Beveridge's insistence that the risk of budget deficits must not be allowed to stand in the way of an effective employment policy and the view expressed in paragraphs 74–79 of the White Paper that the preservation of budget equilibrium should nevertheless remain a primary objective of policy. It is suggested that, if and when the prosecution of a vigorous employment policy threatens to result in an unsatisfactory long-term budgetary situation, the deadlock may be resolved, first, by a long-term policy of lowering interest rates and, secondly, altering the structure of the tax system in such a way as to encourage personal expenditure and private investment without losing revenue.

VI The Location of Industry

65 As has been pointed out above, there is agreement between Sir William Beveridge's book and the White Paper in the view that some control should be exercised over the location of industry, in order to cure structural unemployment, in part at least, by bringing the work to the men. In the passage of his book (paragraphs 223–228) which he devotes to this question, Sir William outlines the conclusions of the Barlow Commission [on the Distribution of the Industrial Population, Cmd 6153, 1940] and of the Uthwatt Committee [on Compensation and Betterment, Cmd 6386, 1942], and expounds a number of considerations (many of which are not relevant to the problem of unemployment) in favour of a general national policy of town and country planning. He concludes that 'For an effective attack upon mass unemployment, as much as for an effective attack on the evils of urban congestion, control over the location of industry is indispensable. This control must be both negative, prohibiting undesirable location, and positive, encouraging desirable location.' (paragraph 228.) He gives no further details of the means by which this general policy is to be implemented.

66 The White Paper, on the other hand, goes into more details as to how the location (or what it prefers to call 'the distribution') of industry should be controlled. It states (paragraphs 26 and 27) that the Government will encourage the establishment of new industries in areas specially vulnerable to unemployment by a series of measures:-

(i)   The Government will require industrialists contemplating the establishment of new factories to notify them in advance so that they may be able to exercise persuasion in the choice of location.

(ii) Power is to be taken to prohibit the establishment of new factories in a district where serious disadvantage would arise from further industrial development.

(iii)   Munitions production will be continued in the 'development
        areas' if it is clear that such production can be continued
        permanently after the war. On the other hand, munitions
        factories which are not likely to be permanently required for
        munitions, will be released as quickly as possible.
(iv)   The Government intends to give priority in the licensing of
        factory building to the areas most vulnerable to unemployment.
(v)   The Government will extend the policy of itself erecting in such
        areas factories for sale or lease to smaller firms.
(vi)   Due regard is to be paid to the needs of these areas in the
        placing of Government orders of all kinds. The Government
        intends to take steps to secure that enterprises which establish
        themselves in these areas will have adequate facilities for
        obtaining the necessary finance.
(vii)   The Government intends also to take such action as may be
        necessary to secure the proper development and modernisation
        of the basic services in these areas, including the improvement
        of communications, of power services, and of housing.

67   It will be seen from the above that the White Paper includes much
more detailed consideration of the practicable measures appropriate to
influence the location of industry than does Sir William Beveridge's book.

VII   The Mobility of Labour

68   In both the documents under consideration it is held that mobility of
labour between occupations presents smaller difficulties than mobility
between localities, and it is for this reason that both documents put
considerable stress upon the importance of influencing the location of
industry. Sir William Beveridge writes, on the basis of the inter-war
experience, that 'The facts of unemployment . . . point to a difference
between the possibilities of occupational and of local transference which
. . . suggest that local movement encounters, at a certain point, obstacles
which cannot be overcome.' (Paragraph 111). The White Paper on
Employment Policy states that 'where a large industrial population is
involved, the Government are not prepared either to compel its transfer
to another area, or to leave it to prolonged unemployment and
demoralisation.' (Paragraph 29.) Nevertheless, there is some difference
of emphasis in the two documents on this question of geographical
transfer. The Government White Paper goes on to state that 'While the
Government do not rely primarily on large-scale labour transference for a
solution of the unemployment problems of particular areas, they are
anxious to overcome some of the obstacles which stand in the way of the
transfer of workers to places where suitable employment is available for
them.' (Paragraph 36.)

69   Whereas Sir William Beveridge has no special suggestions to make
as to the way in which the geographical transfer of labour might be

facilitated, the White Paper makes two positive suggestions. In the first place, it explains how the absence of houses to rent has in the past made it particularly difficult for workers to move from one locality to another; and it states that 'Steps will be taken to secure that a substantial proportion of the new houses erected after the war shall be available at a rent which is within the means of the average wage earner'. Secondly, it proposes that 'Where workers are transferred under approved schemes to a new area, they will be eligible for resettlement allowances to meet the costs involved in their removal and that of their dependents.' (Paragraph 36.)

70   The two documents are also on common ground in pointing to the adverse effects which restrictive practices on the part of workers' organisations may have upon the movement of labour from declining to expanding occupations. (Sir William Beveridge's book, paragraph 235, and the White Paper, paragraph 35).

71   For the rest, there is some considerable difference in the remedies which these two documents propose for increasing the mobility of labour. The White Paper (paragraphs 31–34) lays most stress upon the extension of training facilities. Training schemes are to be undertaken for resettling ex-Service men and released war workers, and these training schemes are to be continued later on a more permanent basis. Workers will not have to wait for long periods of unemployment before they will be provided with opportunities for retraining if such retraining should appear useful; and it is intended that adequate training allowances should be paid which would make the status of the trainee resemble more closely that of a wage-earner, and less that of the unemployed.

72   Sir William Beveridge, on the other hand (paragraphs 230–233), lays most stress on the development of the use of the employment exchanges. He suggests that the use of the employment exchanges should be made compulsory for all juveniles seeking work, so that new entrants to industry may be guided into the expanding, and away from the contracting, occupations and industries. He places very great emphasis on this method of achieving a relative contraction of certain industries, and expansion of others. It is, no doubt, one of the least painful of all methods of labour transference, since the disturbances caused by guiding the choice of new entrants into industry are, no doubt, much less than those due to the removal of an adult worker from an occupation to which he is trained and used, to a new one.

73   But it may be doubtful whether the guidance of new entrants into industry will be anything like sufficient to provide the degree of labour mobility necessary in the post-war world. Sir William Beveridge, in paragraph 216 of his book, suggests that unemployment in coal-mining might be avoided through the Governmental placing of orders for coal for six months or a year ahead on a scale sufficient to employ the desired total of men in the industry; and he goes so far as to argue that, if the public

corporation concerned found difficulty in disposing of this quantity of coal, it would cut down its order for the future while steps were being taken to reduce the supply of labour by means of the guidance of juveniles away from the industry. But it would seem highly improbable that in a world in which (as a result of the present stabilisation and anticipated decline in the numbers of the working population) the ratio of new entrants to the total numbers employed in each industry will become very much less than before, the adjustment in the relative size of different industries can be brought about without the transfer of adult workers.

74   Sir William Beveridge lays stress on the importance of preventing the casual employment of labour in industries like dock and harbour service. He suggests that the war-time experience, whereby this potent cause of chronic underemployment has been removed, should be used in order to devise a system whereby it shall not be allowed to recur in the future.

75   He leaves open the question to be judged in the light of future experience, whether the use of the employment exchanges should be made compulsory for all engagements of labour, and not only for juvenile labour. He is of the opinion that the extension of the use of the exchanges is one of the most important ways of increasing mobility in the labour market, but believes that compulsion may prove to be unnecessary.

76   There is one matter on which Sir William takes a definite and strong line. He argues that 'It should be accepted, as a general citizen duty that if there is a demand for labour at fair wages, men who are unemployed for any substantial period should be prepared to take that work and not to hold out indefinitely for work in their own trade and place', and adds that no men should 'be assisted to be unreasonable by provision of an insurance income. A just consequence of a full employment policy would lie in the stiffening of the conditions of unemployment benefit as regards individuals whose unemployment continues for any length of time'. (paragraph 233.) There can be little doubt that the provision of family allowances and of more adequate unemployment benefit is likely to some extent to reduce the incentive for the unemployed to find new work. An employment policy cannot be successfully carried out unless there is a clearly recognised duty for the unemployed to move into new occupations and new localities if this be necessary. Sir William Beveridge is to be congratulated on the frankness with which he has underlined this essential condition, on which the White Paper does not speak with the same firmness.

VIII   Wages and Industrial Discipline

77   Perhaps the gravest danger to be feared from the prosecution by the state of policies for greatly improved social security and for the maintenance of a high aggregate demand for labour is the removal of the

incentives to work and to be moderate in wage demands. Human nature being what it is, if a man realises that on losing his present job he is almost certain to find another, while his present employer may find difficulty in replacing him, and that in the unlikely event of unemployment he and his family will be generously supported by the state, there is almost bound to be some slackening in industrial discipline and (at least in the case of those paid on a time-rate) in industrial productivity. In these circumstances, trade unions have the maximum incentive to demand, and employers' organisations the maximum incentive to offer, higher and higher wage-rates. If the policies of full employment and improved social security are pushed too far without adequate realisation on the part of the workers of the need for continued industrial discipline and continued moderation in wage demands, the whole policy will be liable to collapse through resulting inflationary pressures.

78 Sir William Beveridge realises these dangers and boldly underlines them in his paragraphs on 'Industrial Discipline' and the 'Determination of Wages' (paragraphs 277–288.) The White Paper on Employment Policy also calls for a moderate wages policy (paragraph 49.)

79 The only question at issue is whether the measures which Sir William proposes for ensuring moderation in wages policy would prove sufficient. He suggests that the TUC should use its good offices in order to achieve 'a unified wage policy which ensures that the demands of individual unions will be judged with reference to the economic situation as a whole'. He suggests further 'not that there should be continuation in peace of the compulsory arbitration which has been accepted in war, but that collective bargains in each industry should in general include a clause for arbitration by an agreed arbitrator, in default of agreement between the parties'; but the right to strike would remain in the background. (paragraphs 286 and 287.)

80 Both Sir William Beveridge and the White Paper realise that a moderate wages policy will be easier to achieve if the Government is able to maintain reasonable stability of prices and, in particular, of the cost of living. The White Paper, however, qualifies its general support for a policy of Governmental price stabilisation when it says that 'The Government for their part are prepared to do what they can to stabilise prices so as to avoid or mitigate changes not rendered inevitable by higher costs, either of imports or of production at home'. (paragraph 53.) In this passage, it is clearly contemplated that if costs rise as a result of wage-rates rising more rapidly than productivity, or of a deterioration in the terms of international trade and a rise in the price of imports, the cost of living must be allowed to go up.

81 There can be no rigid maintenance of the cost of living at a predetermined level (by price subsidies or by other measures) regardless of movements in wage-rates and the price of imports. Otherwise, the Government might find itself committed to paying out ever-increasing

subsidies to the cost of living and thus positively increasing the inflationary gap between spendable incomes and the market value of the supplies of goods and services available for consumption. The facts of life are unfortunately hard. If, when the level of unemployment is held permanently at a low level by an employment policy for maintaining aggregate demand, pressures in the labour market are such as to cause a rapid upward movement of prices, there will be nothing for it but the unfortunate choice between setting a lower target for the level of employment or imposing some form of compulsory wage regulation.

82   It is not so clear from the passages in Sir William Beveridge's book (paragraphs 215, 288, 289–292) whether he fully realises the dangers of a policy of price stabilisation in conditions in which wage-rates are rising immoderately or the terms of international trade have moved substantially against us. He argues that the proper price policy is one 'of maintaining a stable value of money in terms of necessaries, with wages rising both in money terms and in real terms as productivity per head increases'. But he does not say what should be done if wages rise more quickly. He merely underlines the fact that 'it would be unreasonable to expect the trade unions to abstain from using their bargaining strength to the full, unless the Government can give them some assurance that it is pursuing a policy of stable prices. This is the reason why price policy must be an integral part of a full employment policy.' (paragraphs 290 and 291.)

IX   The Machinery of Government

83   Sir William Beveridge has some far-reaching suggestions to make on the reorganisation of the machinery of Government for the purpose of carrying out his employment policy (paragraphs 238–246.) The Treasury is apparently to be wound up; and we are to have in its place a proper Ministry of National Finance which will consider those profound problems of general financial policy which the Treasury, in the past, has so notoriously neglected. The Ministry of National Finance will be supported by a humbler body called the Department of Control, which will exercise those functions of the financial watch-dog which the Treasury has carried out in the past with such stubborn efficiency. Underneath the Minister of National Finance, and watched closely by the Department of Control, will be the various executive spending departments, whose function it will be to carry out the national expenditures as planned in the Ministry of National Finance. Somewhere on the touch-line there is to be a new National Investment Board, which will be independent of the Minister of National Finance, and will have the general powers not only of preparing, but also apparently of carrying out, the general investment plan covering both public and private investment.

84   The Board of Trade's fate is no less forbidding than that of the Treasury. Import and export policy is said 'clearly [to] fall within the purview of the Ministry of Finance . . ., even if the actual administration is

left to a subordinate executive department such as the Board of Trade'. But not only will the Board of Trade lose its control over commercial policy, but a Ministry of National Development is to be set up to rob it of its interest in the localisation of industry.

85 The White Paper on Employment Policy has less ambitious ideas on the subject of the administrative machinery necessary to carry out an employment policy. It does, however, state that 'the Government intend to establish on a permanent basis a small central staff qualified to measure and analyse economic trends and submit appreciations of them to the Ministers concerned'. (paragraph 81.) This reference is presumably to bodies such as the Central Statistical Office and the Economic Section. The conception appears to be that the Treasury, with the aid and advice of this small central staff, should forecast as far as possible the future requirements of general financial policy and determine the lines which that financial policy should take. The planning and timing of public investment and the other forms of control which, with the new conception of policy, the Treasury will be called upon to undertake may no doubt require some new division of functions within the Treasury itself.

86 Apart from this reference to the small central staff and a suggestion that the Board of Trade should take primary responsibility for the localisation of industry (paragraph 30) the White Paper is silent upon the reform of the machinery of Government. Perhaps this silence may be interpreted as suggesting that the Government approves of the unexciting (but perhaps sensible) idea that the Treasury should still be responsible for financial policy, the Board of Trade for the location of industry, and the Ministry of Labour for labour mobility, with whatever Cabinet machinery of co-ordination at the top may be considered most suitable and effective.

X   International Implications of Employment Policy

87 Sir William Beveridge devotes a long chapter to this subject (paragraphs 301–358). This chapter is, however, perhaps the least satisfactory in his book. He points out that there are three possible forms of international economic policy for this country to adopt:-

(1)   We may choose general multilateral trading. By this Sir William means a system in which there is interconvertibility of currencies and in which bilateral payments agreements or barter arrangements are excluded. It is, in fact, a world à la Article VII [of the Mutual Aid Agreement of February 1942 between the UK and the USA].

(2)   The second choice is of a general policy for 'regional multilateral trading'. Sir William makes it clear (paragraph 353) that he has in mind a regional arrangement covering Europe or the British Commonwealth or both together and excluding Soviet Russia and in particular the United States. His idea apparently is that, if we could

obtain agreement between the countries within the region to adopt internal domestic policies for the prevention of slumps and unemployment, we could then safely enjoy a full Article VII mode of life with these countries. At the same time we should all adopt a policy of discrimination against the United States, so long as we considered her an outcast in the matter of domestic employment policy.

(3)   Finally, he gives us the choice of bilateralism. By this he means a system of bilateral payments agreements or barter arrangements whereby we can ensure that other countries spend on our exports as much as we spend on imports from them.

88   In the last paragraph of his chapter (paragraph 358) he compares full multilateralism to an elevator, regional multilateral trade to a staircase and bilateralism to a fire-escape. He tells us 'that in constructing the new edifice' we cannot prudently leave out the fire-escape and staircase until we are sure that there will be no fire and the elevator will always be in action. We are all agreed that there must be ways of escape in case of accident; but what Sir William unfortunately does not tell us in this chapter is whether we are to struggle up and down by the fire-escape, walk on the staircase or ride at ease on the elevator before the accident occurs.

89   It is undeniable that a bilateral system would give some greater measure of stability to our foreign trade. If, when we bought goods from any country, we insisted that we would do so only if they spent an exactly similar sum on our goods in exactly the same period of time, we should, in planning our imports, simultaneously plan the foreigners' expenditure upon our exports. In other words, we should bring under our control the foreign balance which constitutes one of the elements of total national expenditure which it is most difficult to control.

90   But bilateral barter has offsetting disadvantages. Not only the world as a whole, but this country in particular stands to be seriously impoverished by denying itself the economic advantages of multilateral exchange. Moreover, bilateralism necessarily involves discrimination in commercial relationships and will thus inevitably lead to trade wars and diplomatic friction. Finally, we are committed to Article VII which rules out the use of such discriminatory measures which are, in any case, anathema to the United States, on whose close co-operation our future security and prosperity depend. The point at issue, therefore, is not whether bilateralism or multilateralism gives us greater stability and control over our foreign relationships; but whether, the other disadvantages of bilateralism being so obvious, sufficient safeguards can be introduced into a fully multilateral system for it to be made compatible with a high and stable level of domestic employment.

91   Sir William Beveridge states three conditions on which, in his view, multilateralism would be compatible with full employment:- 'First, each of the participating nations must aim at full employment within its

borders and must do so without relying on export surpluses as the principal means to full employment. Second, each of the participating nations must be prepared to balance its accounts with the rest of the world; . . . Third, each of the participating nations must aim at a certain . . . continuity in tariff, subsidy, foreign exchange and other economic policies' (paragraph 315.)

92   It is convenient to consider the first two of these conditions together, because the main reason for fearing uncontrolled depressions in other countries is that they may put an unbearable pressure upon our balance of payments. If an uncontrolled depression were to start in other countries they would spend less on our exports than we, as a result of our domestic policy for maintaining purchasing power, would spend on imports from them. In other words, the result would be to throw the balance of international payments out of equilibrium; and if we could not find, within the rules of the multilateral system, the means of financing the excess of imports over exports which this development would bring with it, we might be obliged to give up our domestic policy for high employment in order to restrain our own purchases on imported supplies.

93   There can, of course, be no two opinions that Sir William Beveridge is entirely on the right lines in suggesting that the ease with which we can carry out our own domestic employment policy will be much increased if we can persuade the other important countries in the world (and the United States in particular) to adopt similar domestic employment policies. If there are no uncontrolled depressions in external purchasing power, our own policy of maintaining domestic national expenditure will be much eased; and any arguments for trying to stabilise and control foreign expenditure on our exports through bilateral barter arrangements or payments agreements would disappear. There has recently been a Cabinet decision that we should support the Australian and the New Zealand Governments in their attempt to obtain, through an international conference, some international agreement on the co-ordination of domestic employment policies; and there can be no doubt that any success which this attempt may have will not only aid our own domestic policy but will remove one of the main obstacles to the achievement of multilateralism à la Article VII.

94   The difficulties of choice between multilateralism and bilateralism begin, however, at this point. Supposing that we cannot assume that there will be no slumps in external purchasing power. Can we devise a multilateral economic system compatible with Article VII which has sufficient safeguards to ensure that its acceptance by us would not remove our freedom to adopt an effective domestic policy? Or should we, on the other hand, in spite of its admitted disadvantages, go for a policy of bilateral trade arrangements which, though they may impoverish us and involve us in acute commercial and diplomatic controversy with our main ally, nevertheless enable us the better to control and stabilise external

expenditure upon our goods? Sir William Beveridge unfortunately sits on the fence.

95   He argues (paragraphs 321–324) that there are two possible ways in which the vicious spiral of international contraction and expansion may be remedied.

96   The first is a discriminatory and selective control of imports. If, for example, the United States falls into a depression, the effect of a reduction of American purchasing power on the rest of the world might be short-circuited if the other countries were free to cease purchasing American goods without cutting down their purchases of goods from each other. This would, of course, involve discrimination against American goods. It is, in fact, exactly the method which is contemplated in the 'Scarce Currency' Article of the International Monetary Fund. Under that Article, if dollars become scarce (as they would do if American purchases from the rest of the world slumped without a corresponding fall in American exports) all other countries would be free to discriminate against American exports.

97   Sir William Beveridge, however, dismisses this as 'a theoretical possibility rather than a measure on which practical reliance can be placed'. But it is not very clear why he does so. In fact the 'Scarce Currency' Article suggests a highly practical arrangement and marks a revolution in American thought on the subject of the responsibility of creditor countries in restoring equilibrium to the balance of payments. Under the 'Scarce Currency' Article, (i) a report would be prepared on the causes which led to the scarcity of a currency, and any such report would clearly point to the responsibility of the uncontrolled American depression for the currency difficulties in the hypothetical circumstances at present under consideration; (ii) all countries would be free to exclude American exports and to buy each others' goods instead; and (iii) it is expressly stated that this freedom would override all pre-existing commercial policy agreements.

98   The second measure which Sir William Beveridge recognises for mitigating the international consequences of depression in a multilateral system is international lending. It is, of course, true that if, when the United States ceased to buy goods, she lent the money abroad instead, other countries could continue to finance the same volume of imports and would therefore be free to maintain their internal purchasing power as before. Certainly there might be some structural unemployment in those countries on whom the decline in American purchases was mainly concentrated; but there would be no reason for the depression in purchasing power to spread throughout the world.

99   There are, however, certain other fundamental measures which might be adopted in order to prevent the hypothetical American depression from so upsetting the balance of payments of other countries

that they were obliged to abandon their domestic employment policies. Of these, one of the most important is, of course, an adjustment in exchange rates. The most astonishing thing in the whole of Sir William Beveridge's book is the fact that in his long chapter on the international implications of full employment, no single reference is made to exchange rates. In the inter-war period, the solid and irreducible minimum of unemployment of a million men, which persisted after the return to the gold standard in 1925, has been ascribed by many authorities to the fact that we returned to the gold standard at too high a parity, thereby overvaluing our exchange rate. In the great depression which developed after 1929 we made one of the earliest and most extensive recoveries. Again many authorities have ascribed this largely to the fact that in 1931 we left the gold standard, and through the consequential adjustment in the sterling exchange rate regained our freedom to indulge in a domestic policy of expansion. The wheel has in fact turned full cycle, when so advanced an advocate of the pure doctrine of freedom for this country to indulge in a domestic employment policy writes a long chapter on the international implications of his doctrine without mentioning the rate of exchange.

100　In this respect, the International Monetary Fund marks an enormous advance. In its Article IV, which deals with the par value of currencies, the principle is laid down that a country which is suffering from a 'fundamental disequilibrium' must be allowed to depreciate its exchange rate, and that such a depreciation cannot be disallowed 'because of the domestic, social or political policies of the member proposing the change'. At the same time, the principle is clearly recognised that countries which do not need to depreciate their currency in order to regain equilibrium should not be allowed to do so. In other words, the International Monetary Fund sets up a system whereby if we were getting into difficulties because we were maintaining domestic expenditure in face of an American depression, we should be allowed to depreciate the pound (as we did in 1931), but the Americans would not be allowed to offset this by an unnecessary competitive depreciation of their currency (as they did in 1933). Sir William Beveridge makes no mention whatsoever of these provisions of the International Monetary Fund.

101　Sir William Beveridge's third condition for the successful working of a multilateral international system is that there should be reasonable stability in the commercial policies of other countries. In other words, countries should not be free to throw each others' employment policies out of joint by violent and unexpected changes in their tariffs or other forms of trade barrier. The commercial policy proposals which have been under discussion in the Article VII conversations would, of course, set such limits to the use of trade barriers as to ensure the desired degree of stability. They would, however, in two other ways ease the problem of maintenance of multilateral economic relations – ways of which Sir William makes no mention in his chapter.

102   In the first place, Sir William asks only for continuity in commercial policy. He admits that countries may still be high tariff or low tariff countries, and he does not require any general reduction of trade barriers. The Article VII commercial policy proposals, however, do demand a general reduction in tariffs and other trade barriers and, in particular, they prohibit (or set strict limitations on) the use of quantitative import restrictions. There is no reason to believe that the reduction in trade barriers would alone make it easier for us to adopt an internal employment policy while depression is generated in the outside world; but it would undoubtedly make some of the other remedial measures more effective. In particular, an adjustment of exchange rates readjusts balances of payments by making the goods of the country whose currency is depreciated so much the cheaper in other markets. If the expansion of that country's exports is rigidly restricted by the quantitative regulation of imports or by prohibitively high tariffs in other markets, then depreciation of its exchange rate will have so much the less effect in readjusting its balance of payments. If this country were to get out of step with the rest of the world because of its domestic employment policy, it could adjust itself the more easily by a moderate depreciation of sterling if it were operating in a world of relatively unhampered trade.

103   Secondly, Sir William Beveridge is naturally unaware of the proposal which forms so prominent a feature of the commercial policy arrangements discussed in the Article VII conversations, by which countries with favourable balances of payments would not be permitted to use quantitative import restrictions, whereas countries with unfavourable balances of payments would be permitted to use them. This is, of course, a further important safeguard. An American depression which caused the United States to have a seriously favourable, and us a seriously unfavourable, balance of payments would automatically give us a freedom of trade regulation which it would deny to the Americans. Here is a fire-escape after Sir William's own heart.

104   It may be useful to summarise the position by enumerating those features of the Article VII world at present under discussion, which will help to make the adoption of multilateralism compatible with that of a domestic employment policy. There are nine such features, the first four of which Sir William Beveridge recognises. The importance of the last five has escaped his attention.

(i)   It is recognised by His Majesty's Government, no less than by Sir William, that an attempt should be made to get international agreement on the co-ordination of domestic employment policies, so that the risk of external depression is reduced to a minimum for each of the co-operating members.

(ii)   Sir William Beveridge lays great stress on the contribution to world stability which might be brought about by the stabilisation of the incomes of the producers of primary products, either through 'buffer stocks' or through long-term contracts covering such commodities. This aspect of commodity policy has also, of course, been prominent in the Article VII conversations.

(iii) Sir William Beveridge recognises that the International Monetary Fund will provide an extra buffer of international credit upon which individual countries can draw when they get into balance-of-payments difficulties. This is, of course, one (but only one) of the ways in which the International Monetary Fund may help to promote the adoption of the domestic employment policies without too rigid a regard to the effect of those policies upon the balance of payments.

(iv) It is generally agreed that countries should be free to control the movement of capital; and this is one of the important principles upon which the International Monetary Fund has been based. Sir William Beveridge underlines this principle in paragraph 347 of his book; but he does not underline the full significance of this. Such control of speculative capital movements would have made an enormous difference to the Great Depression after 1929, when one of the main pressures on the balance of payments of countries which might otherwise have adopted more effective policies for internal expansion was due to the wholesale and unregulated movements of hot money from one centre to another.

(v) As has been pointed out above, Sir William Beveridge entirely fails to appreciate one of the main safeguards which the International Monetary Fund would introduce into a multilateral system, by making it possible (regardless of domestic policies) for countries in balance-of-payments difficulties to depreciate their currencies without the fear of unnecessary competitive exchange depreciation on the part of countries which (perhaps because of an uncontrolled domestic depression) had a favourable balance of international payments.

(vi) The 'Scarce Currency' Article in the International Monetary Fund, as has been explained above, introduces perhaps the most novel and revolutionary improvement into the multilateral system. It would permit all the other countries in the system to isolate themselves from any particular country if, through an uncontrolled depression in that country, it became impossible to finance payments to it without abandoning either the principle of non-discrimination or policies of domestic employment in the other countries. Sir William Beveridge, on insufficient grounds, dismisses the clause as being merely of academic interest.

(vii) In addition to the proposals for an International Monetary Fund, there are those for an International Bank for Reconstruction and Development. Sir William Beveridge, it is true, recognises that a flow of capital from countries with favourable, to countries with unfavourable, balances of payments may enable the latter more freely to adopt domestic policies of internal expansion. But he fails to recognise the second way in which the idea of an International Investment Bank might be developed in the interests of employment policy. Projects of reconstruction and development, which the Bank should sponsor, are to be submitted to the examination of experts. It would be but a natural development of this idea, fully in harmony with developments of modern thought on the subject, that one of the important considerations which the Bank authorities should take into account in examining and sponsoring projects for international investment would be the planning and timing of such development projects in such a way as to aid in the stabilisation of the general level of world demand for goods and services.

(viii) The Article VII proposals for commercial policy suggest a general lowering of tariffs and other trade barriers. Such clearance of the channels of world trade would increase the effectiveness of exchange-rate adjustments as a means of removing any disequilibrium in the balance of payments that might be caused through the adoption of a domestic employment policy in this country. Sir William Beveridge does not recognise this fact.

(ix) Finally, the Article VII commercial policy proposals introduce an important and novel safeguard for countries which may be suffering from a balance-of-payments difficulty as a result, for example, of the maintenance of their own internal purchasing power in a time of world depression. The proposed device is that countries with an unfavourable balance should be free to restrict their imports – a freedom which countries with a favourable balance of payments would not enjoy. Sir William Beveridge is naturally unaware of this proposal.

105   Does an edifice with an elevator and nine fire-escapes meet Sir William's specifications?

16

Economic Planning

This paper was written at the request of Herbert Morrison, Lord President of the Council in the first majority Labour government 1945–51, in September 1945. It was subsequently sent to ministers as 'expressing broadly the principles upon which the [official] Steering Committee [on Economic Development] intended to conduct its work' (Meade Papers 3/10, Meade Diary, 1, 16 and 23 September and 18 November 1945, Public Record Office T230/18 and CAB134/186).

I Introductory

1 The purpose of Economic Planning is to review the economic resources which are likely to be available for the community's use over the period of the Plan (say, during the next five years); to forecast the extent to which and the ways in which these resources are likely to be employed on the basis of current policies and programmes; and in the light of this information to adjust existing programmes and policies in such a way as to ensure that the total claims on the community's resources are neither excessive nor deficient and that each of the main claims receives its due share of resources.

2 The first and foremost purpose is to consider not so much the position of particular industries or regions but rather the overall position of the economy as a whole. Difficulties associated with particular industries or particular regions will be immeasurably easier to manage if the overall balance between supply and demand is maintained. The history of the inter-war years amply illustrates this fact. During those years the difficulty of dealing with the especially depressed sections of the economy was greatly increased by the fact that, for so many of those years, there was an overall deficiency in demand for goods and services. If throughout that period there had been a high demand for labour in many other sections of the economy, it would have been much easier to persuade new enterprise to go to depressed areas where labour was plentiful, and to encourage the movement of labour itself out of the especially depressed occupations and localities.

3 Resources are required for many purposes. They are needed for the maintenance of the Armed Forces and other current Government

services; for the housing programme and other forms of domestic capital development; for the expansion of exports; and for the maintenance and expansion of the current standard of living of the population. The basic question is whether the sum total of all these requirements is likely, on the basis of current programmes and policies, to exceed or to fall below the total resources available for use. An excess of total demands on the available resources will lead to inflationary difficulties; a deficiency will cause deflation, general economic depression, and widespread unemployment. Programmes and policies must be so adjusted as to close any overall inflationary or deflationary gap of this character.

4   Planning should take place in terms of the broad categories of demand upon the community's resources. It would be administratively impossible to plan the future output of every individual service or commodity. Moreover, if there is to be any appreciable freedom of choice on the part of consumers as to what they shall buy or on the part of workers as to what they shall work at, it would not be possible to fix a rigid detailed plan for each particular line of production. Within the planning of the broad categories of use for the community's resources, there must accordingly remain considerable flexibility in detail as to what shall be produced and in what quantities.

5   This does not, of course, imply that no attention should be paid within the framework of the Economic Plan to the implications of the Plan for particular industries and regions. On the contrary, within the picture of the probable future balance between the total demands on the community's resources and the total supply of resources, it will be possible to consider the probable balance between the supply and demand for resources in particular industries. And in considering what changes in programmes and policies would be desirable in the interests of an overall balance, it will be possible to take into account the effect of different policies upon particular sections of the economic system.

6   An Economic Plan of the kind indicated above would fall into two main parts. First, it would be necessary to prepare an Economic Survey which would compare the total economic resources of the community which are likely to be available for employment with the claims which are likely, on the basis of current programmes and policies, to be made on these resources. Secondly, it would be necessary in the light of this Survey to adjust existing policies and programmes in such a way as to bring the total claims on resources into proper balance with the available resources, and to ensure that these resources are used, broadly speaking, for the purposes for which it is desired to use them.

II   *The Overall Economic Survey*

7   In preparing the overall Economic Survey, some common measure must be found for summarising total national claims on resources and the

total resources likely to be available, so that an overall comparison between the two can be made. The most convenient common measure is the monetary measure. Both the resources of the community and the claims made on those resources take many different forms. On the side of resources there is not only manpower (itself not a homogeneous factor); there are also resources in the form of capital equipment, land and other natural resources. On the side of demand, there is an almost infinite variety of different goods and services which are required for various purposes. The most comprehensive common unit of measurement is in terms of money value.

8   For this reason, the best procedure is to consider: on the one hand, the 'target' money national income which the available resources could produce if they were productively employed and if an inflation of prices and money wage-rates were avoided; and on the other hand, the total national expenditure which is involved in the purchase at uninflated money prices of the goods and services required for various purposes.

9   Such a survey of future national income and expenditure can, of course, only be built upon an examination of the underlying real resources and of the real factors underlying the various demands upon resources.

10   A survey of the real factors underlying future developments of the 'target' national income must be based in the first place upon a *survey of the manpower* likely to be available for employment. Such an estimate of the available manpower for each of the coming five years would involve an estimate of the future age and sex composition of the population; an estimate of the unavoidable minimum of unemployment; and an allowance for any changes in the school leaving age, in the probable age of retirement from work, in the number of women who will seek work, in the amount of holidays and in the normal hours of work. That is to say, it involves estimating the amount of leisure in all forms which the people will choose to enjoy at the standards of living which are likely to rule during the period in question.

11   In examining the probable future demands on the community's resources it is necessary to consider the various real programmes underlying the main elements of national expenditure. It is convenient to divide the needs of the community into four basic categories:-

(i)   In the first place, there is the *current expenditure of the central Government and other public authorities* for defence, police, education, etc. The estimation of these future requirements involves the consideration of the various programmes for the future development of the Armed Forces and of other public services.

(ii)   Secondly, there is *public and private investment*, i.e. the use of resources for extending and improving the capital equipment of

the community. This involves the examination of programmes for capital development by a large range of authorities and
institutions. The Central Government is directly concerned in
such matters as Post Office development and programmes for
the development of trunk roads. The local authorities and
other public authorities are concerned with programmes for
municipal housing; for the development of such services as gas
and electricity; and for the capital development of a whole
range of other services. Finally, an attempt must be made to
obtain programmes of industrial capital development. In the
case of nationalised industries (e.g. a programme for the
mechanisation of the coal mines) this will be a direct responsibility of the public body in charge of the industry. In the case of
a number of other industries it should be possible to obtain
somewhat similar programmes. For yet other industries it will
be possible to do little more than make a rough estimate of the
probable future course of investment.

(iii)   Account must also be taken of the balance of *foreign payments*.
It will accordingly be necessary to consider *export 'targets'*, i.e.
a future programme of the demands which exports are likely to
make on the available resources as steps are taken to put the
balance of payments into equilibrium. Similarly it will be
necessary to consider future *import programmes*. On the basis
of future requirements of food, raw materials, and other goods,
considered in relation to the agricultural and other supplies
which are likely to be produced at home, it will be necessary to
estimate and (at least during the period of foreign exchange
shortage immediately ahead) to control both the size and the
main composition of the community's imports.

(iv)   Finally, an estimate must be made of the demands likely to be
made on the community for *personal consumption*, i.e. for
maintaining and improving the current standards of living of the
people. So long as large parts of the consumption field are
directly controlled (for example, by the rationing of clothing or
of food), this will involve a fairly direct estimation of the
supplies which, on the basis of current programmes, it is
decided to allocate to these purposes. In so far as the market for
goods and services is not rigidly controlled, it will be necessary
to estimate how much goods and services for personal consumption people are likely to purchase in view of the probable
developments of the spendable incomes at their disposal.

12   The purpose of all these estimates will be to compare the total
demands on the community's economic resources with the total resources
likely to be available. This involves a consideration of the future course of
productivity. In order to estimate to what extent the future national
requirements of goods and services is likely to be excessive or deficient in
relation to the manpower available to produce those goods and services,
it is essential to consider what is likely to happen to output per man-hour.

The probable future course of productivity is an essential feature of any economic planning, about which our information is at the moment gravely deficient. Even in the best of circumstances there must remain considerable uncertainty about it; and for this reason, if for no other, economic plans must always remain flexible and open to constant revision. It would be absurd to adhere rigidly to a plan to employ X men for a particular purpose, when an unexpected technical change has made it possible to do the same task with ½ X men.

III An Overall Economic Plan

13　On the basis of an Economic Survey of the kind described above, it would be possible to indicate not only the probable dimensions of any future 'inflationary' or 'deflationary' gap, between available resources and the total claims likely to be made on them, but also the alternative ways in which the gap might be closed. The problem will be to consider by how much such major items of policy as the raising of current standards of consumption, the building programme or other schemes for capital development, or the expansion of our exports should be adjusted in order to close an overall gap between available resources and the claims on them, and to ensure that the available resources are used in the desired proportions between these major uses.

14　The means available for adjusting existing economic policies and programmes in such a way as to achieve the desired balance between resources and the claims upon resources will take many and varied forms.

15　In the cases of some items of national expenditure the state itself or some other public authority is responsible for the expenditure involved. For example, in a nationalised coal industry the public authority in control of the industry would be directly responsible for any expenditure on the capital re-equipment of the industry. In the case of the production of military aircraft, the state itself is the sole purchaser. In these cases, the public authority concerned can directly affect the level of expenditure by decisions in regard to the programmes involved. The programme of mechanisation in the coal mines or the aircraft programme can be considered in advance and, within limits, varied so as to fit in with the overall balance between the available resources and the total demand on them.

16　Even in these cases, however, there are, of course, definite limits within which variation can take place solely with the view to filling an overall inflationary or deflationary gap. The primary purpose of the activities in question is to satisfy certain real requirements. The aircraft programme must be laid down in advance primarily with the needs of national defence in mind; and the programme for the mechanisation of the coal mines must be devised primarily from the point of view of the economic productivity and effectiveness of using economic resources for this type of industrial development rather than for other purposes.

17   Quite different techniques are required to control expenditure by private consumers on goods and services for current consumption, by private enterprise for the capital development of unsocialised industries, and by foreigners on our exports.

18   It is essential to draw a distinction between the problems which arise during the period of inflationary pressure immediately ahead and those which will arise in any subsequent period of threatening deflation and depression. During the transitional period of shortage and threatening inflation all sorts of negative restrictions and controls will be appropriate, to prevent producers from producing too much of a particular commodity, from using too many raw materials, from employing too much labour, or from spending too much on other economic resources; and to restrain individual consumers from spending too much on finished products. Theoretically, there is no essential economic difficulty in making such a system of negative controls effective in closing an inflationary gap by pruning the general level of expenditure in the various sectors of the economy.

19   In the period immediately ahead of us the implementation of any overall Economic Plan of the amount of our resources which should be devoted to each of the main categories of national requirements would have to depend largely upon a system of restrictive controls. When there is an excessive demand for resources in every line, the desired allocation of resources can be obtained in so far as it is possible to limit the amount of economic resources which people are permitted to employ in each particular line.

20   In fact, even in the transitional period of overall shortages there will in practice be very strict limitations to what can be achieved solely by a system of negative and restrictive controls. In the first place, such a system of controls cannot be complete, particularly in so far as the direct control over labour is concerned. But, still more important, the transitional period will be one in which changes will be taking place with extreme rapidity. Any limit on, for example, the employment of labour for a certain purpose which was appropriate for next month might be quite inappropriate for the following month; and the question arises whether a system of negative controls could be made administratively sufficiently flexible to ensure that too many resources were not used in any one particular line without leading to serious and unnecessary unemployment. Even during this transitional inflationary period, therefore, it will be increasingly necessary to combine with the system of negative controls a general economic and financial policy which is devised to give people the necessary inducements voluntarily to produce the right things in the right quantities.

21 When, however, inflation gives place to deflation, a system of negative controls will be totally inadequate. It is difficult enough effectively to order a man not to purchase something which he wishes to purchase, not to employ someone whom he wishes to employ, not to produce something which he wishes to produce. It is incomparably more difficult effectively to order him to employ somebody whom he does not wish to employ, to produce something which he finds it unprofitable to produce, to purchase something which he has no desire to purchase. Economic expansion, in the unsocialised sector of the economy at least, must rely, not upon rigid quantitative controls, but upon general economic and financial policies which give the required degree of incentive to produce and to consume.

22 Apart from the possibility of speeding up programmes of public expenditure there are certain broad overall changes which may be useful in stimulating private demand. For example, a reduction in the rate of interest may serve to make all forms of capital development more attractive. Or, if the trouble is a persistent tendency for imports to exceed exports, an adjustment in the rate of exchange might make it more attractive for producers to export to, and less attractive for consumers to purchase from, overseas. A principal instrument of control may well be found in fiscal policy. A reduction in general taxation will leave consumers with larger sums to spend on the purchases of goods and services. Fiscal penalties and inducements might be so devised as to induce private enterprise to programme its development in the amounts and at the times which are in the social interest. Reductions in particular taxes or subsidies of particular kinds may be effective in promoting activity in particular directions.

IV Surveys and Plans for Particular Industries and Regions

23 As has been argued above, the primary objective of Economic Planning must be to examine the overall balance between demand on resources and the available supply of resources. Nevertheless, overall Economic Planning should be of use also in foreseeing the fortunes of particular industries and particular regions. Forecasts of what are likely to be the movements of national demand for the main purposes discussed in paragraph 4 above can be examined in order to consider what is likely to be their effect upon the future demand for the products of particular industries and so upon the employment situation in different industrial, occupational and regional groups.

24 The consideration of the fortunes of particular sections of the economy which a more detailed survey of this kind would make possible, should be of considerable use in considering the adjustment of particular economic programmes and policies. It might, for example, be apparent that a particular industry (for example, ship-building) was likely to be left seriously depressed even after general measures had been taken to

prevent the development of an overall inflationary or deflationary gap. In such circumstances, it would be a matter for consideration whether special measures should be taken to deal with these particular problems of ship-building. It might be decided that the depression in ship-building would only be temporary and that the best way of dealing with the situation would be to take special measures to maintain the demand for new ships over the period in question. Or it might be decided that the future depression in ship-building activity was likely to be chronic. In this case, it might be preferred immediately to initiate measures to assist the movement of labour out of ship-building, or to encourage the entry of new industries into the region affected.

25　Such action differs widely from the rigid planning of the output of particular industries. Rigid quantitative programmes for particular products are not impossible, if the state is either the sole producer or the main purchaser of the goods in question. Thus, the state might fix a rigid quantitative programme for, say, the output of agriculture by offering to purchase over the next five years fixed quantities of output from the agricultural producers at given prices. Or, in the case of a nationalised coal-mining industry, the National Coal Board could fix a rigid quantitative programme for the production of coal over the next five years, regardless of the variations which might take place (for example, as a result of the technical developments of alternative fuel) in the demand for coal.

26　While there is no doubt that short-term production programmes may be of great service it would be exceedingly uneconomic to plan over any considerable period of time the exact production of any particular industry regardless of the changes which may occur in the demand for the product.

27　Similarly, unforeseen changes may occur in the technical efficiency of an industry, so that there would be an alteration in the amount of labour required to produce any given output. It would for this reason also be uneconomic to set a rigid employment target for any particular industry.

28　Whether changes be due to variations in conditions of demand (e.g. the development of a substitute commodity) or to variations in the technique on the supply side (e.g. the development of a new productive process) the relation between prices and costs of production is thereby radically changed. In order that the community may make the best use of its available resources, short-term programmes of production and employment in particular industries must be open to frequent revision, in order that activity may be concentrated on the production (by the most economic methods) of those goods for which the consumers' demand is greatest in relation to their costs of production. In so far as it is desired to introduce an element of stability into the output of an industry or into the volume of employment given in that industry, this should not be done without due regard to the economic cost involved – a cost which can best be estimated by consideration of the excess of the costs in the industry in question over the price obtained for its product.

29   In conditions of peace it is even more essential than in conditions of war to have regard to the prices which consumers are willing to pay for the different products and their relation to the costs of production of the goods in question. In war-time, there is one single aim and object of economic policy, namely to prosecute the war to the maximum and to cut consumers' standards of living to the barest standardised minimum. In peace-time, particularly in the case of a community with high and rising standards of life, there is an infinite variety of competing aims. Apart from the broad overall decisions (as, for example, how much of the resources of the community should be allocated to capital development and how much to raising current standards of consumption), consumers must choose between a large range of alternatives, between various kinds of food, clothing, books, travel, entertainment, and a host of other goods and services. In a community in which consumers' choices are likely to vary considerably as their standards of living rise, and in which there may be frequent technical improvements in the production of various goods and services, the needs of the people can be freely and efficiently met only if due regard is taken, both in private and in socialised industry, to the production of those goods by those methods which the relations between prices and costs show to be the most economic.

30   This is not, of course, to say that the relation between prices and costs must be slavishly followed. There may be many reasons for state intervention to influence what would otherwise be produced or con-sumed. On nutritional grounds the state may wish to encourage the consumption of some foodstuffs and to discourage the consumption of others. On social grounds the state may desire to encourage one mode of life as opposed to another, for example rural life as opposed to urban. But unless due regard is taken of the relation between prices and costs in the various industries concerned, there will be no means of assessing the economic cost of these policies.

V   The Need for Flexibility

31   It should not be concluded that it will in fact prove easy, even in the case of the overall balance between the total demand and supply of economic resources, accurately to foresee future economic develop-ments. Even in the months immediately ahead there are necessarily great uncertainties; and these uncertainties become greater, the more distant is the period which the plan attempts to cover. Indeed, sensible Economic Planning should attempt not merely to forecast the most probable future development, but also to assess the degree of uncertainty which is involved in any such forecast.

32 Some uncertainties are due to lack of statistical or other information; and these it should be possible to remove. But many uncertainties arise from the very nature of the problem, and cannot be removed by any development of statistical or other forms of economic intelligence. To take but one example, the demand over the next five years for resources for house-building must depend upon the technical efficiency of labour employed in house-building. No one can say at the moment what may be the result of a large building programme on building technique. No one can, therefore, say in advance precisely what economic resources it would be appropriate five years hence to devote to the building programme. All that can be done is to assess the most probable requirement on the basis of present information.

33 The moral of this is that the Plan itself should be kept as flexible as possible. Any programme or forecast for 1950, for example, should be constantly and continually revised as 1950 recedes from the fifth, through the fourth, third and second, to the first year of a five-year plan. The figures for the first year of a five-year plan can be reasonably precise, but the degree of precision must shade off until the figures for the fifth year represent merely an impressionistic sketch of what may happen. The overall programmes must be flexible and open to constant review and revision.

34 Such flexibility is even more essential in the plans for particular industries, where changes in technique and changes in demand may necessitate considerable alterations of output and of the use of resources, unless great possibilities of economies and of consequential improvements in overall standards of living are to be missed. Both in the socialised and in the unsocialised sectors of the economy, measures may be taken to ensure that, as judged by the comparison between costs of production and the prices which consumers are willing to offer for the goods in question, resources do in fact turn (albeit with due regard to the difficulties of adjustment) to the most economic production of the things which consumers most desire. Provided that effective steps are taken to maintain the overall level of national demand at the appropriate intensity, the organisation of such flexibility within a general plan should not prove impossible of achievement.

17

Control of Inflation

The Treasury's Budget Committee for the April 1947 Budget asked for a memorandum on the control of inflation from the Economic Section in June 1946. Meade wrote the following (Meade Papers 3/10 and Public Record Office T171/389, Meade Diary, 7 June 1946).

I The Magnitude of the Inflationary Pressure

1 The two Economic Surveys (CP(46) 32 and ED(46) 13 ['Economic Survey for 1946', 30 January 1946, and 'Economic Survey for 1946/47', 3 June 1946, Public Record Office CAB129/6 and CAB134/188]) which have recently been prepared for the Steering Committee on Economic Development have revealed a 'gap' between the 'target' national income and that level of total national expenditure which corresponds to the current departmental plans and programmes. The financial gap so revealed has been reduced from £470 million in the first Survey which was prepared at the end of 1945 to cover the calendar year 1946, to £230 millions in the second Survey which has just been prepared to cover the financial year 1946/47. This reduction is in the main due to the revision of the programme of expenditure on the Armed Forces and their supply.

2 But neither of these figures is in any way an indication of the excess of the total amount of money which individuals, businesses and public authorities would like to spend over the value of the available supplies of goods and services. It is merely a measurement of the self-consistency of existing departmental plans and programmes and shows the excess of the value of the supplies which the various departments wish to use or to see used for various purposes over the supplies that are available. If all direct controls (such as rationing, licensing of purchases and price control) were removed, the excess of the amounts which people would then try to spend over the value of the available supplies at current prices would be very much greater. Some attempt is made in the immediately following paragraphs to indicate the order of magnitude of this inflationary difference.

3 Any calculations of this kind are, of course, uncertain, particularly in so far as they relate to future developments. They purport to represent no more than the nearest estimate that can be made on the basis of the

information currently available. So far as possible they should be subject to frequent revision as the situation develops. It is hoped, however, that they indicate at least the general nature of the problems with which we are faced in the coming months.

(i) The Inflationary Pressure of Demand for Goods and Services for Personal Consumption

4   In the market for goods and services for personal consumption there are at present two fairly distinct, though interconnected, factors at work. In the first place, the accumulation of liquid savings during the war combined with the fact that during the war purchases had to be postponed means that there is an abnormal stored up demand for goods and services. This would constitute inflationary pressure of demand even if the present supplies of goods and services available for consumption were in normal relation to the present level of current spendable incomes, so that the current level of personal savings out of current incomes need not be abnormally high. But at present and in the immediate future – and this constitutes the second potentially inflationary factor – the supply of goods and services for personal consumption is not sufficiently high in relation to the current level of personal incomes to permit current savings to be reduced to a normal pre-war level. These two factors may be examined separately.

(a)   ACCUMULATED SAVINGS AND ARREARS OF CONSUMPTION

5   As the following table shows, the unspent balances accumulated by consumers during the war total something over £6,000 million. Even if there had been no war, consumers would not have spent the whole of their incomes, but would have made some saving. If one allows for this normal saving, the extraordinary war-time balances may be put at about £5,000 million.

	Available personal income (i.e. less direct taxation)	*Personal consumption at market prices*	*Net personal saving*	*Percentage of available personal income saved*
		£ million		
1938	4,300	4,160	140	3.3
1939	4,484	4,271	213	4.7
1940	5,073	4,496	577	11.4
1941	5,565	4,721	844	15.2
1942	5,993	5,004	989	16.5
1943	6,383	5,082	1,301	20.4
1944	6,610	5,335	1,275	19.3
1945	6,915	5,645	1,270	18.4
1938–45	45,323	38,714	6,609	14.6

6   How direct an inflationary pressure these savings represent depends, to some extent, on how they have been absorbed. The pressure is more immediate, the more spendable the savings are. From 1938 to the end of 1945, the estimated currency circulation with the public has increased threefold to £1,342 million, an increase of some £900 million. During the same period deposits with the clearing banks increased more than twofold to £4,850 million. At the end of 1945, the total amount of money in the hands of the public was therefore £6,192 million, an increase of about £3,400 million. This increase must, however, be looked at alongside the prices of goods, for the primary reason why people hold balances of money is to facilitate their purchases of goods. The amount of money in the hands of the public has not increased very much more than the value of the gross national income. By and large, therefore, the increase in money holdings can be treated as a normal increase in cash balances, not (though they have absorbed savings) as balances people will want permanently to deplete by spending. It must also be remembered that only a part of the money held by the public is held by private persons for the purchase of consumption goods. Thus two thirds of bank deposits are held for business purposes. Without full figures of the way the amount of money held by private persons has increased, it is impossible to do more than guess how much of it represents personal savings that may be spent, and how much should be considered normal personal cash holdings. Perhaps as a rough guess £1,000 million of personal savings will have been absorbed as an increase in normal cash holdings. Much of the disproportionate increase in currency holdings, however, may represent the savings of people who are unused to putting their savings into less liquid form; but this would only amount to several hundred millions, and is overshadowed by the vast volume of other forms of small savings.

7   The increases during the war in those Government securities usually regarded as 'small savings' have been as follows (1939–1945):-

Increases from 1938 to 1945:

Post Office and Trustee Savings Banks	£1,567 million
National Savings Certificates	£1,355 million
Defence Bonds	£897 million
	£3,819 million

During the same period the net increase in other public issues has been £5,787 million. It was estimated in paragraph 5 that private saving during the war has been greater than normal to the tune of about £5,000 million. Personal saving must have contributed to other public issues; but it must have been largely absorbed by the increase in normal cash holdings, or by the Post Office Savings Bank, National Savings Certificates and Defence Bonds. The difference in the ease with which they can be spent is a difference of degree. Not only Savings Certificates but also, under present conditions, long-term securities are readily convertible into cash; and they cannot be disregarded in reckoning the money consumers could spend if they wanted.

8   To form some idea of how much of these war-time savings consumers may wish to spend, it is useful to look at the actual ways in which consumers' expenditure has been curtailed during the war.

9   Over the period 1938–1945, it is estimated that total consumption (measured in real not money terms) has been restricted to 80 or 90 per cent of its 1938 level; but the real consumption of *durable* consumption goods has been curtailed much more severely, and averaged only 60 per cent of its peace-time amount. And it is arrears of such goods that consumers are most likely still to wish to make good. The following are the more easily distinguished sorts of durable consumption goods:-

Average over period 1938–1945	*Average consumption in real terms*	*Number of normal years' consumption forgone*	*Value in 1945 prices of war-time deficiency*
	(1938 = 100)	*(1938 = normal)*	*(£ million)*
Furniture & Furnishings	52%	3.9	500
Hardware	59%	3.3	450
Footwear	85%	1.2	450
Clothing	59%	3.3	2,550
Motor-cars (and their running expenses)	35%	5.3	170
	58%		£4,120 million

10   Expressed in this way the war-time deficiencies in durable consumption goods look very considerable. If consumers wished to make them up in whole they might absorb all the war-time abnormal savings now available to be spent. This is, of course, far too simple a way of putting it. Some of the clothes that might have been bought but for the war would by now have been worn out, and will not anyhow be wanted now. Much of the money that would have been spent on motoring would have gone on running expenses that cannot now be incurred. On the other hand, there are other expenses on durable goods not included above, such as the maintenance of private houses. Then again people may by now have grown used to doing without some things, and may not wish to revert to the old peace-time standards. Finally, the prices of different kinds of goods have changed among themselves, and in adjusting to these changes people will not duplicate exactly the old pattern of expenditure that was adapted to different relative prices.

11   Nevertheless it is clear that even when production has been restored to pre-war levels, there will still be backlogs of unsatisfied demand for durable consumption goods that consumers will try to make up; and that,

with the need to satisfy current consumption at the same time it may well take several years to work off the arrears of the past.

(b) THE CURRENT BALANCE BETWEEN SPENDABLE INCOMES AND AVAILABLE SUPPLIES

12   The second factor which we have to take into account is that the current level of supplies of goods and services for personal consumption is insufficient in relation to the current level of spendable incomes to permit current savings to fall back to their pre-war relationship with incomes.

13   The level of personal incomes in 1946/47 may be roughly estimated at about £7,100 million.[1] The value of the goods and services which it is planned to make available for personal consumption is estimated at £6,388 million. At current prices personal savings will then have to be maintained at about £700 million, or about 10 per cent of available income, if an inflationary pressure in the market for consumption goods and services is to be avoided. A portion of spendable income, however, is made up of Forces release leave pay, demobilisation gratuities and post-war credits. Since people demobilised from the Forces are taking most of their release leave before starting in civilian employment, it is probable that much of the former is being spent; but the gratuities and post-war credits are probably being treated as savings. For this purpose they may be treated as savings made in past years, rather than current income that is being saved. If about £150 million is deducted on this account, personal savings would have to total about £550 million out of an available personal income of about £6,950 million; or about 8 per cent as compared with a pre-war figure of 3 to 5 per cent.

14   The Economic Survey for 1946/47 however showed 'gaps' of £230 million between the total value of resources available and the total claims made upon those resources. This 'gap' must mean that some supplies do not reach the planned level. If the whole of this were to fall on goods and services available for private consumption, personal savings would have to be increased to about £800 million; from about 8 to about 11 or 12 per cent of available personal incomes. Even if none of the 'gap' falls on supplies available for personal consumption, savings as a proportion of available income must still be maintained considerably above pre-war, in spite of the fact, emphasised in paragraphs 5 to 11 above, that in present circumstances there are tendencies at work to make people save an abnormally small proportion of income in view of their past abnormal accumulations of savings and the backlog of their demand for durable consumption goods. Including demobilisation gratuities and credits, a net sum of perhaps £400–£450 millions will during 1946 have to be added to the existing total of *abnormal* war-time savings; or considerably more if the 'gap' of £230 millions were to fall on personal consumption.

15   It is impossible to make similar estimates for 1947/48 before a full

[1] On the basis of the forecast of total private income made in the Economic Survey for 1946/47.

Survey for that year has been prepared. Some indication of the trend of personal savings and consumption, however, is to be obtained by examining the figures forecast in the Economic Survey for 1946/47 for the last quarter of the financial year. While the rate of supply of goods and services available for personal consumption (on the assumption that the departmental programmes for such supplies are fully achieved) rises by £200 million, the rate of private income also rises, by about £170 million. It may therefore be doubted whether savings as a proportion of available personal income can, in the last quarter of 1946/47, be allowed to fall at all substantially below the average level needed for the whole year. For the further prospect, on the one hand some increase in personal incomes probably has to be allowed for; on the other side, it is not obvious, barring an increase in productivity, how a further increase in consumption can be met except at the cost of other objectives. As far as can now be discerned, then, there seems little immediate trend towards any further rapid easement of the pressure for consumption.

16   1938 can, of course, be taken only as a very approximate standard of post-war normality. Any general redistribution of incomes that has taken place during the war will probably increase the proportion of incomes that people will want to spend. The existence of large unspent abnormal savings made during the war may well increase the proportion of their current incomes that people want to spend. The increased expenditure on tobacco and alcohol, in spite of their being more expensive, may be partly due to this. As more durable goods become available, this tendency will be strengthened. And the tendency may not be confined to durable goods. Consumers may well want to make up some of their war-time deficiencies in other goods and services. There may for instance be an increased demand for holidays.

(ii)   The Inflationary Pressure of Demand for Investment Goods

17   The present demand for investment goods is, in some ways similar, in some ways dissimilar, to that for consumption goods. There are large balances accumulated during the war that are available to be spent; and the normal demand for investment goods is increased by the demands left unsatisfied during the war. The volume of total gross investment in fixed capital including making good war damage during 1946/47, however, will, on the basis of present plans, be about 5 per cent above the pre-war level.

18   The balances available for private investment are made up primarily of the net undistributed profits of companies, and of unspent depreciation allowances. Between 1940 and 1945 there was little or no net private capital formation; on the contrary arrears of depreciation and maintenance accumulated. Undistributed profits accumulated since 1940 totalled £1,205 million by the end of 1945; and arrears of depreciation and maintenance totalled £1,219 million. To this accumulation must be added such of the past War Damage Compensation payments as have not been

spent; and such war-time depletion of working stocks as has not already been made good.

19   In 1946/47 current company savings (£200–300 million) will be largely supplemented by further war damage payments (£225 million net). The three items together, however, total less than the requirements figures for private net fixed capital formation in 1946/47 (£595 million) and for the building up of working stocks (£300 million); they would not exceed total private investment even if it were reduced by the whole of the £230 million 'gap' shown in the 1946/47 Survey between the value of total resources available and the total demands put upon those resources for all purposes. Unlike consumers' balances, the accumulated balances available for private investment are not still increasing.

20   The urgent demand for private capital formation springs from three causes. In the first place, there is the war-time running down of private capital to make up: the arrears worth £1,200 million at the time will now cost more to replace, to the extent that machinery and building costs have increased. In the second place, there is war damage to property to be made good, as indicated by War Damage Compensation payments still to be paid. Thirdly, there is the need for re-equipment in many important industries.

21   The large-scale housing programme as well as the plans for the re-equipment of the coal, the iron and steel, the cotton, and other industries are not merely an inheritance from the war, but are more fundamental. The cost will greatly exceed the war-time accumulations of undistributed profits or of other capital funds. The inflationary pressure for expenditure on investment goods is not therefore a monetary one of unspent balances seeking for some profitable outlet. It springs from more fundamental underlying factors.

22   In the Economic Survey for 1946/47 it was estimated that the volume of total gross investment in fixed capital including what is possible towards making good outstanding war damage and arrears of depreciation will rise to a rate at the end of the year rather more than 15 per cent greater than the rate in 1938. The increase in working capital required to fill the pipeline of civil consumption is an exceptional item that will not need to be repeated in future years. The volume of capital equipment available will be increased by the release from war production for civilian use of Government factories and equipment that were not included in the war-time totals of private investment. Nevertheless, it is clear that there will continue for some time to be an excess of demand over available supplies in the market for capital goods.

II   Possible Methods of Control

23   Since 1940 the essential bulwark against a potential inflationary

pressure of the kind revealed in the above paragraphs has been the system of direct controls over expenditure, such as price control, rationing, licensing of purchases or expenditure, etc. Of these, the essential anti-inflationary control has been price control, since effective price control, even in the absence of rationing or licensing of purchases, itself effectively limits total expenditure. Those at the head of the queue who are lucky enough to find any of the price-controlled goods obtain their supplies, while those at the tail of the queue have to take their money home to invest in Savings Certificates. Rationing and licensing of purchases introduce the principle of equitable distribution of scarce supplies; but effective price control alone will suffice effectively to limit expenditure.

24   There is, of course, an alternative method of control over a potential inflationary pressure. This consists in bringing the total demand into balance with the total supply by a fiscal policy which keeps the amount of spendable funds in balance with the available supply of goods and services. In present circumstances, this would involve allowing the supply of goods and services available for purchase by the public to increase without an equivalent reduction in taxation, so that the 'gap' between the funds which people have to spend and the value of the supplies available on the market is itself closed.

25   The problem can be tackled on a double front. The pressure can be relieved by a rather quicker increase in the supply of goods and services for ordinary personal consumption, even if this means some slowing down in the programmes for capital development at home or for the restoration of the balance of payments.[2] At the same time, rates of taxation can be maintained, or reduced more slowly than would other wise be the case.[3]

26   In present conditions there is much to be said for a shift in emphasis in our anti-inflationary policy away from too great a reliance on such

[2] A slowing down in the programme for the restoration of the balance of payments could take the form either of a reduction in export targets or of a relaxation of import restrictions. Either course would effectively increase supplies on the home markets; but in so far as it is essential rapidly to establish contacts in export markets, whereas the possibility of future restriction of imports will in any case be unimpaired, the method of relaxation of import restriction would appear to be preferable.

[3] In addition to maintaining the general level of taxation at an appropriate level, it may be possible to choose forms of taxation which, without directly depriving the taxpayer of greater amounts of money, nevertheless leave him with a smaller incentive to spend money on goods and services. High rates of purchase tax which are known to be temporary may have an altogether disproportionate effect in restraining immediate expenditure. Another device would be a tax which differentiated in favour of undistributed profits and against the payment of dividends. Such an arrangement (particularly if it were known to be temporary and likely to give place to a differentiation in favour of the distribution of profits at a later date when there was a threat of deflationary pressure) might induce companies to hold back from distributing a larger part of their profits, with some consequential diminution in the amount which the profit-earning class as a whole has available to spend on goods and services for personal consumption.

direct controls as price control, rationing, etc., and rather more on to a policy designed to restore the essential balance itself between available supplies and spendable funds.

27   In the first place, the war-time apparatus of direct controls is already weakened and is bound to weaken progressively in the future. Effective price control is bound to become increasingly difficult to maintain in face of an excess potential demand for goods and services; and shop-shortages, black markets and the other phenomena associated with this type of control over expenditure are bound to become increasingly irksome.

28   Secondly, too great a reliance on price control and similar direct anti-inflationary controls will harm the incentive to produce. To meet an excess potential demand by means of price control and rationing means that the consumer cannot find the goods available at current prices to mop up all his available buying power; he is forced to save the difference. For this reason, additional increments of income to him lose their value. Indeed, they would become totally worthless[4] to him unless he were to think the day was coming when he would be able to make some use of his accumulated savings.

29   There can be little doubt that this factor has been and is still at work in this country. It is a generally recognised fact, for example, that one of the important causes of voluntary absenteeism among the coal-miners is that they cannot find suitable outlets for the expenditure of the whole of the money incomes which a full week's work enables them to earn. And it must be remembered that this position is not improved merely by an increase in the supply of goods, if at the same time there is a corresponding reduction of taxation which means that the worker does not have to earn more in order to be able to purchase more.

30   Thirdly, in present circumstances, there is an even more compelling argument in favour of shifting the emphasis rather more on to measures designed to remove the underlying lack of balance between spendable funds and available supplies. So long as more or less rigid price control is necessary in order to prevent an excess of spendable funds from leading to an uncontrolled inflation of prices, it will be very difficult to use the mechanism of price adjustment in order to bring about the changes in the economic structure required for a rapid and successful transition from a war to a peace-time economy. For example, there is a crying need to get

---

[4] Germany provides a most illuminating extreme example of the two distinct ways in which inflation may make a currency worthless. After the last war the mark became worthless because of the straightforward astronomical rise in prices which followed an astronomical rise in spendable funds. At present the mark is virtually worthless (and threatens to be replaced by the cigarette as the unit of value!) because effective price control over the very limited supplies of goods means that there is nothing which anyone can buy with the very large supplies of money at their disposal. No one wants to work for money in Germany now. (Between the end of 1938 and of 1944 the note circulation in Germany had increased by 500 per cent, but prices had been allowed to increase only by 11 per cent.)

an increased production of textiles, and for this purpose to man-up the textile industries. A natural solution to this problem would be to increase the incentives to produce more textiles by allowing some increase in the price of textiles, accompanied by a corresponding increase in the wages offered to textiles operatives. But in present conditions of almost universal excess demand, it may be considered necessary to maintain an almost rigid opposition to increases of prices and wages in every sector of the economy, on the grounds that to allow some let-up in one particular sector would lead to sympathetic demands for price and wage increases in many other sectors, which in present circumstances of excess demand could not easily be resisted. In this way a snowball effect might become almost inevitable, and the potential inflationary pressure might begin to translate itself into a real inflation.

31 Nevertheless, if it is the intention of Ministers to plan in a free society, this is a most serious obstacle. If Ministers were prepared to maintain an extensive apparatus of labour direction to accompany price control, rationing, licensing of purchases, etc., it would be possible to deal with the threat of inflation by price controls and simultaneously to direct labour and other factors of production into the production of those commodities the expansion of which was desired. But in the absence of labour direction, it is difficult to see how it will be possible to induce workers and employers to move from the production of what is less urgently wanted to the production of what is more urgently wanted, unless a conscious use is made of price and wage adjustments. In order that this should be possible, it is necessary to aim at a state of affairs in which, while there is an excess demand in some markets (e.g. textiles), there will be little or no excess demand in the majority of other markets. In these circumstances, to allow some let-up on prices and wages in the industries whose products are in particularly short supply would not be made impossible by the general threat of inflation throughout the rest of the economy.

32 There is a fourth disadvantage of relying too heavily on the method of direct controls such as price controls, namely the pure economic cost of managing affairs through the administrative machine rather than by making some use of the price mechanism. There are, of course, many schemes of reform (such as the National Insurance Scheme) which require an extensive administrative apparatus and which are desired on their own intrinsic merits. On the other hand, there are some schemes of administrative control (such as a large part of price control and of various schemes for controlling the purchase or sale of many particular goods and services) the necessity of which is primarily if not solely due to the fact that the failure to stop at source a potential inflationary pressure makes it necessary to find an administrative alternative to the use of the price mechanism.[5]

[5] It would be interesting to know what proportion of the increase of more than one quarter of a million in the whole-time non-industrial staff of the national government between 1939 and 1946 might be attributed to this sort of cause.

33   Nor is it merely the real economic cost of the administration of a miscellany of otherwise direct controls which is at issue. To put rather more emphasis on fiscal measures for influencing the broad direction of national expenditure and to rely rather more upon changes in relative prices and wages to encourage the planned use of resources, would enable a general economic control to be achieved without the petty annoyance of innumerable and extensive particular controls over every form of economic activity (with consequential operations in the Black Market) – a state of affairs which, if it were too prolonged, might bring with it an undesirable reaction against the whole idea of state planning.

34   The above paragraphs have been written mainly from the point of view of the control of inflationary pressure in the market for consumption goods and services. There is, of course, a similar problem in the market for capital goods. In this market, however, the case against putting the main emphasis on direct control is, for the time being at any rate, less strong. If a balance can be restored in the market for consumption goods and services, the present problems of anti-inflationary control will have been largely solved in a way which will restore the desired resilience to the economic system. Consideration of possible ways of streamlining the control of investment can wait until the prior problem of inflationary pressure in consumption markets has received attention.

III   The Problem of Wage-Rates and the Cost of Living

35   Up to this point, no reference has been made to inflationary movements that may start on the side of costs rather than on the side of demand. But in fact, in addition to inflationary developments which may occur because demand is in excess of the available supplies, prices may be pushed upwards because costs of production, and in particular wage-rates and the prices of imported supplies, are increased.

36   These two inflationary influences, although logically quite separate, are nevertheless in fact closely related. Workers are in a strong bargaining position to make successful demands for increases in wage-rates when there is an excess demand for goods and services, and so for labour, in all markets. Moreover, in similar circumstances, employers have the least incentive to resist wage increases, since they know that there will still be a sufficient market for their product at the higher price which will result from the increased cost of production.

37   The following figures (which are illustrated on the graph attached to this paper [not reproduced]) show the annual percentage rate of increase in the general level of wage-rates which has occurred in different periods since the outbreak of war both before and after the initiation in April 1941 of the policy of stabilisation of the cost of living:-

Sept. 1939 – Dec. 1939	12.0 per cent per annum
Dec. 1939 – Dec. 1940	11.6 per cent per annum
Dec. 1940 – Apr. 1941	10.4 per cent per annum
Apr. 1941 – Dec. 1941	7.5 per cent per annum
Dec. 1941 – Dec. 1942	5.6 per cent per annum
Dec. 1942 – Dec. 1943	3.8 per cent per annum
Dec. 1943 – Dec. 1944	5.1 per cent per annum
Dec. 1944 – Dec. 1945	4.8 per cent per annum
Dec. 1945 – May 1946	11.0 per cent per annum

38   It is clear that a continued annual rate of increase of wage-rates of this order of magnitude would hold out serious dangers to the economy. When it is remembered that the pre-war annual rate of increase in productivity (output per man-hour) was of the order of 1½ per cent per annum, it is apparent that an increase of wage-rates at the present speed will inevitably mean a rapid rise in costs of production. Unless costs in foreign countries could be relied upon to rise at a comparable speed or we were prepared to contemplate a process of frequent depreciations in the sterling exchange rate, a continued development of this kind would clearly be disastrous to the expansion and maintenance of our exports on a sufficient scale to restore our balance of payments – quite apart from the domestic hardships and inconveniences of a continued rapid fall in the value of money.

39   The problem with which we are confronted is a difficult one. It is not merely a question of avoiding a rapid continual rise in the general level of wage-rates, but of avoiding too rapid a general rise without rigidly preventing those upward adjustments of particular wage-rates which may be necessary to man-up industries which are badly under-manned. The main principle must be to avoid all increases in wage-rates in all industries, occupations and regions except those which are seriously under-manned.[6]

40   Throughout the war and the more recent period of heavy demand for labour, there has been a steady upward movement in the general level of

---

[6] This is recognised as the fundamental principle which the proposed National Industrial Conference must attempt to achieve. cf. paragraph 17 of the First Report of the Official Working Party on Wages Policy (CP(46)130 [26 March 1946, Public Record Office CAB129/8]):-

'In brief, the changed conditions of the post-war economy make it particularly important that as much restraint as possible should be exercised upon wage increases in the "fully-manned" industries, for the following reasons:-

(a)   In order to allow increased wage-rates in the badly "under-manned" industries to have full effect in making such industries more attractive to labour;
(b)   In order to prevent a generally active demand for labour from causing an upward movement in the level of wage-rates out of relation to increases in the general level of productivity, thus leading to a general inflation of money prices and costs, with seriously adverse effects upon our foreign trade position; and
(c)   In order to avoid increases in labour costs in the "fully-manned" industries which might lead to localised unemployment.'

wage-rates. This is just what one would expect to happen during a period of excess demand for goods and services. One important advantage of adopting a fiscal policy expressly designed to bring the volume of spendable funds more closely into balance with the available supplies of goods and services would be almost automatically to moderate this steady increase of wage-rates.

41   It is a problem of finding a nice balance. One must not, of course, exercise so savage a check on total demand that heavy unemployment would again appear, thus re-establishing a weak labour market merely in order to avoid too rapidly rising money wage-rates. On the other hand, wage policy demands that the general level of demand should not be such as to be excessive in almost every market simultaneously. A more nicely adjusted balance between total demand and total supply would remove some of the forces which are leading to ever-rising money wage-rates. Even so, special additional measures of restraint will be needed in the labour market; for if general demand is maintained at a sufficiently high level to avoid mass unemployment, there will, in the absence of special restraint, be a more marked tendency than in the inter-war years for wage-rates constantly to rise.

42   It is frequently asserted that one of the main factors affecting the level of wage-rates is the movement of the cost of living, and that avoidance of increases in the cost of living is one of the main factors necessary to avoid increases in wage-rates. The attached graph [not reproduced] suggests that the importance of this factor can be overstated. As a matter of fact, wage-rates have increased fairly rapidly and continuously throughout the war and during the year since the war ended. The figures given in paragraph 37 above suggest that the stabilisation of the cost of living in 1941 exercised some moderating influence, temporarily at least; but its effect seems to have been very far from decisive. This experience suggests that the main influence causing the upward movement of wage-rates is, as one might expect *a priori*, the state of demand for labour in the labour market. Wages appear to have risen fairly rapidly so long as there has been a large excess demand for labour.

43   The stabilisation of the cost of living by means of subsidies has serious budgetary implications. At the time of the last Budget [9 April 1946], it was estimated that these subsidies would cost some £335 millions during 1946/47. But already this estimate has been revised to £355 millions. It is thought that by the end of the present year these subsidies may be running at the rate of some £415 millions per annum, as a result of anticipated increases in the cost of domestic and imported food supplies.

44   It is not only the scale of expenditure on these subsidies that is disquieting. This is a form of state expenditure which, so long as the cost of living is stabilised rigidly at its current level, is outside the control of the authorities. In future, as the world food shortage passes, it may be expected that supplies will increase and revert to peace-time norms. If

food supplies returned to the pre-war level and the cost of home-produced and imported supplies remained unchanged, the subsidies would have to rise to no less than £   millions per annum in order to keep the cost of living at its present figure.

45   It is arguable, of course, that this greatly exaggerates the budgetary danger, because, as supplies of foodstuffs revert to more normal levels, the prices payable both to the home farmers and to the foreign suppliers will fall, particularly in the case of wheat, from their present scarcity levels. It is, no doubt, probable that the unsubsidised prices of such foodstuffs will in fact fall in relation to the prices of other goods and services. But it is not at all certain how far, if at all, absolute prices of subsidised commodities will fall. This depends very largely upon the future course of unsubsidised prices in general, both in this country and in the rest of the world. The position may perhaps be summed up in this way. Assuming that supplies reverted to their pre-war levels, that the prices of unsubsidised products settled at their present level 50, 75 or 100 per cent above pre-war, then, in order to maintain the cost of living at its present level, the annual cost of subsidies would be £   millions, £ millions or £   millions respectively.

46   At present, if the cost-of-living subsidies were wholly removed, except for some £80 millions[7] to cover those subsidies (for the finance of cheap milk and of some assistance to domestic agricultural production) which may be desired on their own merits, the direct effect on the present cost-of-living index would be a rise from 132 to approximately 152 per cent of the pre-war level.

47   From the point of view of inflation, such a change would have a twofold effect. On the one hand, in so far as such a rise in the cost of living would induce increases in wage-rates, which would not otherwise occur even in the present conditions of acute scarcity of labour, costs of production would be inflated by a corresponding amount. On the other hand, the removal of the cost-of-living subsidies would diminish by an exactly equivalent amount the existing inflationary pressure in the sense of the existing excess of general demand for goods and services over the available supplies. For example, if £200 millions were added to the cost of the supplies of consumption goods and services likely to be available in 1946/47, the excess of some £400 millions in the personal savings which will be required to avoid inflation during 1946/47 over a more normal peace-time level of savings would be halved. (See paragraph 14 above.)

48   It is highly desirable from the budgetary point of view and from the point of view of controlling the inflationary pressure that a limit should be set to the cost-of-living subsidies and that, as soon as possible, they should be tapered off or, if possible, eliminated. The problem arises whether,

[7] This figure is intended to allow some £30 millions for 'social' subsidies and £50 millions for 'agricultural' subsidies.

from the point of view of the possible adverse effects on wage-rates and on labour relations of the appreciable increase in the cost of living which this policy would entail, there are any means of softening the impact of the readjustment.

49   One possibility would be to introduce a new cost-of-living index number based on the 1937/38 family budget enquiries and, in the future, to focus attention on changes in this as a proper measure of changes in the purchasing power of money. The old cost-of-living index number, being based on the collection of goods and services which a wage-earner consumed in 1904, contains a heavy weight for necessities such as bread and sugar and practically no weight at all for semi-luxuries such as beer, tobacco and entertainments. The question would arise whether it is proper to include in a cost-of-living index number such goods and services as beer, tobacco and entertainments, a large part of the price of which consists of indirect taxation. No encouragement should be given to the idea that price changes which are the conscious result of tax policy should have any bearing upon the fixation of money wage-rates.

50   The following shows the approximate relationship between the present levels of the old and the new cost-of-living indices:-

	Old Index	September 1939 = 100 New Index (a) including beer, tobacco and entertainments	(b) excluding
Subsidised	132	138	132
Unsubsidised*	152	149	144

* Except for £80 million of 'social' and 'agricultural' subsidies.

51   The removal of the cost-of-living subsidies has a much smaller effect on the new index than on the old, because the new index gives a smaller weight to subsidised items. Moreover, if the new index were introduced excluding beer, tobacco and entertainments (which, by reason of the increased taxation on them, have risen very much in price), the new subsidised index is approximately the same as the old subsidised index. The round of wage adjustments which has recently taken place has now brought the index of wage-rates to some 60 per cent above pre-war. It can be properly stressed that this compares very favourably with an unsubsidised index of 144 or 149, quite apart from the fact that weekly earnings have risen more than wage-rates.

52   There would seem to be a strong case for the prompt introduction of the new index number, before the tapering off process of the subsidies was started on any considerable scale. Whether or not the new index should include beer, tobacco and entertainments is a moot point. It is arguable that two new index numbers should be produced and published,

one including and the other excluding beer, tobacco and entertainments. This would at least have the advantage of emphasising the fact that in reality there is no single mystical figure, called *the* cost-of-living index number, which, for all persons and all purposes, accurately measures the cost of living; and if this had the effect of loosening to any extent the connection between wage-rates and the cost of living, such would be greatly to the advantage of a desirable wages policy.

53   Still further to soften the process of adjustment to the removal of the subsidies to the cost of living, some part of the net saving might be used to reduce taxation which falls on the workers or to increase other forms of expenditure which primarily benefit the workers. From £350 millions of subsidies a net saving to the Budget of £200 millions could be achieved if £80 millions of 'social' and 'agricultural' subsidies were retained and £70 millions were used to reduce other forms of taxation or to increase other forms of expenditure.

54   A possibility which springs immediately to the mind is that some part of this £70 millions might be used to reduce duties on beer, tobacco and entertainments, since reductions in such duties would themselves tend to reduce the new index number if it were introduced in its complete form. There is, however, very little to be gained in this way. To obtain a 1 per cent reduction in the new index number would cost no less than some £290 millions in beer duty,[8] £70 millions in tobacco duty or £50 millions in entertainment duty.

55   A more profitable idea would probably be to devote some part at least of the saving on the cost-of-living subsidies to an increase in the payments of national insurance and similar benefits. In the first place, there is already in many minds some link between these benefits and the cost of living, and the pressure to grant some increase in them if the cost of living is raised might accordingly be very great. Secondly, a strong case can be made out on merits for some such adjustment, particularly in the case of children's allowances. It can be forcibly argued that, whereas the cost-of-living subsidies keep the price of food, etc. at an uneconomically low level to everyone (including millionaires with no dependents), the payment of children's allowances (subject to income tax and sur-tax) concentrates the aid upon the poorer families with the largest number of dependents.

56   Moreover, quite apart from any change in the cost-of-living subsidies, there is likely to be considerable pressure for increased financial aid to large families when the Royal Commission on Population produces its report. In this setting, the argument that it was better to concentrate a small amount of money on the large families than to pay out indiscrimi-

---

[8] The new index number contains a very small weight for beer because the 1937/38 family budgets on which it would be based did not cover expenditure by the wage-earner in the public house.

nately a large amount of money to all consumers of bread, potatotes and sugar would have increased force.

57 A further advantage of treating some part of the saving in the cost-of-living subsidies in this way would be further to underline the fact that real income depends upon many factors outside the direct relationship between money wage-rates and the cost of living – factors such as the level of social security benefits as well as of taxation. This might still further help to weaken the link between wage-rates and the cost of living.

58 To raise the National Insurance and Assistance benefits in the ratio of the increase of the new cost-of-living index (excluding beer, tobacco and entertainments), which would result from the suggested reduction by £270 millions in the cost-of-living subsidies, would cost the Exchequer an annual amount of about £30 millions in the present financial year, rising to about £50 millions by 1948, on the assumption that no part of the increased cost was met by increased contributions from employers or employed. In addition, it would be possible to increase the present rate of children's allowances from 5s 0d to 7s 6d a week at an additional cost of about £25 millions a year.

59 The above proposals for tapering off fairly rapidly some £270 millions of cost-of-living subsidies and for using some £70 millions for special compensatory reliefs would result in a net saving of £200 millions. There has not yet been occasion to consider what the balance of the 1947/48 Budget would be like in the absence of these adjustments of cost-of-living subsidies and of any special concessions connected with them. But for the purpose of this paper it is assumed that it will be possible to balance the 1947/48 Budget apart from these adjustments. If the achievement of such a balance should prove compatible with some further moderate tax concessions, then in presentation of the case these other concessions would, of course, also be used as part of the general offset to any rise in the cost of living.

60 On these assumptions, the net saving of £200 millions on the cost-of-living adjustment would represent a true budgetary surplus. The adjustment necessary to bring about this result might be greatly sweetened by appropriating this £200 millions as an annual payment to the new Employment Stabilisation Fund, the institution of which is suggested in the following section (see paragraphs 74 and 75 below). It could then be represented that the new budgetary arrangements were part of the general post-war plan for the maintenance of full employment:- the cost-of-living subsidies were being eliminated; apart from the fact that they were being partly offset by immediate valuable concessions in other taxes or in other expenditure on social security, the whole net saving from the operation was being allocated for the specific purpose of building up a fund, out of which the prevention of unemployment could, in the future, be financed; the abandonment of the rigid price stabilisation policy did not mean the abandonment of economic plans for

stabilisation; on the contrary, it was being used as the instrument for the institution of a new effective system of finance which, over the years, was specifically designed to stabilise the general level of demand for labour.

IV The Implications for Budgetary Policy

61   Of the general principles for central finance, the Coalition Government's White Paper on Employment Policy stated that 'to the extent that the policies proposed in this Paper affect the balancing of the Budget in a particular year, they certainly do not contemplate any departure from the principle that the Budget must be balanced over a longer period' (paragraph 77 of Cmd 6527). It is presumably the accepted doctrine that the maintenance of total demand will require budget deficits in certain years, but that every attempt will be made to offset this as far as possible by budget surpluses in good years. If this principle is adopted, there can be no doubt that next year is a year when, if ever, there should be a budget surplus. There will, as has been seen in Part I, be a strong inflationary pressure. The control of this inflation itself would make it appropriate to maintain relatively high levels of taxation and if it is really desired over the average of years to balance the Budget, there will never be a more appropriate occasion in which to contribute a budget surplus.

62   It must, however, be recognised at the same time that a deflationary pressure may develop a year or two hereafter, rather more rapidly than at present we may expect. If the manpower position revealed in the Economic Survey for 1946/47 (ED(46)13) is considered, it may, at first sight, appear that we must expect a considerable manpower shortage and thus an inflationary pressure to last for a large number of years. The position revealed suggests that even when the main demobilisation is over during the first half of 1947, there will still be insufficient labour to meet all the demands of a normal peace-time economy, even without allowing for the fact that some further expansion of demand for labour for civilian purposes (e.g. for the further development of the export drive, for the restoration of distributive trades to their pre-war level, to offset a reduction in hours of work, etc.) is still to be expected.

63   This conclusion, however, fails to take into account possible developments in productivity. If output per man-hour could be increased by no more than 5 per cent, this would correspond to the product of about 1 million men, a difference in the manpower supply position which might totally alter the picture from one of scarce supplies in relation to demand to one of deficient demand in relation to available supplies. And it must be remembered that a 5 per cent increase in productivity may well be achieved in a relatively short period of time, the average annual rate of progress before the war being probably of the order of 1½ per cent per annum, and there being very considerable possibilities of a fairly sudden spurt in increased efficiency when the first post-war adjustments have been made.

64   In other words, the general principle should be to prepare immediately for effective measures of an anti-inflationary character to restrain total demand and to keep it down in balance with total available supplies, but simultaneously to be ready at relatively short notice hereafter to put the gears into reverse and to stimulate total demand.

65   The treatment of the repayment of post-war [deferred income] tax credits presents an opportunity of observing both these principles. They amount in all to some £800 millions. Their withdrawal now would very considerably increase the existing inflationary pressure and would, therefore, be a very serious embarrassment. Their withdrawal later may be positively of the greatest assistance in stimulating total demand when the need for such stimulation arises.

66   There are two fundamentally different conceptions of the way in which they might be treated:-
  (i)   In the first place, it would be possible to treat them in such a way as to give the greatest possible encouragement to the recipients to treat their refunds as capital sums which they would add to their existing savings and refrain from spending.
  (ii) Secondly, they might be treated primarily as an instrument for controlling consumers' expenditure as a means (additional to variations in National Insurance contributions) of avoiding subsequent depressions in the total demand for goods and services.

67   If (i) is the objective, there is much to be said for paying the credits off at a relatively early date in a relatively large single sum, combined with the maximum propaganda that they should be saved. If they were paid in the form of securities, Savings Certificates or, as is apparently contemplated, savings deposits, and if they were paid at a time when purchases of goods were still subject to rationing, price control, licensing, etc., there would be a good chance that a large amount of them would find their way into ordinary accumulations of savings.

68   If (ii) is the objective, a different treatment would be appropriate. They should be made withdrawable in frequent small amounts (so as to approximate as nearly as possible to income rather than capital receipts) but their withdrawal should be delayed and varied from time to time in the interests of stabilising total consumers' expenditure. For example, the whole credit due to each individual might be repaid immediately in the form of a special interest-bearing savings deposit, but the monthly rate at which these deposits could be drawn upon could be regulated so as to control total consumers' expenditure.[9]

69   Method (ii) is undoubtedly the preferable method. In the first place, method (i) could not in any case be adopted without considerable

[9] The total could be made withdrawable on the attainment of the age mentioned in the last Budget (65 for men and 60 for women).

immediate danger. However successful propaganda were in inducing people to treat the receipt of these sums as a capital receipt which they should refrain from spending, a considerable number of people would in fact tend to treat a considerable part of these receipts as a supplement to their spendable funds. Some very substantial increase to the existing inflationary pressure could not be avoided.

70   Secondly, method (i) sacrifices all the later advantages of method (ii), and fails, therefore, to provide what might prove to be a very effective instrument for stimulating expenditure when the stimulation of expenditure becomes desirable.

71   In the third place, the adoption of method (i) means, over the balance of years, a greater increase in the national debt. If complete success were achieved in persuading people to add those sums to their accumulated savings, then the national debt would be increased by the whole of the £800 million without any stimulation of consumption expenditure. In later years, when it is desired to stimulate expenditure, it will be necessary to run a budget deficit and to increase debt just for this purpose. But if method (ii) had been adopted, the debt which will in any case be incurred when the tax credits are repaid would itself constitute just that debt which was necessary to stimulate expenditure in the subsequent years for the avoidance of a general depression.

72   It may, therefore, be concluded that the best method of dealing with these tax credits would be to repay them all now in the form of a special savings deposit which would immediately become interest-bearing but would, for the time being, remain blocked. The rate of permissible withdrawals from these deposits could be subsequently regulated as and when stimulation of purchases was required for the maintenance of employment.

73   The finance of withdrawals of these tax credits is not likely to be the only special cost which the state will be called upon to meet when the time comes to stimulate rather than to restrict total national expenditure. Various devices are likely to be employed. For example, special help may be needed to promote investment activity. In the case of the reduction of National Insurance contributions, the fact that the scheme as at present proposed does not incorporate the principle of an automatic sliding scale may mean that in fact it will impose some net burden on the Exchequer. Finally, it may in the last resort be necessary to contemplate some special temporary reduction in rates of taxation. All these adjustments can be contemplated provided that it can be ensured that they are counterbalanced by true budget surpluses in times of inflationary pressure.

74   For the finance of such payments in years of threatened depression out of the true Budget surpluses of years of inflationary pressure, such as the present, the following arrangement is suggested. There would be set up in the next Budget an Employment Stabilisation Fund into which an

annual payment of £200 millions should be made out of a true surplus from the ordinary Budget, possibly financed in the first place by a net saving on the cost-of-living subsidies (see paragraph 60 above). Payments would be made out of this Employment Stabilisation Fund in those years when it was necessary to make special arrangements (including the finance of the withdrawal of income tax credits) to stimulate the demand for goods and services.

75   One advantage of this system would be that it might make it possible to run a real budget surplus next year when, from the economic point of view, a surplus is certainly required. Simply to run a surplus and to call it a surplus or a sinking fund might be unacceptable. On the other hand, to explain that a general reorganisation of the financial arrangements was being undertaken in order to plan for full employment, that this special fund was being set up for this purpose, and that the economic circumstances of the time and not merely budgetary orthodoxy required such a surplus for the time being at least, would give an entirely different flavour to the operation.[10]

V   Summary of Conclusions

76   The following is a summary of the main conclusions to be drawn from the above arguments:-

(1)   It is desirable to shift the emphasis somewhat away from price control and on to bringing the supply and demand for goods and services in general more nearly into balance as a means of holding in check the present inflationary pressure: (a) in order that a restored balance between demand and supply in the market for consumption goods and services may help to restore the incentive to work and produce; (b) in order that it may become increasingly possible to allow those adjustments of prices and wage-rates which are a necessary instrument for planning in a free society; and (c) in order to diminish the administrative problems, which result from an excessive reliance upon administrative methods of curbing demand in each particular market separately.

(2)   The possibility should be considered during the period immediately ahead of helping to restore the balance between total demand and total supply of consumption goods and services by a more rapid increase in the supply of such goods and services, even if this involves some moderate reduction in the scale of the existing plans for investment

---

[10] A further and lasting advantage of such a system would be that hereafter the Budget could be treated on the orthodox principles of an annual balance between revenue and expenditure, including the annual contribution to the Employment Stabilisation Fund. Variations in the balance which were required for the purposes of general economic planning against inflation or depression would be thrown on to the separate Employment Stabilisation Fund. Although, in many respects, this is merely a matter of accounting, it might perhaps have considerable political and administrative advantages in helping to achieve a sound financial policy.

or some moderate postponement (through a relaxation of restriction on the imports of consumption goods and services) of the time when our balance of payments will be finally restored.

(3)   Quite apart from other considerations, the budgetary position and the problem of controlling the existing inflationary pressure require that the cost-of-living subsidies should be rapidly tapered off. The possibility should be considered of easing this adjustment by one or more of the following methods:- (a) by the early introduction of the new cost-of-living index; (b) by using some part of the saving in cost-of-living subsidies for the purpose of making some special concessions in taxation or in national insurance and similar benefits; and (c) by making the adjustment the occasion for the institution of an annual payment of £200 millions into an Employment Stabilisation Fund.

(4)   A scheme for the repayment of post-war credits should be worked out whereby the credits are repaid at an early date in the sense that interest would start to accumulate on them, but in such a form that their withdrawal for expenditure could still be blocked and could subsequently be regulated in such a way as to exercise the maximum control over the demand for goods and services for personal consumption.

(5)   The immediate need is for an early budget surplus to control the existing inflationary pressure; but it is equally important to prepare for the later period when it may be desirable to run what will in fact be a budget deficit in order to stimulate the demand for goods and services. For this purpose, an Employment Stabilisation Fund should be set up into which an annual payment of £200 millions should be made from the central Budget – the central Budget hereafter being balanced on orthodox principles and payments from the Employment Stabilisation Fund being made from time to time on the scale necessary to maintain a high and stable level of demand for labour.

18

The Control of Inflation

Meade returned to the problem of inflation in his inaugural lecture as Professor of Political Economy in the University of Cambridge, which he gave on 4 March 1958. He also submitted the published version (Cambridge: Cambridge University Press, 1958) as his written evidence to the Radcliffe Committee on the Working of the Monetary System.

I

The purpose of this lecture is to consider how one can best put a stop to the inflation of prices. But before we try to find the answer it is useful to know whether this is an important question or not. For the extent to which we should be prepared to re-cast our present policies and institutions in order to avoid an inflation of prices will depend upon the importance which we attach to the objective of stable prices.

If it were a question of stopping a serious price deflation, it would be a waste of time to ask whether the objective was an important one. Such a deflationary fall in selling prices, when money wage-rates cannot easily be lowered, will impede economic growth and raise unemployment. This has been a familiar and agreed theme among economists since the Great Depression of the 1930s. But during the last decade prices in this country have been rising by 4 or 5 per cent per annum, and it is worth pausing to ask whether we need to make any very great efforts to prevent a continuing inflation of money prices and costs of this kind. Might we not remain content with policies and institutions which were such as to avoid deflations, even if they resulted in some such degree of continuing price inflation?

Indeed, a moderate and steady rate of price inflation may have some beneficial effects. It may relieve the community from the dead hand of debt. A large national debt, in my opinion, introduces more serious deadening disincentives into the economy than are generally realised. Between 1948 and 1957 the general level of prices rose by some 50 per cent, which is sufficient to reduce by one-third the real value of a given money debt. We did not remove our great war debt by a levy or repudiation; but its weight has been substantially reduced through inflation.

But is this an equitable way of dealing with the problem? The first main argument against inflation is that it causes an inequitable redistribution between property fixed in terms of money and other forms of property and between incomes fixed in terms of money and other incomes. The old-age pensioner and the parents drawing family allowances have received less than was planned for them; and in such cases it is not the rich who have been soaked. Nor is there any reason to believe that it is the millionaire who keeps his property in the form of Consols and life insurance policies, and the widows and orphans who hold ordinary shares. Indeed, the contrary is much more nearly true. It would at least be a much more rational method of redistribution to keep the value of money constant and then consciously to control by other means the real income and wealth of pensioners, parents, widows, and orphans.

It may be argued that an easier, and to that extent more desirable, way of dealing with this aspect of inflation is to take measures to insure the recipients of fixed or sluggish incomes against the evils of price inflation rather than to put a stop to the inflation itself. Thus money wage-rates can be tied to a cost-of-living index. Similarly, proposals have recently been made to tie the money value of old-age pensions or of other social security benefits to the cost of living or to an index of the rise of other money incomes in the economy; and such arrangements would guarantee the recipients of such incomes against future inflations. I do not wish to argue against these proposals. On grounds of social justice it is right and proper that we should decide what real share in the national income we want such people to receive. But I do wish to stress that such measures must not be regarded as making the control of inflation less necessary. Indeed, in certain important respects their institution would make such control even more necessary.

There are certain ways in which the tying of previously fixed or sluggish incomes to a price index would increase the dangers of inflation.

Fundamentally, an inflationary pressure is generated when the slices which various independent competing groups of citizens attempt to take out of the national cake together add up to more than the whole cake. Various groups of workers and producers press up their money wages or profit margins by, say, 8 per cent; since some citizens have incomes fixed in terms of money, this 8 per cent rise in variable wages and profits represents, say, a 6 per cent increase in total money incomes; but only, say, 2 per cent more is being produced; 6 per cent more money incomes chase only 2 per cent more goods, and prices are driven up; and in consequence part of the combined claims of producers with variable incomes for an 8 per cent increase in their real incomes is frustrated by a rise in prices and the cost of living. Now the more rapidly and completely their claims for increased real rewards are frustrated by a rise in the cost of living, the sooner are these groups likely to repeat their claims for yet another substantial increase in money rewards. The larger is the other class of citizens whose incomes are fixed or sluggish in terms of money, the less complete or immediate will be the frustration of those who are pushing up their money rewards. The latter can make real gains at the expense of the former. But the experience of inflation may cause more and more wage-rates, as well as such incomes as pensions, to be tied *de facto* or *de jure* to the cost of living; and in so far as those who previously had fixed or sluggish money incomes now join in the game and have their money incomes raised quickly in response to price rises, they will accelerate the increase in expenditure on the limited real output of the community. The inflationary process will be speeded up and wage demands will follow one upon another so much the more rapidly.

We all have a certain money illusion. We think of our income in terms of money and we have ideas in our head as to what is the proper sort of money price to pay for this or that service or product. A reasonably efficient monetary system for financing transactions and for recording commercial values is of inestimable importance in any modern society. The existence of such a system rests in considerable measure upon our continuing to think in terms of money. Measures like the tying of money wage-rates or of old-age pensions to a cost of living are an invitation to abandon this most desirable habit of mind. The more people concentrate their thoughts not on their money incomes but on their real incomes, the more rapidly will they try to get rid of their money when they expect prices to rise; and this attempt to fly from money into goods will itself increase money expenditure upon goods and will force prices up so much the higher and the more rapidly. The ultimate end is a complete distrust of the currency and the disorganisation of business which ensues when there is no readily acceptable counter for transactions; but some inefficiencies will be introduced into the economic system before this ultimate disintegration is at all nearly reached.

There remains a final, and for a country like the United Kingdom probably a decisive, reason why it is desirable to attempt to control inflation. The United Kingdom has very important trade relations with the outside world. Moreover, her financial relations with outside countries are close and important; indeed, she acts as the banker for a number of other important countries. If money incomes, prices, and costs are inflated in the United Kingdom more rapidly than in other countries, then citizens in the United Kingdom will tend to increase their purchases of imports and they will find difficulty in selling their high-cost produce in foreign markets. We shall lose reserves of gold and dollars. There will be a recurrence of the only too familiar balance-of-payments crisis. The means of dealing with this are limited. Imports might be restricted by import licensing; but if our prices and costs are continually getting more and more out of line with those of our competitors, the strain on our balance of payments will become greater and greater, and the import restrictions will have to become more and more severe. This would be a very serious development for a country like the United Kingdom which has to import so much of its essential raw materials and foodstuffs. Or we could devalue the pound in an attempt to bring down our prices and costs in terms of foreign currencies. But if speculators expected the domestic inflation to continue in the United Kingdom at a rate more rapid than in other countries, they would expect a series of such devaluations to be necessary. They would attempt to anticipate this by getting out of sterling into other currencies; this would cause a heavy loss of gold and dollar reserves or, if it were allowed to affect the rate of exchange, it would drive the foreign exchange value of the pound still lower and would raise the price in terms of sterling of all imports whose prices were fixed in terms of foreign currencies; this by raising the cost of living at home might give rise to still greater demands for increases in money rewards and so extend still further the vicious spiral of higher prices leading to higher wages leading to higher costs leading to higher prices. In the case of a country which, like the United Kingdom, acts as banker for many persons and institutions in the rest of the world, it is especially important to avoid such a distrust of the national currency.

II

I personally find little difficulty in reaching the conclusion that inflation as well as deflation is an evil which deserves a very real effort to avoid. But let us be very clear that there are worse evils than inflation. The stagnation of the 1930s is a much worse evil than the inflation of the 1950s. We must give very careful thought to the question whether a serious attempt to prevent a continuation of the inflation of money prices would lead to a cessation of growth of economic output and to a rise in the general level of unemployment. It is worth a real effort to stop inflation but it must not be done by methods which prevent high and rising production.

In order to decide whether, and, if so, how, price inflation can be stopped without endangering employment and production it is necessary to consider the mechanism through which price rises are generated. There are two closely interrelated factors at work, one operating through the level of money demand for goods and services and the other through the level of money costs of the factors of production and, in particular, through the level of money wage-rates. Let us first analyse each of these two factors separately, and then consider the relationship between them.

Suppose first that all money wage-rates are fixed. Something then causes an increase in the level of total money expenditure on goods and services. When the demand for their finished products goes up producers can do either of two things; they can produce and sell more at an unchanged price or they can raise the price at which they sell an unchanged output. In fact they are likely to react partly in the one manner and partly in the other. If there is much unemployed labour and unused productive capacity, then an increase in demand is likely to lead to a large increase in output and little rise in price. But as demand increases to higher levels, there are likely to arise bottlenecks in one industry after another, as reserves of suitable unemployed labour disappear and productive capacity is strained, until in the end it is impossible to produce more in any industry so that an increase in money expenditure on goods and services will cause only a rise in their prices. In more technical language, with a constant money wage-rate the short-run elasticity of supply of goods in general is likely to be nearly infinite when there is mass unemployment but to fall towards zero as the point of full employment is reached. Thus with constant money wage-rates prices are likely to be at a lower level when demand is low and at a higher level when demand is high. But this does not, of course, explain why prices should continue to rise as they have done over the last decade at a rate of 4 or 5 per cent per annum.

To explain this, we must turn to the other side of the picture. Money wage-rates are not in fact constant and in the last decade they have been rising more quickly than productivity with the result that money costs per unit of output have been rising. In the jargon of economists the supply curve itself has been rising through time. In recent years money earnings per head have been rising by about 7 per cent per annum and output per head by a little over 2 per cent per annum. In consequence labour costs per unit of output have been rising by more than 4 per cent per annum. The steady rise of prices over the last decade is certainly very intimately connected with this steady rise of money costs of production.

But why do rates of money earnings rise more quickly than productivity? In order to answer this question it is necessary to consider the relationship between the demand influences and the cost influences. When the level of demand is high three influences are brought to work which are likely to make wage-rates rise at a rapid rate. First, the high level of demand for finished products will give rise to a high level of demand for labour by producers; the volume of unemployment will be low and the number of unfilled vacancies will be high; and wage-earners will be in a strong position to bargain for increases in rates of pay. Secondly, a high level of demand for finished products will, as we have seen, cause the prices of finished products to be high relatively to any given level of money wage-rates; when prices and the cost of living are high relatively to money wage-rates, workers will have an added reason to demand higher rates of pay to restore the real purchasing power of their wages. Thirdly, when demand rises profits will be raised, either because a larger output is produced at any given margin of profit or else because prices are raised relatively to wage-rates so that a higher profit margin is obtained on any given output; in either case higher profits mean that each employer can afford more easily to pay higher rates of wages and the resistance of employers to wage claims will be lower. In brief, a high level of demand is likely to raise prices relatively to any given level of money wage-rates; but also by reducing unemployment, increasing the number of unfilled vacancies, raising the cost of living, and raising the profitability of industry it is likely to set the conditions in which wages will rise more rapidly than productivity so that there is a continuing inflation of the whole structure of money prices, money costs, and money incomes.

With this brief description of the process of price inflation we are now in a position to consider the measures which might be taken to avoid it. The authorities have at their disposal certain instruments of control through which they can influence the general level of demand for goods and services. They can themselves reduce government expenditure; they can raise rates of taxation so that private citizens are left with smaller tax-free incomes to spend; or by a tighter monetary policy they can make it more difficult for business men to raise funds for capital development. If our analysis is correct such a reduction in total monetary demand will cause some fall in selling prices relatively to money wage-rates and other costs, as producers find the markets for their products becoming less easy. Producers will, however, also react by producing less and employing less labour. In the ways already indicated, the fall in prices, profit margins, and employment will all combine to alter the atmosphere in the labour market, so that money wage-rates rise less rapidly. There is presumably some point at which the total demand for products has been so reduced that the conditions in the labour market have been so eased that money wage-rates rise at an equal rate to the rate of rise in productivity, so that wage costs per unit of output remain constant. This we may call the 'break-even' point.

Thus price inflation *can* be prevented by a sufficiently severe policy of restraint in monetary and budgetary policies; but an essential part of this mechanism is a restriction of total demand which will, *inter alia*, so raise the level of unemployment relatively to the level of unfilled vacancies that the break-even point is reached at which money wage-rates cease to rise more rapidly than productivity. Price stability may be compatible with 3 per cent but not with only 1 per cent of workers unemployed.

We can put the problem in its most dramatic form by asking what would happen if the authorities desired actually to reduce the general level of prices – a situation which might arise in actual fact if an attempt were made to stabilise the general level of prices and if, for some reason or another, prices had temporarily risen above the level at which they were being stabilised. In this case the authorities by more restrictive monetary and fiscal policies would reduce the level of total money expenditure on goods and services. In so far as producers reacted to this by lowering the prices (and so the profit margins) at which they were willing to sell their existing level of output, this would be the end of the story. But suppose that producers' reaction to a fall in the demand for their products were of exactly the opposite kind; suppose that they added a fixed profit margin to their variable costs (such as their wage bill) and that they simply reduced the amount which they produced at this more or less constant 'full-cost' price. When output had been so reduced that the demand for labour fell below the 'break-even' point, wage-rates would rise less quickly than productivity. With fixed profit margins selling prices would come down as labour costs per unit of output fell; and by this process the price level could gradually be brought back to the desired lower level. The pains of price stabilisation can thus be seen to depend upon three factors: (1) the extent to which producers would in fact reduce output and not prices when demand fell, (2) the extent to which wages would continue to rise in spite of a rise in the ratio of unemployed persons to unfilled vacancies, and (3) the speed with which it was desired to bring prices back to the target level if they should diverge temporarily from it.

The nature of the main issues should now be clear. First, should the government take the plunge and say that, whatever happens, it is going to control the level of monetary expenditure so that prices do not permanently rise above a given ceiling? Secondly, if the government does take the plunge, is it possible so to mould the institutional arrangements in the labour market that the 'break-even' point at which wage-rates cease to rise more rapidly than productivity is reached at a satisfactorily high level of employment and production? But these two questions presuppose that the government can in fact exercise a continuous and effective control over total monetary demand. Whether or not existing controls over demand are adequate is a third basic issue. It is to these three questions which we must now turn.

III

What is exactly meant by 'taking the plunge'? The government would announce that in future it was going to make full use of its powers of monetary and budgetary policy in order to maintain the total monetary demand for goods and services at the highest possible level which was compatible with the prevention of some stated index of the selling prices of final products from rising above a stated ceiling. As I shall argue in a moment, if it is decided that price inflation must really be stopped, there are great advantages in the government committing itself to the prevention of some precisely defined index of prices from rising above some precisely defined level. But before this case is argued it is necessary to consider for a moment the nature of the price index to which any such commitment should refer.

Suppost that the cost-of-living index were chosen for this purpose. Suppose then that the terms of international trade were to move against this country because the price of imports had risen. A decline in the real incomes of consumers would have occurred for reasons quite out of the control of the United Kingdom authorities. But in order to stabilise the cost of living when the import component in the cost of living rose, the authorities would have to take disinflationary measures to drive down the price of home-produced goods to offset the rise in the price of imported goods. But unless money wage-rates could be quickly reduced *pari passu* with the fall in the prices of domestic products, there might be a serious growth of unemployment.

An exactly similar difficulty would arise if the government were to decide to raise more revenue by way of indirect taxes. The consequent rise in the price charged to consumers of beer, tobacco, or whatever other commodity was taxed, would have to be offset by a deflation in the prices of other products. Once again, unless wages and other money costs could be as promptly reduced, unemployment might result.

For the same reason, it would be wise to exclude from the index such prices as house rents which are still subject to extensive direct controls. Whether, and, if so, to what extent, rents should be decontrolled is a major issue of economic policy affecting the distribution of income and the uses of house property. But, if a government does decide that rents should be raised by decontrol, it would be irrational and possibly disastrous economically to combine this with another set of rules which involved deflating total demand until the selling prices of other products had been reduced to offset the rise of decontrolled rents.

The best price index to choose for our purpose would thus appear to be one which was specially constructed to cover the selling prices of all domestically produced goods and services except those subject to price control, excluding from such prices the import content of home production and indirect taxes.[1] But, if some such index is chosen, there are powerful arguments in favour of taking the plunge and guaranteeing that it will not be allowed to rise above a given ceiling.

First, the setting of a precise ceiling to a precise price index would have the advantage of calling powerful forces of private speculation to the aid of the authorities. The relevant price index would be frequently and promptly published; if ever it was above the ceiling level, it would be known that the authorities would take disinflationary steps to bring prices down, and private purchasers would have an incentive to postpone their purchases until prices were no longer above the ceiling level; and when the price level was below the ceiling level, purchasers would be induced to speed up their expenditure in order to come into the market before the expansion of monetary demand by the authorities had raised prices once more to their ceiling level. Such speculative postponements and anticipations of private expenditure would powerfully reinforce the actions of the authorities.

Second, a firm commitment to stabilise domestic prices would transform our balance-of-payments problems. Of course, if domestic financial policy is aimed exclusively at the maintenance of domestic demand at the highest level compatible with a ceiling to a domestic price level, then it cannot at the same time be used to control the balance of foreign payments. It will no longer be permissible to take disinflationary measures at home simply in order to discourage the purchase of imports and to release home supplies for export, so as to improve the balance of payments and to stop a foreign drain of gold reserves. But those deficits in the balance of payments which arise from an uncontrolled inflationary rise of prices, costs, and buying power with the United Kingdom would automatically cease; and this would be no mean contribution to the preservation of external equilibrium. It is still possible to imagine circumstances in which, for one reason or another beyond our power of control, the foreign demand for United Kingdom produce would fall off even in these conditions. This would lead to a decline in our exports and so to the growth of a deficit on our balance of payments, which we would not be prepared to offset by engineering an actual deflation in the price level of our own domestic output and in the money incomes of our producers.

The answer to this difficulty is easy to find. The rate of exchange between the pound sterling and foreign currencies should be allowed to vary. If then there were some foreign shift of demand away from our products, the pound would depreciate somewhat; this would cheapen our exports in foreign currencies; and it would raise the price of our imports in sterling. This in due course would so expand our exports and contract our imports as to restore equilibrium to our balance of payments. Meanwhile, if the pound threatened to depreciate excessively, speculators – firm in

---

[1] But including subsidies. It is the net price received by home producers which we want to stabilise.

the knowledge that the sterling price of our own domestic output was to be held stable – would purchase sterling and thus support its value until the long-run equilibrating forces of the exchange-rate change had had time to restore our balance of payments.

But this is much too apologetic a way for me to speak of the balance-of-payments aspect of proposals for setting a firm ceiling to domestic prices. If we really could stabilise the sterling price of our own products, then so long as any price inflation was expected to continue in the rest of the world there would be an underlying tendency for the pound to appreciate in the foreign exchange markets. Even if all foreign inflations were brought under control, there would be more or less equal chances of the pound appreciating or depreciating and in any case no chance of any enormous depreciation of the pound. The only chance of a substantial depreciation of the pound would be the possibility of a serious deflation of money incomes and prices in the United States and elsewhere. But the 1930s have shown that in such circumstances, in order to avoid deflationary influences, overseas countries arc likely to hitch their currencies to the pound rather than to the dollar. Indeed, I would go so far as to argue that the only way in which we can hope to continue to combine the role of international banker with our present very exiguous reserves of foreign exchange is to give the foreigner a firm confidence in the stability of the real purchasing power of our currency rather than in the fixity of its price in terms of other currencies. In such circumstances I would expect it to fare very well.

A third important argument in favour of the setting of a ceiling to a precise price index of selling prices is that it would indirectly help in restraining the inflationary rise of money costs. If there were real confidence that the general level of selling prices would not be inflated, there would be a double restraining influence on wage-rate adjustments. Employers in general would not expect to be able easily to offset increased labour costs by raising selling prices; they would be more resistant to wage demands. On the other hand, the workers would not expect rises in the cost of living arising from domestic inflationary tendencies; and in so far as the expectation of future rises in prices influences their wage demands they would show more restraint. Moreover, the trade unions would realise that too rapid a rise in wage costs might lead now to a redundancy of labour, since it could no longer be offset by a rise of selling prices.

IV

There are, therefore, some very powerful arguments in favour of the government committing itself to a precise ceiling for selling prices. But can we be certain that there would remain no problem on the side of costs? It depends upon how ambitious we are in defining the level of full employment which we hope to attain. As we have already argued, other things being equal, the lower the number of unemployed workers and the higher the number of unfilled vacancies, the more rapidly are wage-rates likely to rise. To repeat our previous example, in conditions of price stability wage-rates might not rise more rapidly than productivity if the unemployment percentage were 3, but nevertheless might do so if the demand for labour were so high that only 1 per cent were unemployed.

But can anything be done to shift the 'break-even' point in the labour market at which wage-rates rise only as quickly as productivity?

It is important to realise that nothing important can be done on the lines of tying wage-rates in particular industries and occupations to changes in productivity in those same industries and occupations. An example will demonstrate this point. Suppose that there are only two products, agricultural output and industrial output. Suppose further that technical progress is such that in the course of the year productivity does not rise in manufactures but rises by 5 per cent in agriculture. If wage-rates remained unchanged, the cost and price of agricultural produce might fall by a full 5 per cent. But the stabilisation of the general level of prices would involve the stimulation of total demand until the general level of prices had been raised back to its old level. This might mean that the price of manufactures had to be raised 2½ per cent above the initial level while the price of agricultural produce was pulled half way back to its initial level, so that it fell by only 2½ instead of 5 per cent. The competition for labour between the two industries might then lead to a bidding up of the wage-rate by 2½ per cent in both industries. In this case the industrial workers would enjoy a rise of wage-rates by 2½ per cent even though their productivity had not increased, and the agricultural workers would enjoy a rise of wage-rates by only 2½ per cent even though their productivity had risen by 5 per cent.

Indeed, the outcome for some time might well have to be even more favourable to the industrial workers whose productivity had not increased. Suppose that when people's real incomes rise (as they would when productivity in agriculture rose) consumers want to buy little more agricultural products but many more industrial products. Then labour will become redundant in agriculture where output per head has gone up but the demand for the product has scarcely risen, and labour will be scarce in industry where output per head has not risen but the demand for the product has increased. There will be a tendency for prices to fall further in agriculture where there is now a glut of produce and to rise further in industry where there is a shortage of produce. This should be allowed to lead to a rise in industrial wage-rates relatively to agricultural wage-rates so long as it is necessary to attract workers from agriculture to industry. The rise in productivity is in agriculture but the consequential rise in wages should be in industry.

When against a background of a stable general average of prices for finished products, there are a series of increases of productivity at varying rates in different industries and occupations, redundancy of labour may appear in some industries, occupations, and regions, and shortages of labour in other industries, occupations, and regions; and there will be no obvious simple connection between the rate of increase of productivity in any one industry, occupation, or region, and the redundancy or shortage of labour in that industry, occupation, or region. Wage-rates must rise in those parts of the economy in which these developments tend to cause a shortage of labour relatively to wage-rates in those parts of the economy in which these developments tend to cause a redundancy of labour. Any attempt to preserve pre-existing differentials by raising wage-rates in the latter group of industries to catch up those in the former group can only lead to a general upward pressure on wage costs which will adversely affect the 'break-even' point in the labour market.

Closely connected with this is another negative conclusion about wage-fixing arrangements. The fixing of money wage-rates must not be regarded as the ultimate weapon for affecting the general distribution of the national income between wage-earners on the one hand and other classes in the community on the other hand. Money wage-rates in general can be pushed up to a certain level at the expense of profits; but in a market in which a ceiling has been set to the prices at which the products of labour can be sold, a rise in wage-rates beyond this point will cause unemployment. Any further redistribution must be sought through other means. For example, measures to prevent monopolies and so to increase competition between producers are likely to raise the demand for labour and so to raise the general level of money wage-rates which is at any time compatible with a constant level of selling prices; the type of taxes which are imposed and, in its broadest sense, the social security system which is in operation will greatly affect the distribution of incomes between various classes of citizen; and as a longer-term consideration, changes might be made in death duties, in the laws of inheritance, and in certain other institutions in order to bring about a more equal distribution in the ownership of property and in the enjoyment of profits themselves. The ultimate redistribution of income and wealth between individual citizens must be sought by means of this kind and not through wage policy.

But are there any positive inprovements which can be made in our present wage-fixing arrangements which might favourably affect the 'break-even' point? I shall not consider such revolutionary changes as that employers' associations and trade unions be made illegal as monopolies in restraint of trade, or that the government itself should fix wage-rates in a comprehensive national wages policy. Present procedures of wage negotiation will certainly continue. But within this framework there are some possible improvements to be made.

The atmosphere of wage negotiations might be much influenced if somebody – perhaps a permanent form of the present Council on Prices, Productivity and Incomes – were required to make regular estimates of the percentage increase in the general level of money wage-rates which would be compatible in the coming year with the preservation of full employment in a regime of stable selling prices. Crystal-gazing about future economic trends is not a thing which I generally recommend. But in this case it is a matter of saying that wage-rates should go up by something like 2 to 3 per cent per annum (which is the order of magnitude of the annual rate of increase in productivity) instead of by something like 7 per cent per annum (as they have done in recent years). The Council should, of course, make the best estimate that it can. But if this year it says 2 per cent when it should have said 3 per cent or *vice versa*, no irreparable damage will have been done. If wages have gone up this year a little less quickly than they should, then they should go up next year a little more quickly than would otherwise have been appropriate. And the need for this will become apparent, because too slow a rise in money wage-rates will, at constant selling prices, lead to a growing scarcity of labour and *vice versa*.

But, as we have already seen, it is necessary not only that the general level of money wage-rates should not go up more quickly than productivity. It is also necessary that wage-rates should go up rather more quickly than the average in those industries, occupations, and regions where a local scarcity of labour is developing, and rather less quickly than the average where local redundancies of labour are developing. In fact there is likely to be a strong tendency for the rate of increase of money wage-rates which the Council on Prices, Productivity and Incomes ruled to be possible on the average for industry as a whole to be treated by the workers in each particular industry as the minimum rise to which they are themselves entitled. If this were so, the announcement of a suitable average wage increase might do more harm than good. This danger would be lessened and the necessary adjustment of relative wage-rates would be helped if a new arbitral body or set of arbitral bodies were instituted for the sole purpose of giving an opinion whether in any particular case a rate of rise of wages appreciably above or below the average was necessary in order, over the next few years, to avoid a serious local shortage or redundancy of labour. If it could be accepted as an obligation by the main parties to wage negotiations always, at the request of either of the negotiating parties or of the government, to refer to this arbitral body for an opinion on this question of fact, the final outcome of negotiations might well be influenced in a salutary manner.

The 'break-even' point in the labour market will also be greatly affected by the degree of mobility of the labour force. Suppose that at any one time it is proposed to reduce the level of unemployment from 500,000 to 300,000 workers. Consider two alternative methods of achieving this objective. The 500,000 unemployed workers will be attached to certain industries, occupations, and regions; and at the same time there will be some unfilled vacancies in some other industries, occupations and regions. If it were possible for the unemployed workers to move readily to the unfilled vacancies, unemployment could be reduced without any very substantial change in the upward pressure on wage-rates in the economy as a whole. For while the bargaining power of labour would be somewhat increased in those parts of the economy from which the labour was moving, it would be somewhat decreased in those parts of the economy into which labour was moving. Contrast this with a policy of reducing the level of unemployment from 500,000 to 300,000 by a general expansion of the money demand for goods and services without any significant mobility of labour. The demand for labour would have to be raised in all industries, occupations, and regions (both in those in which there was a redundancy and also in those in which there was already a shortage of labour) until the market for labour had been expanded by the required 200,000 in the industries, occupations, and regions to which the unemployed were already attached. There would be a great increase in the upward pressure on wage-rates throughout the economy. Thus the 'break-even' point in the labour market can be achieved with a lower level of unemployment, the more mobile is the labour force.

For this reason, if it is desired to combine full employment with price stability, it would be well worth while applying greater thought and expenditure of resources to such problems as the retraining, removal, and rehousing of unemployed workers and their families.

Moreover, there are a number of practices in the labour market which reduce the mobility and flexibility of the labour force. Demarcation rules which prevent one body of workers from shifting from one job to another, apprenticeship rules which prevent the easy entry of new labour into expanding trades, and insistence upon national bargaining which makes it difficult to adapt the conditions of work to the needs of particular producers, are important examples. The more effectively such practices can be restrained, the easier it will be to combine full employment with price stability.

V

We must now turn to the question whether the government in fact has at its disposal adequate instruments of control over the general level of monetary demand for goods and services. We must consider not only whether the authorities can raise or lower expenditures by a sufficient amount but also whether they can make such adjustments sufficiently promptly. For speed is at least as important as size of response.

Inflations and deflations of demand largely feed upon themselves. If prices and profits start on an upward movement, this may well lead to an anticipation of a still further rise; and this speculative optimism may well cause a further increase in demand which will itself drive prices and profits up still more. If it had been possible by a prompt mechanism of control to nip the incipient inflation of demand in the bud, then the inflationary pressures might never have gathered force. An early control of an inflation of demand is likely to require considerably less powerful intervention than a delayed control.

There is an even more serious possibility if action is delayed. Suppose that (for reasons which we shall examine later) there is still a considerable time-lag between any inflationary or deflationary change in the economic climate and the taking of counter-measures by the authorities. It is possible that in these conditions the counter-measures will make the situation worse instead of improving it. Consider a sequence of uncontrolled inflationary pressure which would rise to a peak and then of itself turn down into some deflationary fall in prices, profits, output and employment; we may think of one of the periods of inflationary pressure followed by minor recessions which have occurred in the United States economy since the end of the Second World War. Suppose that the authorities wish to offset this movement; they impose more and more stringent disinflationary measures as the inflationary pressure in the economy becomes more and more intense; but there are delays which mean that the authorities' disinflationary measures are in fact geared to the degree of inflationary pressure to be offset some period – say six months – previously. Consider the effect of this policy at the time when the inflationary boom ends and turns down into a recession. Six months after the top of the boom, when uncontrolled deflationary forces have had six months to gather momentum, the controlled disinflationary forces exerted by the counter-inflationary measures of the authorities will be at their maximum. This might be sufficient to send the economic system into a nose dive of deflation. And conversely, in any situation in which the economic system is naturally moving from the bottom of a recession into a period of economic expansion, the fact that the authorities' reflationary measures will be at their maximum six months after the bottom of the depression, when recovery has had that much time to gather force, might set in motion speculative forces of expansion which would turn a moderate and useful recovery into an undesirable inflation. It is at least possible that delayed counter-measures would make fluctuations greater than they would have been in the absence of all counter-measures. In the words of the poet, delayed action might accentuate the tendency for us to

> . . . swerve
> Along our sinusoidal curve.

Some delay between any undesired disturbance and the corrective action is inevitable. First, there will be a delay between the occurrence of the initial change and its realisation by the authorities. Secondly, there will be some constitutional, administrative, and political causes for delay between the realisation of the initial change and the taking of counter-measures by the authorities. Thirdly, there will be some delay between the taking of the counter-measures by the authorities and the full development of the actual effects of these counter-measures upon the economic situation.

The first of these three delays is common to all forms of control, and I shall not give much thought to it today. But for the response by the authorities to be as prompt as possible much effort should be put into the full and prompt statistical reporting of changes in the main relevant economic variables – prices, employment, unemployment, output, sales, stocks, imports, exports, etc.[2]

As far as the delay between the realisation of the need for action and the actual change of policy is concerned, monetary policy could score high marks. A small and desirable change in conventional procedures would enable the Bank of England to raise or lower the Bank Rate on any working day in the year, and it can already purchase or sell long-term securities in the market in any amounts at any time in order to pump funds into or out of the capital market. Moreover, such open-market opera-

---

[2] Such prompt reporting of actual changes may, of course, be usefully supplemented by information (such as information on producers' plans for future expenditures on capital development) which may help to forecast movements likely to take place in some of the variables after the date for which the last actual values are known.

tions need not be publicised; they can be made as soon as the need for action seems probable; and the Bank should not be inhibited as the situation develops from reversing next week or next month some open-market purchase or sale which it has undertaken today.

But in so far as the lag between a change in policy and its actual effect upon the economy is concerned, monetary policy probably scores badly. Any effect which a rise in the short-term rate of interest may have upon the holding of stocks may be reasonably prompt in its effect; but this is not likely to be the main ultimate effect of a change in monetary policy, and the other ultimate effects are all likely to be delayed. When the Bank of England takes steps to reduce the liquidity of the commercial banks, the latter may be induced to reduce their advances to industry. But with the British overdraft system this process is likely to be delayed. The process must consist of being less willing to grant new overdraft facilities, of increasing pressure on clients to repay their outstanding borrowings from the banks concerned, and of negotiating reductions in the limits of unused overdraft facilities. But these things all take time, and if there is a natural inflationary pressure in the economy, business men are likely to continue for a time to make increased use of unused overdraft facilities, so that total advances may well continue to grow for some time after the change in monetary policy. The change in monetary policy may well involve an almost immediate sale of long-term securities by banks and so an almost immediate rise in long-term interest rates. But any effects which this may have upon expenditure upon capital development are likely to be delayed, since dearer money is likely to affect projects which are now being planned for future execution rather than projects on which funds are now being spent.

As far as budgetary policy is concerned, changes in public expenditure score badly from the point of view of both the types of delay now under discussion. Changes in rates of expenditure on public services require considerable consideration of the various public policies involved and are likely to make a considerable political fuss. Moreover, even when a decision has finally been taken to change the level of some government expenditure the consequential change in that level is likely to mature only gradually as the new plan replaces the old.

Changes in rates of taxation are likely to score badly where monetary policy scores well and to score well where monetary policy scores badly. As the tax system is at present organised, there are serious delays between the realisation of change in the economic situation and the offsetting change in rates of taxation. There are Parliamentary and constitutional difficulties in changing rates of tax except at Budget time; and there are real administrative difficulties in making frequent changes in many tax rates. Thus with present PAYE procedures a change in rates of income tax requires the preparation and distribution to all employers of new tax-deduction schedules; or a change in the rates of purchase tax leads to awkward problems of profit or loss on stocks in retailers' hands of goods which have paid tax at the old rates. In any case, a change in tax is a matter of considerable political concern, so that politicians will often have strong incentives to make no change until the need for change has become extreme.

But changes in many taxes are likely to win high marks in so far as the lag between the application of the new rates and the realisation of its effects on expenditure is concerned. For example, a change in the rate of tax collected under PAYE will immediately affect the weekly pay packets of millions of wage-earners; or a change in the rate of purchase tax will very promptly affect the price which all consumers have to pay for the goods in question. It is, of course, probable that some part of the impact effect of such changes may fall upon the savings of wage-earners and other consumers, in which case to this extent there will be no immediate effect upon the amount of goods which they try to purchase. But the change is likely to affect real expenditure fairly quickly.

In short, a widespread tax would constitute an ideal instrument of control if only it were technically capable of rapid and frequent change and if an institutional arrangement could be found to make such changes politically possible.

VI

In an Annex to the White Paper on Employment Policy issued by the Coalition Government in 1944 (Cmd 6527) the proposal was made that the workers' and employers' weekly contributions to national insurance might be varied in order to stabilise the general level of money demand for goods and services.[3] Technically, this is among the best forms of levy which could be used for our purpose. It would be possible to make administrative arrangements for prompt and, if necessary, frequent variations in the amount of the levy.

The effect on demand would be marked and prompt in so far as the contributions of the employee or of the self-employed were varied, since this would immediately affect the amount of spendable incomes. A change in the employers' contribution would affect the profitability of business and thus would ultimately affect expenditure out of profits; but such an effect would be uncertain in amount and delayed in its operation. Moreover, a rise in the employers' contributions would raise costs of production; and it would be anomalous to attempt to restrain a rise in money prices by an instrument which directly raised money costs. It would be preferable, though not absolutely essential that the scheme should exclude variations in employers' contributions.

But could a device of this kind be operated on a scale which was sufficient for the stabilisation of demand? At present national insurance contributions are levied at a fixed rate regardless of the earnings of the contributor in question. For this reason it may be difficult to raise the rate of contribution very significantly because an increased contribution which could fairly easily be borne by a well-paid worker might represent a very heavy burden to a low-paid worker. This difficulty would be diminished if the levy in question were expressed as a proportion of the

[3] In fact under the post-war legislation reforming the national insurance system [the National Insurance Act of 1946] the Treasury is already endowed with the power to vary national insurance contributions for this purpose.

contributor's actual earnings, as has been proposed in some recent suggestions for the reform of our national insurance arrangements. An additional payment of 1 per cent of the earnings of those concerned would raise something like £150 million a year; and the device could thus be used to exert a really important influence over total demand.

From the point of view of fairness of tax burden an even more acceptable alternative might be a scheme whereby the rate of income tax was subject to a positive (or negative) supplement which could be varied quarterly. Since many workers are exempt from income tax it could not have so widespread an effect upon the weekly pay packet as a variation in national insurance contributions. Moreover, it would be administratively more difficult. But it might nevertheless prove a feasible alternative. The income-tax allowances for dependents and for earned income, the amounts of income subject to reduced rates of income tax, and the standard rate and the reduced rates of income tax would all, as now, be fixed once a year at Budget time. But each quarter positive (or negative) supplements to the standard rate and to the reduced rates of tax could be announced. As far as personal incomes were concerned, which, like dividends, could be treated only on an annual basis, the amount of tax liability at the end of the year would be so adjusted that the annual rate of tax was equivalent to the average of the four quarterly supplemented rates which had been announced in the course of the year. But weekly, monthly, or quarterly earnings at present subject to PAYE deductions or income tax would be treated for such deductions on a quarterly instead of an annual basis. Each quarter a new period would start for the reckoning of PAYE deductions on the present cumulative principle, and new tax deduction schedules would be used if a change had been announced in the quarterly supplements to the rate of tax.[4] At the end of each year tax payments under PAYE would be so adjusted as to make the total tax paid on the whole year's income correspond to an annual rate of tax on that income equivalent to the average of the four quarterly supplemented rates announced during the year.

I do not want on this occasion to argue the detailed merits and difficulties inherent in these particular schemes. My present intention is only to illustrate the point of principle: it would, in my opinion, be both desirable and possible, at some administrative cost and inconvenience, to devise some form of widespread levy on personal incomes which could be used to make frequent and prompt variations in spendable incomes.

It is, of course, necessary to treat stabilisation policy as a co-ordinated whole. A particularly important example of this truth is provided by the intimate relationship which would have to exist between those in charge of monetary and banking policy and those in charge of the special stabilisation levies. If variations in national insurance contributions were the chosen instrument, arrangements would have to be made to separate the book-keeping of the normal insurance contributions from the excess or deficiency of the contribution which was imposed for stabilisation

---

[4] To avoid delay it might be feasible to have alternative tax deduction schedules printed in advance to correspond to various positive and negative supplements to the normal rates of tax.

purposes. This could be achieved by instituting a Stabilisation Fund separate from the ordinary National Insurance Fund. In times of inflationary pressure when contributions had been raised above their normal level, the Stabilisation Fund would receive the revenue from these supplementary contributions. In times of deflationary pressure when contributions had been reduced below their normal level, the Stabilisation Fund would pay out to the National Insurance Fund an amount sufficient to make up this shortfall in its revenue. A similar Stabilisation Fund could be set up to receive from, or to pay to, the Exchequer the proceeds of the special supplements on rates of income tax, if that were the chosen instrument. In either case what the Stabilisation Fund did with its balances would most powerfully affect monetary conditions. Suppose, for example, that when it was receiving funds the Stabilisation Fund invested in Treasury Bills or ran up a deposit balance with the Bank of England; and suppose that when it had to pay out funds, it sold Treasury Bills or ran down or overdrew its account with the Bank of England.

The liquid reserves of the commercial banks would in this case be subject to an automatic drain equal to the total of the supplementary stabilisation levies in times of inflationary pressure. If, for example, £150 million per annum were being drawn out of the commercial banks for the payment of additional levies on personal incomes to the Stabilisation Fund, this would cause the liquid reserves of the commercial banks to decline at a rate of £150 million per annum. As the total liquid reserves of the commercial banks (including cash, money at call, and bills) are now about £2,000 million, it can be readily seen that this would represent a powerful automatic force leading to a deflationary monetary policy. And conversely, in times when a counter-measure was required to offset deflationary pressures in the economy, the special reductions in levies on personal incomes would introduce automatically both an increase in the flow of money receipts to consumers to stimulate demand and also an increase in the liquidity of the banking system to enable the banks to adopt a reflationary monetary policy.

Variations in special stabilisation levies could thus be so operated as to enforce a powerful and continuing monetary disinflation so long as they were kept above the normal, and *vice versa* when they were reduced below the normal. But whether or not it would be desirable to link these monetary effects with the direct effects of variations in special stabilisation levies upon consumers' expenditure would be a matter for consideration in each particular situation. It might be desirable to offset them in whole or in part by means of open-market purchases or sales of long-term securities by the Bank of England or by shifts between long-term securities and short-term assets on the part of the Stabilisation Fund itself.

The extent to which reliance should be put upon the various instruments of control – the supply of money, the structure of the national debt, normal rates of tax, or variations in special stabilisation levies – will depend upon the particular conditions of each case. How far is speed of response important in the particular circumstances of the case? Which instrument will raise or lower demand in a particular sector of the economic system affected by some special temporary disturbance? Does the balance-of-payments situation require controls which will operate very directly on the demand for imports and for domestic products which could be exported?

Another basic consideration is the choice between instruments of control which affect expenditure on capital development and those which affect the demand for consumption goods. In my previous discussion of the 'break-even' point in the labour market I argued as if the rate of rise of productivity were a given phenomenon about which one could do nothing. But this is not entirely true; and the more quickly output per head can be made to rise, the more quickly can money wage-rates be raised without leading to any rise of costs per unit of output. One way in which productivity can be raised is by maintaining a high rate of investment in new capital equipment. To fight a current inflation by measures which can cut down on current consumption rather than on investment will permit a higher future rate of increase of productivity and will thus alleviate future inflationary pressures. On the other hand, the measures necessary to restrain current consumption may well themselves intensify the immediate pressure for increased money wage-rates in an attempt to restore their real standard of living on the part of the wage-earners. Capital development and the consequential rises in productivity are not merely – indeed not mainly – needed for the purpose of controlling inflation; they are wanted for their own sake in order to raise real income and standards of living. But they have an important effect upon the inflationary process; and in so far as it is possible to choose weapons of control which will maintain present rates of investment at the expense of present rates of consumption without thereby causing an immediate increase in the demand for higher money wage-rates, future inflationary forces will be reduced.

But although stabilisation policy must, for these reasons, be treated as a single co-ordinated whole, there is, nevertheless, reason for making certain broad distinctions between responsibility for the various weapons of control. The ordinary Budget is used primarily to influence the distribution of income and property, to determine the broad choice between investment and consumption over a period of years, and to subsidise particular activities (such as agriculture) at the cost of others (such as industry); in addition it could and should be used generally to exercise a steady disinflationary or reflationary force during a continuing period of inflationary or deflationary pressure; but it is not well contrived to exercise prompt and frequent disinflationary or reflationary influences over total demand, changing the pressure from month to month as the driver of a motor-car continually presses his steering wheel now slightly to the right and now slightly to the left. Such guidance could be exercised in the monetary sphere by the Bank of England and in the fiscal sphere by the proposed system of variations in some special stabilisation levy on personal incomes.

It can be argued that policies of this latter type should be entrusted to bodies which have been given full power of operation of their stabilisation weapons independently of the government. Chancellors of the Exchequer cannot reasonably be expected in all political situations to take prompt but unpopular action to reduce spendable incomes. They may be greatly tempted to wait and see, and thus to let undesirable tendencies develop much too far unchecked. This danger might be met by some self-denying ordinance by the political parties, removing stabilisation policy from the ordinary political machine.

This end might conceivably be achieved by devising an automatic sliding scale for the operation of the stabilisation devices. Thus in the Coalition Government's White Paper of 1944 it was suggested that the rates of national insurance contributions should vary automatically with variations in the percentage of workers unemployed. When the unemployment percentage went up to a stated level, the rate of contribution would automatically be reduced by a stated amount; and *vice versa*. This suggestion is open to two serious objections.

In the first place, experience since the war has shown that it is practicable to keep the unemployment percentage consistently at a much lower absolute level than was then envisaged. The unemployment percentage is not likely to prove the sensitive and variable index which would be appropriate for the workings of an automatic stabilising device of this kind.

But there is in fact a more fundamental objection to the use of any automatic device of the kind envisaged in the Employment Policy of the White Paper. It is exceedingly difficult to decide to what extent any particular counter-measure to offset inflationary and deflationary developments would be successful in its objective. The economic process in a developed country like the United Kingdom is a complicated system of interrelationships. An increase in incomes will after a time-lag lead to an increase in the demand for goods and services which in turn after some time-lag is likely to lead to some further increase in incomes paid out to wage-earners and other producers of these goods and services. Increases in expenditure are likely to cause at first some fall in stocks and subsequently both some increases in prices and, after another time-lag, some increase in amounts produced and put on the market for sale. But if prices are rising at a certain rate and have been rising for a certain time, people may be led to speculate upon a continuing rise of prices and they may thus be induced to spend still more on their current purchases of goods; and the rate at which the production of goods is growing may itself influence the amount which is spent in buying new machines and in building up stocks of raw materials and semi-finished goods, in order to keep capital equipment and stocks in balance with a higher rate of output.

Every economist could mention many more dynamic relationships of this kind between movements of prices, costs, profits, wages, tax payments, savings, consumption, investment, output, employment, amounts of money, and rates of interest – to say nothing of the influence of imports, exports, and foreign capital movements. It is into a complicated dynamic system of this kind that the authorities have to introduce their stabilising measures to offset inflationary and deflationary developments of demand in the economic system. Unfortunately much more work must be done on the analysis of such dynamic interrelationships in the modern economic system before anything can be said with much assurance about the precise effect of any particular stabilising device. Even if it were possible to take some simple criterion (such as the divergence of selling prices above or below some stated ceiling) as the criterion for some stabilising device like variations in national insurance contributions, it would be probable that disinflationary action, and thus the extent of the rise in the level of national insurance contributions, should be intensified not only in accordance with the extent to which the price level is above the ceiling level, but also in accordance both with the speed with which it is still rising and with the extent to which it has been consistently too high over the past. Thus disinflationary action should be strong if prices are too high, have been high for a long time, and are still rising rapidly. If prices are too high but are already falling rapidly, it may be time to relax the disinflationary pressure in order to make sure that the fall in prices does not overshoot the mark. It may be that when we know much more than we do at present about the nature of reactions within the dynamic economy with which we have to deal, it will be possible to invent an effective automatic formula for stabilisation in which the level of the special stabilisation levy is made to depend automatically on the size, the rate of growth, and the past extent of the divergence between the actual level of prices and the level at which it is desired to stabilise prices.[5] But that time is still far off. For the moment, those who are in charge of the operation of such a device must be left with some discretion by trial [and] error to use it in the most effective way to achieve the desired stabilisation.

If this is so, the only way to make the operation of such a device independent of *ad hoc* government decision would be to set up a separate independent statutory body – let us call it the Stabilisation Commission – charged with the task of making variations in the level of the special stabilisation levy at its discretion, but only within the limits laid down by Parliament and only for the purpose of achieving some precisely defined objective, such as the maintenance of total demand for goods and services at the highest possible level compatible with the prevention of some precisely defined price index from rising above a precisely defined ceiling.

The disadvantages of any such arrangement are clear. Budgetary policy, monetary policy, and variations in a special stabilisation levy make up such a closely knit whole that it is inappropriate to have more than one authority with final responsibility for them. Let me give only one example of the problems which might arise if normal budgetary policy were in the hands of the government but special variations in, say, national insurance contributions were in the hands of an independent commission. Suppose that the government were under strong political pressure to reduce taxation at a time of inflationary pressure. If the Chancellor of the Exchequer held the rates of normal taxes at inappropriately low levels, the Stabilisation Commission would have the responsi-

[5] For a technical discussion of this point see the article by A. W. Phillips in *The Economic Journal* for June 1954 entitled 'Stabilisation Policy in a Closed Economy' [Vol. 64, pp. 290–323].

bility of offsetting this by holding the rates of national insurance contributions more or less permanently at abnormally high levels; and this might give an undesirable twist to the distribution of the normal burden of taxation. The only way to avoid this would be to make the Chancellor ultimately responsible for both types of taxation and thus responsible for maintaining a sufficiently strict general monetary and budgetary policy to prevent the need for a permanent use of abnormally high rates for the special stabilisation levies which were intended to be used only for short-term stabilisation purposes.

And yet there is real substance in the argument for removing these month to month stabilisation devices as far from the ordinary political arena as possible. Perhaps a good working arrangement would be to set up a separate Stabilisation Commission to initiate variations in the special stabilisation levies but to put the Commission under the ultimate control of the Chancellor of the Exchequer. The government, by legislation or otherwise, would in this case openly commit itself to the precise objective of maintaining total demand at the highest possible level which was compatible with the prevention of prices from rising above a stated ceiling; two independent bodies, the Bank of England and the Stabilisation Commission, would be given the responsibility for making changes in monetary policy and in the special stabilisation levies for the attainment of the same objective, but they would be subject to final direction by the Chancellor of the Exchequer. To assist the proper co-ordination of the various stabilising devices the Treasury, the Bank of England, and the Stabilisation Commission might be advised by a single expert secretariat; and to ensure a proper public understanding and appreciation of the stabilisation policy this secretariat might be required to publish an annual report on the stabilisation policies of the Treasury, Bank of England, and Stabilisation Commission. By such means a full co-ordinated stabilisation policy might be achieved, removed in some degree from the immediate rough and tumble of party politics.

VII

The basic question which I have discussed in this lecture is whether or not the government should put a stop to price inflation once and for all by committing itself so to control the general level of money demand for goods and services that prices are not permitted to rise above a stated ceiling. I have argued that it should be possible to do this, but have pointed out the very real dangers of such a policy, unless wage-fixing methods are suitably reformed. I have illustrated my argument by making a number of positive proposals for the application of such a policy:

First, that the government should accept openly a precise commitment to use its powers of financial policy so as to maintain the highest possible level of demand for goods and services compatible with the prevention of a precisely defined price index from rising above a precisely defined ceiling.

Second, that this price index should be composed of the prices of all home-produced goods and services, exclusive of the prices of imports and the import-content of home production, and exclusive of prices (such as rents) which are subject to important price controls, all prices to be reckoned after the payment of indirect taxes and the receipt of subsidies.

Third, that arrangements should be made for prompt and frequent variations in some suitable widespread levy on personal incomes as an additional means of controlling demand.

Fourth, that a Stabilisation Commission, subject to the ultimate control of the Chancellor of the Exchequer, should be set up to determine and operate these variations in the special stabilisation levies.

Fifth, that the Treasury, the Bank of England, and the Stabilisation Commission should share a common technical secretariat to give advice on stabilisation policies, and that this secretariat should publish an annual report on the stabilisation policies which had been adopted.

Sixth, that some body like the Council on Prices, Productivity and Incomes, should at regular intervals publish an estimate of the average rates of rise in money wage earnings per head which it considered would be compatible with the preservation of full employment in these conditions of stable selling prices.

Seventh, that arbitral bodies should be set up to which employers, workers, or the government could refer for a judgement whether the workers involved in any particular wage negotiation should obtain a rise in wage earnings appreciably above or below the average in order, over the next few years, to avoid a serious local shortage or redundancy of labour.

Eighth, that more extensive provision should be made to ease the retraining, removal, and rehousing of workers who become redundant in their existing jobs.

Ninth, that restrictive practices in the labour market should not be exempt from public scrutiny and control.

Tenth, that if financial policies were concentrated on domestic stability in this way, variations in the rate of exchange between the pound and other currencies could and should be made much more freely as a means of preserving equilibrium in the balance of payments.

I have put forward these proposals in a very positive tone of voice. But whether or not the government should actually take the plunge depends both upon questions of fact such as how much unemployment would in fact be necessary in any given circumstances to avoid a cost inflation and also upon value judgements such as how much unemployment it would be worth risking in order to achieve price stability. I have not tried in this lecture to answer either of these questions; I have tried only to elucidate some of the processes at work. The detailed proposals which I have put forward so brashly are intended mainly as illustrations of these processes. I rather think that I myself believe in them; but my main purpose has been to use them as illustrations of the basic issues.

VIII

One final word. My lecture has been about the control of inflation, because that is the problem with which we have become so familiar in recent years. I do not myself believe much in forecasting economic events. But it is at least possible that in the not too far distant future inflationary pressures may give place for a time to deflationary forces. A more serious American recession than anything which we have experienced since the end of the Second World War is always a possibility. In such an event we should have to put the engines of financial policy rapidly and massively into reverse. One of the main virtues which I would claim for proposals of the type which I have outlined today is that they are equally well designed to stimulate expenditure and to keep selling prices up in a period of deflationary pressure as they are to prevent price rises in an otherwise inflationary situation; and it is even more important to be in a position to offset any future deflation than to stop the present inflation.

19

Wages and Prices in a Mixed Economy

The second Wincott Memorial Lecture, delivered at the London School of Economics on 29 September 1971 and published as Occasional Paper 35 by the Institute of Economic Affairs (London, 1971), pp. 7–36.

I Introduction[1]

I need not dwell on the fact that we find ourselves not merely in an inflationary situation, but in a situation in which the rate of inflation has itself recently been rising rapidly and has been combined with an exceptionally high level of unemployment. This 'stagflation' is illustrated by the following figures:[2]

	1966	1967	1968	1969	1970	1971 (1st Qtr)
Percentage rise in						
(i) Weekly Money Earnings[a]	6.5	3.3	8.1	7.8	12.0	12.7[b]
(ii) Retail Prices	3.9	2.5	4.7	5.4	6.4	8.6[b]
Percentage of Employees Unemployed[a]	1.53	2.40	2.43	2.42	2.62	2.97

[a] Seasonally adjusted.
[b] Increase over corresponding period in 1970.

Since 1966 there has been a marked rise both in the level of unemployment and in the rates of inflation of wages and prices.

II Inflation: 'Anticipated and Explosive'

But should not the stagnation trouble us much more than the inflation?

---

[1] I am greatly indebted to Professor E. H. Phelps Brown, Sir Alec Cairncross, Mr John Gratwick, Mr Graham Hutton, Mr L. F. Neal, Professor W. B. Reddaway, Professor B. C. Roberts and Mr Z. A. Silberston for extensive comments on an earlier draft of this lecture. As a result I have greatly simplified the positive proposals which I put forward and to which, of course, I commit no one but myself.

[2] Taken from Tables XVIII and XX of F. W. Paish, *Rise and Fall of Incomes Policy*, Hobart Paper 47, 2nd edition (London: Institute of Economic Affairs, 1971).

Perhaps price stability does not matter. After all money is but a veil and it is from the enjoyment of a large output of real goods and services that the real standard of living arises. There is undoubtedly a very large element of truth in this assertion; and before one embarks on the rather formidable task of trying to remodel society so as to make full employment compatible with price stability, it is worth while asking what, if any, is the real disadvantage or danger in price inflation.

For this purpose it is useful, I think, to distinguish between two types of inflationary situation, which I will call 'anticipated' and 'explosive' inflation. By an anticipated inflation I mean a situation in which the future upward movement of the general level of prices is fully and accurately foreseen and is taken into account in all private and public contracts and other financial arrangements. The well-known distributional inequities of inflation would cease to exist because no one would be on a fixed money income; the old-age pensioner would have a money income which would rise in line with the cost of living.

Nor need there be any balance-of-payments problem. If the fully anticipated rate of inflation in the United Kingdom was 1 per cent per annum higher than the fully anticipated rate of inflation in the United States, then the sterling exchange rate would have to be depreciated in terms of dollars by 1 per cent per annum in order to keep sterling and dollar prices in line with each other. But if both inflations were fully anticipated, this would not present any insuperable problem. This need not lead to any speculative capital movements. The rate of interest would, of course, have to be 1 per cent per annum higher in the UK than in the USA so that any gain on the exchanges by moving from sterling to dollars would be offset by loss of interest.

Nor need this external need for a higher rate of interest in the UK present any fundamental internal domestic problem. A fully anticipated 1 per cent per annum rise in all prices raises the yield on capital investment by 1 per cent per annum because it presents a 1 per cent per annum capital gain on all real capital goods. To maintain the same domestic relationship between the supply and demand for funds for investment, the money rate of interest must therefore be raised 1 per cent per annum, if money prices are all known to be rising by 1 per cent annum.

This situation could, however, give rise to a domestic liquidity problem. It is conceivable that the future movements of the general level of prices (i.e. a specified price index) is sufficiently accurately foreseen for one to be able to talk of a fully anticipated inflation; but this would not imply that the future movement of every individual price was precisely foreseen. Particular uncertainties will persist and people will wish to hold liquid funds in order to meet unanticipated events. But if because of a rapid rate of price inflation the rate of interest on money loans is, say, 15 per cent per annum and if at the same time the rate of interest on liquid balances of money is zero, there will be a heavy cost in remaining liquid. This could lead to real economic inefficiency; economic decision-makers would, simply because of the monetary inflation, not be willing to preserve those socially desirable defences against uncertainties and risks which in a non-inflationary situation the holding of money balances would provide.

This disadvantage of anticipated inflation could itself be removed by the payment of a rate of interest on money balances equal to the anticipated rate of increase of prices. So far as deposit money is concerned, this presents no insuperable problem. It is a more difficult institutional problem to arrange for a rate of interest to be earned on the notes and coin which one carries round in one's pocket or holds in one's till. The retailer would be tempted not to hold much change; and you and I would be tempted not to have much cash in our pockets. There would be real inconveniences in shopping and one might even find oneself stranded without one's bus fare. But this, which is I think the only insuperable disadvantage of a fully anticipated inflation, is in my opinion a rather minor matter.

The situation is totally different when one considers what I have called 'explosive' inflation, which arises in a monetary economy when the various groups in the community are so acting as to make demands on real resources that, for one reason or another, it is impossible to fulfil. Let me give an example. Suppose output per man-hour to be rising by 3 per cent per annum; and suppose that wage-earners are demanding increases in wage-rates designed to raise their real take-home pay by 4 per cent per annum. It is possible that for a short time this gap can be closed by reductions in taxation or by a squeeze on profit margins. But at some point prices must start rising by 1 per cent per annum (the difference between wage per man and output per man) unless profits are first to be reduced to zero and then turned into ever-increasing losses. But when prices and also the cost of living starts rising by 1 per cent per annum, wage-earners must demand wage rises of 5 per cent per annum in order to obtain a rise in real income (take-home pay) of 4 per cent per annum. But now prices and so the cost of living will start to rise by 2 per cent per annum (the difference between the increase of 5 per cent per annum in wage per man and the 3 per cent per annum increase in output per man). Wage-earners will now demand wage increases of 6 per cent per annum in order to achieve a real increase of 4 per cent per annum; this will however cause the cost of living to go up by 3 instead of 2 per cent per annum; and so on in an explosive inflationary spiral. You cannot get more than a pint out of a pint pot. The attempt to do so must lead to an ever-increasing rate of inflation, the actual rate always being higher than the anticipated rate.

An analogous situation can arise if each of two groups in society is trying to get a share of the national income which is incompatible with the share demanded by the other group. Consider two groups of workers, group A and group B, each of which considers that it is right and proper that it should receive a differential 10 per cent above the other. Both start with a wage of 100: A then demands 110 to restore what it considers to be the proper differential. B then demands 10 per cent above that figure, namely 121, in order to restore what it considers to be the proper differential. A then demands 10 per cent above that, namely 132.1; and so on in an infinite series. Moreover, as soon as A in its demands seeks not merely 10 per cent more than the present level of B, but 10 per cent more than what B will get in the future given the past experience of the rate of rise in the earnings of B, the percentage rate of inflation will explode; the rate of rise will become more and more rapid as both groups add their impossible, because incompatible, demands on to the past rate of inflation. If A is trying to leap-frog over B's back at the very same moment that B is leap-frogging over A's back, not only is the sky the limit, but both players will shoot off into the empyrean at an ever-increasing speed.

Money will have ceased to be a reliable counter or *numeraire* for useful trading calculations. It will have become involved in a set of very real incompatibilities, the removal of which presents the basic anti-inflationary task.

III   Conditions for Full Employment Without Inflation

I conclude that it is worth real effort to understand and to take steps to control such an inflation. There has in the past been considerable dispute about some aspects of the mechanism of this inflationary process. I do not intend in this lecture to devote much time to the details of controversies about the relative importance of demand-pull versus cost-push influences on wage-rates and prices. But certain broad aspects of the mechanics of the inflationary process – aspects which are, I think, luckily fairly obvious and widely accepted – are essential for my present purpose. The national income measured in terms of money or, what with appropriate definitions comes to the same thing, the money value of the nation's production, depends upon two things: the real quantities of goods and services produced, and the money prices at which these goods and services are valued. Money prices and costs are directly determined by wage bargains, by the decisions of manufacturers as to what profit margins to charge, and similar decisions in individual markets. The quantities of goods and services produced are subject to upper limits set by the full employment of labour or the capacity use of capital equipment; but below these limits the quantities which can be sold at any given prices and thus the quantities of labour employed and of other inputs purchased by manufacturers will depend upon the total amount of money expenditures by consumers on consumption goods and services, by the government on public services of various kinds, by producers on investment in additional capital equipment, and by foreigners on the country's exports.

The total level of these money expenditures can undoubtedly be greatly influenced by governmental fiscal and monetary policies. Conscious and calculated demand control has, indeed, become a familiar and accepted feature of governmental policy since the general acceptance of Keynesian ideas at the end of the Second World War. I assume the possibility of effective demand control for the purpose of this lecture without discussing at all how it may be achieved.

I would, however, like to digress for one moment to emphasise that while fiscal and monetary policies may differ in important ways in their effects on different elements of total money expenditure, they are nevertheless both methods of influencing total money expenditure, i.e. the total money demand for goods and service. Those who see some magical effect on prices to be derived from a control of the supply of money other than through its effect on money demands for goods and services are surely chasing a will o' the wisp. Those economists who place their bets on monetary policy have, of course, always believed that changes in the supply of money operated through their effects on the money demand for goods and services, as can be seen from Professor Milton Friedman's exposition in last year's Wincott Lecture on *The Counter-Revolution in Monetary Theory*.[3] We may agree then that both fiscal policy and monetary policy can affect inflation only by influencing money demands for goods and services, and any resulting restraints on money demands may in both cases *either* restrain the volume of real output which is sold at unchanged prices *or* restrain the prices charged for the same quantities of output *or* cause partly the one effect and partly the other. There is, however, no obvious reason to believe that fiscal policy and monetary policy will differ in any essential way in their relative effects on prices and outputs.

The complete inflationary process thus depends on two rather separate sets of processes:

(i) the processes by which money wage-rates and prices are determined, and

(ii) the processes by which total money expenditures are determined.

There are, of course, most important interrelationships between these two sets of processes, and it is in the assessment of these interrelationships that difficulties arise in the full analysis of the inflationary process. Thus a controlled restriction of total money expenditures would almost certainly not leave the course of money wages and prices totally unaffected and exert its full effect solely on the quantities of goods and services sold. Manufacturers in fixing their profit margins presumably pay some attention to the buoyancy of the markets in which they are selling their goods, and there is presumably at least some level of unemployment which would reduce the incentive of trade unions to insist on a given level of wage increases.

On the other hand, it is obvious that the total level of money expenditure may be affected by the level of money wages, since a rise in money wage-rates, if employment does not fall, will increase wage incomes, the prospect of which may well increase money expenditures on consumption goods. But the degree and speed of the effect of unemployment and excess capacity on wage- and price-fixing and the degree and speed of the effect of wages and prices on incomes and expenditures are both difficult matters to analyse and to measure. I do not intend to enter into these matters in this lecture.

---

[3] Occasional Paper 33, Institute of Economic Affairs, December 1970.

However, it is clear that in order to achieve full employment without price inflation, two separate conditions must be fulfilled:

first, the government must be able by fiscal and monetary policies to keep total money expenditures at the level necessary to provide a market for the full-employment capacity level of output at uninflated money prices; and

second, the wage–price fixing processes must be such as to ensure, at this full-employment, capacity level of real activity, both that money wage-rates are not pushed up more quickly than output per head is growing and also that profit margins are stabilised.

In this lecture I shall assume that we do know broadly how to control the total level of money expenditures at whatever level we desire. It is on the second of these two conditions that I wish to lecture, namely the problem of restraining the wage–price fixing processes so as to avoid, or at least much reduce, price inflation at full-employment levels of output.

IV Recent Changes in the Labour Market

Let me start with wage restraint which, as I shall argue later, is the basic problem. Until very recently it was possible to argue that a reasonably moderate restraint of total effective demand (such as to maintain the unemployment percentage at about 2½ per cent) would damp down the labour market sufficiently to avoid an undue rate of inflation of money wage-rates. Professor Paish has shown very convincingly that for the years 1952–66 the level of demand for labour had a clear effect on the rate at which money wages were increased, the relationship being such that with an unemployment percentage of 2½ one could expect an annual increase of incomes from employment of about 4 per cent per annum.[4]

But there has of recent years been a most dramatic and marked change. This can be seen clearly from the figures I quoted at the beginning of this lecture (page 321), which show that weekly wage-earnings rose in 1970 by 12 per cent, while the unemployment percentage was no less than 2.6 per cent. In 1970–71 the highest rates of rise of money wage-incomes have been combined not with the lowest, but with the highest, unemployment percentages since the end of the Second World War. Professor Paish has analysed this dramatic change. He reaches the conclusion that, whereas on the basis of the 1952–66 experience one would have expected the unemployment ruling between the middle of 1969 and the middle of 1970 to have been associated with an increase of 3.8 per cent in the money incomes earned from employment, in the result this increase in money earnings was no less than 13.7 per cent – some 10 points higher than one would have expected from previous experience.[5]

[4] F. W. Paish, *op. cit.*
[5] F. W. Paish, *op. cit.*, p. 70.

How can one explain this very dramatic increase in the amount of wage inflation associated with a given level of demand in the labour market? No one, I think, can at present give a confident answer to this question. There are many possible factors at work and very probably it is the combination of many different influences which has caused so large a change. I will do no more than to refer you to Professor Paish's analysis and to summarise briefly five possible influences.

(1) Theoretically one could explain the change if there had been a dramatic increase in structural unemployment, i.e. in unemployment that was highly concentrated in particular regions or occupations. Money wage-rates are much more easily pulled up by an excess demand for labour than they are pushed down by an excess supply of labour. If a given total of unemployment takes the form of a mass of unemployment in one particular market combined with a scarcity of labour elsewhere, the upward movement of wages where there is scarcity is likely to be rapid; and this is likely to be combined with little if any deflation of wage-rates where there is heavy unemployment. If the same total of unemployment were evenly spread over all labour markets, so that there was no scarcity of labour anywhere, the upward movement of wage-rates would almost certainly be much less marked.

There is not, however, any evidence of a dramatic increase in concentrated, structural unemployment sufficient to explain the dramatic change in the rate of wage inflation. We can dismiss this influence as an explanation. I have mentioned it at some length, however, because it does point one moral. An important element in any long-run policy designed to combine full employment with price stability should consist of policies to deal with structural unemployment: to bring new industries to depressed areas, to re-train unemployed workers, to enable unemployed workers to find houses to rent in regions of expanding demand, and to break down restrictive practices in the labour market which prevent workers in contracting occupations and industries from being admitted to work in more prosperous trades. For the less unemployment is concentrated in depressed, contracting regions and occupations, the lower will be the general level of unemployment needed to prevent an inflation of money wage-costs. But this has always been true; it is not a new phenomenon which will explain the sudden present intensification of the wage problem.

(2) There have in recent years been two very important changes in the labour market – namely, the institution of redundancy payments and of more generous income-related unemployment benefits – which have reduced the terrors of temporary forced unemployment. One likely result has been that in pressing wage claims trade unions and similar bodies have been less sensitive than before to any given level of unemployment among the workers concerned. This may well have exerted an appreciable influence, though it is difficult to imagine that it explains the whole of the change.

(3) A third influence may be found in the fact that the great recovery in the balance of payments after 1967 necessitated a reduction in the standard of living below what it would otherwise have been. In conditions

of full employment you cannot import less and export more real goods and services without cutting down some forms of domestic consumption or other use of real resources. Higher prices of imports and higher direct and indirect taxes were among the necessary means which the then Chancellor of the Exchequer had the political courage to face. But wage-earners may not automatically accept lower incomes and higher prices without an attempt to restore the situation through more urgent demands for increased money wages. The real restraints on consumption after 1967 may well have intensified the pressures for increased money wage-incomes.

(4)   This development may have made wage-earners more conscious of rises in the cost of living and more insistent that it is real wages rather than money wages in which they are interested. This in turn could well lead to an explosive inflationary situation of the kind which I outlined at the beginning of my lecture. Suppose that in a given situation a rise of 3 per cent per annum in the real wage-rate is what would correspond to the rise in the real productivity of labour. Suppose that last year the cost of living went up by 6 per cent. Suppose finally that workers demand a money wage increase of 10 per cent, because they aim at a rise in the real wage of 4 per cent (i.e. 10 per cent rise in money wages minus 6 per cent to cover the rise in the cost of living = 4 per cent rise in the real wage, i.e. take-home pay). Then money wage-costs per unit of output will rise by 7 per cent (i.e. 10 per cent in the money wage-rate minus 3 per cent rise in output per head). Prices must be raised this year by 7 per cent instead of by last year's 6 per cent if profit margins are to be maintained. In this way a more-and-more definite and deliberate attempt to achieve an over-optimistic target of improvement in the real wage-rate by adding a precise figure to offset last year's rise in the cost of living can lead to a rapid acceleration of price, and so in turn of wage, inflation. I strongly suspect that something of this kind may have been happening.

(5)   Any or all of the influences which I have already discussed may have initiated stronger pressure by trade unions and similar bodies for wage increases. Such pressures having resulted in a marked increase in the rate of rise of money wage-rates may have given individual trade unions an unexpected glimpse into the very large monopolistic powers which they possess for pushing money wage-rates up and which they have not fully exploited in the past. The consequence may have been a basic change in their attitudes. The order of magnitude of what is regarded as a reasonable annual claim may have been more or less permanently changed; and trade union leaders may have become much more acutely aware of their powers to obtain concessions through the threat to disrupt basic economic activities.

V   Proposals for Restraining 'Explosive' Wage Inflation

If it is really important to restrain this sort of explosive wage inflation and if it is impossible nowadays to do so merely by restricting the total demand for labour to a moderate and tolerable degree, what can be done about it?

One possibility is to attempt a full-scale governmental incomes policy, which involves, first, laying down criteria to determine the legitimacy of wage increases and, second, instituting some governmental machinery to see that these criteria are observed. This procedure in my opinion is neither desirable nor practicable. The criteria must cover such matters as productivity agreements, the treatment of very low wages, the correction of acute shortages of labour in particular markets, the maintenance of equitable differentials, and so on. The effective application of these criteria to basic rates and to overtime rates, to piece-rates and to hourly rates of wages for labour of different skills over a wide range of occupations and industries in a large number of firms in different localities would involve a most far-reaching incursion of governmental control into the whole of the private, free-enterprise sector of the economy. *This is in itself very undesirable*; and the experience of the valiant efforts of the now-defunct Prices and Incomes Board makes me wonder whether in any case so detailed and far-reaching an exercise is practicable.

Another possibility is to work for what is known as a voluntary incomes policy, i.e. to hand over this same formidable task not to a governmental institution but to the joint decision of the TUC and the CBI. I believe this solution to be equally undesirable and equally impracticable. If it could be worked, it would mean that what were in essence public rules and regulations of the most far-reaching importance to the individual workers and employers concerned were determined by the decisions of two private monopolistic organisations in no way responsible to the democratically elected government. If the TUC and the CBI had the power over their members to make this solution possible, then in my opinion they would be usurping powers which properly belong to the government. Fortunately experience suggests that they do not possess the powers necessary to make this solution a practicable one.

I think we must squarely face the fact that trade unions *are* monopolistic organisations in which individuals have banded together to fix a price for what they are selling and that with the present rules and regulations these particular monopolistic bodies have too great a bargaining power.

This is, I know, largely for historical reasons a very emotive subject; and I want to make it clear from the outset that I am not just advocating trade-union bashing. It is true that a trade union is a monopolistic organisation. But even those who, like myself, would like to see as much freedom for private enterprise and trade as is feasible in modern conditions recognise that 'monopolistic' arrangements are often not merely inevitable, but even positively desirable. No one, I think, would suggest that transport by rail or the generation of electricity should be conducted by a very large number of small competing units. The fact that trade unions are monopolistic organisations does not automatically condemn them; and indeed they perform a number of very important, necessary functions. Many of their most important functions in representing the interests of the workers to the managers on many aspects of the conditions of their work and employment have nothing directly to do with wage-fixing. Moreover, where there would otherwise be a very large number of workers facing a very small number of employers, trade unions are needed to provide bargaining power in order to offset the monopso-nistic, exploitative powers of the limited number of employers. Simple, straightforward trade-union bashing is not the answer. But this does not, of course, imply that there should be no social control over their activities. Indeed, in no other sphere of economic life does one consider it desirable that a monopolistic organisation should not be subject to social controls of one kind or another over such matters as the prices it charges or the amounts it supplies.

I think that we must consider the possibility of some simple, practicable means of control over the bargaining powers of the trade unions; and I propose the following very simple scheme.

(1) The government lays down from time to time a 'norm' for the annual percentage rise in wage earnings. Let us speak of this norm as x per cent per annum; and I will discuss later the value of x.

(2) Any group of employers and employees would, however, be perfectly free to reach agreement on any wage or salary bargain, whether or not it implied a rise of earnings above the x per cent per annum norm.

(3) There would, however, be a recognised system of tribunals or courts to which, in the case of a trade dispute about wages or salaries, the matter could be referred in order to obtain a judgement as to whether the increase in pay which was claimed did or did not exceed the x per cent norm.

The functions of these wage tribunals or courts would be very limited, simply and solely to determine whether a particular pay claim would cause the earnings of the workers concerned to be more than x per cent higher than they were a year ago. Even so their task would not be an easy one. It may be remembered that the award of the Wilberforce Commission[6] in February 1971 after the December go-slow of the workers in the supply of electricity was claimed by some to represent a rise of some 20 per cent and by others to represent a rise of little over 10 per cent. The essential task of the tribunals would be to decide whether, taking into account such matters as fringe benefits and the probable effects on overtime, the cost to the employer of employing a given amount of the labour concerned would be raised by more than x per cent. Such a determination might take a little time; and the tribunals would have to be empowered to issue interim judgements which could later be revised by a final determination.

(4) If it were ruled by the tribunal that the pay claim under consideration exceeded the norm of x per cent, then, but only then, regulations would come into force to curb the bargaining power of the workers concerned in pressing the claim. The sort of regulations which

---

[6] *Report of a Court of Inquiry into a Dispute: Electricity Supply Industry*, Cmnd 4594, HMSO, February 1971.

might be appropriate would be: that any workers who went on strike in favour of the claim would lose any accumulated rights to redundancy payments in their existing jobs; that any supplementary benefits paid for the support of their wives and children would become a liability of the trade union that was supporting the strike or, failing that, would be treated as a debt of the individual worker concerned; and that the trade union would be liable to a tax on any strike benefits which it paid out to its members. On the other hand, there would be no curbing of trade unions' bargaining powers in respect of claims which did not exceed the x per cent norm.

The choice of an actual number for the x per cent norm would give the government an important new weapon for the management of the economy. In the present situation it would not be practicable to fix x immediately at a level which would avoid all further inflation. Acute problems of comparability during the transition to stability would arise, since some workers (group A) will have just received, say, a 15 per cent rise in pay, while another group of workers (group B) is caught by the new arrangement just before it has demanded its 15 per cent rise. To set a norm of 3 per cent in such conditions would be grossly unfair to group B. Perhaps an initial norm of 10 per cent might be set.[7] Then as the inflation tailed off the norm could be reduced until some level compatible with general price stability was achieved. What this ultimate level should be would depend upon many things: the severity of the curbs imposed on those who pressed claims which exceeded the norm; the degree to which the government restricted total effective demand and thus maintained a restrictive pressure in the labour market; the extent to which restrictive practices in the various labour markets were controlled; and so on. The norm would merely provide the government with one extra dimension in its control of the economy.

VI Supply and Demand in the Labour Market

I hope that the general philosophy behind these proposals is clear. Free wage-bargaining would in general persist. Any wage agreed between workers and employers would be permissible. No strike or lock-out would be made illegal by these proposals. But there would be serious financial curbs on claims which are both excessive and resisted by employers.

The result would be an absolute minimum of governmental intervention in labour markets. There would, for example, be no need to define legitimate productivity agreements in order to define a permitted

---

[7] Professor Reddaway has suggested to me that the norm might take the form of, say, 30 per cent over the last three years rather than of 10 per cent over the last year. That is to say, the curbs on bargaining power would be applied if a current wage claim would cause wage-earnings this year to be more than 30 per cent in excess of what they were three years ago rather than if it would cause wage-earnings to be more than 10 per cent in excess of what they were one year ago. Such a rule would certainly ease the problem of fairness in the transitional period and might well be a more acceptable form for the long run as well.

exception to a norm for wage increases. Since any agreement reached willingly between employers and employed would be permitted, it would not matter whether or not it could be called a productivity agreement.

Similarly, the difficult – indeed, in my opinion, insoluble – problem of the definition by some governmental body of equity in the comparability of one wage with another would disappear. Comparability might well be taken into account, as it is now, in the determination of wages in a wage-bargain; but that would be a matter for the employers and employees concerned to determine. It is, however, an important negative merit of the proposals which I have put forward that they do not interfere arbitrarily with existing wage comparabilities. My proposals refer equally to all employees whether wage-earners or salaried professionals and whether in private or public employment. In my opinion it is manifestly unfair, and for that very reason I suspect ultimately impracticable, to try to contain inflation by government resistance to wage claims by public servants without any similar resistance to wage claims in the private sector. My proposals would apply equally in all sectors.

In a similar way it would not be the duty of any governmental body to determine whether a specially high wage-rate might be offered to meet a scarcity of labour in a particular labour market. That also would be left to the free determination of the employers and employed in the market concerned. Successful, expanding employers would be free to offer any wage they liked to attract the labour they needed. Wage drift of that kind should not, and with my proposals would not, be frowned upon.

The proposals I have put forward thus have the merit that they in no way impede an upward movement of earnings in markets where there is an excess demand for labour relatively to earnings in markets where there is an excess supply of labour. The wage-rate is the price of labour; and in our sort of mixed economy prices have an important role to play in helping to achieve an efficient use of economic resources. A high market price for a particular resource ruling in a particular market where that resource is scarce will

(i)   help to attract the resource to that market from other markets where it is in more plentiful supply; and
(ii) help to induce the users of that resource where it is scarce to economise in its use.

Both these influences are desirable in the interests of economic efficiency.

I do not wish to imply that the use of resources should simply be left in all cases to the free play of uncontrolled markets. Far from it. Let me take an example. I believe that the social costs of road transport are much higher than those of rail transport. Heavy taxation of road transport used to finance the carriage of heavy goods traffic by rail would in my view be much in the social interest. But after allowance is made for any such interventions and controls there will result a certain demand for railwaymen and a certain demand for road transport workers; and if the other state interventions are correct it will be economically efficient to meet these labour demands. Has the wage-rate a rôle to play here?

Labour is, of course, a very special case, and there are many ways in which it should not be treated just like any other commodity. Men and women and children should be generously supported in childhood, sickness, unemployment, old-age, and other times of dependent need. Moreover, as I shall argue later, radical fiscal and similar measures outside the wage system should be taken to influence the distribution of income and wealth which should not be determined simply by the forces of supply and demand in the labour market. But if such fiscal measures are adequately developed, then relative wage-rates as between different skills, regions, occupations, industries, etc., can be used for the double purpose, first, to induce individual employers to economise in the use of labour where it is scarce and to make free use of it where it is plentiful, and, secondly, to attract labour from firms where it is in plentiful supply to firms where it is scarce.

In so far as labour cannot move easily between regions and occupations, the first of these functions is very important both for the maintenance of full employment and for ensuring the most economic use of available labour resources. If computer programmers are scarce, it is important that they should be used only on the most important and productive tasks; and a high cost for employing a computer programmer will help to cut out wasteful uses of scarce ability. If unskilled workers are available in large numbers in a particular market, it is important that useful tasks they could perform should not be made unprofitable by a high cost for the employment of such workers.

But it is important to promote the movement of labour from uses of low to uses of high social productivity. It is probable that at present the incentive to move from a sector where pay is low to a sector where pay is high is less important than the incentive to move from a sector where there is unemployment to a sector where job opportunities are good.[8] But this does not, of course, automatically ensure the movement of labour from points of low to points of high productivity. Job opportunities for new entrants may be poor in a highly paid occupation just because the cost of labour is maintained there at an artificially high level, and there may be a high unsatisfied demand for labour in another sector just because labour is cheap there. The more readily relative wages can be allowed to respond to true scarcities and surpluses of labour, the less likely are such situations to arise and the more nearly will opportunities for employment be equalised in all sectors. But the more nearly this position is realised, the more important will differences in pay become relatively to differences in job opportunities in attracting labour from depressed to prosperous occupations.

But for this to happen one very important condition must be fulfilled. There must not be any extensive network of restrictions on the entry into particular labour markets. Limitation of entry to a trade to persons trained as apprentices, when the number of apprentices permitted to train is unnecessarily limited or the time and expense of apprenticeship

[8] The evidence for this conclusion is highly persuasive but not conclusive. See 'Note' at the end of this lecture (pages 340–42).

are unduly extended; trade union insistence on pre-entry closed-shop arrangements, whereby only trade unionists may work in a particular sector of industry and the trade union itself limits the number who may join it; professional examination requirements which demand qualifications or time spent in training which are not essential for the proper performance of the professional service; all these and similar restrictive practices may make it impossible or unnecessarily difficult for people to move into a particular labour market. An exceptionally high rate of pay to such a group of workers may be needed to restrict the demand to the artificially restricted supply; but the high rate of pay is not needed to attract labour; indeed, it is paid solely because the labour which would be attracted is artificially excluded.

For this reason a proper set of policies for the control of wage inflation cannot be divorced from a proper set of policies for the removal of unnecessary restrictive practices in labour markets. I cannot in this lecture cover this aspect of the subject, which is a matter for legislation to amend the rules of trade unions and professional associations about the qualifications for employment on particular tasks. The recent Industrial Relations Act is, of course, highly relevant here in its banning of closed shops which might restrict the entry of new labour and in its insistence that a union should admit all persons who are reasonably qualified for the trade in question.

The difficult problem here is, of course, the definition of what qualifications are reasonably needed for a particular job. In many cases where the employer is a business concern which is technically quite capable of judging for itself what skill is necessary and whether any particular applicant has in one way or another acquired that skill, there is really in effect little need for any systematic process of definition of the required skill and for the exclusion of those without that skill. But in some jobs these simple conditions are not fulfilled. This may be the case with certain industrial skills. It is certainly the case with specific professional skills where the 'employer' (for example, the citizen in ill-health or in conflict with the law) needs the services of a professional person (for example, a doctor or lawyer) who is highly trained in techniques which the 'employer' does not begin to understand. Some system for an independent determination of the necessary skills and for an independent judgement on who has and who has not acquired those skills is necessary in cases of this kind. The machinery for this purpose will inevitably depend very largely upon the opinions of the professionals concerned: doctors will know more about the requirements of medical knowledge and lawyers more about the requirements of legal knowledge than anyone else. But even doctors and lawyers are human and will not want their position to be undermined by an avoidable inflation of their numbers. It would seem that the final decision on professional qualifications must not be left to the closed guild of the existing professionals. Some independent body must decide, relying, however, inevitably very largely on the advice of the professionals.

VII   A Critical Look at the Proposals

I fear that I have been tempted to stray somewhat from my main theme. The central point is simply that the proposals I have put forward for the curbing of wage inflation do nothing to impede the movement of relative wages in response to the true relative scarcities of labour in different markets. Any wage-rate freely agreed between employer and employed is permissible.

But may not this very fact mean that my proposals will be ineffective as an anti-inflationary device? It can be argued that there will always be some important sectors where, to maintain smooth relations with the workers, employers will be willing to grant excessive inflationary wage increases and where these increases will set the tone for excessive claims elsewhere to maintain existing differentials and comparabilities.

I do not think that this need be a fatal flaw. Proposals of the kind I have made for the curbing of inflationary wage increases are not, of course, a panacea for all our evils. In particular they are no substitute for monetary and fiscal policies which will properly prevent an excessive inflation of demand. The proposals I have made in this lecture will increase the bargaining power with which employers can resist excessive wage claims; they must be combined with a control of total money demand which means that over the whole range of economic activity producers do not find it easy simply to pass on higher money costs in charging higher money prices without losing sales.

Consider one recent example, namely the wage settlement by Ford in April of this year involving a 16 per cent rise in pay for two successive years which was widely considered to set an unfortunate inflationary pattern. It must be remembered that this wage increase was not given readily, but only after a seven-week strike. Suppose that a 10 per cent norm had been ruling and that the strikers had known that they would lose all their accumulated rights to redundancy payments if they struck for more than this. Suppose that the trade unions concerned had known that they would incur a liability for all supplementary benefits paid to the workers' families and, say, a 100 per cent tax on any strike pay they distributed. Suppose further that the Industrial Relations Act had been in force, ensuring that Ford could employ any labour[9] which was available. Suppose finally, as I shall later propose, that Ford had had to compete

[9] The wage claim made by the Ford workers was based largely on a demand for comparability with the earnings of workers in car manufacture in the Midlands. But has this any more force than comparability between the earnings of Ford workers and the earnings of workers with similar qualifications in and around Dagenham? The pay of Ford workers might be low relatively to that of other workers in the Midlands but high relatively to that of other workers in and around Dagenham. What is the correct comparability? Suppose that in the absence of artificial restrictions the other workers in and around Dagenham could readily and effectively change their occupations to that of car manufacture, but that the geographical movement of car workers from Dagenham to the Midlands was difficult and expensive. There would be a large available supply of workers seeking employment at Ford; and the rate of rise of wages there should be restrained. But if occupational mobility between other workers and car manufacture in and around Dagenham were truly difficult and expensive, while regional mobility for car workers were easy and cheap, suitable labour for Ford at Dagenham would become scarce and an exceptional wage rise would be appropriate.

with foreign cars imported free of all duty. Would it not have been likely that the dispute would have been settled for a rate of rise of wages that did not exceed the ruling 10 per cent norm and did not, therefore, bring into operation the curbs I have suggested?

That my proposals allow wide freedom for wage flexibility on supply–demand grounds may give rise to another type of criticism, namely that they do nothing to discriminate in favour of exceptionally rapid rises for exceptionally low wage-earners. I believe myself to have a strong egalitarian philosophy, and yet I would reject this criticism. Wage-rates, like all prices, have a dual effect. If they are set on supply–demand principles they can help to ensure that the most effective use is made of the available labour; but at the same time they are a major determinant of the distribution of income. The best arrangement in my view is to allow the market wage-rate charged to the employer of labour to be set on supply–demand principles to ensure that employers economise in scarce types of labour and make full use of plentiful types of labour, and then to modify, very radically if necessary, the resulting distribution of income by means of fiscal policies of one kind or another.

The removal of restrictive devices which maintain high earnings in particular professional or industrial occupations by limiting entry to those occupations will itself do something to raise wages in lower-paid outside occupations. It will make it more possible for low-paid persons to move into high-paid jobs; and this will not only help those who do move but, by reducing the supply of labour in the low-paid occupations, will improve the position of those who are left behind.

Upward pressure by trade-union action on money wage-rates in general is not an effective means for redistributing income as between the general body of wages on the one hand and the general body of incomes from property on the other. Experience suggests that the result is in the main merely an inflation of money prices as profit margins are restored or, if prices cannot be raised, some increase in the general level of unemployment. This does not, however, mean that trade unions never have any rôle to play in improving distribution. Particular groups of workers may, of course, be being sweated or exploited because unorganised competitive workers without monopolistic bargaining power are being employed by a set of tightly organised, monopsonistic employers. In such circumstances the organisation of workers' interests through a trade union or some form of government wage council is the answer. But even when all monopsonistic exploitation has been removed, a low wage may be needed in some labour markets in order to give scope for the full employment of the labour available in that market. In such conditions the imposition of a substantially higher minimum wage or the exceptional pushing up of the wage-rate on the grounds of equalising this particularly low wage-rate with the higher earnings available to other workers may well lead to the unemployment of the less-qualified workers. Far better in my opinion is to have some system for the subsidisation of low incomes rather than to impose a minimum wage-rate or otherwise artificially to 'jack-up' the wage-rates of well-organised (but nevertheless low-paid) workers.

There are a wide range of fiscal devices for the redistribution of income and wealth. In this lecture I cannot possibly discuss them at length. They include such measures as the reform of death duties and of the laws of inheritance designed to produce a much greater equality of inherited property; specially favourable opportunities for the accumulation of property by those who are less well-off; the progressive taxation of high incomes and the direct subsidisation of low incomes; the bringing into the tax net of exempt incomes, such as the Schedule A value of owner-occupied houses, so that property owners may not receive substantial slices of tax-free income; the development of social benefits and of educational and other opportunities for upward mobility; and so on. I would advocate a radical development on these lines; and if such a development were achieved *pari passu* with the reform of wage-fixing institutions on the lines I have advocated, it would perhaps help to make the application of the supply–demand principle to wages politically more acceptable.

VIII   Bringing Profits and Prices into the Net

There remains one further fundamental matter which I must discuss. I have so far spoken solely about the determination of *rates of pay*, i.e. of wages and salaries. But should not the same principles be applied to other forms of income and, in particular, to profits and profit margins?

I agree wholeheartedly that just as some social control of the kind which I have outlined is necessary over the exercise of monopolistic bargaining power of trade unions and similar professional organisations, so some social control is needed over the exercise of monopolistic power by the producers and sellers of commodities. In addition I would argue that, just as in the case of wages and salaries, any further redistribution of income and wealth should be a matter for fiscal and similar policies and not for wage and price control. Thus the curbing of monopolistic powers by producers of products will help to restrain profit margins; but if a further move in the direction of redistribution of income is required from rich to poor this should be achieved by progressive taxation and similar fiscal devices and not by additional direct controls over selling prices or profit margins.

Up to this point, I would agree, the case for social control over prices or profit margins is on all fours with the case for social control over wages and salaries. But the methods of application of control must be quite different in the two cases and for this reason the two sets of problems should be tackled by two different sets of institutions. This does not, of course, imply that they should not be tackled simultaneously and with equal vigour.

The reason why different methods of attack are appropriate is simple. The sort of wage bargains which may need social control are typically those that take place between a monopolistic organisation on the supply side (namely, a trade union) and a monopsonistic organisation on the demand side (namely, an employers' association or a large-scale single employer) – what we economists call a case of bilateral monopoly. Such a case can be handled by my suggestion for taking steps to regulate the bargaining strength of the parties in this bilateral bargain. But this is not at all the typical situation in a case of a monopolistic sale of a product. A large-scale manufacturer of cars does not strike a bargain over the price of cars with a consumers' association, or with one large-scale consumer. There are many independent, unorganised consumers facing the large-scale monopolistic seller. This situation cannot be controlled by measures designed to affect bargaining strengths on one side or the other.

But measures can be taken to curb monopolistic action by producers and to encourage price competition among them. First, there are the measures designed to curb the growth of monopoly power by restricting mergers, combines, and similar developments and measures designed to outlaw restrictive practices by producers. I cannot in this lecture discuss these measures which we associate with the work of the Monopolies Commission and with the operation of the Restrictive Practices Act. It would, however, be possible for these measures to be supplemented by more specific controls over certain prices. Detailed governmental control over all selling prices is, in my opinion, impracticable and undesirable for just the same reasons which I argued earlier in the case of detailed governmental control over all wages and salaries. But there is much to be said in favour of a system of the following kind. An official council might be set up with the specific duty of bringing complaints to government departments who would be empowered to refer to the Monopolies Commission the question whether in a particular case a particular producer was charging prices which represented undesirable monopolistic profit margins. If such were ruled to be the case, the producer in question could be required to reduce his prices accordingly.

There are other less direct ways of preventing monopolistic abuses and encouraging competition. I will mention two controversial possibilities. First, the present arrangements whereby undistributed profits are taxed less heavily than distributed profits should be reversed. If the finance of capital development from ploughed-back funds was heavily discouraged by taxation, companies would have to compete on the open capital market for new funds, which would promote competition in favour of the most promising new enterprises. Second, the discouragement of advertising through the taxation of advertisement expenditures, the removal of advertising from television, and so on, could induce producers to compete more by charging lower prices rather than by spending money on advertising, much of which is designed to build up the monopolistic market power of the producer by 'bamboozling' the consumer into thinking that there is something unique about a particular brand.

IX Free Imports Most Effective Weapon

But far and away the most effective way of promoting competition and curbing monopolistic powers would be to admit the free import of goods from all foreign sources; and this would also make producers who had to face foreign competition more willing to resist inflationary wage-claims.

This possibility opens up the whole question of our financial and economic relations with the rest of the world. Membership of the European Economic Community would, of course, open us up to the direct competition of the manufactures of Germany, France, Italy, and the Benelux countries. A North American Free Trade Area or a unilateral move back to our ancient and honourable free trade policy would be even more effective from this point of view.[10]

But whatever form it takes, free importation raises basic problems of the mechanism for maintaining equilibrium in our balance of payments. There must be some effective means other than import restriction for us to combine full employment at home with a balanced balance of payments. One method would be to allow the exchange rate to vary so as to reconcile our own domestic policies for the control of demand and the regulation of wage inflation with the needs of external economic and financial conditions; and this is the method which I would myself advocate.

There is, however, serious talk of the EEC developing into a monetary union in which there would not only be free trade between the members, but in which the members would share a common money or, at least, operate a system of rigidly and immutably fixed exchange rates. If we are seriously to contemplate such a possibility, I suggest that there are three basic necessary conditions, all of which must be simultaneously satisfied.

First, the members of the monetary union must have an effective joint monetary and fiscal policy to stabilise total monetary demand within the monetary union as a whole. If recessions of total demand within the monetary union as a whole were a real possibility, the adjustments of cost–price structures in the UK necessary to reconcile full employment with a balanced balance of payments might be altogether too large to be manageable.

Second, the members of the monetary union must be assured in one way or another of extensive currency reserves to finance substantial imbalances in the balance of payments, since relative cost–price adjustments between the members will undoubtedly be necessary from time to time and cannot be expected to operate very quickly.

Finally, membership of a free-trade monetary union would make some governmental control over the degree of wage–cost inflation in the UK absolutely essential. Without it we would be continually subject to the risk that we should have to face prolonged periods of unemployment and low levels of economic activity in the interests of balance-of-payments equilibrium. Whether or not the particular proposals which I have put before you would be sufficient for this purpose is a question which only experience of them could answer. For the time being I must, alas, leave you to form your own unaided judgement.

---

[10] I have given a more detailed analysis for and against these alternatives in *UK, Commonwealth & Common Market: A Reappraisal*, Hobart Paper 17, 3rd edition (London: Institute of Economic Affairs, 1971). [See Volume III, Chapters 16 and 17.]

Note on the Measurement of Influences Affecting the Allocation of Labour

Recent investigations[11] have suggested that differences in wage-earnings play a relatively small part in attracting labour from one occupation to another. It is implied that labour is re-allocated among occupations rather by the fact that jobs are offered in expanding sectors while unemployment rules in contracting sectors. The basic method of these investigations is to compare over a series of years (i) the rise in earnings, and (ii) the increase in employment in various sectors, in order to see whether exceptionally high increases in pay have been associated with exceptionally high increases in the labour available. The result has in general been to find (1) that changes in employment have been very great relatively to changes in pay and (2) that there is little if any positive correlation between rises in pay and rises in employment.

If changes in employment were due solely to changes in the demand for the various products of labour, the absence of a positive correlation between wage increases and increases in numbers employed would imply that relative wages played a small part and that some other mechanism (such as unemployment in contracting industries and good job opportunities in expanding industries) had been the main factor leading to the movement of labour.

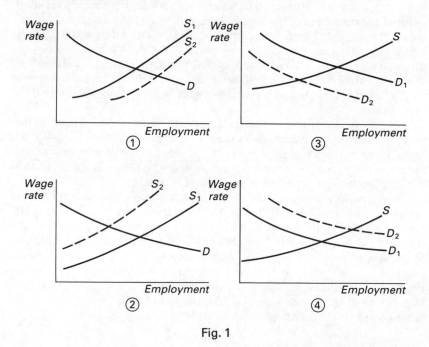

Fig. 1

[11] W. B. Reddaway, 'Wage Flexibility and the Distribution of Labour'. *Lloyds Bank Review*, no. 54 (October 1959), pp. 32–48; Report by an Expert Group for the OECD, *Wages and Labour Mobility*, OECD, 1965.

But suppose that there have also been important changes on the supply side in various labour markets. (And there have in fact been at least some very important changes of this kind such as the increase in the supply of white-collar workers due to the expansion of educational opportunities or the reduction in the supply of coal-miners because of the abnormal age distribution of coal-miners after the Second World War.) Then one would expect to find relative pay declining where employment had been increased because of the increased supply of labour, and pay increasing where employment had declined because of the scarcity of the supply of labour.

Consider an economy in which there were changes over a period of time in the following four sectors (Fig. 1):

In sector (1) the supply of labour at any given pay has risen; in sector (2) the supply of labour has fallen; in sector (3) the demand for labour has fallen; and in sector (4) the demand has risen. In all cases both supply and demand are very sensitive to changes in pay. The scatter diagram between percentage changes in employment and percentage changes in pay would be as in Fig. 2.

The movements of employment would be very large compared with movements in pay and there would be no correlation between the two. Yet supplies of labour and demands for labour are both very sensitive to relative changes in pay, and we need not rely on any other mechanism to explain the re-allocation of labour.

This Note is not intended to deny the great importance of relative job opportunities. It is merely maintained that in the absence of any distinction between the importance of shifts on the demand side and shifts on the supply side in labour markets, the method used does not provide any conclusive evidence of the unimportance of relative pay as such in attracting labour.

It is strange that those who put so much emphasis on job opportunities have not made the direct comparison between relative levels of unemployment (and/or of vacancies) and relative expansions of the labour supply in various sectors. To what extent is there exceptionally low

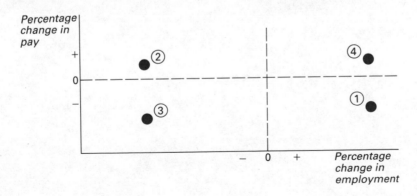

Fig. 2

unemployment in contracting occupations (because workers are moving elsewhere and the supply is diminished) rather than exceptionally high unemployment (which is driving workers to seek jobs elsewhere)? It would be interesting to know.

20

The Keynesian Revolution

From Milo Keynes (ed.), Essays on John Maynard Keynes *(London: Cambridge University Press, 1975), pp. 82–88*

Was there ever a Keynesian Revolution and, if so, what was it? Any short answer to these questions, particularly if it is designed to be of interest to those who are not professional economists, is bound to be a gross oversimplification. Not only are the problems themselves of some technical complexity; but one of the outstanding features of Keynes' mind was its intuitive subtlety and flexibility. As a result commentators have found it easy to make quips about Keynes' inconsistencies, but the fact that Keynes was trying continuously to relate his very extensive experiences in the real world of affairs in an intuitive manner to the revision of standard economic theory was of the essence of his genius. His thinking never stood still and his critique of the existing corpus of economic doctrine was constructed out of many and various – and in some cases rather subtle – components.

In spite of this, one can, I think, pick out one rather simple and precise relationship which is the quintessence of Keynes' intellectual innovation. I shall concentrate solely on this one single feature, which has not only changed the typical economist's approach to his problems but has also had a far-reaching effect on government economic policies. There are in fact two distinct, though closely related, Keynesian Revolutions: first, the theoretical revolution in economic analysis; and, second, the practical revolution in governmental policies. I will discuss each of these in turn.

Keynes' intellectual revolution was to shift economists from thinking normally in terms of a model of reality in which a dog called *savings* wagged his tail labelled *investment* to thinking in terms of a model in which a dog called *investment* wagged his tail labelled *savings*. Let me explain. Investment is defined as the flow of expenditure of money on additions to the real capital equipment of the community (additions to plant, machinery, stocks of goods, houses, etc.) and savings is defined as that amount of their flow of incomes which people decide not to spend on consumption goods (food, clothing and so on). Before the Keynesian Revolution a normal way of starting to think about the relationship between savings and investment would have been in terms of models of the following kind: out of given real incomes people decide to spend a certain amount on consumption goods: they save the remainder; these savings flow on to the money and capital markets and constitute what is directly or indirectly available for borrowing by entrepreneurs and others to spend on new capital equipment; if savings go up, more funds are available on the capital market; the cost of borrowing falls; accordingly more is spent on investment in real capital goods; if people do not decide to increase their savings, it is not possible to finance an increase in investment.

It was thinking of this kind which lay behind the notorious 'Treasury view' of the 1920s and early 1930s. At that time the United Kingdom was experiencing a period of heavy unemployment of labour and underutilisation of industrial capital equipment. Lloyd George and others (including Keynes himself) were advocating a policy of public works (i.e. public investment schemes) to put the unemployed to work. The Treasury view, which opposed these proposals, was that if savings were borrowed for public works there would be just so much less savings available on the capital markets to finance private investment. The result would be merely to substitute less productive public investment for more productive private investment.

There was clearly something wrong with this line of argument in a period of mass unemployment. In a period of full employment, when it is impossible to produce more goods and services in general, the argument would hold. If people are buying a given amount of consumption goods, then there is left over a certain amount of resources to produce capital equipment. In conditions in which these productive resources are fully employed, if the public sector takes up more of these investment resources it must drain them from the private sector. But in a period of mass unemployment this conclusion does not necessarily hold. More goods and services can be produced for all uses. An increase in public investment does not necessarily imply any reduction in private investment or in consumption. The Treasury view was applying to conditions of mass unemployment a mode of thought that was suitable for conditions of full employment.

Keynes started at the other end. His reasoning ran on the following lines. Drop the assumption that there is a given level of real income. Suppose instead that we start with a given level of the flow of investment expenditures. This is sensible because investment is in fact influenced primarily by outside or 'exogenous' influences such as the confidence and expectations of business men in the case of private investment and governmental decisions in the case of public investment. These investment expenditures will generate the payment of wages, rents, interest, profits, etc. to those engaged in producing the capital equipment in question. Those engaged in the production of these capital goods will save some of the incomes so earned but will spend the rest on consumption goods. The producers of these consumption goods will thus earn incomes, part of which they will save but part of which they will in turn spend on other consumption goods, thus generating still other incomes which will be partly saved and partly spent on consumption, and so on. This process will generate a converging series of ever-diminishing waves of expenditures which will result in a finite level of demand for goods and services to meet both the original investment demand and the subsequent induced demands for consumption goods. The level of economic activity so generated may or may not be sufficient to provide full employment for the available productive resources in the community. If it is insufficient, why not do something to increase the original injection of the flow of investment expenditures into the system?

Such was the famous Keynesian Multiplier, expressing total income as a multiple of investment. This relationship could be expressed in another way. Investment expenditure could be regarded as an injection from outside of a flow of purchasing power into an income-generating system; savings could be regarded as a leakage of purchasing power out of this income-generating system. Given an initial injection of investment demand into the system, incomes would be generated by a succession of waves of induced demand for consumption goods until the resulting leakage out (savings) was equal to the original injection in (investment). The greater the level of investment and the lower the proportion of their income which people decide to save, the higher would be the level of the resulting effective demand for goods and services and so the demand for output and for the employment of labour.

It was an easy extension of this mode of thought to realise that private investment was not the only element of demand for goods and services that might best be regarded as an exogenous injection from outside into the income-generating cycle, and that savings was not the only possible leakage of purchasing power out of this income-generating cycle. Government expenditure on goods and services of all kinds also constitutes an injection of purchasing power into the system which can be exogenously determined by government policy; and corresponding to this injection there is a leakage of purchasing power out of the income-generating system in the form of the direct and indirect taxes which people must pay out of their increased incomes and expenditures. The demand for a country's exports may also be regarded as primarily determined by what is going on in other countries outside the country in question and thus may be regarded as representing another injection from outside of purchasing power into the system, and corresponding to this there is a leakage of purchasing power out of a country's income-generating process in so far as its citizens spend their incomes on imports rather than on home-produced goods. We may regard the system then as one in which

$$
\text{the flow of}
\left\{
\begin{array}{c}
\text{investment} \\
+ \\
\text{government} \\
\text{expenditure} \\
+ \\
\text{exports}
\end{array}
\right\}
\text{into the system} =
$$

$$
\text{the flow of}
\left\{
\begin{array}{c}
\text{savings} \\
+ \\
\text{tax} \\
\text{revenue} \\
+ \\
\text{imports}
\end{array}
\right\}
\begin{array}{c}
\text{out of the} \\
\text{system}
\end{array}
$$

The left-hand side is the Keynesian dog and the right-hand side is the Keynesian tail. The inflow on the left-hand side, by a series of repercussions, raises the demand for consumption goods until incomes are earned on such a scale that there is an equal outflow on the right-hand side.

But how was one to judge between this Keynesian view and the then prevailing Treasury view? Suppose that a policy of substantial public works expenditures were adopted and that the increased borrowing for the finance of this programme did cause such an increase in the rate of interest and the general difficulty of acquiring finance that competing private projects were stifled, so that there was no net increase in investment. If this happened, then there would be no net additional investment to be financed but also no net additional finance in the form of savings generated through a Keynesian Multiplier. The Treasury view would be justified. Suppose, however, on the other hand that the public works expenditures did not supplant existing investment expenditures, then there would be a net additional injection of investment demand into the system which would generate additional incomes and so additional savings on a scale sufficient to finance the new public works. The Keynesian view would be justified. Both results might seem at first sight to be equally plausible. Is it a pure toss-up which happens?

Keynes argued for the validity of his view through his analysis of the basic nature of the money and capital markets. People hold money for two broadly distinguished purposes. First, they must hold a stock of active money to finance the turnover of their business, commercial, and domestic purchases and sales of goods and services. Second, they may well choose to hold additional sums of idle money as a liquid asset in preference to other forms of capital asset. It is true that if they hold idle money on which the yield is low or non-existent, they will lose the yield in interest or dividends or rents which they might have obtained if they had put their funds into other less liquid assets. But there are certain advantages in holding some part of their funds in the form of liquid money, which is a safe asset which can be used quickly and readily to meet unforeseen contingencies; and there will be an additional reason for holding money rather than other assets, if it is thought that the current market prices of such assets (such as security prices on the Stock Exchange) are on the high side so that they are more likely to fall than to rise in the near future. Such was Keynes' Liquidity Preference theory, expressing the fact that the higher the price of non-liquid assets such as Stock Exchange securities and the lower their yield, the greater would be the relative attraction of holding idle balances of liquid money instead of other income-earning assets.

Armed with this Liquidity Preference theory Keynes could justify the Keynesian view in the following way. Suppose that increased borrowing by the government through the sale of additional government bonds to finance a public works programme did initially tend to cause some fall in the price of such securities and thus some rise in the rate of yield on them. The Keynesian view would be substantially correct if a fall in security prices and a rise in interest rates (1) had little effect in discouraging other competing investment projects but (2) had much effect in inducing people who were holding idle liquid balances of money to purchase other assets such as securities which were now somewhat cheaper and provided a somewhat higher yield. For in this case the fall in security prices and the rise in interest rates would be quickly checked by those who were using their idle liquid balances for the purchase of these securities; and any small increase in interest rates which did nevertheless occur would have a negligible effect in cutting back existing investment projects. On the other hand, the Treasury view would be substantially correct if a fall in security prices and a rise in interest rates (1) had much effect in discouraging other competing investment projects but (2) had little effect in inducing people who were holding idle liquid balances of money to purchase securities which were now cheaper. For in this case there would be nothing to prevent a heavy decline in security prices and rise in interest rates; and this would have a very marked effect in cutting back on existing investment projects.

The Keynesian effect could, of course, always be made to operate by means of monetary policy. If, when the government issued new bonds to finance public works, there was not a sufficient shift out of existing liquid balances of idle money to prevent a substantial rise in the cost of borrowing, a suitable purchase of government bonds by the banking system with newly created money could play the necessary role in preventing any increase in the cost of borrowing or difficulty in finding finances for existing investment projects. In the absence of a suitable monetary policy the effect could in theory be partly of the Keynesian and partly of the Treasury variety; but it was Keynes' contention that in fact – particularly at a time of great economic depression with an excess of idle funds waiting for profitable outlets – the nature of the demands for money and for other capital assets was such to justify his view, even in the absence of an expansionary monetary policy.

Thus the Keynesian theoretical revolution can be expressed in terms of the combination of his Multiplier theory with his Liquidity Preference theory. It would, however, do a grave injustice to many earlier and contemporary economists to suggest that they were oblivious either of the fact that exogenously determined changes in such variables as investment could affect the level of activity in the economy or of the importance of the nature of the demand for money in influencing such effects. On the contrary, much analysis of the trade cycle and of other phenomena had been based on relationships of just this kind. But nearly all intellectual revolutions have their roots in the work of forerunners. It was Keynes' great contribution to start with investment wagging savings and to build modifications on to that model, rather than to start with savings wagging investment and to build modifications on to that model.

Since Keynes made us all think in these – at that time apparently topsy-turvy – terms, there has been much sophisticated work attempting to incorporate these and other relationships into dynamic models of the whole system; but nearly all such models start now from the basic Keynesian original.

Such in my opinion was the essence of Keynes' intellectual revolution.

The revolution in practical governmental policy is of much greater importance and significance for the welfare of mankind. But it can be expressed and discussed in many fewer words. It is now universally recognised by governments, at least throughout the industrialised free-enterprise world, that it is one of their primary duties to control the level of total effective demand for goods and services. If demand is insufficient to provide full employment, it is the government's duty to raise it by stimulating the injections (investment, government expenditure, and/or exports) and/or by discouraging the leakages (by reducing the proportions of income saved, paid in taxes, or spent on imports). If demand is excessive, then it is the government's duty to restrain the injections and to encourage the leakages. This general task of controlling the level of total effective demand throughout the economy was not recognised to be a duty of government before the Second World War; it has been generally so recognised since the war.

How far is this revolution in government policy due to Keynes or how far simply to the bitter experience of the wastes of mass unemployment between the two world wars? One cannot give any precise answer to this question. But one can at least assert with confidence that Keynes' great intellectual contribution hastened the change and that the execution of this new governmental obligation is nowadays conceived in Keynesian categories.

The overall stabilisation of a modern economy must be thought of in two parts: first, a stabilisation of effective demand in the sense that the real demand for real goods and services of all kinds for all purposes must be kept at a level which will provide full employment, but not more than full employment, for the available real resources of labour, land, capital equipment, etc. in the economy. But that, alas, as we are learning by bitter experience is not the whole of the story. In conditions of modern industrial and trade union organisation such a level of real demand has come to be habitually accompanied by an inflationary upsurge of money costs and prices. Keynes, if anyone, can be regarded as the architect of the system designed to maintain effective real demand at the full-employment level. Would that he were alive to exercise his ingenious and fertile mind on the problem to which the very success of his construction has in large measure contributed – namely the problem of making a high and sustained level of *real* economic activity compatible with a restraint of those inflationary rises in *money* prices and wage-rates which are so naturally demanded and so readily conceded in conditions of a sustained high level of demand for the goods and services in question.

21

The Meaning of 'Internal Balance'

Meade's Nobel Memorial Lecture, delivered in Stockholm on 8 December 1977, and reproduced in The Economic Journal, *vol. 88 (1978), pp. 423–435.*

I

It is a special privilege for me on this occasion to have my name associated with that of Professor Bertil Ohlin. By the younger generation of economists we are no doubt both regarded as what in my country and now in his own are now termed senior citizens; but I am just that much younger than Professor Ohlin to have regarded him as one of the already established figures when I was first trying to understand international economics. His great work (Ohlin, 1933) on *International and Interregional Trade* opened up new insights into the complex of relationships between factor supplies, costs of movement of products and factors, price relationships, and the actual international trade in products, migration of persons, and flows of capital. Of the two volumes which I later wrote on International Economic Policy – namely, *The Balance of Payments* and *Trade and Welfare* (Meade, 1951, 1955) – it is in the latter that the influence of this work by Professor Ohlin is most clearly marked.

Professor Ohlin also made an important contribution to what now might be called the macro-economic aspects of a country's balance of payments. In 1929 in the *Economic Journal* he engaged in a famous controversy with Keynes on the problem of transferring payments from one country to another across the foreign exchanges. In this he laid stress upon the income–expenditure effects of the reduced spending power in the paying country and of the increased spending power in the recipient country. In doing so he made use of the usual distinction between a country's imports and exports; but in addition he emphasised the importance of the less usual distinction between a country's domestic non-tradeable goods and services and its tradeable, exportable and importable, goods. I made some use of this latter distinction in my *Balance of Payments*; but looking back I regret that I did not let it play a much more central role in that book.

II

Indeed I realise now, looking back with the advantage of hindsight, that my two books were deficient in many respects. From this rich field of deficiencies I have selected one as the subject for today's lecture, because it raises an issue which in my opinion is at the present time perhaps the most pressing of all for the maintenance of a decent international economic order.

The basic analysis in *The Balance of Payments* was conducted in terms of static equilibrium models rather than in terms of dynamic growing or disequilibrium models. The use of this method of comparative statics was a result of Keynes' work.

Keynes (1936) in *The General Theory* applied Marshall's short-period analysis to the whole macro-economic system instead of to one single firm or industry. In this model additions to capital stocks are taking place; but we deal with a period of time over which the addition to the stock bears a negligible ratio to the total existing stock. Variable factors, and in particular labour, are applied to this stock with a rising marginal cost until marginal cost is equal to selling price – an assumption which can be modified to accommodate micro-economic theories about determinants of output and prices in conditions of imperfect competition. The rest of the Keynesian analysis with its consumption function, liquidity preference, and investment function can be used to determine the short-period, static, stable equilibrium levels of total national income, output, employment, interest, and so on, in terms of such parameters as the money wage-rate, the supply of money, entrepreneurs' expectations, rates of tax, levels of government expenditure, and the foreign demand for the country's exports. The model can then be used to show how changes in these parameters would affect the short-period equilibrium levels of the various macro-economic variables. Keynes was not, I think, interested in the process of change from one short-period equilibrium to another, though he was very interested in the way in which expectations in a milieu of uncertainty would affect the short-period equilibrium, in particular through their effect upon investment. If my interpretation is correct, he judged intuitively that the short-period mechanisms of adjustment were in fact such that at any one time the macro-elements of the system would not be far different from their short-period equilibrium values; and he may well have been correct in this judgement in the 1930s.

The Balance of Payments was essentially based on macro-economic models of this kind. What I tried to elaborate was the international interplay between a number of national economies of this Keynesian type. For this purpose I discussed the different combinations of policy variables which would serve to reconcile what I called 'external balance' with what I called 'internal balance'. By 'external balance' was meant a balance in the country's international payments; and although this idea presents, and indeed at the time was realised to present, considerable conceptual difficulties, nevertheless I still instinctively feel that it is not a foolish one. But can the same be said of the idea of 'internal balance'? Does it mean full employment or does it mean price stability?

I don't believe that I was quite so stupid as not to realise that full employment and price stability are two quite different things. But one treated them under the same single umbrella of 'internal balance' because of a belief or an assumption that if one maintained a level of effective demand which preserved full employment one would also find that the money price level was reasonably stable. The reason for making this tacit or open assumption was, of course, due to a tacit or open assumption that the money wage-rate was normally either constant or at least very sluggish in its movements. In this case with the Keynesian model the absolute level of money prices would be rather higher or lower according as the level of effective demand moved the economy to a higher or lower point on the upward-sloping short-period marginal cost curve. But there would be no reason to expect a rapidly rising or falling general level of money prices in any given short-period equilibrium position.

This may have been a very sensible assumption to make in the 1930s. It is more doubtful whether it was a sensible assumption to make in the immediate post-war years when *The Balance of Payments* was being written. In any case if I were now rewriting that book I would do the underlying analysis not in terms of the reconciliation of the two objectives of external balance and internal balance, but in terms of the reconciliation of the three objectives of equilibrium in the balance of payments, full employment, and price stability.

Why did I not proceed in this way in the first place?

I was certainly aware of the danger that trade union and other wage-fixing institutions might not permit the maintenance of full employment without a money cost–price inflation. But I suppose that writing immediately after the war I adopted the basic model which was so useful before the war and simply hoped that somehow or another it would be possible to avoid full employment leading to a wage–price inflation. Having done so I found that there remained quite enough important international relationships to examine even on that simplifying assumption. That is not perhaps a very strong defence of my position, but I suspect that it is the truth of the matter.

I am well aware that I could now adopt a more sophisticated line of defence of my past behaviour. It is quite possible to define as the natural level of employment, that level which – given the existing relevant institutions affecting wage-fixing arrangements – would lead to a demand for real wage-rates rising at a rate equal to the rate of increase of labour productivity. One has only to add to this the assumption that one starts from a position in which there is no general expectation of future inflation or deflation of money prices to reach the position in which the maintenance of this natural level of employment is compatible with price stability. If this natural level of employment is treated as 'full employment', one has succeeded in defining a situation of 'internal balance' in which 'full employment' and 'price stability' can be simultaneously achieved.

One could then go on to discuss the many institutions which affect this so-called full employment level. Decent support of the living standards of those who are out of work may mean that unemployed persons are legitimately rather more choosy about the first alternative job which is offered to them, quite apart from the existence of a limited number of confirmed 'sturdy beggars' who prefer living on social benefits to an honest day's work. The obligation to make compulsory severance or redundancy payments when employees are dismissed may make some employers less willing to expand their labour force in conditions in which future developments are uncertain. Monopolistic trade union action may put an extra upward pressure on money wage demands which means that unemployment must be maintained at a higher level in order to exert an equivalent countervailing downward pressure. Some statutory wage-fixing bodies in particular occupations may exert a similar influence.

It is not very helpful to squabble about definitions. There is, however, a very real difference of substance between those who do, and those who do not, consider these labour market institutions to cause very real difficulties. Is it necessary to achieve some radical reform of these institutions in order to make reasonable price stability compatible with reasonably low levels of unemployment? Or is it a fact that, if affairs could for a time be so conducted as to remove the expectation of any marked future inflation of the money cost of living, we would find that even with present institutions the natural level of unemployment would not be at all excessive? I myself would expect that in many countries including the United Kingdom the recasting of labour market institutions would still be found to be of crucial importance.

As far as the less important question of definition is concerned, I prefer to think of 'full employment' and 'price stability' as being two separate and often conflicting objectives of macro-economic policies. Anyone who has this preference can, of course, be legitimately challenged to define what is meant by full employment. Perhaps I would be driven to the extreme of defining full employment as that level of employment at which the supply–demand conditions would not lead to attempts to push up the real wage-rate more rapidly than the rate of increase in labour productivity if there were perfect competition in the labour market – no monopsonistic employers, no monopolistic trade unions, no social benefits to the unemployed, no obligations on employers to make compulsory severance or redundancy payments to dismissed workers, and so on – though I am not at all sure whether this extreme form of definition has much meaning. However, in so far as full employment could be defined somewhere along these lines, one would end up with price stability and full employment as separate macro-economic objectives in any real world situation with labour market institutions as one of the instruments of policy. This is the way in which I like to think of macro-economic problems.

If one adopted this approach, how should *The Balance of Payments* be recast? In the basic model we would have the three targets of external balance, full employment, and price stability. If one continued to think in terms of matching to each 'target' a relevant policy 'weapon', one could divide the weapons into three main armouries: the first containing the weapons which directly affect the level of money demands (e.g. monetary and budgetary policies); the second containing the weapons which directly affect the fixing of money wage-rates; and the third containing the weapons which directly affect the foreign exchanges, such as the fixing of rates of exchange, measures of exchange control, and commercial policy measures designed directly to affect the total value of imports and exports.

My subsequent education in the rudiments of the theory of the control of dynamic systems suggested to me that this was not the best way to have proceeded. One should not pair each particular weapon off with a particular target as its partner, using weapon A to hit target A, weapon B to hit target B, and so on. Rather one should seek to discover what pattern of combination of simultaneous use of all available weapons would produce the most preferred pattern of combination of simultaneous hits on all the desirable targets. With this way of looking at things no particular weapon is concentrated on any particular target; it is the joint effect of all the weapons on all the targets which is relevant.

There is no doubt that this is the way in which a control engineer will look at the problem and that in a technical sense it is the correct way to find the most preferred pattern of hits on a number of targets simultaneously. For a considerable period between the writing of *The Balance of Payments* and the present time I was fully enamoured of this method.

I am now, however, in the process of having second thoughts and of asking myself whether the idea of trying to hit each particular target by use of a particular weapon or clearly defined single armoury of weapons is really to be ruled out. This onset of second childhood is due to a consideration of the political conditions in which economic policies must be operated. It is most desirable in a modern democratic community that the ordinary man or woman in the streets should as far as possible realise what is going on, with responsibilities for success or failure in the different fields of endeavour being dispersed but clearly defined and allocated. To treat the whole of macro-economic control as a single subject for the mysterious art of the control engineer is likely to appear at the best magical and at the worst totally arbitrary and unacceptable to the ordinary citizen. To put each clearly defined weapon or armoury of weapons in the charge of one particular authority or set of decision makers with the responsibility of hitting as nearly as possible one well-defined target is a much more intelligible arrangement.

Of course there are obvious disadvantages in any such proposal. Thus the best way for authority A to use weapon A to achieve objective A will undoubtedly be affected by what authorities B and C are doing with weapons B and C. It depends upon the structure of relationships within the economic system how far these repercussions are of major importance. Perhaps a mysterious dynamic model operated inconspicuously in some back room by control experts for silent information of the authorities concerned might be useful; and in any case in the real world it would be desirable for the different authorities at least to communicate their plans to each other so that, by what one hopes would be a convergent process of mutual accommodation, some account could be taken of their interaction. But in the modern community there is, I think, merit in arrangements in which each authority or set of decision makers has a clear ultimate responsibility for success or failure in the attainment of a clearly defined objective.

III

There are six ways in which each of three weapons can be separately aimed at each of three targets. Some of these patterns make more sense than others. In this lecture I can do no more than give a brief account of that particular pattern which, as it seems to me at present, would make the best sense if one takes into account both economic effectiveness and also comprehensibility of responsibilities in a free democratic society.

With this pattern:

(1)   the instruments of demand management, fiscal and monetary, would be used so to control total money expenditures as to prevent excessive inflations or deflations of total money incomes;

(2)   wage-fixing institutions would be modelled so as to restrain upward movements of money wage-rates in those particular sectors where there were no shortages of manpower and to allow upward movements where these were needed to attract or retain labour to meet actual or expected manpower shortages. This should result in the preservation of full employment with some moderate average rise in money wage-rates in conditions in which demand management policies were ensuring a steadily growing money demand for labour as a whole; and

(3)   foreign exchange policies would be used to keep the balance of payments in equilibrium.

This pattern implies the use of the weapons of demand management to restrain *monetary* inflation and of wage-fixing to influence the *real* level of employment and output. Many of my friends and colleagues who share my admiration for Keynes will at this point part company from me. 'Surely', they will say, 'you have got it the wrong way round. Did not Keynes suggest that the control of demand should be used to influence the total amount of real output and employment which it was profitable to maintain, while the money wage-rate was left simply to determine the absolute level of money prices and costs at which this level of real activity would take place?' I agree that this is in fact the way in which Keynes looked at things in the late 1930s when it could be assumed that the money wage-rate was in any case constant or rather sluggish in its movements. What he would be saying today is anybody's guess; and I do not propose to take part in that guessing game except to say that he would be appalled at the current rates of price inflation. It is a complete misrepresentation of the views of a great and wise man to suggest that in present conditions he would have been concerned only with the maintenance of full employment, and not at all with the avoidance of money price and wage inflation.

Whatever Keynes' policy recommendations would be in present circumstances, I would maintain that the way in which I have distributed the weapons among the targets is in no way incompatible with Keynes' analysis. In the 1930s Keynes argued, rightly or wrongly, that cutting money wage-rates would have little effect in expanding employment because its main effect would be simply to reduce the absolute level of the relevant money prices, money costs, money incomes, and money expenditures, leaving the levels of real output and employment much unchanged. It is a totally different matter, wholly consistent with that Keynesian analysis, to suggest that the money wage-rate might be used to influence the level of employment in conditions in which the money demand was being successfully managed in such a way as to prevent changes in wage-rates from causing any offsetting rise or fall in total money incomes and expenditures. If one is going to aim particular weapons at particular targets in the interests of democratic understanding and responsibility, it is, in my opinion, most appropriate that the Central Bank which creates money and the Treasury which pours it out should be responsible for preventing monetary inflations and deflations, while those who fix the wage-rates in various sectors of the economy should take responsibility for the effect of their action on the resulting levels of employment.

Earlier I spoke of 'price stability' as being one of the components of 'internal balance'. Yet in the outline which I have just given of a possible distribution of responsibilities no one is directly responsible for price stability. To make price stability itself the objective of demand management would be very dangerous. If there were an upward pressure on prices because the prices of imports had risen or indirect taxes had been raised, the maintenance of price stability would require an offsetting absolute reduction in domestic money wage-costs; and who knows what levels of depression and unemployment it might be necessary consciously to engineer in order to achieve such a result? This particular danger might be avoided by choice of a price index for stabilisation which excluded both indirect taxes and the price of imports; but even so, the stabilisation of such a price index would be very dangerous. If any remodelled wage-fixing arrangements were not working perfectly – and it would be foolhardy to assume a perfect performance – a very moderate excessive upward pressure on money wage-rates and so on costs might cause a very great reduction in output and employment if there were no rise in selling prices so that the whole of the impact of the increased money costs was taken on profit margins. If, however, it was total money incomes which were stabilised, a much more moderate decline in employment combined with a moderate rise in prices would serve to maintain the uninflated total of money incomes.

The effectiveness of the pattern of responsibilities which I have outlined rests upon the assumption that there is a reasonably high elasticity of demand for labour in terms of the real wage-rate, since success is to be achieved by setting a money wage-rate relatively to money demand prices which gives a full employment demand for labour by employers. I have no doubt myself that in the longer run the elasticity of demand is great enough. But what of the short run? What if in every industry there is a stock of fixed capital in a form which sets an absolute limit to the amount of labour which can be usefully employed, while, for some reason or another of past history, there is more labour seeking work than can be usefully employed? There will be unemployment in every industry; and any resulting reduction in money wage-rates combined with the maintenance of total money incomes would merely redistribute income from wages to profits.

I have explained the danger in its most exaggerated form; but it would remain a real one even in a much moderated form. There should, of course, never be any question of the wholesale immediate slashing of wage-rates in every sector in which there was any unemployment. Any such arrangement would, for the reasons which I have outlined, be economically most undesirable even if it were politically possible. What one has in mind is simply that in a milieu in which total money incomes are steadily rising at a moderate rate, money wage-rates should be rising rather more rapidly in some sectors and less rapidly or not at all in other sectors according to the supplies of available labour and the prospects of future demands for labour in those sectors. There would be no requirement that any money wage-rates must be actually reduced.

Putting more emphasis on supply–demand conditions in the settlement of particular wage claims could only work if there were general acceptance of the idea by the ordinary citizen; and such acceptance would depend *inter alia* upon a marked change of emphasis about policies for influencing the redistribution of the national income. I have for long believed that it is only if, somehow or another, the ordinary citizen can be persuaded to put less emphasis on wage bargaining and more emphasis on fiscal policies of taxation and social security for influencing the personal distribution of income and wealth that we have any hope of building the sort of free, efficient, and humanely just society in which I would like to live. But that raises a host of issues which I cannot discuss today.

There is, however, one feature of this connection between the supply–demand criterion for fixing wage-rates and the attitude of the wage-earner to his real standard of living on which I do wish to comment. Suppose, for example because of a rise in the world price of oil or of other imported foodstuffs or raw materials, that the international terms of trade turn against an industrialised country. This is equivalent to a reduction in the productivity of labour and of other factors employed in the country in question. If money wage-rates are pushed up as the prices of imported goods go up in order to preserve the real purchasing power of wage incomes, money wage costs are raised for the domestic producer without any automatic rise in the selling price of the domestic components of their outputs. Profit margins are squeezed. The demand for labour will fall unless and until profit margins are restored by a corresponding rise in the selling prices of domestic products. But such a rise would in turn cause a further rise in the cost of living, followed perhaps by a further offsetting rise in money wage-rates, with a further round of pressure on profit margins. In fact workers are attempting to establish a real wage-rate which, because of the adverse effect of the terms of international trade, is no longer compatible with full employment. The resulting rounds of pressure on profit margins, rises in domestic selling prices, further rises in money wage-rates, further pressure on profit margins, and so on, may result in stagflation – a level of employment below full employment with a continuing inflation of money prices.

This story may in fact help to explain what has happened recently in some industrialised countries, but my purpose in telling it is merely to give a vivid illustration of the fact that an effective combination of full employment with the avoidance of inflation necessarily requires that wage-fixing should take as its main criterion the supply–demand conditions in the labour market without undue insistence on the attainment and defence of any particular real wage income. The latter must be the combined result of domestic productivity, the terms of international trade, and tax and other measures taken to affect the distribution of income between net-of-tax spendable wages and other net-of-tax incomes.

IV

So much for the specification of targets and for the distribution of weapons among targets; we must now ask 'What about the detailed specification of the weapons themselves?'

If the velocity of circulation of money were constant, a steady rate of growth in the total money demand for goods and services could be achieved by a steady rate of growth in the supply of money, and this in turn could be the task of an independent Central Bank with the express responsibility for ensuring a steady rate of growth of the money supply of, say, 5 per cent per annum. It is a most attractive and straightforward solution; but, alas, I am still not persuaded to be an out-and-out monetarist of this kind. It is difficult to define precisely what is to be treated as money in a modern economy. At the borderline of the definition substitutes for money can and do readily increase and decrease in amount and within the borders of the definition velocities of circulation can and do change substantially. Can we not use monetary policy more directly for the attainment of the objective of a steady rate of growth of, say, 5 per cent per annum in total money incomes, and supplement this monetary policy with some form of fiscal regulator in order to achieve a more prompt and effective response? For this purpose one would, of course, be well advised to call in aid the skills of the control engineer, in order to cope with the dynamic problems of keeping the total national money income on its target path. Am I to be regarded as a member of the lunatic fringe or as an unconscious ally of authoritarian tyranny if I express this remaining degree of belief in the possibilities of rational social engineering?

I find very attractive the idea that this monetary control should be the responsibility of some body which was not directly dependent upon the government for its day-to-day decisions but which was charged by its constitution independently to achieve this stable but moderate growth of money incomes. But there is real difficulty in endowing any such independent body with powers to use fiscal policy as well as monetary policy to achieve its objective.

Let me take an example. Suppose that overseas producers of oil raise abruptly the price charged to an importing country; and, to isolate the point which I want to make, suppose further that the oil producers invest in the importing country any excess funds which they receive from the sale of an unchanged supply of oil, so that there is no immediate need to cut imports or to expand exports in order to protect the foreign exchanges. The abrupt price change will, however, tend to cause a deflation of money incomes in the importing country whose citizens will, out of any given income, spend less on home-produced goods in order to spend more on imported oil, the receipts from which are saved by the oil producers. With the scheme of responsibilities which I have outlined it is now the duty of the demand managers to reflate the demand for goods and services in the importing country in order to prevent a fall in money incomes in that country.

There are at least two alternative strategies for such reflation.

In the first place, the taxation of the citizens of the importing country might be reduced so that, while they have to spend more on imported oil, they have just so much more spendable income to maintain their demands for their own products. In this case the government directly or indirectly borrows funds saved by the oil producers to finance the larger budget deficit due to the reduced tax payments by the domestic consumers. No one's standard of living is immediately affected.

If this solution is adopted, the importing country faces an ever-growing debt to the foreign oil producers with no corresponding growth of domestic or foreign capital to set against it. If this is considered undesirable, the private citizens must not be relieved of tax; their current consumption standards must be allowed to fall as a result of the rise in the price of oil; and the reflation of domestic income must be brought about by measures which stimulate expenditure on extra real capital development at home, the finance of which will mop up the savings of the oil producers. Such action will depend upon monetary policies rather than, or at least as well as, upon fiscal action.

I have told this particular story simply to make the point that the choice between fiscal action and monetary action must often depend upon basic policy issues which should certainly be the responsibility of the government rather than of any independent monetary authority. Perhaps the best compromise is an independent monetary authority charged so to manage the money supply and the market rate of interest as to maintain the growth of total money income on its 5 per cent per annum target path, after taking into account whatever fiscal policies the government may adopt. One would hope, of course, that there would be a suitable discussion of their plans and policies between the government and the monetary authority; but the latter would be given an ultimately independent duty and independent choice of monetary policy for keeping total money incomes on their target path.

The difficulties involved in the specification of the weapons of demand management are real enough; but they fade into insignificance when they are compared with the problems of remodelling wage-fixing arrangements in such a way as to ensure a greater emphasis on supply–demand conditions in each sector of the labour market.

I can think of five broad lines of approach.

First, one can conceive of wage-fixing in each sector of the labour market by the edict of some government authority. An efficient use of this method would be extremely difficult in a modern economy with its innumerable different forms and skills of labour in so many different and diverse regions, occupations, and industries. It would, I think, in any case ultimately involve a degree of governmental authoritarian control which I personally would find very distasteful.

Secondly, there is the corporate state solution in which a monopoly of employer monopolies agrees with a monopoly of labour monopolies on a central bargain for the distribution between wages and profits in the various sectors of the economy of the total national money income which the demand managers are going to provide. I suspect that, in the United Kingdom at any rate, any such bargain would be very difficult to attain without leaving some important, but relatively powerless, sectors out in the cold of unemployment or of very low wages. In any case I ought to reveal my prejudice against being ruled by a monopoly of uncontrolled private monopolists.

Thirdly, the restoration of competitive conditions in the labour market would in theory do the trick, since the competitive search for jobs would restrain the wage-rate in any sector in which there was unemployed labour and the competitive search for hands by competitive employers would raise the wage-rate in any sector in which manpower was scarce. There is little doubt in my own mind that in some cases trade unions have attained an excessively privileged position and that some reduction of their monopoly powers might help towards a solution. But I do not believe that any full solution is to be found along this competitive road. On the employers' side it may be impossible to ensure effective competition where economies of large scale severely restrict the number of employers. On the employees' side the whole of history suggests the powerful psychological need for workers with common concerns to get together in the formation of associations to represent their common interests. Moreover, reliance on individual competition might well involve the reduction, if not elimination, of support for workers who were unemployed and of compulsory severance or redundancy payments to workers whose jobs disappeared. But what one wants to find is some effective, but compassionate and humane, method which applies supply–demand criteria for the fixing of wage-rates for those in employment without inflicting needless hardship and anxiety on those particular individuals who are inevitably adversely affected by economic change.

Fourthly, there are those who see the solution in the labour-managed economy in which workers hire capital rather than capital hiring workers. In such circumstances there would be no wage-rate to fix. Workers would share among themselves whatever income they could earn in their concerns after payment of whatever fixed interest or rent was necessary to hire their instruments of production. These ideas are very attractive; but, alas, there is, I think, good reason to believe that satisfactory outcome on these lines is possible only in those sectors of the economy where small-scale enterprises are appropriate and where conditions make it fairly easy to set up new competing co-operative concerns.

Finally, there remains the possibility of the replacement in wage bargaining of the untamed use of monopolistic power through the threat of strikes, lock-outs, and similar industrial action by the acceptance of arbitral awards made by trusted and impartial outside tribunals – awards which would, however, have to be heavily weighted by considerations of the supply–demand conditions of each particular case, if they were to achieve what I have suggested should be the basic objective of wage-fixing arrangements.

This is the civilised approach; but I am under no illusion that it is an easy one. It relies upon a widespread acceptance of the idea that some such approach is necessary for everyone's ultimate welfare and, in particular, as I have already indicated, upon the belief that there are alternative fiscal and similar policies to ensure social justice in the ultimate distribution of income and wealth. But even if in the course of time such a general acceptance could be achieved, some form of sanction for its application in some particular cases would almost certainly be needed. The punishment of individuals as criminals for taking monopolistic action to disturb a wage award does not hold out much hope of success, but is it pure dreaming to conceive ultimately of a state of affairs in which (1) in the case of any dispute about wages either party to the dispute or the government itself could apply for an award of the kind which I have indicated and (2) certain financial privileges and legal immunities otherwise enjoyed by the parties to a trade dispute would not be available in the case of industrial action taken in defiance of such an award?

Perhaps this is merely an optimist's utopian fantasy; but I can think of nothing better.

V

So much for the attainment of price stability and full employment through the instrumentalities of demand management and wage-fixing; we must now ask 'What about the attainment of external balance through foreign exchange policies?'

In my view the appropriate division of powers and obligations between national governments and international institutions is that the national governments should be responsible for national monetary, fiscal, and wage policies which combine full employment with price stability and that external balance should be maintained by foreign exchange policies under the supervision of international institutions.

Variations in the rate of exchange between the national currencies combined with freedom of trade and payments should in my view be the normal instrument of such foreign exchange policies, but this is not to say that there will never be occasion for the use of other instruments of foreign exchange policy. Special control arrangements may be appropriate where the removal of an international imbalance requires wholesale industrial development or structural change, or where abrupt changes in the international flow of capital funds require special offsetting measures, or where differences in national tax regimes would distort international transactions in the absence of offsetting measures. But where such exceptions to the free movement of goods and funds arise, these should be under the rules and supervision of appropriate international institutions.

After the war we managed to lay the foundations of an international system of this kind with the pivotal institutions of the International Monetary Fund, the International Bank for Reconstruction and Development, and the General Agreement on Tariffs and Trade, a system which for a quarter of a century resulted in a most remarkable expansion of international trade. In my opinion there was one important original flaw in this system, namely the insistence on the International Monetary Fund's very sticky adjustable peg mechanism for the correction of inappropriate exchange rates. But even this flaw has now gone as the International Monetary Fund seeks to find the most appropriate rules for running a system of international flexible exchange rates.

Yet we seem now to be faced with the possibility of a gigantic tragedy, with this initial success being fated unnecessarily to end in calamity. Why is this so? In my view the answer is obvious; it is simply because so many of the national governments of the developed industrialised countries have failed to find appropriate national institutional ways of combining full employment with price stability.

If they could do so, not only would the domestic tragic waste and social discontent of heavy unemployment in such countries be removed, but the international scene would be transformed. The pressure for the use by developed countries of massive import restrictions rather than of gradual and moderate changes in exchange rates to look after their balances of payments would, I suspect, be very greatly reduced. It is the spectacle of imports competing with the products of domestic industries in which there is already serious unemployment which is the greatest threat to the freedom of imports into the developed countries. With full employment and price stability at home the balance of payments could with much more confidence be left to the mechanism of flexible foreign exchange rates. The developed countries would then have less difficulty in giving financial aid to the third world; and, what in my opinion is even more important, they could much more readily accept the inflow from the third world of their labour-intensive products.

In this lecture I have marked an occasion which is concerned with international economics with a lecture on internal balance. But I suggest that in present conditions this is not anomalous. I do not, I think, exaggerate wildly when I conclude by saying that one – though, of course, only one – of the really important factors on which the health of the world now depends is the recasting of wage-fixing arrangements in a limited number of developed countries.

References

Keynes, J. M. (1936). *The General Theory of Employment, Interest and Money*. London: Macmillan.

Meade, J. E. (1951). *The Theory of International Economic Policy. Vol. I. The Balance of Payments*. London: Oxford University Press for the Royal Institute of International Affairs.

Meade, J. E. (1955). *The Theory of International Economic Policy. Vol. II. Trade and Welfare*. London: Oxford University Press for the Royal Institute of International Affairs.

Ohlin, B. (1933). *International and Interregional Trade*. Harvard University Press.

22

On Stagflation

The text of Meade's Snow Lecture which was broadcast on BBC Radio 3 in November 1978; from The Listener, *14 December 1978, pp. 778–784.*

I am much honoured by the invitation to give this, the second Snow Lecture; and I, like all of us, am greatly pleased that Lord and Lady Snow are both here on this occasion.

I have chosen Stagflation as the topic for my lecture. This nasty word 'stagflation' has been invented to describe the even nastier state of affairs in which the economy is simultaneously both stagnant and inflationary, the main symptoms of the disease being the appearance, at one and the same time, of heavy unemployment and of a rapid rate of rise of money prices.

This relatively new disease has recently spread as an epidemic through the community of countries of which we are a part – namely, the industrially developed, free-enterprise, liberal, mixed-economy democracies; and its possible consequences should be taken very seriously.

For if one wished to undermine the structure of a liberal society one might find it difficult to choose between a policy of debauching the currency by a runaway inflation or a policy designed to ensure a prolonged period of heavy unemployment. Germany in the early 1920s experienced a complete runaway inflation which reduced the value of the mark virtually to zero and ruined many members of the middle class; and this was followed in the early 1930s by a horrific period of mass unemployment which impoverished practically the whole community. Runaway inflation followed by mass unemployment brought the curse of Hitler upon Germany. To combine inflation and unemployment simultaneously could be an even surer recipe for disaster.

Of course I am not for one moment suggesting that our immediate danger is anything comparable to that of the dreadful inter-war German experience when the rate of explosive price inflation and the level of mass unemployment were of quite different orders of magnitude from anything which we are at present experiencing. But there is one ominous feature of the experience of recent years which does, I think, suggest that the position should be taken very seriously. In this country over the last decade or two, each level of unemployment has been associated with ever higher rates of inflation as the years have passed; and it is not difficult to see why this phenomenon of stagflation might well get progressively worse unless something fairly radical is done about it.

Let me illustrate by means of the following simple arithmetical parable. Suppose that we are all organised into powerful pressure groups of trade unions, professional associations, giant business corporations, industrial cartels and the like, each tight group prepared to use its monopoly powers to enforce its own claims on the national income. Suppose that we all demand a rise in our real standards of pay of, say, 5 per cent a year; but suppose that productivity per head is rising only by, say, 2 per cent a year. We all start this year by demanding our 5 per cent rise in money pay. This causes money costs per unit of output to go up by 3 per cent, since improved productivity will account only for 2 per cent of the 5 per cent rise in money wage-costs. Except in so far as profit margins are excessive, reductions in output and increases in unemployment can be avoided only if total money demands for goods are allowed to expand so that producers can sell their outputs at prices inflated by 3 per cent to cover the 3 per cent rise in their costs. In this case, the cost of living will go up by 3 per cent. Next year we will demand an 8 per cent rise in pay of which 3 per cent is designed to offset the current rate of inflation of the cost of living and 5 per cent to give us the real rise in our standards which we are demanding. But this 8 per cent rise in money wages will cause a 6 per cent rise in money costs on our assumption that improved productivity continues to reduce costs only by 2 per cent per annum. If selling prices are to keep in line with costs and unemployment is thus to be avoided, selling prices must rise by 6 per cent. The following year, therefore, we all demand a wage increase of 11 per cent, of which 6 per cent is designed to offset the inflation of the cost of living and 5 per cent to give us our real rise. And so on. Each year the rate of price inflation increases, probably in an explosive manner as soon as we start to put forward wage claims designed not merely to make up for past rises in the cost of living but to anticipate future increases in the rate of inflation.

Attempts to get a quart out of a pint pot will, of course, always be frustrated; but the process can have some very unfortunate side-effects. It leads to an increasingly serious problem of uncontrolled inflation or an increasingly serious problem of unemployment or some combination of the two.

There is another kind of explosive mechanism which may also be at work. People are very concerned with wage differentials. Jones feels badly used not simply because his pay is low but also because he has lost out in comparison with Smith. Suppose that candlestick makers consider that they should be paid 5 per cent more than butchers and bakers and that at the same time butchers and bakers consider that they should be paid at least as much as candlestick makers. Starting from the same wage the candlestick makers demand a 5 per cent rise. The butchers and bakers respond quickly with a demand for a similar 5 per cent rise, in order to keep in line with the candlestick makers. The candlestick makers then respond with another 5 per cent demand in order to get ahead once more, to which the butchers and bakers respond with another 5 per cent demand in order to catch up once more. And so on. In vain attempts to escape from the frustration of this leap-frogging process each group may put forward its claims more and more rapidly and may put forward on each occasion larger and larger claims in an attempt to offset in advance the anticipated counter-claims of the other group. In these conditions the rate of wage inflation will quickly explode; and if, in an attempt to control an explosive inflation, selling prices are not allowed to rise as rapidly as wage costs, unemployment will result. Once again we encounter stagflation.

By 1975 the situation in this country had become very serious indeed. In that year, demands for wage increases of no less than 30 per cent were not uncommon; and we may then have been near the edge of the precipice, from which we have withdrawn by means of some commonsensical, effective *ad hoc* measures. But is the problem really solved? At present we are pleased to have got the rate of rise of wage earnings down to some 15 per cent per annum and the rate of price inflation down to some 7 per cent. But productivity is certainly not rising by the 8 per cent gap between a 7 per cent rise in selling prices and a 15 per cent rise in rates of pay, so that money wage-costs are rising more rapidly than selling prices. Thus we face a demand for return to free collective bargaining at a time when, merely to prevent the rate of inflation from starting once more on an upward path or to avoid a further rise in unemployment as profit margins are squeezed, there must be further substantial reductions in the rates of rise of money wages. If we wish to do even better and to bring inflation down farther from what really is still a hideously high rate and actually to reduce unemployment below what is still an abnormally high level, the need for further wage restraint is still more marked. But in fact we hear talk once again of wage claims of 20 per cent or more. May we not be standing once more on the edge of the precipice?

This state of affairs leads to a cruel dilemma for those who are responsible for the country's financial policy. Before each Budget the Chancellor of the Exchequer can rely nowadays upon receiving much conflicting advice, some urging expansive monetary and budgetary policies designed to stimulate monetary expenditures on goods and services in order to create jobs and reduce unemployment and others urging restrictive policies to reduce money expenditures in order to keep down prices and fight inflation. And this conflict of advice shows itself not only within the country but also internationally between countries. Thus the government of a country like Germany which has a lower rate of price inflation and a favourable excess of exports over imports is urged to expand its internal demand for goods and services by the authorities in other countries like the United Kingdom with its higher rates of price inflation and its perpetual threat of an excess demand for imports. Surely, it is argued, it is the duty of Germany, which has only a moderate rate of domestic price inflation, to adopt an expansionary domestic policy which will help to increase the demand for its own products and also for imports from countries like the United Kingdom; for this will help to reduce unemployment in both Germany and the United Kingdom and at the same time to correct an imbalance in international payments by increasing the imports of the surplus country, Germany, and the exports of the deficit country, the United Kingdom. But the Germans may very understandably be reluctant to expand their own domestic demands because they wish, above all, not to stoke up their own domestic price inflation. And in the light of their past history who can blame them for that?

I hope that I have said enough to give you at least a vague idea of the nature of the disease and of my reasons for believing it to be a serious one and for doubting whether we have yet found a cure.

Let us go back in history to the great depression of the 1930s in order to trace the history of the disease. At that time, there developed a great deficiency of effective demand for goods and services throughout the world economy. Men and machines lay idle and foodstuffs and raw materials piled up in unused heaps, although at the same time impoverished citizens throughout the world were in crying need of food, shelter, warmth and clothes, to say nothing of some of the amenities of life. This poverty in the midst of potential plenty was a phenomenon which many of us regarded as both foolish and wicked. It was in these circumstances that Keynes elaborated his system of thought whereby in such conditions the governments of the world might in concert stimulate effective demands for goods and services – demands the satisfaction of which would relieve poverty and the fulfilment of which would at the same time provide work for the unemployed.

The weapons recommended for this process of stimulating effective demand were of three kinds. First, public authorities might themselves spend more on public works of various kinds – road-making, housing projects, capital development in nationalised industries, and so on. Second, the Central Bank could take steps to increase the supply of money and to reduce the rates of interest at which funds could be borrowed for investment in capital development of every kind in the private sector of the economy. Third, rates of tax might be reduced and social benefits and similar governmental outlays increased in order to leave the ordinary tax-paying citizen with a larger amount of tax-free income to spend on goods and services. The immediate increases in incomes caused by these initial increases in expenditures on goods and services would lead to further secondary increases in expenditures and so in incomes, which in turn would lead to further tertiary increases, and so on, through the repercussions of Professor Lord Kahn's famous multiplier effects.

Keynes was strongly opposed in the 1930s to any attempts to expand employment by the alternative means of a reduction of money wage-rates, and this for two reasons. First, he considered that it would be largely ineffective. Reduced wage-costs can provide an incentive to employers to take on more labour only if reduced wage incomes do not lead at the same time to an off-setting reduction in the workers' demands for the products of industry. Keynes gave reasons for believing that in the conditions of the 1930s the main effect of reductions in money wages would be to cause a fall in all money costs, money prices, money incomes, and money profits, leaving the levels of real employment and real output much unchanged. Second, he pointed out that there were immense political difficulties in inducing an effective and fair all-round cut in money wage-rates, whereas the alternative policy of stimulating demand for the products of industry would be not only more effective and reliable, but also incomparably fairer and easier politically.

This Keynesian technique of demand management, as it came to be known, was never designed to cope with all forms of unemployment. In a dynamic economy, there will always be some people on the move from contracting to expanding activities, and they will be without work during this frictional process of movement. Moreover, structural industrial situations can arise in which workers remain unemployed in spite of a strong demand for their products because of an inadequate supply of specialised machinery or of a few specially skilled workers needed to co-operate with them in the productive process.

Keynes never intended that his demand management techniques should be used to cope with such frictional and structural unemployment, but only with what we may call general unemployment; namely, with those situations in which there is widespread unemployment of labour and of capital equipment of all kinds, due to a general deficiency of demand for the products of industry.

It is, of course, impossible to draw a hard and fast line between these different types of unemployment. Even at the bottom of the most severe General Depression there may be some few industries producing new products in which the available specialised equipment and specialised labour force are insufficient to cope with the demand. As general demand is stimulated, there will be more and more particular bottlenecks of this kind where demand is excessive in relation to potential specialised productive resources. It is difficult to say at what precise point one should regard general unemployment to have disappeared and the remaining pockets of unemployment to be wholly frictional or structural cases; but at some point the line must be drawn.

Keynes was a practical man. He did his great work on these subjects in the 1930s when there was heavy unemployment in an atmosphere of falling rather than rising money costs and prices. He was not then concerned with the danger that a policy of demand management for the reduction of unemployment might be frustrated by an explosion of money wage-costs. But I can vouch from personal knowledge that in the discussions of plans for post-war reconstruction he was very conscious of this danger for the post-World War Two economy.

Thus during the 1930s Keynes was preaching the doctrine that governments should take on one more important fuction; namely, that of demand management. During the war, thought was given to post-war reconstruction; and in the historic White Paper of 1944 on Employment Policy general demand management for the maintenance of full employ-ment was officially recognised to be a proper governmental function. Nor was this great revolution of thought confined to the United Kingdom. In the United States a similar governmental obligation to be concerned with maintaining a high level of employment was recognised by an Act of Congress. Indeed, when Keynes died in April 1946 at the very moment of transition from War to Peace Economy he left a world in which virtually all the governments of our type of country were explicitly or implicitly committed to the Keynesian policies of demand management.

There followed a quarter of a century of the most unparalleled economic growth and prosperity. We in this country are sometimes apt to think of it as a period of failure. This is the exact opposite of the truth in that our standards of living have never grown at a faster rate. Our problem during those years was that other countries were doing even better than we. I know that *post hoc propter hoc* is not convincing logic. But the great post-war economic settlement has in my view a lot to do with this period of unprecedented economic success, built on the two foundations of domestic demand management and of the international freeing of trade and payments through the International Monetary Fund and the General Agreement on Tariffs and Trade – and Keynes was a principal architect of both the domestic and the international elements of this reconstruction.

But over the last few years it has all turned sour and we are now cursed with the epidemic of stagflation. What has happened?

In my view there are two main factors at work: first, the temptation for the politicians to use the tools of demand management for the overstimulation of the economy and, second, the uncontrolled power of labour monopolies to press for wage increases.

In the good old days – or, as I prefer to put it, in the bad old days – of the Gold Standard and of Balanced Budgets, there was little or no opportunity for the authorities to exercise discretionary power over the level of total demand. The supply of money and the consequential ease or tightness of funds on the capital market had to be managed by the Central Bank with the overriding purpose of keeping the sterling price of gold fixed in a free world market for gold. The rigid conventional requirement that the government's Budget should be balanced except in extreme crisis such as that of a major war made it impossible to vary government expenditures and taxes so as to stimulate demand through budget deficits. The Keynesian revolution replaced both these rigid conventional constraints – indeed, one might almost call them constitutional constraints – with the simple hope that politicians would have the good sense to use their discretionary powers over monetary and fiscal policies in a disciplined manner.

But expansion of demand is always more attractive politically than contraction. Making funds available at cheaper rates for house purchase, paying larger child benefits or old-age pensions, reducing the rate of income tax – all these are policies which provide immediate specific benefits to specific groups of voters. The inflationary dangers which may result are vague, dispersed, and delayed; and a week is a long time in politics. On the contrary, to contract demand hits certain specific citizens clearly and immediately, and the advantages of avoiding inflation are vague, dispersed and delayed. As a result the stimulation of the economy through demand management techniques has on balance been overdone.

Let me remind you that after 1922 in the inter-war period in this country the unemployment percentage, except for one or two months, never fell below 10 per cent and in 1932 rose to 23 per cent. After the Second World War for many years we drove the economy at unemployment percentages of 1.5 per cent and 2 per cent, while 3 per cent was regarded by some as a threat of serious unemployment. There is no doubt in my mind that Keynesian stimulation of demand has been used to tackle frictional and structural as well as general unemployment. This has led to a general inflationary situation; and as people have come more and more to expect and anticipate price rises so, by the processes which I described earlier in this lecture, the inflation rate has tended to explode.

Closely connected with this are the effects of the quite lunatic way in which we nowadays set about fixing money wage-rates. Organised associations of labour have been given every kind of legal immunity and privilege to take monopoly action (by way of strikes, boycotts, closed shops, etc.) in order to achieve what each separate group judges for itself to be the proper reward for its own particular work. These monopolies are separate from and independent of each other. They leap-frog in attempts to impose inconsistent differentials and in conjunction they strive to obtain a quart out of the available pint pot. This is generally called free collective bargaining. But English is a rich language and I prefer to call it 'uncontrolled monopoly' rather than 'free collective' bargaining. Combine this system of uncontrolled monopoly bargaining with a so-called Keynesian governmental undertaking that, whatever happens to the level of money wages, demand will be stimulated sufficiently to avoid any general unemployment, and you have a set of institutions which might well have been expressly designed to set in motion and to maintain that process of explosive inflation which I described at the beginning of this lecture – particularly if you add for good measure the political probability that demand will in fact be overstimulated beyond the point needed to avoid general unemployment. It is a recipe for disaster, which can be averted from time to time by the temporary reinstatement of strict monetary and fiscal constraints which will result in unemployment and a stagflating economy as the upward pressure of rates of pay meets the reimposed downward pressure of the monetary and fiscal constraints.

Once upon a time, there were two men working on a long stretch of a single-line railway track, when they saw two express trains coming at full speed towards each other, one from each end of the track. As they stepped off the track, one man said to the other: 'That's a bloody silly way to run a railway.'

Please do not mistake me for a Fascist Beast whose one obsessional desire is to bash the trade unions and to grind the faces of the poor. I am, in fact, a rather old-fashioned Radical who really does believe in Liberty, Equality and Fraternity – without, I may add, holding the view that putting anyone who disagrees with you under the guillotine is the most obvious way to express one's belief in Liberty or Equality – or, for that matter, in Fraternity.

I could lecture you for hours on the desirability of many positive social and economic policies for the promotion of these three great objectives – by national health and educational systems which help to equalise conditions and opportunities and to break down class barriers, by systems of industrial relations which do not involve managers treating workers as a different species of animal and *vice versa*, by tax and social security measures for the promotion of a more equal distribution of income and wealth, and by the prevention of excess monopoly profits through the promotion of competition, through the outlawing of restrictive business practices, and, where undue monopolistic power is inevitable, through price control or the nationalisation of the enterprise.

But these are not the topics of my lecture today. Nor am I concerned today with the great victory for the principle of freedom of association which was won in the past by the removal of outrageous restrictions on the rights of workers to form free trade unions.

Freedom of association does not, however, imply any right to limit the personal freedoms of those who do not choose to join, or are prevented from joining, the association. Thus measures which prevent the employment of additional labour in an exceptionally well-paid occupation except on terms imposed by those who are already enjoying the privilege of working in that occupation seem to me a very doubtful way of increasing personal liberty (since it limits the freedom of choice of occupation by the outsider) or of increasing equality (since it prevents lower-paid persons from entering a higher-paid occupation) or of demonstrating the Brotherhood of Man between those inside and those outside the charmed circle. Indeed, what I am concerned with today is precisely the implication of constructing an economic system on the principle not of limiting restrictive monopoly powers, but of positively endowing large powerful independent groups with a panoply of monopoly powers to enforce their claims on the community – which implies, of course, powers to attempt to enforce conflicting claims on each other. That, I am asserting, is a bloody silly way to run an economy.

What, then, must we do to be saved?

As far as the need for monetary restraint is concerned I cannot go the whole way with the monetarists, who rely simply upon controlling the growth of the total supply of money. This in my view is to throw out the baby with the bath-water. Even with a controlled supply of money, total expenditures can still vary very greatly as transactions are financed by a given stock of money passing more or less rapidly from hand to hand or by the use of trade credits and other substitutes for money. Rather let Keynesian techniques of demand management continue to be used; but let us revise the precise purpose for which they are used. In place of what Parliament used to recognise as the constitutional constraints of the Gold Standard and the Balanced Budget, let Parliament now recognise as a strict constitutional financial restraint, a sacred rule that fiscal and monetary policies should be used, not directly to maintain full employment, but to maintain a steady rate of growth of, say, 5 per cent per annum in the total money demand for goods and services and so in the total money national income.

Keeping total national income on a steady 5 per cent per annum growth path would normally indirectly result in a steady 5 per cent per annum growth in the total money demand for labour. But if for any reason profit margins rose during any year, a 5 per cent growth in the total expenditure on goods and services would during that year cause total profits to rise by more than 5 per cent and total wages by less than 5 per cent. A variant of the proposed constitutional rule for financial restraint would be that total demand should be so managed as to keep, not the total national income but rather the total national wage bill on a steady 5 per cent per annum growth path. There is much to be said for this variant which is more in line with the existing political debate. Any governmental percentage guide-lines for increases in wage-rates would simply be replaced by an effective use of demand management techniques which actually kept the total wage bill on a given annual percentage growth path. And that would be that, leaving it to wage-fixing arrangements to decide how the increase would be divided between increased employment and increased wage-rates in the various sectors of the economy.

But whichever variant of the rule was adopted, it would remain important that profit margins as well as money wage-rates should be restrained. As I have already argued, the appropriate measures for this purpose are the promotion of competition among producers – an important element of which is competition with imported products – the outlawing of restrictive business practices, and price control or nationa-lisation where strong monopolistic elements are unavoidable.

There are, of course, very serious problems involved in the imple-mentation of either variant of the constitutional rule for financial restraint. Can suitable political institutional arrangements be devised whereby Parliament could effectively commit itself to such a financial restraint? And is the technical economic problem soluble? The economic system consists of a very complicated network of dynamic interrela-tionships with all sorts of delays between the various interactions. With what degree of success can one hope to find forms of monetary and fiscal control which will affect expenditures promptly enough and, even with the help of the most skilled control engineers, to devise working rules for their use so as effectively to keep total money expenditures on a predetermined steady growth path? I have no time now to discuss these important issues.

But clearly one necessary condition for the feasibility of any such rule for monetary and fiscal policies is that it should be accompanied by a suitable reform of wage-fixing arrangements. If money wage-rates were allowed to go up by 15 per cent in any year, the total wage bill could be restricted to a rise of 5 per cent in that year only by a devastating deflation of the total demand for the products of industry sufficient to reduce by 10 per cent the number of persons in employment over whom the restricted wage bill was to be spread or, in other words, to add a net figure of two million or more to the number of unemployed.

What is needed is some accompanying form of wage-fixing arrange-ments which in each sector of the economy would resist wage increases in so far as they would increase unemployment or prevent the expansion of employment in that sector. In any occupation, trade, industry or region in which there was a scarcity of labour relatively to the demand, a *rise* and not a *fall* in wage-rates is needed to attract workers to that sector and so to *increase* employment in that sector; and remember that this principle would be operating against a background in which on the average over all the sectors of the economy the money demand for labour would be expanding at a steady rate so that sooner or later there would be a competitive need in each typical sector to raise its wage-rates to maintain its labour force. In any sector in which labour was specially scarce, wages would need to rise faster than this average. In any particular sector in which there did still exist an excess supply of labour a rise in wage-rates should be avoided in order not to accentuate the problem of unemployment. The cure for unemployment in such sectors must rely partly upon a gradual improvement in that sector as it enjoyed some share of the general steady 5 per cent per annum expansion in the total demand for labour and partly upon redundant labour being attracted to those other sectors in which employment opportunities were expanding and in which the competitive demand for a limited supply of labour was bidding up the wage-rate and making employment more attractive.

What sort of institutional changes would be appropriate for this purpose?

Some would advocate an official incomes policy covering wage-rates in the different sectors of the economy. As an *ad hoc* crisis measure I fully support the present Government's use of such techniques to bring us back once more from the edge of the precipice of runaway inflation. But I dislike the implications of a system of central authoritarian wage-fixing as a permanent long-run solution of the problem. It is impossible to decentralise such a system. Either it implies the universal application of some simple crude rule, like the present 5 per cent rule, which is bound to lead eventually to unbearable anomalies in an economy such as ours with its great diversity of skills, of industrial, occupational, and regional conditions, and of methods of payment. Or else it involves a gradual invasion by the central authorities into the detailed arrangements in every economic activity, thus constituting a serious infringement of the freedoms and efficiencies of a more decentralised competitive market system.

Some would advocate a getting together of the Big Boys of the CBI and the TUC to decide on the division of each year's 5 per cent increase in the total wage bill. I dislike this corporate state solution because I think that the Big Boys in powerful monopoly positions in sensitive sectors of the national economy would be likely to obtain an undue share of the lolly, thus condemning the Little Boys to low wages or causing unemployment, results which would be both inefficient and unfair.

Some would advocate a transformation of existing enterprises into labour-managed, worker-owned co-operatives in which the fixing of wage-rates would not arise, since the workers would simply divide between them whatever share they could earn of the steadily growing demand for goods and services in general, after paying any necessary rents or interest on the land and capital equipment which they had hired. I am afraid that I believe that this attractive solution can be expected to work well only in those activities which are labour-intensive rather than capital-intensive in their technologies, in which small-scale enterprise is possible, and in which the entry of new competing co-operatives is relatively easy. But where it is possible it should be greatly encouraged. The desire for some such release from the restrictions imposed on regular industrial employment may perhaps be already observed in such phenomena as special arrangements for the self-employment of the drivers of a company's road vehicles, the so-called lump of self-employed workers in the building industry, and widespread moon-lighting by industrial workers in secondary jobs, movements which in some cases are motivated by a desire to evade the tax gatherer but in some cases also to escape governmental and trade union restrictions imposed on regular employment.

Some would advocate trade union bashing and a return in the labour markets to a régime in which the competition of workers for jobs and of entrepreneurs for workers would bid up wages where labour was scarce and bid down wages where labour was plentiful. I do not believe that a full solution is possible on these lines. Economies of scale mean that in a number of sectors there cannot be a large number of competing employers; and unfair bargaining positions would arise where a large number of competing individual workers faced a strictly limited number of employers. Moreover, it goes against the whole of history to overlook the real psychological need for groups of workers to form associations to represent their common interests. And in its full form this competitive solution would involve the denial of any substantial unemployment benefit, redundancy payments, and the like in order to induce unemployed workers to compete more effectively for jobs; and I would strongly oppose the ungenerous treatment of those who are unlucky enough to be unemployed.

But as some of you may already have guessed, I do see much merit in a free competitive market system; and although for the reasons which I have just given it is not desirable to seek a full solution of the wage-fixing problem by a complete restoration of unmitigated competition in labour markets, it is nevertheless necessary that the present excessive monopoly powers of the trade unions should be restrained.

What is the civilised way to deal with these problems? Let us continue to treat generously those who are unfortunate enough to be unemployed. Let us do nothing to discourage the formation of free trade unions and similar associations to represent the common concerns of different groups. Let profit margins be restrained by the measures which I have already mentioned. Let the distribution of income and wealth between individuals be influenced by fiscal and similar measures. But in place of industrial action to determine personal incomes by the accidents of monopoly bargaining power let there be a resort to arbitration in cases of dispute, a main criterion of such arbitral awards being to restrict such wage increases as would impede the expansion of employment in any sector of the economy. All this taking place in a financial environment which assured a steady rate of growth in the total demand for labour.

This would be compatible with a simple return to what I have called uncontrolled monopoly bargaining, but with one essential difference. Either party to a trade dispute and the government itself could be given the right to refer that dispute for an arbitral award of the kind which I have outlined. Industrial action would still remain possible; but penalties of one kind or another could be imposed if such an arbitral award were resisted. There are many possibilities. One would be to rule that the legal immunities granted to the parties to a trade dispute by the present Trade Union and Labour Relations Acts would be denied in the case of industrial action taken in opposition to any such arbitral award.

This set of arrangements would mean that there was no restriction whatsoever on any wage bargain freely agreed between any group of workers and employers. But when, against the background of a strictly restrained total market for goods and services, employers decided to resist a claim, it could be made subject to an arbitral award. Even so it would not be a criminal offence for the workers or employers concerned to take industrial action against the terms of the award; but in that case they would be liable to damages in connection with breach of contract or restraints of trade or other acts in the same way as any other group in society.

I put forward this set of ideas very tentatively. Their detailed implications would clearly need much careful examination. But in any case, while it may all sound very fine in principle, is there any prospect of such a solution by arbitral awards being acceptable? Of course, I realise that its immediate adoption is not politically possible. In the sort of decent, free, democratic society in which – thank goodness – we are still privileged to live, what is politically impossible today can be made politically possible tomorrow only by developing a general understanding of the problem and building up a general consensus in favour of the needed changes, either through eloquent persuasion of the kind to which you have been submitted today or, perhaps more effectively, by the rather less pleasant educative process to which, I fear, we are likely to be exposed by actual events in the months ahead.

I am an economist and have tried to give you an economic solution for an economic problem. Please do not argue that I am a rotten economist on the grounds that the economic solution is politically unacceptable. The really difficult part of our present problem *is* political; and on that I would be incompetent, even if I had the time, to express any worthwhile opinion. There is clearly a long and dreary haul ahead of us. I can only express the hope that our politicians can successfully use their skills to make clear to the man and the woman in the street the nature of our problems and to steer the development of our institutions in the directions which I have described.

One final word. Some of you may be surprised that I should have lectured on stagflation in the United Kingdom without mentioning the balance of payments. Alas, one cannot cover the whole of economics in one lecture. But if we avoided inflation through the adoption of domestic policies of the kind which I have outlined, our balance-of-payments problems would be eased out of all recognition. Keeping the domestic money national income or wage bill on a predetermined steady growth path would, however, mean that further domestic monetary contractions or expansions could not be used as an instrument for removing any residual balance-of-payments problems. The domestic policy which I have advocated implies, therefore, that we must not commit ourselves to any international monetary régime which would prevent us from making those adjustments in the foreign exchange rate which would from time to time still be needed on balance-of-payments grounds, unless we are prepared to rely on direct controls over imports and other foreign payments as the means for regulating our balance of payments. The proposals which I have made for domestic policies leave quite open the choice between exchange-rate adjustments and direct controls over imports and other foreign payments, though I would myself greatly hope that the instrument of exchange-rate adjustment would be chosen and would be found adequate. In any case our first priority should be to control our own domestic inflation. And how much more dignified it would be to set about putting our own house in order rather than to spend our time blaming our troubles on others – on the Japanese for producing better cars and on the Germans for controlling inflation more effectively than we do. But I must not keep you for the extra hour or two that would be needed for a proper development of the international aspects of our problem.

23

Comment on the Papers by Professors Laidler and Tobin

The papers by David Laidler and James Tobin – 'Monetarism: an interpretation and an assessment' and 'The monetarist counter-revolution today – an appraisal' – and comments on them by Meade and by R. C. O. Matthews were first presented at the Royal Economic Society Conference on 'Monetarism – An Appraisal' in London in July 1980. They were published in The Economic Journal, *vol. 91 (1981), pp. 1–55.*

We have been privileged to hear two expositions of the nature of monetarism which have greatly increased our understanding of the many issues involved. Professors Tobin and Laidler have distinguished between many nuances of analysis and of policy prescription covered by the term 'Monetarism'; and I shall accordingly devote my time to the congenial task of constructing a taxonomic classification of the distinctions which they have drawn and which demonstrate so clearly the foolish crudity of simply dividing the universe into Monetarists and Keynesians. This classification is shown in Table I.

What then are the distinguishing features of a Monetarist? I start with a basic threefold division into (1) Non-Keynesian Monetarists; (2) Keynesian Monetarists; (3) Keynesian Non-Monetarists. (I shall treat as empty the logically possible class of (4) Non-Keynesian Non-Monetarists.)

I shall say little about my first class which contains the Non-Keynesians because I agree fully with both Professors Tobin and Laidler on their analysis of the wrongheadedness of this group. In my terminology – I am now on line 1 of my schema – the Non-Keynesians are those who believe that the best macro-economic models are built on the assumption of flexible price mechanisms which continuously clear markets, so that no excess unsold supplies or excess unsatisfied demands exist, one implication of this being, of course, that all unemployment is best treated as voluntary in the sense that the unemployed man or woman has chosen to remain unemployed rather than to cut his or her wage demand sufficiently to find a job.

I find this assumption of continuous market clearing so unlike what goes on in most markets in our sort of developed economies that I would reject these Non-Keynesian models as being of no serious use in analysing our macro-economic behaviour. In fact through trade unions and

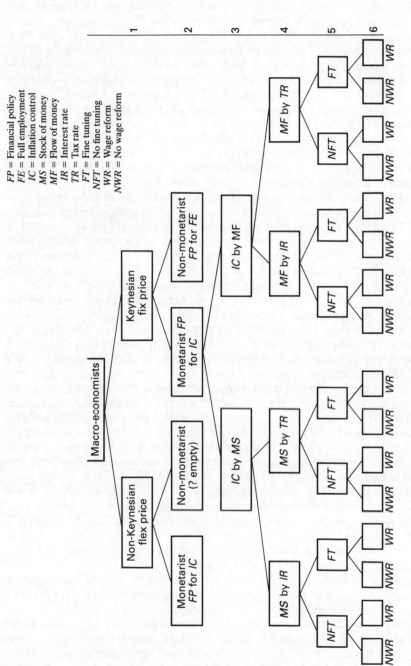

FP = Financial policy
FE = Full employment
IC = Inflation control
MS = Stock of money
MF = Flow of money
IR = Interest rate
TR = Tax rate
FT = Fine tuning
NFT = No fine tuning
WR = Wage reform
NWR = No wage reform

Table I

customary conventions workers set and insist on the rate for the job; and our theories of what is needed to offset the monopsonistic powers of a small number of employers facing a large number of workers in imperfect markets provide a very good explanation of such behaviour. Similarly the existence of oligopolistic markets for the sale of products which make it impossible to calculate at all precisely the price elasticity of demand for a single manufacturer's output provides a well-known explanation of the practice of setting selling prices for manufactured products on the basis of a conventional mark-up of the variable costs of production. At current prices stocks build up or run down and the lengths of order books rise or fall; employers have more or less difficulty in recruitment of the labour which they seek at current wage-rates and workers have more or less difficulty in finding work at the ruling rate for the job.

This is not, of course, to assert that such indications of excess supply or excess demand do not induce price setters to revise their prices. Indeed, for labour the Phillips curve is all about the degree and speed with which excess demands or supplies will cause the rate for the job to be adjusted; but if there are significant time-lags in various markets between the appearance of excess demands or supplies and the consequential adjustment of prices, prolonged dynamic cumulative disturbances of real incomes, outputs, and employments will occur. And this is surely of the essence of macro-economic control.

The models built by the Non-Keynesian Monetarists are very ingenious. They often lay stress on the assumption of rational expectations. I find this assumption also very implausible given the extreme complication of the real world in which we live; but their work on that subject has certainly emphasised for me the importance for macro-economic analysis of the ways in which economic agents formulate their expectations and, in particular, of the ways in which the effect on expectations of the announcement of economic policies may affect the outcome of those policies. But, as Professor Tobin has stressed, it is the assumption of continuous market clearing which constitutes the basic dividing line; and this assumption seems to me to fly in the face of facts.

I turn to line 2 of my schema to discuss the distinction between my second and third main classes: namely between Keynesian Monetarists and Keynesian Non-Monetarists. I hope that I shall be forgiven if I introduce these distinctions by expounding briefly my own beliefs (which are, I think, much in harmony with those of Professor Tobin) and then asking in what class or sub-class I should be numbered.

First of all then, my creed: I believe in demand management operated largely through finely tuned tax policy designed not to control the level of real output and employment, but to keep the level of the flow of total money expenditures on goods and services on a steady growth path, combined with a reform of wage-fixing arrangements which, against this background of a steady rate of growth in the overall money demand for the products of labour, sets wage-rates in each sector of the economy primarily for the purpose of promoting employment in that sector.

Am I a Monetarist?

Some would argue that there is a prior question, namely: Am I a

Keynesian? After all in the 1930s Keynes argued that it was no good trying to cure unemployment by cutting money wage-rates and that expansionary demand management should be employed to provide fuller employment; this would seem to be incompatible with any view that demand management should be used to restrain the inflation of money flows and that wage restraint should be used to provide employment. One may perhaps deny the title of Monetarist to anyone who believes that demand management should be designed primarily to maintain the level of real outputs and employments rather than to restrain monetary inflation; but I do not believe that it is appropriate to deny the title of Keynesian to anyone who believes that demand management should be largely designed to restrain monetary inflation, provided that it is combined with wage restraint to promote employment. Let me argue the case as follows:

Keynes in the 1930s was against using cuts in wage-rates to expand employment because in the absence of positive offsetting expansionary financial demand-management policies this would lead merely to a reduction in all money prices, costs, and incomes with little or no effect on the volume of unemployment and output. But he would not, I think, have denied that a cut in wages combined with positive expansionary demand-management policies sufficient to prevent the fall in money wage-rates from causing any fall in total money expenditures on goods and services would lead to an expansion of output and employment. I can hear him say that it is a silly proposal in circumstances in which there was already a deflation of money wages and prices, no threat of general inflation, and much greater political ease and administrative feasibility in simply relying on the restoration and maintenance of total money expenditure. But in a world threatened with explosive inflation of money incomes and prices to recommend the alternative of using wage restraint to promote employment, combined with positive financial demand-management policies to keep total money incomes and expenditure on a given growth path in spite of any adjustments of money wage-rates may make much better sense and, I would claim, is in no way at variance with Keynes' basic analysis. I defend my claim to the title of Keynesian.

But can I avoid the title of Monetarist?

In the taxonomic schema which is before you I have made the distinctive feature of a Monetarist to be the view that financial policies should be aimed primarily at the control of inflationary money expenditures. This makes me a Keynesian–Monetarist. But there are at least four other possible criteria for Monetarism, discussed in the papers of Professors Tobin and Laidler, and enumerated on lines 3, 4, 5, and 6 of my schema.

(1) The first is shown on line 3 of my schema. If it is held that a distinctive feature of a Monetarist is the belief that financial policy should be so devised as to keep the *stock* of money (some form of M) on a steady growth path, then I can avoid the description of being a Monetarist, believing as I do that the aim should be to keep the *flow* of money expenditure (some form of MV) on a steady growth path. After all, the purpose of the Monetarist must be to control M so as to influence MV in

such a way that this control of PT restrains movements of P. If so, why not keep one's eye directly on MV, i.e. on PT, rather than on M? Professor Tobin makes this point; and at the end of section IV of his paper Professor Laidler discusses the ways in which the adoption of a particular definition of M for the purpose of monetary control can affect financial habits and institutions and so the demand for the particular brand of M. Can we not tempt him to join us in keeping his eye on PT rather than on M?

(2)   A second possible distinctive feature of a Monetarist, noted on line 4 of my schema, is to rely wholly on monetary policy and not on fiscal policy as the means for the control of inflation. If this is a necessary criterion of a Monetarist, once again I fail to qualify. It is perhaps worth while pointing out that there would be nothing illogical for those whose aim is to control M rather than MV to do so by pumping money into or out of the system by fiscal changes which affect the Public Sector Borrowing Requirement rather than by changes in banking policies whose impact effect is on interest rates and the other terms of lending to the private sector. Indeed, if it were a necessary criterion for a Monetarist to dismiss fiscal policy as an instrument of control of inflation, then Mrs Thatcher and Sir Geoffrey Howe with their insistence on reducing the Public Sector Borrowing Requirement would fail the test. So perhaps I am safe on this one.

(3)   Line 5 of my schema presents a much more serious threat to my claim to be a Monetarist, since I believe not only in fiscal policy, but in finely tuned fiscal policy, as an instrument for the control of MV. The discussion of the merits of fine tuning is often confined (as it is I think in both Professor Tobin's and Professor Laidler's papers) to the use of demand-management policies and, in particular, of fiscal policies for the maintenance of a high level of employment and real output. But fine tuning does not, I think, in itself refer to the use of any particular instrument or the pursuit of any particular objective, but rather to the possibility of making frequent and prompt variations in whatever instrument is being used for whatever purpose. Suppose Sir Geoffrey Howe were to devise a special tax that he could put up and down like Bank Rate from week to week in order to pump money into and out of the system in order to keep the stock of money on a given growth path, you might be surprised but you would not, I think, argue that he had ceased to be a Monetarist. It is on similar grounds that I would argue that similar fine tuning of a tax to keep MV on a given growth path does not disqualify one from being a Monetarist simply because one is fine tuning rather than rough tuning the tax. I ought to stick to my self-imposed humdrum taxonomic task of classifying classes, but I cannot resist the temptation of making a brief digression on the merits of fine tuning. I believe that in a 'fixprice' world there can be cumulative forces affecting real incomes, output, and employment working through the multiplier, the accelerator and the influence of expectations whose effects it is important to nip in the bud; that future developments are very difficult to foresee; that the work of A. W. Phillips and others has shown how important is the influence of time-lags in any dynamic control; that in consequence prompt and frequent variations of control are necessary; and that we cannot hope to

achieve the necessary finely tunable controls unless we consciously devise taxes that can be so varied. Fiscal fine tuning to control MV has not failed; it has never been seriously tried.

(4)   Line 6 brings me to the final test of my claim to be a Monetarist. It runs on one's attitude to reform of wage-fixing institutions. Is a Monetarist allowed to believe that such reform is an essential element of a macro-economic policy for the control of inflation? The Keynesian Non-Monetarist holds the view that demand-management policies should be devised to maintain full employment and that if, as may well be the case, this leads to the threat of an explosive wage-cost-push inflation, then an incomes policy is a necessary ingredient of any macro-economic policy to control inflation. But such persons make no claim to be Monetarists. But what about someone who thinks that demand-management policies should ideally be used to control MV, but that this should be done if, and only if, wage-fixing arrangements can be suitably reformed to promote employment, so that the control of PT is compatible with a full-employment level of T? Can he claim to be a Monetarist?

The concept of a Natural Rate of Unemployment, derived from the expectations-adjusted Phillips curve, as that rate which, given the existing wage-fixing institutions, would avoid any acceleration or deceleration of the rate of inflation, is an illuminating one. But it is possible that with wage-rates fixed through uncontrolled monopoly bargaining by bodies which are more concerned with the real standards of those in employment than with the numbers of unemployed, the Natural Rate will be unnaturally high; indeed some would go so far as to say that it becomes not merely a useless, but indeed a meaningless concept. I for one have in mind an alternative concept which one may perhaps in old-fashioned Keynesian terms call the Full Employment Rate of Unemployment. Admittedly it is not a very precise notion but its definition would run on the following lines: 'The Full Employment Rate of Unemployment is that rate which would result if, against the background of a steady growth in the demand for labour and taking into account the need for fixing the rate for the job in imperfect monopsonistic markets, rates of pay in each sector of the economy were adjusted so as to promote employment in that sector rather than to promote the standard of living of those already in employment in that sector.'

All this may be dismissed as a mere play on rather imprecise words. If one agrees on the desirability of certain reforms, does it matter whether one says that they will help to reduce the Natural Rate of Unemployment or whether one says that they will help to preserve Full Employment? In fact there is a real difference of emphasis between those who think that one can control inflation through demand-management policies and that existing wage-fixing arrangements can then be left to produce, after a tiresome but not fatal time-lag, a tolerable level of employment and those who like myself, and, I think, Professor Tobin, would not accept this. May we nevertheless call ourselves Monetarists?

Just to confuse the issue I have devised my schema in such a way that as you move to the *Left* you become more and more certainly a Monetarist and as you move to the *Right* more and more certainly a Keynesian and less and less certainly a Monetarist. I am down there at the bottom in the sixteenth box on the extreme Right of line 6. Ought I to be dismissed and moved one step further to the Right to join many of my Cambridge colleagues in the Keynesian Non-Monetarist box on the extreme right of line 2?

The papers of Professors Tobin and Laidler have prompted me to arrange in this schema the distinctions which they have drawn. They have done me the great service of clarifying my mind on how many issues there are at stake. In the last row of my schema there are no less than sixteen boxes. But that is (*i*) without including and sub-dividing the two big classes of Non-Keynesian Monetarists and Keynesian Non-Monetarists, (*ii*) without any reference to differences of view on the treatment of the balance of payments, (*iii*) without any reference to what I will call the control engineer's view that instead of linking each instrument of policy to one particular objective all instruments should be simultaneously and jointly planned to get the best combined result of all targets simultaneously, and (*iv*) with the use sometimes only of distinctions of analysis (as in line 1) and sometimes only of distinctions of policy recommendations (as in lines 2, 3, 4, 5 and 6). Time pressses and I must leave you to complete the taxonomic classification, though I must warn you that you will need a very large piece of paper to do it all adequately. Meanwhile on your behalf I would like to thank Professors Tobin and Laidler for their papers and, in particular, for the illumination which they throw on the absurdity of dividing economists crudely into Keynesians and Monetarists.

24

A New Keynesian Approach to Full Employment

This text of a lecture given in Copenhagen on 5 May 1983 to mark the centenary of Keynes' birth was published in both the Nationaløkonomisk Tidsskrift, *vol. 121 (1983), pp. 299–316, and* Lloyds Bank Review, *no. 150 (October 1983), pp. 1–18.*

I am greatly honoured by the invitation to speak at this conference to celebrate the centenary of the birth of John Maynard Keynes. Personally, like many others, I owe more to him than I can express. In my very first years as an economist I had the inestimable privilege of being a member of the small group, including Richard Kahn, Joan and Austin Robinson, and Piero Sraffa, which in 1930/31 met weekly to discuss and develop the analysis in Keynes' *Treatise on Money* which had just been published. In fact to some extent we played the role of midwives at the birth of the ideas which Keynes was evolving for inclusion in his *General Theory of Employment Interest and Money*. Later on in the war years when Keynes was working in the Treasury from 1940 until his death in 1946, I was employed as a member of the Economic Section in the Cabinet Offices; as a result I had the privilege of seeing him at work on domestic and international war finance and on plans and preparations for domestic and international reconstruction. I admired him beyond measure; and he has been the decisive influence in the formation of my ideas about, and attitudes towards, economic policies and institutions. He was a man of magical personality and with a fantastically wide span of interests and occupations, ranging from the manipulation of public and private finances to the collection of pictures and books and the promotion of the ballet. I will not attempt to describe the richness of his personality. But there is one feature of his character which I would like to stress. Beneath the wit, the charm, and the magic of his personality there lay an overpowering desire to build a freer, more sensible, more efficient, fairer, and better domestic and international society. He devoted his life to this effort and indeed in the end killed himself by overwork at it. I stress this because of the fashionable attempts to ascribe all our present economic ills to Keynes. To one who has attempted to work beside him in this task, such a depreciation of such a man appears both absurd and obnoxious.

I am, I fear, no scholar; and I would fail badly in the task if I attempted to pay my tribute to his memory by recounting and appraising the development of his thought on economic policies and institutions. Instead I am going to discuss the present problem of heavy unemployment which is common to all the countries of the free-enterprise mixed-economy industrially developed world. This is certainly a problem for the cure of which Keynes, if he were alive, would be pouring out a stream of new ideas – each one being not necessarily completely consistent with its predecessor; and I feel that it is fit that a disciple of Keynes should pay tribute to him by attempting, however inadequately, to carry on that discussion.

I am one of that generation of young men and women who in the 1920s and 1930s in the United Kingdom turned to economics because of the prevailing mass unemployment. We believed that it was both stupid and wicked to do nothing about poverty in the midst of potential plenty, that is to say, to allow resources of men and machinery to rust in involuntary idleness when there were so many real needs to be satisfied. We fell under the spell of Keynes. We believed that effective demand could be stimulated, and the production of useful things thus be restarted, by a combination of monetary policies to ease the terms on which funds could be borrowed for capital development, of fiscal policies which would expand public demand for goods or services or would leave people with larger tax-free disposable incomes to spend themselves on goods and services, and of foreign-exchange-rate policies which would prevent too much of the increased demand from expending itself on imports and thus causing an intolerable balance-of-payments problem. During the 1930s there continued to be a tug-of-war both in debate and in policies between these ideas and the more orthodox attitudes to financial questions.

During the war in the United Kingdom there was much discussion of post-war plans; and in 1944 the war-time Coalition Government of Conservative, Liberal, and Labour members published a White Paper on Employment Policy in which the government accepted the duty of maintaining a high and stable level of employment. In the simultaneous international discussions which resulted in the setting up of the International Monetary Fund and the International Bank for Reconstruction and Development and in the signing of the General Agreement on Tariffs and Trade, the idea of governmental responsibilities for maintaining effective demand and so a high and stable level of employment played an important role. Keynes himself was one of the chief architects of this domestic and international structure.

There followed a quarter of a century of the most prosperous and most rapidly growing international economy. In the United Kingdom the standard of living grew more rapidly than ever before in its history, although we were often apt to regard it as a period of failure because we were not growing as rapidly as the majority of other similar economies. One must not, of course, argue *post hoc propter hoc*. Many scholars tell us that there were good reasons for the buoyancy of real demands and economic activity in this period which had nothing to do with the conscious adoption by governments of Keynesian financial policies to stimulate demand. However, it is at least true that governments did not adopt anti-Keynesian restrictive policies of a kind which would have inhibited this golden age of prosperity; and it may be that expectations by business men that governments would if necessary live up to their newly accepted responsibility for the maintenance of a high and stable level of employment encouraged the atmosphere of confidence in which the current expansion took place.

However this may be, the interesting question for a Keynesian is not whether it was Keynesian policies which caused the period of prosperity, but rather why it was that Keynesian policies were not adopted in the subsequent period of world depression to stimulate demand in order to restore a high and stable level of employment.

The immediate answer to this question is obvious. During the 1930s when the *General Theory* was being written mass unemployment was combined with stagnant, and indeed for much of the time with slowly falling, money prices and wage-rates. An expansion of effective demand which was desired in order to deal with the mass unemployment of men and other resources could then be regarded as positively desirable also in order to put a stop to the fall in money prices with its undesirable effects on the real value of indebtedness; at any rate there was no overriding fear that it would lead to a rapid and possibly explosive inflation of money prices, money costs, and money incomes.

In the 1970s and 1980s the situation was, of course, completely different. The growth of heavy unemployment was accompanied by a rapid price inflation and indeed in the United Kingdom at times with the threat of a real explosive, runaway inflation. The authorities were faced with a tragic dilemma: should they expand in order to put an end to the tragic waste of idle resources or should they restrict expenditures at the risk of causing more unemployment and bankruptcies in order to stop the inflationary explosion? In my view we would all now be fighting – and most probably fighting with considerable success – the world depression with Keynesian anti-depression policies and we would never have heard of monetarism, Mrs Thatcher, or President Reagan if it had not been for the threat of excessive and explosive price inflation.

But it may be asked, was not the threat of explosive price inflation itself the result of the previous adoption of lax, expansive, Keynesian, financial policies? I do myself believe that during the 1950s and 1960s, in the United Kingdom at least, the policies for financial expansion were overdone. We then ran the economy at unemployment levels of 3 per cent, 2 per cent or even 1 per cent as compared with the range of 10 per cent to 20 per cent in the inter-war period; and there was a perpetual underlying tendency for wage and price inflation. There may well during these years have been some undesirable demand-pull inflation. But certainly in the case of the United Kingdom it is very difficult to ascribe the inflationary pressures in the 1970s and 1980s to the pull of excess demand. Profit margins during this period were very markedly eroded, which clearly suggests that the immediate cause of continuing price inflation during this period of declining effective demand and increasing unemployment was the upward pressure of wage costs and imported material costs the effects of which in causing a price inflation were in fact slightly damped down by the reduction of profit margins.

The dilemma of the choice between expansionary policies for full employment and restrictive policies for the battle against inflation is a very real one, and one which Keynes would certainly have recognised. It is indeed a total misrepresentation of that great man to represent him as an irresponsible inflationist. I can vouch for this myself personally. I had a number of discussions with him in the last years of his life on this topic as the government's post-war plans were under discussion. He was acutely aware of the fact that the success of Keynesian employment policies ran a great danger of being frustrated by inflationary pressures and in particular by inflationary wage-cost pressures.

If there were textbook perfect competition in the labour market, upward pressure on money wage costs would not occur in times of heavy unemployment. Wage contracts are set in terms of money; if there were unemployed workers seeking work in a perfectly competitive labour market, they would be undercutting existing money wage-rates. I am not arguing either that it is possible, or that it would be a good thing if it were possible, to introduce perfectly competitive conditions in the labour market. Indeed I strongly oppose measures which would involve the elimination of any social support for the unemployed in order to sharpen their appetites for jobs, and the prohibition of any trade union or similar arrangements in order to reduce the defences of those in work from inroads by the unemployed. In the case of the labour market, workers' organisations are needed to offset the monopsonistic bargaining powers of large-scale employers and to improve the workers' information about market conditions; and social support for those who in a dynamic economy are bound from time to time to be unemployed for no fault of their own is clearly needed on humanitarian grounds. Institutional arrangements which impede the forces of competition are not always wrong But where they exist their actions should be subject to appropriate social control. What I *am* arguing is that the application of this principle to labour market arrangements lies at the heart of our present troubles.

The basic function of a trade union is to obtain the best possible rate of pay for those employed in the sector concerned rather than to set a rate of pay in that sector which will open up opportunities of employment to the greatest possible number of outsiders – to those in less well-paid jobs or to those who are wholly unemployed, including in particular the unemployed school leavers among the least privileged sections of society. There is nothing morally wrong with this attitude; it is the proper function of a trade union official to look after the interests of his own employed members; but it needs to be exercised within accepted social restraints. It has, however, one most important implication for our present problems.

As a depression develops with falling demand and growing unemployment a trade union may exercise great restraint in its wage claims because those in employment whose interests it represents will fear that they may lose their jobs if they price their services too high. But when demand starts to rise again this element of wage restraint will disappear; as soon as unemployment begins to fall, those in employment will feel no threat to their jobs and will have an incentive to enjoy the advantages of a growing demand for their products by improving their own rates of pay rather than by opening up to the outsiders opportunities for new jobs in their sector. This will be particularly true if the depression of demand has been severe and has lasted for some time, since in this case many elderly workers who have lost their jobs during the recession will no longer be seeking work. They will have been replaced by school leavers who have never been in jobs and who have, therefore, never been trade union members. Those who are still in employment will have little direct interest in such unemployed outsiders. It is for reasons of this kind that in my opinion we would be foolish to believe that any current restraints in wage claims which are due to the past process of recession can be relied upon to continue during any future period of recovery.

The real inflationary danger from an upward pressure of wage claims is not so much from a persistent but constant rate of price inflation, provided that it is not excessively high, but rather from an explosive inflationary situation in which the rate of price inflation threatens continually to increase. This can happen if monopolistic wage claims are inconsistent either absolutely with the rate of increase of productivity or relatively with each other.

Thus suppose that we all demand a 5 per cent per annum rise in our real standards of pay though output per head is rising only at 2 per cent. This year we demand a 5 per cent rise in money pay. This causes costs to rise by only 3 per cent since output per head is rising by 2 per cent. This 3 per cent rise in costs may at first eat into profits, but sooner or later it will cause selling prices to rise by 3 per cent per annum to cover the rise in costs. But when the cost of living starts to rise by 3 per cent per annum, we shall all demand a money wage increase of 8 per cent – 3 per cent to cover the cost of living and 5 per cent to give us the real increase at which we aim. The 8 per cent rise in money pay will cause a 6 per cent rise in costs after allowing for increased productivity. We shall then demand a rise of 11 per cent in money pay – 6 per cent to offset the cost of living plus 5 per cent to attain our real target; and so on in an explosive inflationary spiral.

A similar result can occur as a result of inconsistent relative wage claims. Suppose group A insists on being 5 per cent ahead of group B, while group B insists on being at least on a level with group A. Group A obtains its 5 per cent rise; group B follows with a 5 per cent rise to catch up; group A responds with a further 5 per cent rise to keep ahead; and so on. This leap-frogging process may well speed up as each group in turn realises that it has failed to achieve its objective. Once more we have an explosive inflationary spiral.

At this point it may well be asked why, if my analysis of the power and effect of monopolistic wage-fixing institutions is correct, they did not display their devastating inflationary possibilities during the golden age of full employment of the 1950s and 1960s, but rather suddenly started to do so during the less prosperous and ultimately depressed conditions of the 1970s and 1980s. Certainly in the United Kingdom there does seem to have been a rather sharp change in this respect at the end of the 1960s and the start of the 1970s. To what could it have been due?

A first possibility is that there was simply a progressive increase in the institutional power of organised pressure groups which in addition became more and more willing to exert their own power to enforce their own ambitious claims. I am no sociologist and I have no idea why such changes of attitude should occur rather abruptly, if they do so occur; but it is interesting to note that this was just the period when aggressive student unrest rather suddenly swept through our world.

A second possibility for which there seems to be some hard evidence is that for one reason or another the 1970s were a period when output per head rose less rapidly than before. People may well have carried over into a period of less rapid growth of output per head claims to which they had got used during a previous period of more rapid growth and which, though over-ambitious and highly inflationary in the new period, were not so over-ambitious or inflationary in the previous period.

A third development was, of course, the fourfold increase in the price of imported oil set by the OPEC oil producers in the first half of the 1970s. Such a development can best be thought of as a reduction in the output per head of the goods needed for domestic consumption, since it means that each unit of home-produced goods for export will exchange for a smaller amount of imports needed for home consumption. To put it another way, at any given level of domestic prices and costs (including the money wage-rate) the cost of living will be higher because of the direct and indirect element of oil consumption in that cost. Any attempt to raise the money wage-rate to offset the higher cost of imported oil would trigger off an explosive upward spiral of wages chasing prices of the kind which I have described, since people would be seeking a real rate of pay which was inconsistent with the lower productivity of their exported output in terms of imported consumption.

Suppose my analysis of the present wage-fixing problems to be broadly correct. What should a Keynesian like myself recommend as a possible way out of our present troubles?

An Orthodox Keynesian would, I suppose, recommend that we should use the whole panoply of financial policies – monetary policy, fiscal policy, and foreign exchange rate policy – to expand the effective demand for goods and services until we had regained a high level of employment and that we should then design these policies to stabilise the demand for labour at that level. Some Orthodox Keynesians hold the view that the danger of this leading to an explosive wage-cost–price inflation is greatly exaggerated and that some gentle persuasion and nudging on the labour front could keep inflationary pressures within tolerable bounds. Other, and in my view more realistic, Orthodox Keynesians fully recognise the inflationary dangers of such a policy and would urge that Keynesian expansion of demand for full employment be combined with an effective centralised incomes policy to prevent rates of pay from rising in an explosive inflationary manner.

I myself find difficulty in accepting these recommendations on the ground that such a centralised incomes policy, while it would in my view certainly be needed if an Orthodox Keynesian expansionary policy were adopted, would require a degree of intervention and control over money wages and prices which might well be impossible to administer and would in any case be unacceptable if an effective alternative approach could be found. While accepting the basic Keynesian analysis of effective demand and while recommending the full panoply of Keynesian financial policies for the management of demand, I am led to stand the Orthodox Keynesians on their heads in an upside-down posture which I will call that of New Keynesianism.

Incidentally, before I explain what I mean by this gymnastic exercise, let me make it clear that I am not necessarily labelling Keynes himself as an Orthodox Keynesian, and I am not suggesting that he would necessarily need to be stood on his head if he were still with us. He would, I feel sure, still qualify as a Keynesian; but what particular brand of Keynesianism he would now be promoting is anybody's guess – probably some imaginative and constructive brand of his own. How I wish that he could be with us in our present troubles.

Let me explain what I mean by the reversal of functions between what I have called Orthodox, and what I have called New, Keynesianism. The Orthodox Keynesian doctrine is to use financial policies to achieve satisfactory levels of real effective demand and so of the *real* national income and, if necessary, to control the fixing of money rates of pay so as to prevent unacceptable rates of *money* price inflation. By New Keynesianism I mean a policy of using the whole panoply of Keynesian financial policies to maintain a steady but moderate rate of growth of total monetary expenditures on domestically produced goods and services and so of the national *money* income, and against this background to reform wage-fixing institutions so as to promote *real* output and employment in each sector of the economy.

Recent experience has persuaded me that we do need some monetary anchor. I do not like the idea of using for this purpose a fixed monetary price of gold or indeed of a composite basket of standardised primary products. I am not attracted by the idea which is implied by Orthodox Keynesianism that one should by central control fix the money price of labour instead of the money price of gold or of some basket of commodities. Nor do I see any merit in selecting one particular form of liquidity – M_1, M_2, or M_3 – and keeping this particular stock of assets on a steady growth path while investors are free to shift their funds into and out of this particular kind of property. But I do see great merit in looking directly at the total national money income and controlling money expenditures with the whole armoury of fiscal, monetary, and foreign-exchange-rate policies so as to keep the total of available money incomes on a steady growth path. Against this background money wage-rates could play their proper role on a decentralised basis in matching supplies and demands for labour at full-employment levels.

It is not technically difficult for an economist to devise blueprints for suitable wage-setting institutional arrangements, taking into account for each country its historical background, and its laws, customs, and existing institutions. In the case of the United Kingdom I personally would suggest a combination of some reforms of labour law to restrain certain of the trade unions' excessive monopoly powers and of some increases in legal and institutional constraints or controls over the setting of selling prices by monopolistic businesses, in order to make it difficult for them to play a part in the inflation of money wages, costs and prices. Against the background of a resolute financial policy designed to maintain the total money national income on a moderate and steady growth path, I would like to see some central representative body set up to assess the economic effects of such a policy and as a result to announce a norm or average increase in the rate of pay which would in these circumstances promote the attainment and maintenance of a high and stable level of employment. I would recommend the institution of a national structure of pay tribunals to which either party to a dispute about rates of pay could refer the case, the duty of the tribunal being to make an award which corresponded to the current national norm, unless the setting of a somewhat higher or lower award seemed to it to be desirable in order to promote employment and output by balancing supply and demand for labour in the particular sector under examination. I would like to see the application of certain sanctions against those who took industrial action against the terms of such an award. All this might be combined with a special inflation tax on increases in rates of pay which exceeded the norm by some stated percentage.

I do not want to dwell on these particulars since they would obviously need to be designed differently to suit the conditions of each country. But I would like to emphasise two points: first, that in my opinion a really radical reform of wage-setting institutions is essential for the health and welfare of our sort of free democratic world; and, second, that obtaining general acceptability of any such set of reforms is essential for their working and politically far and away the most difficult domestic economic problem.

I fear that this calls for a revolution in present attitudes. A decentralised system for setting rates of pay in each sector of the economy in such a way as to promote output and employment in that sector means that wage-fixing cannot be used as a main instrument for achieving a more equal and fair distribution of income. The appallingly difficult task is to persuade people to think of the wage-rate not primarily as an instrument for achieving a desirable distribution of income as between wages and profits and as between different types of labour, but primarily as an instrument for promoting the full and efficient employment of labour. This does not mean that we should be unconcerned about these distributional problems. What it does mean is that somehow or other the emphasis must be decisively shifted onto other measures – such as welfare services, social benefits, and taxation – to achieve a socially acceptable distribution of income and property.

Indeed, such a shift of emphasis is desirable not only for the promotion of employment but in the direct interests of a decent redistribution of income as well. For it is true, at least in the United Kingdom, that for the relief of real poverty reliance on tax arrangements, social benefits, and welfare services is a more efficient tool than adjustment of low pay. The fact is that the correlation between poverty and low pay is surprisingly low; there are many low-paid workers who are not in poverty, being members of a family with other earners and few dependents, and many who are not low paid but are in poverty, being members of a family with no other income but many dependents with, perhaps, special needs. Taxation, social benefits, and welfare services unlike rates of pay can be moulded to fit needs and resources.

I am myself convinced that for the reasons which I have already discussed the application of Keynesian expansionary policies is held up by present attitudes and institutions which connect wage claims with the attainment of absolute or relative levels of real income (which may well be inconsistent with what is in fact attainable) rather than with the promotion of output and employment. This is, in my view, already the basic impediment for planning for prosperity. But if we peer into the future the implications of this clash between the use of the wage-rate to obtain a desirable real income target and its use to promote output and employment may become even more formidable. I refer to the possible, though by no means certain, implications of the new technological revolution through which we are passing in communications, information services, data processing, control systems, etc. – what for short I will call Chips and Robots.

It is certain that Chips and Robots will substantially increase the total amount that could be produced with any given amount of Men and Machinery; but a basic question to which the answer is, I think, uncertain is whether it will make Men less valuable in production relatively to Machinery – whether, that is to say, it will raise the return on capital relatively to the real wage offered to the worker – and if so how much.

If Chips and Robots turn out simply to raise productivity without basically affecting the relative marginal products of labour and capital, there will be no long-run fundamental increase in the problem of reconciling full employment with a decent distribution of income. The owners of capital will receive a real income, say, twice as great, but the real rate of pay in that case will also be twice as great. No doubt there will be less employment because, if we can judge from past history, the higher real income of the worker will be taken out largely in increased leisure – shorter working hours, longer holidays, earlier retirement, etc. But this is compatible with an unchanged distribution of real standards between workers and owners of capital; and it does not imply any lasting increase in involuntary unemployment, though during the process of change, as employment is reduced in occupations taken over by Robots and is expanded in occupations in which labour remains important relatively to machinery, there will be serious problems of structural and frictional unemployment.

But the situation would be quite different if Chips and Robots turned out to make capital very much more important relatively to labour. Imagine for a moment the extreme possibility. Let us suppose that Robots can produce everything, including manufacturing and replacing each other, and that they require an absolute minimum of labour to attend them. The wages of labour are transformed into profits earned on Robots. But the ownership of property is at present much less equally distributed than the ability to work; and the profits on the Robots would thus be more highly concentrated than the previous wage earnings. Although output per head might be immensely increased, either competition among workers for the small number of jobs would reduce the real wage absolutely to a very low level or else, if by trade union or similar action the real wage was held up, there would be a large volume of involuntary unemployment among those who were not privileged to get the few jobs available at the fixed rate of pay.

No doubt the change will be nothing like as stark as I have just depicted it. But if it turns out that Chips and Robots have a substantial influence of this sort on the distribution of real income as between income from property and income from work, it is possible that reliance on the existing mechanisms for the redistribution of income through taxation and social welfare would not be enough. In this case attention would have to be paid to two other possible developments.

The first would consist of measures to redistribute the private ownership of property so that society becomes a property-owning democracy, in which the representative citizen was a representative owner of property as well as a representative potential worker. The national income, including the products of the Robots, would again be more equally divided and the workers' decreased employment would again become voluntary leisure rather than involuntary unemployment.

The second development would be by means of what I will call topsy-turvy nationalisation, by which I mean socialisation of ownership with privatisation of management instead of socialisation of management with privatisation of ownership. With the nationalisation schemes with which we are familiar in the United Kingdom the government takes over for centralised public management the actual physical machinery and equipment (e.g. the railway lines and rolling stock), but in compensation it issues national debt to the previous owners who continue to receive interest on their capital. By topsy-turvy nationalisation I mean a process whereby the management of the physical equipment (e.g. the Robots) is left in the hands of a multiplicity of small competing privately managed companies, while government by means of a capital levy, wealth tax, or death duties gains an unencumbered ownership of shares in these competing companies. It could hold these shares directly; or could invest the capital in various privately operated investment trusts whose job it would be in competition with each other to invest the money in turn in what they considered to be the most promising companies operating the Robots. By this means all part of the profits of such companies would indirectly accrue to the government, which could use the revenue to finance a social dividend or other form of social benefit to the generality of citizens, who would thus receive an income other than their income from work, so that once again involuntary unemployment could be transformed into voluntary leisure.

Now I personally believe that a society which combined elements of redistributive taxation and social welfare with elements of property-owning democracy and topsy-turvy nationalisation would in any case be a very desirable kind of society to live in, though I have no desire to hide the fact that I have said nothing about the very difficult measures which would be needed to produce a real property-owning democracy or to achieve any considerable degree of topsy-turvy nationalisation. I wish only to point out that it might conceivably in the future become necessary to face these difficulties, if we wanted to combine full employment in a free-enterprise society with a tolerable distribution of income.

But our immediate unemployment problem is not primarily due to Chips and Robots. In two years from 1979 to 1981 the volume of industrial production in the United Kingdom fell by some 15 per cent, at which depressed level it stagnated. By no stretch of the imagination can more than a very small part of this sudden collapse be ascribed to the introduction of new technologies. A major part of our present trouble remains a case of lack of Keynesian effective demand complicated by the threat of an explosive inflation if Keynesian expansionary policies were introduced.

So much for the problem of wage-fixing. The other half of the problem of restoration of Keynesian full employment relates to the management of the total money demand for the products of a country's economy by means of fiscal, monetary, and foreign exchange policies. When I planned this lecture, I had intended to devote equal attention to both halves of the problem; but since in my opinion it is the wage-fixing problem which is the basic impediment to a successful Keynesian attack on unemployment, I make no apologies for having devoted a disproportionate amount of my time to its discussion. In the short time that remains to me I can only state very briefly and very dogmatically my own views on financial demand-management policies without really adequate discussion of them.

Let me start by considering the position of a single country – let us call it New Keynesiana – which alone is going to attempt to devise its financial policies on the New Keynesian principle of adjusting total money expenditures on its domestically produced goods and services so as to keep the total of its domestically produced money income on a steady growth path. The first basic question is whether it should rely primarily on monetary or on fiscal policies for this purpose. If, as I would hope, the country concerned is attempting to remain a member of an open world economy without reliance on controls of capital movements, it will in my opinion have to rely on its domestic fiscal policy rather than on its domestic monetary policy for the control of total money expenditures on goods and services. With freedom of international capital movements it will not be able to set its domestic monetary policy, that is to say its domestic structure of interest rates, without regard to interest rates in other countries. Even if it allows the foreign exchange value of its money to float freely, it cannot set its domestic interest rates seriously out of line with interest rates in the rest of the world without causing an intolerable overshooting of the foreign exchange value of its currency away from any reasonable equilibrium level.[1]

[1] The influences at work may be illustrated by the following much oversimplified numerical fable. Suppose the rate of interest in the USA to be 20 per cent and in the UK to be 10 per cent, and that this divergence were confidently expected to last for three years and then to stop. If in these conditions the £ depreciated by some 30 per cent below the natural competitiveness level which was expected to rule in three years' time when the divergence of interest rates was expected to cease, the expected yields on the present investment of funds in the USA and the UK would be equalised. An owner of £s who bought $s now would gain some 30 per cent over the next three years from the 10 per cent higher rate of interest enjoyed in the USA, but he would lose 30 per cent by the fact that he would pay now 30 per cent more £s to buy the $s than he would receive at the end of the three years when he bought back the £s at the natural competitiveness rate of exchange.

Thus New Keynesiana would be using its wage-fixing institutions to maintain employment and designing its budgetary balance to keep its total money national income on a planned steady growth path. It would be wise in my opinion to allow the exchange value of its currency to float fairly freely, but to employ its domestic interest rate structure to influence international capital flows in such a way as to maintain, without too great a reliance on the use of its foreign exchange reserves, a rate of exchange which maintained a reasonable degree of competitiveness of its main products relatively to similar products of other countries. In other words, it would attempt by the use of monetary policy to induce continuous adjustments of the money rate of foreign exchange which reflected divergences between movements in its own domestic money costs and prices and the rate of inflation of such money costs and prices in its main competitor countries.

The competitiveness of New Keynesiana's products *vis-à-vis* similar products of its main competitors would have to be measured by some index of the ratio of its own money costs measured in its own domestic currency to money costs in foreign countries converted at the ruling rate of exchange into New Keynesiana's domestic currency. Let us call this the real rate of foreign exchange as contrasted with the money rate of exchange. The question remains at what level should it choose to stabilise this real rate of exchange. Let me discuss the answer to this question by considering the following horror story.

Suppose that everything is going along nicely when, alas, New Keynesiana is faced with a serious world depression which greatly reduces the world demand for her exports at the current real rate of exchange, i.e. at their current relative competitiveness. The fall in the demand for her exports will threaten to cause a reduction in the total money demand for her products and on New Keynesian fiscal-policy grounds she will offset this by increased government expenditures, or perhaps rather by reduced taxation, to promote an offsetting increase in public or private expenditures on goods and services. The country's demand for imports will thus be maintained in spite of the reduction in the world's demand for her exports. Suppose New Keynesiana attempts to finance this current account deficit on her balance of payments by a rise in domestic interest rates to attract foreign funds on capital account. This rise in interest rates will discourage domestic investment in capital development of all kinds; and to offset this additional threat to the maintenance of her money national income on its planned steady growth path, her fiscal policy will need to be further relaxed and her budget deficit still further increased.

Thus New Keynesiana will be confronted with a persistent budget deficit and ever-growing national debt with its ever-growing interest burden, and will almost certainly be simultaneously faced with a continuing loss of foreign exchange reserves or a continuing building up of official debts incurred in foreign currencies, since it is most unlikely that she could or should finance the whole of the current account deficit by raising domestic interest rates sufficiently to attract private funds.

If she cannot ride out this tempest, what can she do about it?

A first possibility is that she should impose restrictions on her imports to divert away from foreign products on to New Keynesiana's own products a sufficient amount of domestic expenditures to replace the reduction in the world's expenditure on her exports. This would deal simultaneously with both her balance-of-payments and her budget deficit problem; and it would be perfectly permissible under the GATT articles for her to employ import restrictions on balance-of-payments grounds in such circumstances. Yet in spite of this, I greatly hope that New Keynesiana would be able to avoid this solution. Freedom of commerce is still a very fragile structure; and I greatly fear that if New Keynesiana were to adopt this policy, although for her it would be perfectly justifiable on good macro-economic grounds, it would inevitably lead to protectionist retaliation by other countries which, since they were not preventing their own domestic depressions, would have no macro-economic justification for protection but nevertheless would have exceptionally strong protectionist political pressure from their depressed industries. There is in addition another very formidable problem connected with the imposition of import restrictions on balance-of-payments grounds: should such restrictions be discriminatory or not? Should two deficit countries be obliged pointlessly to restrict imports from each country or should they be allowed to discriminate against imports from the surplus countries only? And if various countries had various degrees of deficit or surplus on their balances of payments, what would be the appropriate structure or degree of discrimination if the problem were to be tackled by import restrictions? The experience of commercial and financial arrangements after World War II suggests that this is a very formidable political and economic issue.

A second possibility for New Keynesiana is, of course, to depreciate her real exchange rate. Ultimately it may be assumed that by making her products more competitive, demand at home and abroad will be sufficiently diverted on to New Keynesiana's products as to cope with the problem and thus to relieve both the balance-of-payments problem and the budget deficit problem. But because of the time-lags involved in the adjustment of channels of trade to new price relationships, the immediate and temporary effect may be a worsening of these two problems. The rise in the price of imports due to the exchange depreciation may immediately make the balance-of-trade deficit even greater than before. It will only be when price changes have had time to reduce the demand for foreign products and to increase the demand for New Keynesiana's products that the situation will be relieved. During the downward slope of the infamous J-curve the strain on the balance of payments and thus on the budget will be magnified. The exchange-rate variation will achieve an ultimate solution, but at the expense of a temporary once-for-all worsening of the deficits both on the balance of payments and on the budget.[2]

---

[2] Two colleagues of mine (David Vines, economist, and Jan Maciejowski, control engineer) have been engaged on applying New Keynesian principles to a dynamic model of the UK economy, which they have used in an attempt to answer the question: What would have happened in the 1970s and 1980s to the UK economy if these New Keynesian policies had been applied in spite of the world depression? The horror story related above for New Keynesiana reproduces what their enquiries suggest would have happened in this period to the UK. These results will be included in Vines, Maciejowski, and Meade, *Stagflation, Volume 2, Demand Management* (London: Allen & Unwin, 1983).

There is, of course, a third and better solution, namely by means of international co-operation which would avoid the ravages of such fluctuations in world economic activity; and indeed for very obvious reasons the smaller the country, the more important it becomes for New Keynesiana to rely on such international action. An international order for a free-enterprise world of New Keynesianas could be constructed more or less on the following principles.

Each member country would set a target for the planned growth of its own domestically produced money income. Each member country would devise its own fiscal regulator mechanisms for keeping money expenditures on this target path. Each country would design its own institutions for the control of prices and the setting of rates of pay for the promotion of its own real output and employment. These would all be national responsibilities, though international exchange of information and ideas about them would no doubt be useful.

International decisions and obligations would relate to interest-rate policies, foreign exchange rate policies, and the provision and use of international reserves and liquidity. The principles of operation can be enumerated under the following five headings:

(i) Agreement would be needed on a structure of targets for the members' real foreign exchange rates, these rates being chosen so as to ensure a reasonable level of competitiveness for each member's products relative to the products of the whole group of countries.

(ii) Agreement would be needed on a structure of domestic interest rates. The levels of these rates relatively to each other would influence the international flows of capital funds and thus the demands for the various national currencies; and they would accordingly be set in such a way as to help to preserve the agreed target real foreign exchange rates without undue reliance on the use of official foreign exchange reserves. This structure of relative domestic interest rates would need to be continually surveyed and revised as experience showed that such revisions were needed for the attainment of the target real exchange rates.

(iii) The absolute level of the whole structure of domestic interest rates would, if necessary, be subject to revision in an upward or downward direction, without disturbance of the relative levels needed to preserve the real exchange-rate targets. Thus if the majority of members were finding it difficult to maintain their domestic money income targets without the stimulus of undesirably large budget deficits, the occasion would have arisen for a general reduction in the whole structure of interest rates, which would stimulate domestic investment expenditures in the countries concerned and would thus reduce the need for stimulus by budget deficits. And conversely an upward shift of the whole structure of domestic interest rates would be appropriate in conditions of an otherwise widespread need for excessively high taxation and budget surpluses to prevent an undesired inflation of money national incomes.

(iv) The case for a revision of the real exchange-rate targets would arise if one country or group of countries was having to run undesirable budget deficits to prevent domestic deflations of their national incomes, while another was having to run undesirable budget surpluses to prevent domestic inflations. In this case a depreciation of the real exchange rates of the former group and appreciation for the latter group, together with an appropriate reduction of domestic interest rates in the former group and increase in the latter group, would be appropriate. When these changes had had time to work themselves out the exports of the former group would have risen and of the latter would have fallen relatively to their imports; and this shift of world demand for the products of the two groups of countries would reduce the deflationary influences and so the need for budget deficits in the first group of countries and *vice versa* in the second inflationary group. These changes would be furthered by the reduction of interest rates in the former group of countries which would promote domestic investment and thus further reduce their need for stimulus through budget deficits, and *vice versa* in the second inflationary group of countries. And the change in relative interest rates would be compatible with the preservation of the new target real exchange rates, since the former group of countries would have more favourable balances of payments on current account and would therefore need less inducements to attract funds from abroad on capital account, and *vice versa* for the other group.

(v) However, during the period needed for the changes in real exchange rates to work out their effects on the balance of trade (that is to say, during the period of the downward slope of the infamous J-curve) the problems of the two groups of countries might well be intensified rather than relieved, since for the time being the balance of trade of the former group of deflationary countries might be worsened instead of improved; and *vice versa* for the other group. There would during this transitional period be a very strong case for relying upon the use of foreign exchange reserves or other forms of official finance to cover the temporary balance-of-payments deficit of the former group at the expense of the temporary balance-of-payments surplus of the latter group, rather than to attempt to maintain the new real target exchange rates by a temporary but wholly perverse rise, instead of a fall, in the domestic interest rates in the former group and a temporary but wholly perverse fall, instead of a rise, in interest rates in the latter group. The covering of the perverse downward section of the J-curve is the occasion *par excellence* for the official financing of temporary imbalances in international payments.

I have no time to discuss these rules adequately, but only to assert dogmatically that in my opinion arrangements on these lines would enable national New Keynesian policies to be woven into an effective international whole.

So I will end this long rigmarole by asking the question: 'Can we restore Keynesian full employment?' The answer is 'Certainly Yes; but only on the two conditions of a suitable reform of national wage-fixing institutions and a suitable reform of international financial institutions, both of which reforms are essential economically but will be extremely difficult if not impossible to achieve politically.' It is the politicians, not the economists, who have the really difficult task.

25

Wage-Fixing Revisited

This revised and expanded version of the fourth Robbins Lecture at the University of Stirling on 25 October 1984 was published as Occasional Paper 72 by the Institute of Economic Affairs (London, 1985), pp. 15–47.

I am greatly honoured to be giving the fourth in this series of lectures instituted in honour of Lionel Robbins, who for 15 years was my close colleague and chief in Whitehall and the London School of Economics. This is not the occasion for a full personal appreciation of my old friend and colleague. I pay my tribute to him today simply by choosing for my lecture a subject matter which I know interested him, because we often discussed it together when we co-operated in work on the 1944 Government White Paper on Employment Policy.

The Problem of Stagflation

That document, published by a coalition of Conservative, Liberal, and Labour Ministers, marked the official acceptance for post-war economic policy of the Keynesian thesis that it was properly one of the functions of government, through its fiscal, monetary and exchange-rate policies, to control effective demand for the products of labour and thus to maintain a high and stable level of employment. It was certainly the enthusiastic and, as we thought, well-grounded hope of people like Lionel and myself that we would never again experience the heavy mass unemployment of the 1930s. Many other economic problems would remain – concerning, for example, education, health, housing, monopolies, the distribution of income and wealth, incentives and efficiency, pollution, the use of exhaustible resources, and so on – but not the old problem of the waste of resources through mass unemployment. And for a quarter of a century our hopes and expectations were fulfilled.

But now we are back with apparently persistent unemployment in this country of some 12½ per cent. Nor is this problem confined to the United Kingdom. It is worse in the UK than in most of the other free-enterprise developed countries of the world; but practically all of them are suffering from it to a larger or smaller extent. There have, of course, been a number of notable developments in the world economy, such as the

OPEC setting of oil prices and the rapid development of chips, robots, information technologies and all that – events which obviously have important effects upon the demand for labour. At the same time, there are important technical economic problems involved in the financial relationships between budgetary, monetary, and balance-of-payments policies as means for expanding the demand for the products of labour. Thus, thank goodness, there remains a delightfully rich collection of problems for economists to research into and to squabble about. Do not, however, let them throw dust into your eyes. Behind all these special problems and technicalities lies one simple basic economic malaise which is very easy to diagnose but very difficult to cure.

Why is it that we do not now set to work to reduce the present 12½ per cent unemployment by Keynesian measures to promote effective demand? Despite the technicalities of budgetary, monetary and foreign-exchange policies, it is not because we could not expand money expenditures on the products of labour if we decided to do so. Nor is it because there are no useful things to be done or to be made; indeed, throughout the economy people and institutions are being required to economise and cut back on what they desire to do and to consume. Nor is it because in some lines of activity modern technologies are reducing the demand for labour; there remain many useful sectors in which higher output would call for increased employment. The basic reason is well-known. Governments do not expand money expenditure because they fear, and justifiably fear, that it will lead to an inflationary rise in money prices – perhaps to an explosive, runaway inflation – rather than to increased sales of a larger quantity of products at uninflated prices.

All governments of the free-enterprise, developed countries are now confronted to a smaller or larger degree by this dilemma of stagflation: Should they expand total money expenditures in order to increase the demand for the products of labour and so to reduce unemployment at the risk of causing an inflationary price explosion? Or should they restrain total money expenditures on the products of labour in order to reduce the rate of price inflation at the risk of maintaining an undesirably high level of waste through unemployment? The basic problem is really straightforward: How can we ensure that, so long as there is a substantial volume of unemployed resources, an increase in total money expenditures will lead to an increase in employment, output and sales at uninflated money wage-rates and prices rather than to an increase in the money earnings and prices of the existing volume of employment, output and sales? This question is very simple to understand but very difficult to answer.

I shall start by dismissing rather cursorily two possible extreme forms of answer.

The Promotion of Competition

The first of these types of response would be to rely solely on the ruthless restoration of competitive conditions in all markets so that labour and other resources would be both able and willing, so long as they were unemployed, to offer their services at a rate of pay which undercut the earnings of existing employed resources. If this could be achieved, money costs and prices per unit of output would fall so long as there was any substantial unemployment; if, at the same time, money expenditures on the products of labour were being maintained by Keynesian financial measures, the volume of output and employment would be effectively expanded. The search for such competitive conditions would call for the abolition of all trade union privileges and immunities and of a host of other governmental interventions in agriculture, housing and many other sectors, as well as an effective set of policies and institutions to restrain monopolistic restrictive agreements.

As I shall indicate later, I am myself in favour of many moves in this direction. But there are good reasons for believing that it would be both undesirable and ineffective to go the whole hog in this direction.

The undesirability of such an extreme approach becomes obvious as soon as it is realised that it would involve the ruthless cutting down, if not abolition, of all support for the unemployed and their dependents in order to drive them back into the labour market at whatever reduction in rates of pay might be necessary to find them jobs within their reach without undue delay. With rapid technological change many people will, through no fault of their own, become unemployed; and a rich developed community should surely search for some solution which enables such victims of progress to be treated with relative generosity.

Indeed, current technological changes may make even more desirable than at present the development of arrangements for the support of incomes outside the labour market. It is possible that machines (such as robots) may become more productive at the margin than men in many sectors of the economy. The ownership of capital is much more concentrated than is the ability to work, and the result in a purely competitive market could then be that a few owners of the robots received a large income from the profits of industry while the displaced men competed at starvation wages for employment as butlers by the owners of the robots. I paint this silly extreme picture merely to illustrate vividly the possibility that modern technologies *may* shift the distribution of income somewhat in a fully competitive society from earned to unearned income. The shift will not, of course, be anything like as dramatic as in this extreme case.

The new technologies will undoubtedly increase average output per head. As a result, the real income of the worker may well be maintained at an *absolute* level as high as, or even higher than, previously, even though at the margin (which in a fully competitive economy is what counts in determining market values) the value to the producer of an additional man falls *relatively* to that of an additional machine. The maintenance of the absolute level of workers' real pay may well be promoted by an expansion of investment in real capital equipment, stimulated by the high profits in industry and leading in turn to an increased demand for men to operate the additional machines. But, even in this case, the possible labour-saving nature of the new technologies in a fully competitive economy would cause wage earnings to fall relatively to profits. There would remain a strong argument on distributional grounds for supporting relatively low incomes by payments outside the wage system in order to reconcile distributional *desiderata* with the maintenance of wage payments at rates which were low enough relatively to profits not to impede the employment of labour.

The Effects of Imperfect Competition

But even if these possible effects of the new technologies could be disregarded, it is questionable whether, in the absence of other measures which I will discuss later, the mere ruthless pursuit of competitive conditions would serve to solve the problem. We live inevitably in conditions of imperfect competition. In many sectors of the economy technological considerations make it necessary to produce on a scale which is large enough relatively to the size of the market for the product to leave room for only a limited number of competing producers. Moreover, these producers in many cases produce different qualities and brands of the product, and they may well be somewhat protected in their regional markets by transport costs. For all these reasons, such concerns will be faced with a falling demand curve – that is to say, with a choice of selling a restricted amount if they charge a higher price or an expanded volume if they charge a lower price. Indeed, if we ask any producer of manufactured goods whether he can sell just as many units of his existing product as he chooses at his current selling price, he will answer (with very few exceptions): 'Of course not. If I want to sell more, I must cut my price or improve the quality of my product or spend more on advertising and other selling costs.' This is likely to remain the typical situation even if all artificial restrictions on competition were removed.

That we live inevitably in a world of imperfect competition of this kind has a most important implication. Let us suppose that money expenditure on the products of industry is increased by Keynesian expansionary policies. An individual producer will experience an increase in the demand for his product. In conditions of imperfect competition he will then be faced with a choice: Should he take the increase out in the form of a higher price for his existing volume of sales or should he sell a larger quantity at an unchanged price? The more imperfect are the competitive conditions in the market, the easier will it be for the individual producer to choose to raise his price without a major loss of sales; and the more the generality of producers choose to raise their prices rather than increase the volume of their sales, the easier will it be for each individual one of them to raise his own price as his competitors' prices rise. Thus, by a process of action and reaction the less perfect the market the greater the ease of price inflation relatively to product expansion.

The fact that it is open to producers to raise prices as an alternative to increasing output and sales does not, of course, in itself mean that it will be profitable to do so. Profits can be increased by selling more at an unchanged profit margin per unit of output as well as by charging a higher profit margin on the existing volume of output. If the alternative of increased output is chosen, this implies a higher volume of employment. Let us suppose then that unemployed labour is brought into employment at the current money wage-rate with the result that there is more employment at the current money wage-rate, an unchanged profit mark-up on the labour cost of production per unit of output, but a higher total profit in industry due to the expanded volume of output.

Let us suppose now that the labour force is unionised. It is the function of a trade union leader to achieve the best possible conditions for the employees whom he represents and who constitute a group of what may be called 'lucky insiders'. It is not his job to seek the maximum possible expansion of job opportunities for the unemployed, the 'unlucky outsiders'. When he sees an expansion of the market leading to a rise in total profit without any rise in the rate of pay for the existing labour force, his natural reaction will be to demand a rise in the rate of pay so that the existing workers as well as the existing shareholders can participate in the enjoyment of the fruits of the expanded demand for the firm's product. In conditions of imperfect competition it will be relatively easy for the individual employer to respond to such industrial pressure from the workforce by conceding a rise in the rate of pay and preserving his profit margin through a corresponding rise in his selling price.

This sort of reaction will, of course, be the more likely the stronger is the trade union organisation. But I do not believe that it depends solely on organised monopolistic trade union action. Let us suppose that there was no trade union representation in the firm concerned. It is in the interest of the employer to maintain good relations with his workforce. Thus, even from the most selfish profit-making point of view it might well be considered wise to share to some extent the fruits of an expanded demand for the firm's product with the existing employees and thus to engage their loyalty and reap the production benefits derived from the efforts of a contented workforce. In practice, I think we do observe these relationships in the real world. Both in the UK and the USA we observe an expansion of demand leading partly to higher output and partly to an inflation of money wages and prices. The price inflation is worse in the UK where there is a much stronger monopolistic union organisation, but it also exists in the USA where such organisation is much weaker. Where technical conditions of production make imperfect competition inevitable, even the most ruthless attempts to restore competition will not ensure that a Keynesian expansionary policy will lead to increased output and employment without an inflation of money costs and prices, even though there is a substantial volume of unemployed labour.

A Centralised Incomes Policy

At the other extreme, we could attempt to solve the problem not by aiming at perfectly competitive conditions but by the extension of government control and intervention in the market in the form of a centralised control of rates of pay. The argument for such a policy is simple. If it were illegal to raise the rate of pay – or, rather, to raise the rate of pay by more than a certain restricted annual percentage – and if this requirement could be effectively enforced, then it would be possible to ensure that, so long as there was a substantial volume of unemployment, an expansion of the demand for the products of labour through expansionary Keynesian financial policies would lead to an increase of employment and output rather than to an inflation of money costs and prices.

In its extreme form this solution must also be rejected because, to be effective, the policy would have to be applied in a way which involved either many undesirable side-effects or an intolerably complicated, expensive and pervasive governmental interference with market forces.

Let us consider the policy in its most straightforward form in which it was made illegal for an employer to raise any *rate* of pay by more than x per cent in any year. The cost of a unit of labour must be reckoned in terms such as money earnings per hour of work. But there are innumerable ways in which labour can be paid: by an hourly rate, by overtime rates for additional hours of work, by means of an incremental scale in which rates of pay rise according to length of service, by different rates of pay for different grades of labour, by piece-rates per unit of product produced, by a share in the firm's profits, by means of fringe benefits in the form of pension arrangements, free or subsidised meals, social amenities, cheap loans, and so on. To ensure that the money value of real pay per hour of work was not raised by more than a limited amount would, in the end, involve consideration of the effects of adjustments as between normal time and overtime, of promotions of labour from one grade to another, of the distinction between a rise in schedule and a movement on a schedule of length-of-service pay, of adjustment of piece-rates, and of fringe benefits. Any precise control covering all rates of pay for all workers in all employments would clearly raise intolerable problems of intervention by the controlling body.

Moreover, to avoid serious inefficiencies it would be essential to allow exceptions to any rigid limitation of the permitted increase in rates of pay. Over the years demands change, technological advances take place, and different primary resources become scarcer or more abundant. For the economic system to be at all efficient, it must be possible for the prices of scarce resources to be raised relatively to the prices of abundant resources. Labour of a grade, training and geographical location that is scarce must be allowed to earn a higher rate of reward than labour of a type which is abundant and unemployed; and, even with general unemployment at 12½ per cent, there will always be some grades of labour which are in short supply. As demand is expanded it must be possible for the rate of pay of labour which is in short supply to rise relatively to that of labour which is in excess supply. An effective centralised wage policy would thus be complicated still further by the need for the authority concerned to differentiate between the limits set on wage increases for different groups of workers.

It would be possible to impose a severe financial penalty on any employer who was convicted of paying an excess rate of pay; but the policing and administration of a permanent centralised system of wage control would either be ineffective, leaving many loopholes which would in the end discredit the system, or would become intolerably expensive, complicated and distorting.

If the two extreme approaches of a perfectly competitive economy and a centralised pay policy are ruled out, we are left with the question whether an effective intermediate approach is available. It is my belief that a set of policies and institutions could be devised which in themselves would not be administratively impossible nor lead to unacceptable side-effects. They would thus not be open to the same objections as the two extreme responses which I have just dismissed. But in putting these constructive ideas forward, I run the risk of making myself look ridiculous.

Wages, Full Employment, and the Welfare State

What I shall propose would admittedly be totally impracticable politically unless there was a widespread political consensus that it would constitute a much more sensible way than at present of conducting our affairs; and the possibility of such a consensus is particularly likely to appear a mere pipe-dream in the present atmosphere of extreme confrontation and conflict in industrial relations. It is my belief that our problem is soluble in a free society only if there is general acceptance of two ideas: first, that wage-rates should be set with much more emphasis on their effects on output and employment and with much less emphasis on their effects on the real incomes of those already in employment; and, second, as a necessary corollary of the first, that the emphasis should be shifted away from wage-rates and onto fiscal and similar measures to ensure an acceptable distribution of income and wealth. I believe that this second condition requires a really radical reform of our present social security and welfare arrangements, and a really radical reform of direct taxation and of the taxation of accumulated and inherited wealth, which would be clearly seen as an effective alternative approach to a more acceptable distribution of the increased real national product that would result from full employment and wage restraint. This, the positive part of our welfare problem,[1] raises problems of the greatest importance and difficulty. I shall not discuss them here, though I wish to emphasise that I personally regard their acceptance and implementation as essential conditions for my attempt to shift the emphasis away from wage-setting as an instrument of distributional fairness.

Holding this view, all that I can offer is a blueprint of the arrangements which would, I think, be practicable and effective *if* such a consensus of opinion could be achieved politically. It is, I am well aware, a very big 'if'.

Before I do so, however, I hope that you will excuse me if I very briefly express an opinion on the political background. I believe that the present

---

[1] I discussed this aspect of the problem in a T. H. Marshall Memorial Lecture entitled 'Full Employment, New Technologies and the Distribution of Income' given at the University of Southampton in November 1983, *Journal of Social Policy*, vol. 13 (1984), pp. 129–46.

Government was right in its determination to put an end to the threat of explosive inflation of money costs and prices, and that this inevitably called for a curbing of the excessive privileges and immunities of labour monopolies. But, in my opinion, it missed a great opportunity by relying solely on negative labour-law measures, combined with whatever restriction of money expenditures and consequential rise in unemployment was needed to keep down the rate of wage inflation. It has thereby gained the reputation of seeking confrontation with a lack of compassion which is now erupting in serious civil disorders.

In my opinion, the prospect for an ultimate new political consensus on these problems would have been much better if, from 1980 onwards, the Government had introduced the legislation which was certainly needed to curb the excess monopolistic powers of labour organisations merely as a negative item in a whole range of *positive* policies to ensure full employment in an efficient but compassionate welfare state. The positive elements in such a programme might have covered:

(i)   the planning of financial policies so as to ensure a predetermined growth in the total money demand for the products of labour;

(ii) the development of some central co-operative machinery for assessing a guideline norm for the average growth of rates of pay which would have been compatible, in these financial conditions, with the attainment and maintenance of full employment;

(iii) the institution of a system of impartial pay tribunals to settle wage claims in place of the present chaos of uncontrolled monopoly bargaining backed by the threat of industrial action;

(iv) the institution of opportunities for employees to participate in decision-making in their enterprises;

(v)   the strengthening of measures to promote competition and to restrain monopolistic restrictions on the part of employers and producers, including the control of selling prices in cases of monopolistic production of standardised products;

(vi) a thorough-going reform of the present wasteful and inefficient muddle of tax and social security arrangements so as to concentrate support at much improved rates on the poorest and most needy members of society;

and, perhaps above all,

(vii) a radical reform of the taxation of income, expenditure, wealth and inheritance designed to promote a more acceptable distribution of income and property.

Such an approach would have presented the surgical operation against the excessive privileges and immunities of labour monopolies as a necessary negative ingredient in a positive programme to implement the existing post-war consensus in favour of full employment and the welfare state. In the rest of this paper I intend to confine the discussion to alternative wage-fixing arrangements which might have played the negative role in such a comprehensive positive programme.

The Curbing of Labour Monopolies

Let us then simply assume that there is a widespread, confident public belief that, through the Government's financial policies, the total demand in money terms for the products of labour will be expanded over the next 12 months by, say, 8 per cent and that this will lead to an acceptable development of employment opportunities if money rates of pay are raised on the average by, say, 5 per cent.

If it could be firmly established, such a financial background would undoubtedly be helpful in restraining inflationary wage settlements; there would be an obvious implication that, if in any particular sector the rate of pay rose by more than the 5 per cent norm, either the pay rise must be lower in some other sector or there would be an inevitable rise in unemployment. The question then remains whether the combination of such a financial background together with certain curbs on the monopolistic powers of trade unions would be sufficient to ensure the necessary degree of moderation in average wage settlements.

There is no doubt that such curbs would help. There are, however, limits to the extent to which we should be prepared to restrict the monopolistic powers of labour organisations. A basic principle applied to curbing restrictive *business* practices is that independent producers should not be allowed to agree upon minimum prices below which they will not sell their products. To apply this principle to labour organisations would be to outlaw all agreements among individual workers not to work at wages below some agreed minimum, that is to say, to remove all trade union bargaining power. The argument against this 'final solution' is simple and conclusive. The scale of production normally involves a single employer (such as a joint-stock company) engaging a large number of employees. In conditions of imperfect competition this will result in an unfair bargaining position unless the many employees can get together to form a single unit to bargain with the single employer.

Many of the curbs introduced by the present Government do not endanger this legitimate degree of labour organisation. Outlawing secondary action to prevent one group of workers from industrial action other than in support of a claim against their own employer, or outlawing arrangements designed tightly to restrict the entry of new workers into a particular occupation through a pre-entry closed shop or through the unnecessary restriction of new trainees – none of these curbs forbids the combination of a group of workers to bargain as a unit with their own employer.

The logical outcome of this line of argument would be to confine trade unionism to what might be called independent company unions. More accurately, this would involve outlawing agreements among otherwise independent employers not to pay wages above some agreed maximum rates and outlawing all trade unions except those which were confined to the employees of a single independent employer. Each employer would bargain independently with a union confined to his own employees. Such a solution would in any case present severe administrative difficulties, particularly in deciding in a world of interlocking company structures what constituted a single independent employer. And, even if the definition of a single independent employer could be made precise, it would always be easier for such employers than for their employees to reach informal agreements which in practice covered a wider range.

The device of independent company unions, if it were practicable, would in current conditions have one considerable advantage. At present in the UK there is a marked difference between the relative prosperity in the southern regions and the extreme depression and mass unemployment in the northern regions of the country. A reduction in the rates of pay in the depressed regions (with their massive armies of surplus labour) relatively to rates of pay for similar workers in the prosperous regions (with their scarcities of trained workers) would enable new enterprises to start up in the former. But a single national union which insists on a single 'rate for the job' to rule throughout the country excludes the depressed regions from economic developments at a rate of pay which would be much more attractive than the dole to the local unemployed, even though it was not as high as that earned by the fortunate dwellers in the south.

The application on a national scale of the strict principle of 'equal pay for equal work' is in effect one example of the conflict of interest to which I have already referred (p. 402) between the 'lucky insiders' who are already in employment (in this case in the south) and the 'unlucky outsiders' who are unemployed (in this case in the north). Separate unions setting different rates of pay with different companies in the north and the south would help to resolve this aspect of the problem.

But the institution of one-employer-one-union could not in practice be relied upon to solve the whole problem satisfactorily. It would leave some bodies with much more strength than others. Let us take as an extreme example the employees of a national electricity grid where technical considerations would require one employer, and thus one compact trade union, for the whole of the country's electricity supply. The company union would still have enormous wage-bargaining power since, by taking industrial action, it could hold the whole country to ransom. It is this sort of consideration which underlines the inadequacy of any attempt fully to solve the problem by particular curbs on the monopolistic powers of labour organisations. They will always leave some groups with much more clout than others; and it is totally unsatisfactory that the pattern of rates of pay should be set in such a manner.

A Possible Role for Pay Tribunals

The civilised way to deal with this aspect of the problem is to replace the system of wage settlement through uncontrolled monopoly bargaining, backed by the threat of industrial action, with a system of awards through an impartial wage tribunal. Any such body would, of course, need to work according to some agreed set of principles. In general, we might envisage a nationwide structure of tribunals to which a pay dispute could be referred, the tribunal being required by statute to make an award which, against the background of the agreed guideline norm for the average rise in rates of pay, would put strong emphasis on the promotion of employment and output in the sector of the economy under review.

There are many different forms which such a structure might take, but there are certain general principles on which it should be based:

(i)   There should be a single, uniform structure of pay tribunals, but they should as far as possible deal with particular, decentralised wage settlements. What is required is that, against the background of a moderate rate of growth of the total of money expenditures on the products of labour, the rate of pay should be permitted to rise relatively in any particular sector of the economy in which there was a scarcity of labour and to fall relatively where there was an excess supply of labour. The different cases should be judged separately. At the same time, it would be essential to avoid the dangers of leap-frogging inflation that arise from a set of totally independent arbitral bodies, where one *ad hoc* body decides that butchers and bakers need to be paid rather more than candlestick-makers while another *ad hoc* body decides that candlestick makers should be paid rather more than butchers and bakers. Different awards must be made for different groups, but by a unified structure of tribunals.

(ii)   The principle that a tribunal's award in any particular case should be designed to promote employment in the sector under review is admittedly intended to restrict upward inflationary pressures on money rates of pay. But it does not, of course, imply that there should be an unlimited downward pressure on every individual rate of pay. Pay in any sector may need to be raised to attract labour where it is in short supply, just as it may need to be lowered to expand the demand for labour where it is in excess supply. The guideline norm for the average of pay throughout the economy would provide a useful benchmark against which a particular case should be judged.

(iii) There is another aspect which must be borne in mind in considering the argument for a rise, or that against a fall, in a particular rate of pay. In an occupation which requires a special training or which is conducted in a specially isolated location, the existing labour force may be tied to the occupation because of the difficulty of moving to an alternative job. A reduction in the rate of pay might have little or no immediate effect in reducing the supply of labour. But in the longer run, in particular as older workers retired and new entrants to the labour force went elsewhere, a low rate of pay might cause a marked shortage of labour. Indeed, while a lowered rate of pay might have a negligible short-run effect, a rise in the rate of pay might be required to sustain an adequate supply of labour in the long run. The principle of setting rates of pay to promote activity in any one sector should be interpreted as setting rates required to promote long-run sustainable activity.

(iv) It is, of course, always possible that, as a result of technological changes and historical developments, the supply of labour in a particular sector of the economy is largely in excess of any permanently sustainable level of demand. In such a case, the unmodified criterion of promoting employment would justify an immediate, almost unlimited, reduction in the rate of pay. But such violent downward movements would be socially unacceptable; and it would, therefore, be wise to set a limit to which a pay tribunal could restrict the rate of pay in any sector relatively to that which would correspond to the general guideline norm. For example, if the guideline average norm were for a 5 per cent rise in rates of pay, the tribunal might be required to award at least a 2 per cent rise, though the workers in the sector concerned would, of course, be free to agree with their employers to accept a lower rate in order to protect their jobs.

(v) But it is not only sharp reductions in a rate of pay which would be socially unacceptable. People are deeply concerned with their pay relatively to the pay of workers in other sectors of the economy. A serious fall in a worker's pay relatively to that of other workers is felt to be as unacceptable as – perhaps even more unacceptable than – an absolute decline in pay which does not disturb relativities. In the long run it is essential that rates of pay should fall relatively in sectors in which there is an excess supply of labour and should rise relatively in sectors in which there is an excess demand for labour. However, just as it is suggested in (iv) above, that there should be some restriction on the rate at which the absolute level of pay should be cut, so there might also be some restriction on the speed at which a rate of pay should be eroded relatively to rates of pay in other sectors. For example, a pay tribunal might be required never to grant an award which would reduce the current ratio of a particular rate of pay to the average rate of pay throughout the economy by more than, say, 3 per cent below what that ratio had been on average over, say, the last five years.[2] Such a formula would, of course, imply that, if a relativity had slipped down sharply, the tribunal could not impede any current rise in the rate of pay which was needed to restore the relativity to within 3 per cent of what it had been over the previous five years.

---

[2] This would allow a steady continuing erosion of a relativity by no more than (approximately) 1 per cent per annum, regardless of any excess supply of labour. A reduction each year of the relativity by 6 per cent of its existing five-year average would be needed to allow a steady continuing erosion of the relativity by (approximately) 2 per cent per annum.

(vi) There is much to be said in favour of the principle that, in considering a pay dispute, the tribunal should be required simply to choose between the latest claim submitted by the employees and the latest offer made by the employer, and to grant as its award the one more likely to promote sustainable activity in the sector concerned. This principle has the great merit of reducing the task of the tribunal to choosing between two ready-made sets of proposals instead of requiring it to work out its own detailed solution, even though it would in practice have much less knowledge than the parties themselves of the particular circumstances of the case. Moreover, a simple restricted choice between latest claim or latest offer would encourage the parties themselves to reach agreement without reference to the tribunal since, in formulating its own latest offer or latest claim, each side would have to confine itself to proposals likely to promote sustainable employment and output.

(vii) The principle behind the tribunal's award should be the promotion of the long-run sustainable output of the sector concerned rather than of long-run sustainable employment. In the production of any product for which the demand is inelastic, employment may be maintained through restrictive labour practices requiring two men to do the job of one. Disputes often involve matters other than simple rates of pay and it should not be the intention to promote the maintenance of employment by means of unnecessary restrictive practices. The promotion of output as an objective implies the promotion only of necessary employment.

(viii) Finally, in devising a particular structure, it should be remembered that a basic purpose of the whole operation is to remove the inequality of bargaining power which would otherwise occur where a single employer has the advantage over a large number of independent, competing, potential employees.

A Possible Blueprint for Pay Tribunals

The following is an example of a set of arrangements designed to meet these eight requirements.

There would be a national structure of impartial pay tribunals to which any group of employees could refer their claim in the event of a dispute with their employer. The presumption of the tribunal would be in favour of the employees' claim, which it would automatically accept as its award unless the employers could show beyond all reasonable doubt that they had made an offer which satisfied three conditions: first, that it presented the prospect that output would be sustainable in the long run at an appreciably higher level than would be possible if the employees' claim was accepted; second, that their offer did not imply a rate of increase in the sector's rate of pay which was below the guideline's average norm by more than, say, the three percentage points suggested in (iv) above; and, third, that their offer did not imply setting a pay relativity for the sector which would be more than, say, 3 per cent below what it had been on average over, say, the last five years, as suggested in (v) above. Only if it satisfied these three conditions would the employers' offer become the tribunal's award.

If such a structure were accepted, it would be appropriate to abolish competely all the legal privileges and immunities which were conferred on trade unions by the famous 1906 Trade Disputes Act. Support for the bargaining power of the workers would now be provided by extending to them alone the right of appeal to an impartial body to get their claim imposed upon the employer, rather than by the method which has proved so disastrous of granting them legal privileges to use at their own discretion a wide range of uncontrolled monopolistic pressures which would otherwise be illegal.[3]

In addition to the removal of all such immunities, a further range of sanctions against resort by the employees to industrial action rather than appeal to the pay tribunals might be provided by such measures as: making any supplementary benefit payable to the families of strikers a loan repayable by future attachment of their earnings; ruling that any strike action implied the ending of the striker's contract of employment and thus the loss of any benefits – such as the amount of a future redundancy payment – which depended upon length of service; and the imposition of fines on the funds of a trade union body which was supporting direct industrial action. In the case of the employers, the problem of sanctions is readily met by making the non-observance of the award a criminal offence, subject to the imposition of fines at a penal rate, and thus presenting them with the stark choice of accepting the award or closing down their business.

Such a system could, in principle, be applied in the public service as well as in private industry provided that the public authority was prepared to announce cash expenditure limits as a measure of its demand for the service in question. In the light of the expected guideline norm to be earned elsewhere, the tribunal would then have to judge the rates of pay needed to attract suitably qualified employees before deciding whether it was clear beyond reasonable doubt that the employing authority's wage offer would attract sufficient employees to sustain the public service at a markedly higher level than could be financed within the given cash limits at the rate of pay claimed by the employees.[4] Such a decision would admittedly involve a difficult judgemental assessment by the members of the tribunal concerning the interpretation of the public expenditure

---

[3] Sir John Donaldson, Master of the Rolls and former President of the National Industrial Relations Court, in an address to the Engineering Employers' Federation early in 1984, advocated a move away from the special freedoms of trade unions to engage in industrial action towards an extension of their rights to obtain impartial settlements of disputes. (*The Times*, 15 February 1984).

[4] In addition, the tribunal would support the employing authority's offer rather than the employees' claim only if it did not reduce the growth or relativity of pay below the limits set in (iv) and (v) above.

plans, the level of qualifications required in the service, and the rates of pay required to provide and sustain the largest possible scale of well-qualified service within the planned expenditure constraints. Since the employing authority could, if it thought fit, always refuse to accept the employees' claim unless the employees took it to the tribunal, the system could act as an effective restraint on excessive inflationary increases throughout the public service. But since the tribunal would be required always to start with a presumption in favour of the employees' case, this restraint would be effective only if the employing authority could make out a strongly convincing case against the claim of the employees. The system would admittedly present considerable difficulties; in spite of its inadequacies, however, I personally cannot think of a better alternative to replace the still greater inefficiencies and inequalities of the 'tooth-and-claw' of so-called industrial action.

There remains one other basic unsolved problem. However effective the proposed system of pay tribunals might be in its application to the public service and in coping with pay disputes in the private sector, it would not cover possible voluntary agreements between employer and employees which led to an undesirable inflation of money wage costs and selling prices. If my earlier analysis is correct, there is a real danger that, in conditions of imperfect competition, the effect of an expansion of money expenditures on the products of a particular firm may result in a mutual agreement between employer and employed to devote an undue proportion of the increased sales revenue to raising the money incomes of the existing workers and shareholders rather than to reducing unemployment through the expansion of the firm's capital investment, its employment of labour, and its output and sales at the existing rates of earnings and prices.

A Tax on Inflationary Wage Settlements

This problem might be tackled through the imposition of a special anti-inflation tax levied on employers who granted increases of pay above some permitted level, the intention being to make it too expensive for employers to be willing to grant such excess increases.[5] The scheme would require the official announcement of a precise limit to permissible tax-free rises in pay, a limit which might well be related to the guideline norm for the average of pay increases discussed above. Thus, if an average guideline norm was set at 5 per cent over the coming 12 months, an upper limit of, say, 8 per cent might be set, above which all rises in pay would be subject to tax. Such an upper limit would then match the lower limit of, say, 2 per cent below which, as already suggested, employers' offers would be ruled out-of-court by the proposed pay tribunals.

The tax would have to be operated in some such manner as the following. The employer would have to record the total of the pay of his

---

[5] Richard Layard, *More Jobs, Less Inflation* (London: Grant McIntyre Ltd, 1982) for a concise statement of the case for this type of tax.

employees and the total number of man-hours worked in his business during each quarter, thus providing a figure of average earnings per hour's work. The figure for the current quarter would then be compared with the corresponding figure in the same quarter of the previous year. If earnings per hour's work had risen by less than the permitted 8 per cent, there would be no tax liability. But if, for example, it had risen by 10 per cent, the employer would be liable to the special inflation tax on the excess 2 per cent of his total wage bill for the quarter.

Such a tax would clearly present a number of problems both for the employer and for the tax enforcement authorities. To cover such matters as overtime, part-time work, and variations in employment over the quarter, it would be necessary to record total hours worked rather than average numbers employed. It would not be feasible to apply the limit of pay rises to each category and grade of workers separately; it would have to be applied crudely to a general average for the business as a whole, and the system would thus give a bias in favour of the expansion of unskilled workers at low rates of pay to replace skilled workers at higher rates of pay. Moreover, it would be difficult – and perhaps impossible – to include in the definition of pay the value of many fringe benefits, and this would give a bias in favour of granting pay increases in the form of such unrecorded benefits.

Awkward administrative problems could arise if, in any quarter, a particular business experienced very exceptional conditions – such as a strike or a holiday closure for reorganisation; in such conditions a figure for earnings per hours worked would be unavailable or much distorted. There would be problems in starting up the scheme since a firm which happened to have had a specially high or a specially low earning per hours worked in the previous year's base-period would be treated particularly leniently or harshly in subsequent quarters. Special arrangements would be required to deal with the setting-up of new firms – probably a wholly tax-exempt running-in period.

Many administrative problems would be considerably eased if it were possible to exclude a host of small-scale employers. This would much reduce the number of cases for tax enforcement and would confine the difficulties of administration to businesses which would be better able to deal with the accounting problems. On the other hand, it would itself present a number of new problems. There would be employers at the margin whose employment was sometimes above and sometimes below the dividing line. There would be mergers of businesses which raised the total employment above the dividing line, and, more importantly, the break-up of employing bodies which drove the total employment by each individual fragment below it. In general, there would be the problem of determining what in practice constitutes an employing unit in the case of interlocking corporate structures with partially or wholly owned subsidiary interests.

These are all real problems. It is, however, extremely easy to find such problems with any proposed tax measure. Indeed, if the present income tax arrangements did not exist, academic economists who presented an exact blueprint of all the current income tax provisions and anomalies would be laughed out of court by the commonsensical members of the establishment for being so ridiculously out of touch with administrative realities. I personally do not think that the inflation tax must be rejected out of hand on these grounds.

There are, however, two further complicating factors which must be borne in mind. In the first place, if it is to act as an effective restraint, the tax on increases in pay above the upper limit would have to be imposed at a very high rate. Since the base of the tax would be the rise in rates of pay between one year and the next, a rise in this year's rate of pay would raise the tax-exempt level of pay for every future year. Thus the tax charge on a £1 rise in this year's rate of pay gives an employer the tax-exempt right to offer to an unlimited number of workers for an unlimited number of years a rate of pay £1 higher than otherwise. To put the problem in a different way, let us suppose a £1 rise is postponed for one year. No exemption is gained from the tax on the £1 rise; only the interest on the postponement of the tax payment for one year is gained. The tax charge may have to be very high to restrain the increase.

In the second place, in order to prevent gross inequalities or the avoidance of the tax, it would be necessary to complicate the procedures suggested for the operation of the proposed pay tribunals. Any wage claim submitted to a pay tribunal would, if necessary, have to be scaled down by the tribunal to ensure that it did not involve an increase in rates of pay above the upper limit set for the exemption from the inflation tax. Otherwise it would be possible for the tribunal to impose on the employers an excess wage claim which the latter had opposed but which would make them compulsorily liable to the inflation tax. This anomaly would be totally unacceptable. It would not be satisfactory to deal with it by ruling that the employers would be exempt from the tax if the settlement had been imposed on them by the tribunal. For, in that event, employers and employees who wished to agree voluntarily on an excess increase in the rate of pay – and the tax is specially devised to prevent such agreements – could by tacit arrangement circumvent the tax: the employees would put their excess claim to the tribunal against which the employers would put in a feeble and unacceptable counter-offer. The employers would lose their case and thus be compelled by the tribunal to do exactly what they wanted to do, namely, to pay a tax-exempt excess increase in the rate of pay. The anomaly must be ruled out by any necessary scaling-down of the wage claim before the tribunal reaches its decision.

The final question arises whether, in view of these limitations, complications and difficulties, the game is worth the candle. We may perhaps conclude that a scheme could probably be devised provided that it confined itself to the discouragement of severely excessive wage settlements by a limited number of large employers of labour.

The Outcome in a 'Share Economy'

There is another possible approach to the problem of encouraging business to respond to increases in demand by expanding output rather than raising selling prices. It has recently been claimed that, for the general run of private enterprises, a solution to the problem of ensuring full employment without inflation can be found by a change in the method of paying the workers.[6]

To take a simple example, if in a given firm the existing wage bill were £8 million and the other incomes (that is, net profits, rent, interests, etc.) generated in the firm totalled £2 million, then instead of receiving their existing payment in the form of a fixed wage, the workers would be offered an 80 per cent share in the total incomes generated by the firm – or what may alternatively be called an 80 per cent share in the value of the firm's net product.

So long as the value of the firm's net product remained unchanged at £10 million, the incomes of the workers and of the owners of the capital invested in the concern would be unchanged at £8 million and £2 million respectively. But the change might give a two-fold stimulus to the workers' contribution to the value of the firm's net product and so to the incomes of the workers and the capitalists.

In the first place, as with all schemes of a profit-sharing character, the workers' participation in the outcome of the firm's activities might help to diminish their sense of alienation from the employers and increase their incentives for efficient operation, since their own incomes would depend directly on the firm's profitability. Thus the value of the firm's net product might be expanded even in the absence of an increased input of labour or capital resources into the firm.

In the second place – and this is the important thrust of the argument – the change of mode of payment to the workers will transform the incentives of the employers to employ more workers. As long as each worker must be paid a given money wage, the employers will take on workers only up to the point at which the extra worker increases the value of the firm's net product by at least as much as the extra worker's wage. But if the workers as a whole are paid 80 per cent of the value of the firm's net product, the employer will receive his 20 per cent of whatever is produced, so that an additional worker will be taken on so long as he or she adds anything, however small, to the value of the firm's net product – or until the employers can find no more unemployed workers to employ. This is the basic claim made for the replacement of the familiar 'wage economy' by a 'share economy' in order to promote employment without inflation.

However, the proposed scheme may need an important modification. Let us suppose that the firm is managed in the interests of the existing owners of the capital invested in it. Let us then consider the planning of a new investment project which would add a net £100,000 to the value of the firm's output without any net addition to the number of workers in employment. Under the share system, 80 per cent of this additional value would accure to the existing wage-earners and only £20,000 out of the £100,000 would accrue to those who had found the finance for the new

[6] Martin L. Weitzman, *The Share Economy: Conquering Stagflation* (Cambridge, Mass. and London: Harvard University Press, 1984).

development, with an apparent consequential serious disincentive for capital developments.

This would, of course, raise the earnings of the existing workers. If, as a result, the employers were enabled to offset this rise with an equivalent reduction of the 80 per cent share allotted to wages without losing their labour force, the reduction in the yield on the capital investment would be avoided. But if they could not rely on such downward flexibility of the share allotted to wages, capital investment projects would be discouraged by sacrificing to labour its 80 per cent of the yield.[7]

The opposite sort of situation would arise in an unmodified share economy if the firm's decisions about employment, investment and output were taken in the interests of the existing workers. In this case the managers would have an incentive, regardless of the effect on the value of the existing shares, to raise new funds for investment in new capital equipment, provided that the investment added anything, however small, to the value of the firm's net product, since the existing workers would enjoy their 80 per cent share of that addition. But they would have a contractionary, rather than an expansionary, attitude to the employment of new workers. Let us suppose that a new worker could be attracted to the firm for a weekly payment of £100 and that his work would add £100 to the value of the firm's net product. In a wage economy his employment would leave the position of the existing workers unchanged. But in a share economy the capital shareholders would receive £20 of the £100 addition to the value of the firm's net product; only £80 would be left to add to the total of the workers' incomes; and thus the existing workers would not be able to offer £100 to attract the new worker without a loss of £20 to themselves.[8]

This effect could, of course, be offset by a downward pressure on the

---

[7] This discouragement of investment by existing firms might well be accompanied by investment in capital equipment for the setting-up of new firms, particularly if new firms were free to pay their labour by offering an attractive wage instead of an 80 per cent share in the firm's net product. The restriction of capital investment by the existing share economy firms would have raised the rate of gross marginal yield on capital (that is, the yield before the deduction of the workers' 80 per cent share of the marginal yield); and this would open up attractive possibilities for other competing firms. But the entry of new firms is impeded by setting-up costs, by the need to produce on a sufficient scale to enjoy any economies of large-scale production, and by the problems of invading on a sufficient scale what may be an imperfect market for their products. In any case, it is no real solution for the running of a share economy merely to proliferate the number of firms each of which, if it was faced with an inflexible share ratio, would have an incentive economically to restrict its own capital investment relatively to its employment of labour.

[8] This disincentive is quite different from the familiar disincentive to employ more workers in a labour co-operative in which all partners, new and old, are paid the same reward. The existing partners will in this case wish to maximise income per worker and will, therefore, hesitate to expand the labour force if it might cause a reduction in the value of net product per head, even though it is clear that the new partner will be keen to join the partnership in return for a reward which is less than his addition to the value of the firm's net product. In the case of the share economy discussed in the text, there would be the prior and additional disincentive due to the fact that the whole of the addition to the value of the firm's net product will not be available for payment either to the new or to the existing workers, since a share of it will accrue to the owners of the capital.

share of the product allotted to capital which was sufficient to offset the capitalists' unearned gain from the new worker's output.

Unless, therefore, sufficient flexibility in the shares allotted to labour and capital could be ensured, a share economy run in the interests of the existing capital shareholders would tend to be expansionary in its employment decisions and contractionary in its investment decisions. If it were run in the interests of the existing workers, however, it would tend to be expansionary in its investment decisions and contractionary in its employment decisions. This would introduce a new and direct conflict of interests between capitalists and workers in the firm's plans for employment and for capital investment.

Labour–Capital Partnerships

To remove this potential conflict of interest is of the utmost importance. As I have already argued, a major advantage of the share principle might be that making the workers' income depend upon the success of the firm's operations might help to remove the sense of alienation between 'us' (the workers) and 'them' (the employers). This sense of alienation could only be increased by excluding workers from participation in the main decisions about investment and employment which in a share economy would so directly affect their pay. Indeed, to remove the sense of alienation requires arrangements for workers' participation in decision-making as well as arrangements for their participation in the enjoyment of the fruits of the firm's success.

It is, however, possible to avoid these conflicts of interest between capital and labour by arrangements which ensure appropriate adjustments in the shares of the product allotted to capital and labour. Let us consider the following sketch of a suitable labour–capital partnership.

When our firm with 80 per cent wage income and 20 per cent other income shifts on to the partnership system, a certain number of share certificates would be issued. Each share certificate would carry exactly the same right to a dividend and, subject to what I shall say later, exactly the same right of shareholders' votes at the shareholders' annual general meeting, so that all shareholders, whether capitalists or workers, would have the opportunity of full participation in decision-making. Share certificates would be issued to all existing workers and capitalists in proportion to the incomes which they were deriving from the firm. The immediate effect would thus be that everyone's income was unchanged. Every worker's or capitalist's income would, however, now be received in the form of a dividend on his or her share certificates instead of the payment of a wage, rent, interest, or profit. The issue of share certificates would, however, be divided into two types: 80 per cent of them would be labour share certificates issued to each individual employee *pro rata* to his existing wage earnings in the firm, while the remaining 20 per cent would be capital share certificates issued *pro rata* to the existing ultimate beneficiaries from the rest of the firm's income, that is, to the holders of the firm's equity, the firm's creditors, and so on.

Capital share certificates would in all material respects be similar to a company's ordinary shares and would be freely tradeable between willing buyers and sellers on the Stock Exchange or elsewhere. Labour share certificates would, however, be tied to individual employees and would be cancelled whenever the particular employee retired. There would, of course, be an agreed retiring age with agreed pension rights. The employee would naturally be free to resign earlier from employment; but if he did so he would have to give up his holding of worker shares. However, if he were unwillingly dismissed (except in the case of serious misconduct, illness, etc.), he would retain his worker shares until the normal age of retirement.

Investment in additional capital equipment in such a firm would be financed by the issue of additional capital share certificates. Let us suppose that a new issue of capital share certificates which increased the total issue of share certificates (that is, the total of capital and labour share certificates) by 1 per cent would, at current market valuations, raise new funds for a capital development project which was expected to increase the total value of the firm's net product by 2 per cent. The operation would be profitable for all existing shareholders, whether workers or capitalists, since it would increase by 2 per cent the amount of income available for distribution between a number of claimants which had increased by only 1 per cent. By the issue of additional capital share certificates, new investment could thus be financed whenever it was agreed that such investment would add more to the value of the firm's total net product than to the cost of raising the new funds to finance it.[9]

The same principle could be applied to decisions to expand the employment of labour. Let us suppose that an additional worker could be attracted to the firm by the issue to him of an additional number of labour share certificates which represented a smaller percentage addition to the existing total issue of both types of share certificates than the expected percentage addition to the firm's total net income due to the new worker's production. Once again, the total of the firm's distributable income would go up proportionally more than the number of claims on it; and all existing claimants, both capitalist and labour, would gain by expansion so long as the cost of attracting the new labour was less than the new worker's net addition to the value of the firm's product.

The Principle of Equal Pay for Equal Work

The solution sounds very simple; and, indeed, it is very simple. But there

[9] In so far as the firm used part of its own income to finance its investment project, the same principle could be applied. The expenditure on the new project would be accompanied by the issue of new additional capital share certificates equal at current valuations to the expenditure on the new capital project. These additional capital share certificates would then be allocated to all shareholders, whether capital or labour shareholders, *pro rata* to each individual holding. Thus workers as well as capitalists would acquire capital share certificates (which they would be perfectly free to hold or to sell as they chose) to represent that part of the firm's income which had been withheld from distribution on their existing share certificates.

lies behind it a most important implication. Let us consider a successful firm of the kind we are now discussing in which

The existing income per worker is	£100
The addition to the value of the firm's output due to an additional worker would be	£ 80
The additional worker's existing income is	£ 60

If the additional worker is offered a new issue of labour share certificates which would provide him with an income of, say £70, everyone will gain. The new worker will earn £70 instead of £60, and there will be an additional £10 (that is, the excess of the new worker's contribution to the firm's income of £80 over his own income of £70) to be distributed among all the existing shareholders, both capital and labour shareholders. But it means that the new worker will be working for a pay of £70 at the same workbench as an old-established worker who is being paid £100 for the same work. Is this fair and acceptable or does it too grossly offend the old-established principle of equal pay for equal work?

I believe that it is the practicable way of solving the problem of expansion of firms in conditions of imperfect competition, and that it should be acceptable because it is not as unfair as may appear at first sight. It means that lucky insiders would welcome outsiders into their companionship on terms which improve the welfare of the outsiders even if they are not so good as the terms already enjoyed by the insiders. But it should be remembered that, in these conditions, the new hands will in time become old hands and will in a successful enterprise come to enjoy the privileges of old-established insiders. Let me illustrate from my previous numerical example in which the retirement of an old hand would result in:

Reduction of income payable to the retired worker	£100
Loss of firm's output	£ 80
Addition to incomes of remaining insiders	£ 20

An old hand retires; his labour certificates are cancelled; this reduces the existing claims on the firm's income by £100; but that total income is reduced by only £80 as a result of the reduction of employment by one worker; the remaining claimants have an additional £20 to distribute among them. Thus the newcomers will gradually participate in the monopolistic-success-rents enjoyed by the old hands.[10] The partnership

---

[10] The existing capital shareholders will take their 20 per cent of the gain, with the consequence that the existing employees will take over only 80 per cent of the retired employee's monopolistic rents. If it were desired that the existing employees should take over the whole of the retired employee's rent, a more complicated arrangement would be needed. The loss to the firm's income due to the retirement of the old employee would have to be estimated, so that the net gain to the whole partnership (that is, £20=£100−£80) could be agreed between capital and labour shareholders. A corresponding proportion of the retiring employee's labour share certificates (that is, £20/£100=20 per cent) would then be distributed *pro rata* as additional labour share certificates to all existing labour shareholders.

is one in which the new partner starts in a modest way; but if the partnership is and continues to be a successful one so that there is a monopolistic-success-rent to be distributed, the newcomers will gradually come to share in that rent. If such arrangements are the price to be paid for economic expansion, they do not seem to me to be unacceptably unfair. Indeed, some people may well argue that their very fairness is an additional recommendation for them.

Conflicts and Risks in Labour–Capital Partnerships

It should be noted that all of the major decisions which I have so far discussed involve no conflict between the interests of capital and labour shareholders. Indeed, the whole object of the exercise is to devise a set of arrangements whereby both partners bear the risks and enjoy the fruits of success; and this is for the most part achieved by the principle that the dividend paid on capital share certificates is the same as the dividend paid on labour share certificates, with the consequence that any decision which is to the advantage of one partner will also be to the advantage of the other.

There are, however, inevitable exceptions to this rule.[11] One obvious example would be a decision to devote part of the firm's resources to the provision of social amenities or fringe benefits for the workers which would not confer any direct benefit on the capital shareholders. Another could arise from a decision to promote a worker from one grade of work to a higher-paid grade, a decision which would involve the issue of additional labour share certificates to the promoted worker. Promotions are, of course, a proper and desirable phenomenon – indeed, a necessary one if able persons are to be retained in the firm's service. But they could in theory be misused; if they were made on a wholesale scale which was unnecessary for the success of the firm's activities, they would result simply in a shift of part of the firm's income from capital shareholders to labour shareholders. Earlier in this paper I suggested that all share certificates, whether capital or labour, should have the same voting rights and thus the same ultimate influence in decision-making. But, in most concerns, the labour votes would outnumber the capital votes, while the opposite would obtain in a few very capital-intensive concerns. It might therefore be necessary to rule that, for certain types of decision, the agreement of representatives of both types of partner would be required.

There is one final point. I have sketched the principles of a capital–labour partnership on the assumption that the shift to the share system is 100 per cent complete for both the capitalists and the workers. This is not necessary, and indeed in many cases will be undesirable. Thus the partnership may want to be free to borrow some capital funds on fixed-interest contracts with the creditors – for example, overdrafts from

---

[11] One example of such an exception would occur if the procedure for dealing with retirements outlined in the preceding footnote were adopted. The capitalists would gain from a high, and the workers from a low, estimate of the loss to the firm's total income to be expected as a result of the old employee's retirement.

the bank, if nothing else; and on the shift over to the share principle some of the debenture or mortgage creditors of the firm may be unwilling to convert their assets into capital share certificates. On the labour side, the firm may well desire to be free to hire certain grades of labour – temporary or part-time workers or consultants – on fixed-wage contracts. Even more important, some of the existing workers may prefer to remain on wage contracts; and, indeed, all the workers might desire, as an insured fall-back in the case of the firm's poor performance, to remain on fixed-wage contracts for some part of their pay.

I suggested earlier a set of rules which would normally allow a worker to hold his worker shares until the age of retirement, unless he voluntarily resigned his employment at an earlier age. This would mean that a worker could, if necessary, be dismissed as redundant, but that in the case of involuntary redundancy he would be entitled to continue to receive his dividend upon his worker certificates until he reached the normal retirement age. In this case, existing shareholders would have an incentive to dismiss a working colleague as redundant only if they judged that what he contributed to the value of the firm's net product had fallen below the amount of the fixed-wage element in his pay, since any dividends payable to him would remain a charge on the firm's income whether he was made redundant or not. Thus, by choosing any given mix between a fixed-wage payment and a dividend on worker share certi-ficates, a worker would thereby in effect have chosen to distribute his risks in a corresponding mix between unemployment and fluctuations in pay.

All of these mixes between fixed payments and share dividends can be readily incorporated into the structure of a capital–labour partnership. The firm's net surplus may be defined as the value of its total net product less expenditures on fixed-interest, fixed-rent, and fixed-wage contracts. Capital and labour share certificates can then be issued and distributed to those who have a claim to the firm's remaining net surplus. The rules and activities of the partnership can then proceed on the principles outlined in my sketch. These principles will to a larger or smaller degree promote a non-inflationary expansion of successful businesses if – but only if – it is recognised that, when outsiders are offered jobs, they must not expect to receive immediately the same reward as old-established partners even if they perform exactly the same service to the enterprise. This is the crucial condition.

Conclusion

And so at last I come to the close of this rigmarole of provisions for a Utopian blueprint of wage-fixing institutions which really would enable us to achieve full employment without inflation. The question remains whether I have merely made a consummate ass of myself or whether I am an inspired prophet of a new order.

I am, I assure the reader, not ass enough to believe that a whole new system could be introduced overnight by a series of legislative enactments. My blueprint can, I well realise, have a use only in so far as the inspection of an ideal ultimate target may help to inform the gradual step-by-step process of persuading people of the need for change in a particular direction and of introducing partial institutional changes towards it. And, surely, such partial changes are possible – at one point a co-operative institution to agree upon a guideline norm, at another point some reform of capital taxation, at another some sensible co-ordination of income tax and social security, at another some promotion of arbitral procedures which attach some weight to effects on employment, at another some experiments in labour–capital partnerships, and so on and so on. My Utopian blueprint is not meant to imply more than gradual movement in a given direction. Nevertheless, I would remain a pessimist if I had to abandon all hope that the emphasis in the minds of the man and woman in the street and at the workbench might ultimately be shifted away from wage-setting onto fiscal and welfare measures as the appropriate means for influencing the distribution of income.

Index